Society and Economic Growth

Society and Economic Growth

A Behavioral Perspective

of Social Change

[JOHN H. KUNKEL]

NEW YORK

OXFORD UNIVERSITY PRESS

LONDON 1970 TORONTO

To Those Who Dream of the Future

Preface

The study of social change and economic development attracts many who dream of a future when the human spirit will no longer be shackled by deprivation and suffering. Mere dreams, however, especially if they are combined with no more than a vague desire to help, will lead to failure, for the social, political, and economic problems of developing nations can be solved only by those who are willing to engage in objective analysis and hard work. If men's efforts to improve the qualities of life are to be successful, the inspiration provided by dreams must be fused with knowledge of human limitations and the operation of social and psychological principles.

Much of the literature on social and economic change is quite abstract and somewhat removed from the everyday concerns of men in developing nations; creative personalities, capital-output ratios, and a twelve per cent investment rate are among the topics that have received considerable attention. But what of the men who live, who build and hope, work and die? Many discussions of industrialization have a strangely ethereal quality about them, for the men who perform the tasks involved in economic growth appear merely as fleeting shadows in the kaleidoscope of critical minimum efforts and problems of capital formation. Yet the activities of men, no less than social and economic factors, provide the substance for any understanding of the problems and promises of modernization. This book is designed to integrate men and behavior into the analysis of economic growth on the basis of recent work in sociology, psychology, and anthropology. A behavioral model of man and the social systems perspective are here combined to delineate the roles of individuals and their activities in the social changes that attend industrialization.

J. H. K.

Contents

ix

List of Figures

xiii

Acknowledgments

I wish to express my appreciation to the publishers and authors of the following works for permission to use quotations appearing in this book:

Banfield, Edward C., *The Moral Basis of a Backward Society*. Glencoe: The Free Press. Copyright © 1958 by The Macmillan Company.

Buckley, Walter, *Sociology and Modern Systems Theory*. Copyright © 1967. By permission of Prentice-Hall, Inc., Englewood Cliffs, N.J.

Fillol, Tomas R., *Social Factors in Economic Development: The Argentine Case*. Cambridge: Massachusetts Institute of Technology Press, 1961.

Foster, George M., *Tzintzuntzan: Mexican Peasants in a Changing World*. Boston: Little, Brown and Company, 1967.

Hagen, Everett E., *On the Theory of Social Change: How Economic Growth Begins*. Homewood: The Dorsey Press, Inc. Copyright © 1962 by the Massachusetts Institute of Technology.

Hagen, Everett E., (ed.), *Planning Economic Development*. Homewood: Richard D. Irwin, Inc. Copyright © 1963 by the Massachusetts Institute of Technology.

Holmberg, Allan R., "Changing Community Attitudes and Values in

Peru: A Case Study in Guided Change," in Richard N. Adams et al., *Social Change in Latin America Today: Its Implications for United States Policy.* New York: Harper and Brothers, for the Council on Foreign Relations, 1960.

Homans, George C., *Social Behavior: Its Elementary Forms.* New York: Harcourt, Brace & World, Inc., 1961.

Reproduced from *The Achieving Society* by David C. McClelland, by permission of Van Nostrand Reinhold Company, 1961, New York.

Myrdal, Gunnar, *Asian Drama: An Inquiry Into the Poverty of Nations.* New York: Pantheon Books. Copyright © 1968 by the Twentieth Century Fund.

Papanek, Gustav F., *Pakistan's Development: Social Goals and Private Incentives.* Cambridge: Harvard University Press, 1967.

Reining, Conrad C., *The Zande Scheme: An Anthropological Case Study of Economic Development in Africa.* Evanston: Northwestern University Press, 1966.

In addition I want to thank the American Anthropological Association for permission to quote from George M. Foster's "Peasant Society and the Image of Limited Good," and the Society for the Psychological Study of Social Issues and Eliezer B. Ayal for permission to use material from Ayal's "Value Systems And Economic Development in Japan And Thailand."

Finally, I express my appreciation to the editors of *Economic Development And Cultural Change,* the *Journal of Social Issues, Social Science Quarterly,* and the *Pacific Sociological Review,* for permission to reprint portions of my articles that appeared in their pages.

Society and Economic Growth

i *Introduction*

Wherever he turns, man is confronted by inescapable evidence of social change. The ubiquity and high rate of change, dominant features of the present and recent past, have led to the rise of increasingly urgent questions and complex problems. Social scientists have presented a number of answers and solutions, but present knowledge is not sufficient for the tasks that lie ahead. Not only the fact of social change but also the results of its analysis have increased man's uncertainty concerning the future and his ability to cope with it.

While social change is evident all over the world, it is especially one type of change—economic development—that has recently captured the center of interest. The term refers not only to the rise of secondary industry but also to the associated political, social, cultural, and psychological changes in the conditions of human existence. Its hallmark is the improvement of living conditions. This is usually expressed in terms of per capita income and productivity, death and morbidity rates, the supply of food and other goods, average educational attainment, and a host of additional characteristics which, together, are thought to constitute the "good life."

Economic development—whether it is only a dream, a painful transition from hope to reality, or an almost accomplished fact—is the domi-

3

nant motif of the present and future for much of mankind. More and more millions of men are exerting increasing pressure for the elimination of the disease, poverty, and ignorance which heretofore have been their lot. As a result, the analysis of industrialization and its problems has become an ever more urgent task, and information in this area is rapidly accumulating. Unfortunately, present efforts are not equally distributed among all aspects of economic growth; generally speaking, major emphasis so far has been placed on various economic characteristics, while social, cultural, and psychological aspects have often been neglected. The first aim of this book is to assess present knowledge of those characteristics of industrialization which usually are labelled "noneconomic," and to outline the contributions which sociology can make toward the comprehensive analysis of the process.

He who surveys the manifold phenomena of social change and economic development in the world today, who contemplates upon the undulations of recent history or ventures to predict the seething future, cannot help but search for explanations, for principles to account for today's events, for a glimpse of what is to be. The uneasiness which arises from the often cataclysmic events of the past, the fear inspired by present upheavals, and the dread borne from knowledge that the only certainty of the future is the alteration and disappearance of much that we cherish today, drive men to search for an understanding of the turbulent social world. A simple description, however, is not enough. A consistent explanatory system of thought—some kind of theory—would not only bring order into observations but also provide a "meaning" for events and enable man to predict, however hesitatingly, that which is to come.

Much of our knowledge of economic development is in the form of abstract economic formulas and descriptions of specific situations. Although both are useful, the early stages of theory construction require, in addition, the development of meaningful, valid concepts and the formulation of propositions which can be tested. The second aim of this book, then, is to provide such components for a theory of social change, and especially of economic growth.

There is much pressure to plan for economic development and to deliberately accelerate the often sluggish pace of modernization, for the material benefits so evident in the western world have increased the feelings of relative deprivation in the as yet nonindustrialized nations. Unfortunately, these efforts often are not so much a reflection of adequate information and the utilization of sociological and economic principles as they are the result of the simple—and often desperate—human desire for improvements in the quality of life. But the combination of ignorance and desire provides no assurance of success, and many programs have failed. The third aim of this book, therefore, is to outline the social factors and principles which, as far as is known today, are likely to be involved in programs of economic growth.

The titles of recent works are good indicators of the gamut of phenomena involved in the analysis of the social, cultural, and psychological aspects of economic development. "The Great Ascent" [1] which people in the industrializing nations envisage in the near future, "The Passing of Traditional Society" [2] which is deplored by the few and ardently hoped for by the many, and knowledge that "Man Takes Control" [3] of his destiny to an ever increasing degree, are topics which reflect the depth of both the problems and emotions engendered by the rapid pace of alterations in the lives of millions. And when Myrdal entitles his ten-year study of industrialization in a large part of the world "Asian Drama," [4] the allusion to tragedy, to men caught up in the whirlwinds of others' making, is real and powerful.

Two of these books begin with charming stories of individuals buffeted by the forces unleashed in the development of modern industrialized nations. The present work does not begin with a story, and individuals such as the grocer of Balgat or Juan of Las Bocas do not appear. This is because emphasis is placed less on the experiences of particular persons or nations and more on the statement and investigation of hypotheses which may be abstracted from the experiences of men and the descriptions of social events. In order to accomplish this task, a variety of studies performed by men in several disciplines will be analyzed, ideas derived from the work of many investigators will be evaluated, and various approaches to the study of social change will be weighed against available data. The result is a somewhat abstract discussion, but frequent descents

1. Heilbroner (1963). The titles are located in the Reference section at the end of the book, under author's name and publication date.
2. Lerner (1958).
3. Erasmus (1961).
4. Myrdal (1968).

to the world of living men will render the whole project meaningful to bystanders and relevant for the participants.

Most studies of the noneconomic aspects of industrialization categorize their subject matter in terms of academic disciplines, describe a host of psychological and sociological characteristics, and investigate the complex roles of bureaucracies, governmental elites, vital rates, religious ideals, educational institutions, and so forth.[5] Recent discussions of the "Three Worlds of Development," [6] "Rich Lands and Poor," [7] and the "Springtime of Freedom," [8] for example, concentrate on several large-scale characteristics and trends of nations and subcultures. These and other studies [9] provide not only an overview of economic development but also place the process within the context of today's political realities, yesterday's historical heritage, and the present state of sociological knowledge. In short, they present pictures of industrialization which are equivalent to paintings viewed at a distance of several yards. The major units of the composition are easily discerned, their relationships are clearly evident, the (historical) perspective is flawless, and the scope of the conceptualization is astounding. Without a doubt much of reality is captured in all its breath-taking complexity. Often, however, the basic elements and specific relationships involved in the production are not amenable to detailed analysis. Characteristics of the canvas, paints, and brush strokes are lost—or at least overwhelmed by the grandeur of the overall impression.

The present work differs from most other studies in that it focuses on the basic elements and relationships that make up the multivariate social components of economic development. It attempts to recognize the fact that many complex phenomena—such as the extended family—have features which are both detrimental *and* conducive to industrialization,[10] and that an adequate understanding of any social process requires the analysis of its constituent parts. In effect, this book with its emphasis on men and behavior presents an investigation of the same pictures of industrialization, but the paintings are now viewed from a distance of a very

5. For example Jacobs (1966), Morris (1967).
6. Horowitz (1966).
7. Myrdal (1957).
8. McCord (1965).
9. Etzioni (1968), Levy (1966), Moore (1967), Rostow (1960), Smelser (1963), Worsley (1964), Zimmerman (1965).
10. Litwak (1960a, 1960b).

few inches. Not all of the features are clearly evident, and the total composition is at times difficult to discern. The (historical) perspective is limited, and it may not be easy to appreciate the unity of the whole. Nevertheless, the procedures and basic elements which are involved in the production—the nature of the canvas, the characteristics of the paint, the various types of brush strokes—are easily apparent.

Just as the complete understanding of any painting depends on both the appreciation at a distance and the minute examination of the elements which produce the over-all effect, so the understanding of economic development is furthered by the study of men, behavior, *and* social processes. Clearly there is no conflict between these two procedures: each contributes answers to questions raised by the other, and thus the results are in every sense complementary.

The study of a complex subject such as industrialization, fraught as it is with emotions, unanswered questions, and ethical implications, should be prefaced with a brief statement concerning the investigator's theoretical and philosophical preconceptions.[11] First, it is assumed that the evaluation of economic development and its consequences at present is incomplete and often reflects opinions rather than facts. Since industrialization involves both benefits and costs,[12] it is possible that "The Great Ascent" may not be worth making, and that not all characteristics of industrialism [13] necessarily represent a distinct improvement over earlier conditions of human life. Second, this book assumes that vital decisions—for example the specification of plans for accelerating industrialization—should be based on ideas and propositions that have been validated by the best available analytical procedures and empirical evidence. Finally, it is taken for granted that the quest for economic growth is essentially voluntary. A nation chooses to industrialize, and it selects and employs various procedures to attain its goals. Social scientists can offer suggestions and advice, but they cannot determine the path that a nation must take.

11. For a good discussion of this topic, see Myrdal (1968), especially chapter 2.

12. As described, for example, by Lewis (1955:420–30).

13. For a description, see Kerr *et al.* (1960).

ii *Methodological Considerations*

Requirements of Development Analysis

The study of economic development, like that of any other social process, requires in its early stages that the investigator concern himself with questions concerning the adequacy and validity of the concepts he will employ, the variables he will include in his analysis, and the data and measurements he will utilize.[1] Although these and other methodological questions are important, they are often left unanswered, and development analysis has its share of poorly defined terms, vague and ambiguous concepts, variables that are difficult to measure and relate, and propositions that cannot be tested or rejected. Since no analysis can be better than its constituent elements, it may be useful to indicate what kinds of concepts, procedures, data, and propositions should be included in the study of social aspects of economic development.[2]

First, the major concepts must have empirical referents, or be related to them through logic or other procedures that are amenable to objective

1. For examples of value-laden answers, see Chase (1962), Juenger (1956), and Krutch (1953).

2. The following discussion is based on Dumont and Wilson (1967), Gross (1959), and Zetterberg (1965). For an early proponent of this position, see Lundberg (1939, 1961).

examination and replication. Material objects such as taxes and roads, and associated phenomena such as investments in social overhead, for example transportation systems, may become part of the analysis. "Friction of space," defined in terms of time and effort required for movements from one place to another, or "infant mortality rate," may also be included since these concepts are based on empirical referents and have generally accepted specific definitions. The behavior of individuals, the products and other results of human activities, and the written or spoken ideals of subcultures, are other phenomena that may be included. Conversely, concepts such as societal "adjustment," the "integration" of cultural elements, the "internalization" of values, or "dynamic equilibrium" should be employed sparingly, for their definitions are still subject to debate and their empirical referents are vague. The very term "economic development" falls into the second category, for there is as yet no agreement as to its meaning or empirical referents. Gross national product, labor force distribution, per capita income, demographic variables, and the per capita production of coal, steel, and electricity, have been employed as indicators of development, but it is questionable whether any one of these elements reflects the essence of industrialization. Consequently, while it is quite acceptable to speak of "economic development," the analysis of the process is restricted to the specific variables which are assumed to indicate "development."

Second, the phenomena which are included in the analysis, and the relationships among them, must be measurable. Even this simple requirement, however, is lacking in many areas of present development analysis. Since economic and demographic statistics are plentiful,[3] industrialization has been viewed mainly in terms of demographic indicators such as infant mortality and other rates,[4] or economic indicators such as income or gross national product.[5] While international comparisons in terms of these indicators are useful and can be easily made, the application of several indicators to one nation is likely to produce inconsistencies. Japan, for example, ranks "high" on some criteria of development and "low" on others,[6] and some development hypotheses are supported by middle

3. Kuznets (1956–1967) has collected vast amounts of economic information, while the United Nations' *Demographic Yearbooks* provide a wide variety of population statistics.
4. Hauser (1959a).
5. For example Leibenstein (1957), Pesek (1961), Stockwell (1960).
6. Hollerman (1964).

eastern experiences while others are not.[7] The measurement of social aspects of economic development is still rudimentary.[8] The variety of statistics is increasing, but their reliability and meaning are still subject to debate. Literacy, educational attainment, political stability, the distribution of radios, and the degree of need-achievement have been measured with some success,[9] but more encompassing concepts such as "national integration" or "social development" still have a weak foundation. Gross judgments can be made, of course, but their accuracy is not yet sufficient to make concepts such as "integration" or "development" useful components of scientific analysis. When such amorphous elements are included in the study of industrialization, the analysis can be no more specific or meaningful than present knowledge of these elements. The requirement of measurability therefore means, in effect, that at least for the time being the concepts and phenomena in development analysis will have to be relatively simple.

Third, inferences and abstractions should be based on objective criteria and involve generally agreed-upon procedures. This means, usually, that the inferences and abstractions made by one investigator should involve data and procedures that are available to and can be replicated by other qualified observers. For example, high agricultural productivity can be readily inferred from a low percentage of a nation's labor force in primary industries; but the inference that a boy has unconscious guilt feelings because he is assumed to hate his father, involves procedures that are difficult to replicate or validate. In general, inferences derived from empirical evidence are more trustworthy than inferences derived from theories, but whether one is to be preferred to the other depends on the circumstances and characteristics of the study. When "other qualified observers" are employed to replicate and validate an investigator's inference, they should not be drawn from a small coterie of adherents to the same theory. Psychiatrists from one "school," for example, will have little difficulty in agreeing with one another's inferences, but this does not necessarily validate such inferences, for men in other fields or of other psychological persuasions may not agree. Inferences, then, should be open to *replication in general.* Even general agreement on an inference is not equivalent to validation, however, and thus any inference, no matter how wide its acceptance, should be viewed as little more than a meth-

7. Shorter (1966).
8. For example Naroll (1956).
9. For examples, see Lerner (1958), Lipset (1960), McClelland (1961).

odological hypothesis subject to continuous evaluation. In the study of economic development, especially, the paucity of data and the complexity of many processes require a large number of inferences; the testing and validation of inferences therefore should be a major concern of any investigation.

Fourth, the relationships among elements included in the analysis of economic development should be testable and refutable.[10] In order to accomplish this, the phenomena and their relationships will usually have to be relatively simple, with clear empirical referents, and measurable in terms of objective criteria. The formulation of propositions that are testable and have some predictive value, then, includes all of the previous requirements and is the major goal of development analysis.[11] The fact that experimentation is quite difficult in this area, and that the time span necessary for the adequate testing of hypotheses is often enormous, does not diminish their importance. Rather, limitations such as these simply indicate the need for ingenuity on the part of the investigator and the careful construction of theories so that the testing of a few propositions will have repercussions for a large part of the theory. Only when hypotheses are vague and involve amorphous elements and relationships do the present limitations of social science methodology have devastating consequences.[12]

One attempt of meeting these requirements is based on the assumption that the often complex social processes and phenomena involved in economic growth consist of a large number and variety of much simpler components, especially individuals and their actions.[13] Emphasis on behavior, in turn, requires information concerning the (social) determi-

10. For a compendium of propositions currently available, see Kushner *et al.* (1962).

11. For a discussion of this position and its fate in current sociology, see Gibbs (1968).

12. For examples of theories and hypotheses that are extremely difficult to test by means of presently available methodologies, see Barringer *et al.* (1965), Eisenstadt (1964), Hoselitz (1960a & b), Levy (1966), Moore (1964), and Parsons (1964).

13. While sociologists have written volumes on action theory—for example, Parsons (1951) and Weber (1947)—few have rigorously maintained, or been able to follow the implications of, a strictly behavioral perspective. Indeed, the classic formulations of the "action-approach" contain a welter of concepts and propositions dealing with mental states, personality systems, cultural systems, cathectic-cognitive orientations, and so forth. "Action," then, has taken on a rather broad meaning and is no longer synonymous with "behavior." Throughout the present work, however, the two terms will be considered as being synonymous.

nants of action and the nature and form of (social) relationships. Psychologists have analyzed behavior for decades, social psychologists have investigated the structure of small groups and the influence of the person's immediate social context, and thus there is sufficient information in these areas to formulate propositions concerning the determinants of behavior and the role of an individual's social environment. Furthermore, it should be possible to analyze the structure and operation of larger social phenomena in terms of these basic elements and relationships, and to summarize the results in the form of higher-order hypotheses. When these are combined with propositions concerning the systemic properties of large social units and their effects on the constituent behavioral elements, the explanation and prediction of social processes should be within grasp.[14]

The Components of Social Phenomena

INDIVIDUALS

Most social phenomena become apparent only through the actions of men, consequently it is the individual and his behavior which constitute the basic elements of the sociologist's subject matter. Many students of economic development begin with the same postulate and devote much effort to the analysis of entrepreneurs, men with achievement motives, workers in factories, voters, etc. As Lerner says, we know that "The Industrial Revolution . . . worked itself out through millions of individual lives; that many suffered, others prospered, while their world was being reshaped in the modern image." [15] To be sure, it makes good sense to speak of a "death rate," but it is the individual man who dies; and when sociologists analyze the characteristics of a population, such as "median educational achievement," the summary measure is made up of men who have attended school for a certain number of years. The empirical referent of most sociological concepts is man; not physiological or chemical conglomerations, but "the man of flesh and bone, who is born, suffers, and—above all—dies, who eats and drinks, plays and sleeps, who contemplates and loves." [16] As one student of industrialization has observed,

14. For the description of a similar procedure, see Homans (1964a). For an early example of this type of analysis, see Homans (1951).
15. Lerner (1958:43).
16. Unamuno (n.d.:7), author's translation.

"the great dramas of societal transition occur through individuals involved in solving their personal problems and living their private lives." [17] In the course of their work, sociologists summarize and abstract, they emphasize certain human aspects and disregard others, but the ultimate source of their data—no matter how rarefied the final propositions—is the individual. As Levi-Strauss puts it in his *Tristes Tropiques*: "I had been looking for a society reduced to its simplest expression. The society of the Nambikwara had been reduced to the point at which I found nothing but human beings." [18] One need not be ashamed of this, but at the same time one must remember that much of what man is—for example what he eats, how he drinks, when he plays, or where he sleeps—depends on the society of which he is an inextricable part. To understand man, then, one must understand the social system, even as one must understand man in order to understand the social system.

BEHAVIOR

From this discussion it is apparent that the sociologist's interest in the individual is not directed toward unique personality characteristics, psychological predispositions, or the emotional make-up of persons. Rather, interest focuses on the individual because the individual is the locus of action, because the individual behaves. Any investigator who describes and analyzes social phenomena is concerned, essentially, with action, for there is little in society that does not lead to, or is not the result of, the activities of men. As Moore says, "let us now be clear on an elementary point: individuals behave"; [19] Homans concludes on the basis of many years' work that "if a serious effort is made to construct theories that will even begin to explain social phenomena, it turns out that their general propositions are not about the equilibrium of societies but about the behavior of men." [20] Groups as such do not behave, and when the consequences of an action, such as the building of a nation, are ascribed to groups, this ascription is a semantic convenience.

Social psychologists have been especially aware of such methodological shorthand expressions, and have spent a great amount of time and effort in dissecting the actions of "groups." The results of such dissections

17. Lerner (1958:74).
18. Levi-Strauss (1961:310).
19. Moore (1967:181).
20. Homans (1964:818).

are usually statements concerning the factors which affect the behavior of individuals, for example their productivity or their co-operation with others, or which determine the final result, that is, "group action." [21] The distinction between "group action" as a methodological or semantic convenience, and "individual action" as empirically demonstrable reality, cannot be repeated too often. When social phenomena are analyzed and explained, or when a program of fostering change is instituted, the blurring of this distinction may lead to the asking of incorrect or meaningless questions and the proposing of wrong and often useless answers. A conservative elite may be said to oppose a nation's modernization, for example, but the explanation requires an analysis of the determinants of behavior patterns, which are summarized by the words "conservative" and "oppose," as they are performed by certain individuals and not by others.

When it is granted that only individuals behave, the next question is: how can the behavior of individuals be analyzed? This is an important topic because the activities of any man form an almost continuous stream throughout his life. The division of the behavior stream into manageable units and useful categories has been a problem of interest to several sociologists.[22] It is generally agreed that muscle twitches are of no interest and that an accurate and exhaustive description of a person's actions during even a small part of an average day is of little significance.[23] Generally speaking, sociologists are interested in "meaningful" actions. But what are "meaningful" actions, and what are the criteria for differentiating behavior patterns that are meaningful from those which are not? Since sociologists are not interested in individuals as isolated entities but rather as members of groups, "meaningful" action may be provisionally conceived in terms of the reactions of other people. Thus, an individual's actions are meaningful if they produce reactions in other people; conversely, other people's activities are meaningful if a person reacts to them and if this reaction in turn triggers further action on the part of others. In short, meaningful action is part of a behavior chain and derives its "meaning" from the chain.[24] Most chains sooner or later involve two

21. See, for example, Thibaut and Kelley (1959), Proshansky and Seidenberg (1965).
22. For example Adler (1956, 1960).
23. As described, for example, by Harris (1964).
24. For a similar view, see Mead (1934).

or more people, and each person's behavior is a link in the total chain of events. *Behavior, then, must always be considered in a social context and in a time perspective.*

In the description and analysis of social phenomena, the behavior of men is usually combined into patterns of varying length and complexity. The specification of such units depends on the focus of the analysis, and all that need be remembered is that any such unit is composed of the many activities of several men. "Cooperation in slash-and-burn agriculture," for example, is a complex unit of action which may be a significant component of ecological analysis,[25] just as "block voting" may be important in another type of study.[26]

The recognition of behavior as a basic component of social phenomena raises the question of the determinants of action. The simple description of behavior leads to statements of correlations among actions; it is only when behavior is analyzed in terms of its determinants and consequences that the formulation of propositions becomes possible. Many psychologists, and some sociologists who are captivated by their theories, postulate that the individual's internal state, such as his motives, needs, and personality, plays a major role in determining specific actions. Other investigators, some psychologists and many sociologists, attempt to explain behavior by assuming that men behave in certain ways because they have learned particular actions in a specific environment. Here emphasis is shifted from man's internal state to the values and norms of the subculture and society to which he belongs. Thus the study of behavioral determinants leads not only to psychological factors but also to the actions of men who constitute the individual's context. "Other men," then, are an important component of behavior-oriented analysis, requiring the sociologist to concern himself with subcultures, organizations, and other large and complex entities.

GROUPS

Sociologists often find that concern with the behavior of individuals is inconvenient or needlessly cumbersome, and that summary measures of behavior are useful and essential components of analysis. For example, information that the crude birth rate in the United States was 17.9 per 1000 in 1968, as a summary measure of certain behavior patterns

25. Kunkel (1967).
26. Lipset (1960).

of millions of individuals, is a useful and necessary element of demographic analysis.

Individuals have also been combined into one or another type of "group," such as subculture, community, and elite. While the empirical referents of these units consist of persons, the question arises whether such groups are real. Warriner has pointed out that the term "group" may be considered from several points of view, and concludes that groups are real in the sense "that 1) the group is just as real as the person, but that 2) both are abstract, analytical units, not concrete entities, and that 3) the group is understandable and explicable solely in terms of distinctly social processes and factors, not by reference to individual psychology" [27] or by emphasis on the internal state of individuals. He concludes that according to the "realistic" view of groups, "social phenomena have their reality only through [the] expression of actors." [28]

Two major problems encountered in discussions of human groups as undifferentiated units are reification and anthropomorphism. The layman is not the only one who speaks of a society that decides, the community that wants change, or an elite that opposes modernization. Even social scientists are capable of writing that "an innovation, to be successful, requires . . . a supporting social structure onto which it can be grafted." [29] Perhaps it is only convenience of expression or the limitation of language which is at fault; but all too often such conveniences become part of development analysis and conceptions of reality. Concern with men and behavior provides one solution.

Models of Man

One of the most important questions facing the sociologist interested in men and behavior is: what are the characteristics of man? The specific postulates and assumptions concerning individuals—usually summarized as a "model of man"—are largely derived from psychological principles and reflect the "school" to which the investigator adheres.[30] Since every psychological "school" has a tendency to produce its own model of man, much of the diversity of development analysis can be

27. Warriner (1956:550).
28. Ibid. p. 554.
29. Foster (1962:162).
30. For an extended discussion of models of man, their characteristics, and their implications for research, see Simon (1957). The relevance of models of man in economic development is discussed by Opler (1968).

explained in terms of the different models which are employed. A model of man differs from more diffuse "conceptions of man" or views of "human nature" in that it has a much narrower scope; it is a *selective* set of propositions whose purpose is not to exhaustively describe or define all of the nature of man, but to make statements concerning those aspects of individuals which are necessary for subsequent theoretical and practical issues.[31] At the same time, models of man are usually broader than "personality" as that term is generally used by the psychologist, since they may include additional elements such as propositions concerning the relationship between behavior and the social context. Although a model may include "personality" characteristics, the terms are not synonymous.

One of the best-known models of man is that of Malthus.[32] His concern with population characteristics and trends led him to postulate that men must eat, that they engage in sexual relations, and that they will not voluntarily limit the number of their children. These three propositions do not constitute a complete description of man, but they do contain the elements essential to Malthus's interest. On the basis of this model, together with some added assumptions about the rate of increase in population and food supply, he constructed his theory. The importance of a model for subsequent theoretical and practical work may be illustrated by the reversal of one of these propositions. If one were to postulate that man *does* voluntarily limit the number of his children, for example through the employment of preventive checks, what would happen to the theory? Malthus's conclusion concerning man's misery would no longer follow, and different programs of action would appear "logical."

Malthus's theory illustrates a further—and crucial—characteristic of models of man: their constituent propositions usually reflect the "best" scientific knowledge available at one time. Additional information, further experimentation, and improvements in methodology may necessitate alterations in the model, and perhaps the elimination of certain propositions or the formulation of new ones. Models of man, then, actually have the status of hypotheses in that their components are subject to change as scientific knowledge accumulates. At any one moment, however, models may be considered the "givens" of an analysis.

Most sociologists do not employ an explicitly formulated model of

31. The following discussion is based in large part on Kunkel and Garrick (1969).
32. Malthus (1960); for a different, recent example, see Lenski (1966).

man and use, instead, an often implicit set of more or less vague assumptions concerning man. For example, investigators of need-achievement assume that men are characterized by a variety of needs, students of cognitive dissonance assume that men strive for congruence in their perceptions, Parsons assumes a rather complicated internal state consisting of value orientations and need dispositions, and Homans assumes that men learn behavior patterns through differential reinforcement.[33] While it is probably not necessary to present an explicit model of man in every study, the evaluation of research results and the convergence of theoretical efforts in the field of economic development will be greatly facilitated by the open formulation of the models which various investigators employ in their work. Implicit models of man cannot help but lead to implicit theories, and only the explicit and clear statement of a model of man can contribute to the formulation of an explicit theory containing specific concepts, legitimate abstractions, and clear-cut testable hypotheses.

Students of economic development who emphasize behavior require models of man which include propositions concerning a) *the determinants of behavior* and b) *the relationships among activities and among individuals.* Since most of the models that have been described by psychologists are basically attempts to explain behavior, these two requirements are easily met by a number of different psychological theories. Within the great variety of models there are enough similarities, however, so that it is possible to group most of them into two major, although somewhat heterogeneous, groups.[34] These categories are defined in terms of characteristics important to those who are interested in economic growth and therefore may appear somewhat unorthodox to the psychologist. Since not all models can be discussed in this chapter, it is only by means of such categorization that a systematic analysis of models can be attempted and that their implications for development analysis can be outlined and evaluated.

PSYCHODYNAMIC MODELS

There are today a large number of psychodynamic theories which have given rise to several models of man—for example those of Freud

33. Brehm and Cohen (1962), Parsons (1951), Homans (1961).
34. For a discussion of the philosophical foundations of these two groups of models, see Allport (1955).

and Jung [35]—which emphasize man's internal state and explain behavior in terms of a variety of internal characteristics.[36] The general propositions of psychodynamic models that are relevant to sociological investigations may be stated as follows: [37]

1. Men are born with certain internal elements such as drives, needs, instincts, libido, etc.

2. Societal norms and values are internalized and may limit or modify some of these elements.

3. The resulting combination of original and modified elements, together with the internalized societal factors, form an internal state usually called personality, which is the major determinant of action.

4. A stimulus impinging upon a person causes a state of tension (or disequilibrium) in the internal state (which is unpleasant).

5. Behavior is a consequence of the individual's and personality's tendency to return to a state of equilibrium (which is pleasurable).

6. The internal state, much of it unconscious, is created largely in early life and is extremely difficult, if not impossible, to change later on.

Since the social context which is introduced into the system is usually that of childhood, and more specifically that which was filtered through the behavior patterns of parents, adult personality characteristics and the actions arising from them are often quite independent of the adult's social environment. The explanation of activities therefore demands not only inferences concerning the present internal state but also an analysis of the distant past. A further complication arises from the assumption that internalized norms and values may block certain drives or instincts, thereby preventing the discharge of psychic energy,

---

35. For brief descriptions, see Hall and Lindzey (1957).

36. For an extensive analysis of psychological concepts, models, and theories, see Marx (1963).

37. This discussion of psychodynamic models of man is based largely on Hall and Lindzey (1957), Munroe (1955), and Wolman (1960). Many models have not been presented in systematic form, and ambiguities in components and relationships among them abound. Thus it is no easy task to summarize the models of man arising from the diverse psychological theories available in the literature. The propositions below are designed to indicate the general characteristics of psychodynamic models; specific models based on specific theories would differ from the general model mainly in terms of the particular elements of the internal state and their relationships postulated by a particular theory. However, adherents of particular theories and models of man should have no difficulty relating these to the very general propositions discussed in the following pages.

i.e. action. Such internal blockage or conflicts among the various components of the internal state are usually described in terms of repression, frustration, sublimation, or reaction-formation.[38] Dissimilarities between observed behavior and the actions predicted by psychodynamic theory are often reconciled by the utilization of these concepts.

The two best known psychodynamic models in the recent development literature appear in the theories of Hagen and McClelland. Hagen,[39] following Freudian theory, postulates an internal state consisting of anxiety, rage, various needs, aggression, etc. In addition there are several processes such as repression, reaction-formation, and identification. Childhood experiences modify the original internal state and create personality, many components of which are unconscious. In later life, external stimuli "trigger" the operation of various factors and processes of the internal state, resulting in observable action. Since the immediately surrounding social environment has a minimal effect on the behavior which occurs at any moment, the understanding and prediction of behavior requires substantial knowledge of the operation of the internal state. For example, the congruence of the activities of sons and fathers is explained as follows:

> There is a still more subtle and compelling reason for his partial identification with his father. Along with his love and admiration for his father, the boy is jealous of him and hates him. But if he perceives that his father loves and values him, this hatred and jealousy cause the boy to feel guilt. He will sense rejection of him by his father at times, for example, when he attempts to come between his father and his mother. He seeks some explanation of this rejection. His father being loving, he cannot blame his father, and so he blames himself, and for this reason too feels guilt. To protect himself from this guilt and fear of rejection, he incorporates into his own personality standards of conduct which he believes to be those of his father. By doing so (a) he tries to prove to himself that since he is like (or is) his father, he cannot really hate his father, and so need not feel guilty, and (b) he tries to reassure himself that since he is his father, his father does not really wish to reject him.[40]

38. For example by Wolman (1960:254–56).
39. Hagen (1962).
40. Ibid. p. 136.

A somewhat simpler model of man, requiring far fewer inferences concerning the internal state, has been presented by McClelland.[41] He postulates that behavior is largely determined by a constellation of motives, such as the need for achievement, for affiliation, and for power. Motives are established largely in childhood, especially through family and school socialization, and are expressed in behavior at a much later date. Need structures (or motivational complexes) are not likely to change much in later life. Like Hagen, McClelland concludes that the contemporary social context plays a relatively minor role in affecting behavior, and that the explanation and prediction of action rests upon knowledge of internal needs. Unlike Hagen, however, McClelland provides objective procedures and empirical data for the assessment of his model's components.

Implications for Economic Development. Psychodynamic models in general, and the above two examples in particular, have important consequences for the analysis of industrialization and the formulation of action programs, which may be summarized as follows:

1. The explanation of behavior must concentrate on man's internal state. The exact focus of attention will vary from model to model, of course, but would include in most studies a rather complex set of elements. Since much of the internal state is assumed to be unconscious, the determinants of behavior may not be evident unless the individual is psychoanalyzed.

2. Since the various aspects of man's internal state which determine behavior are largely created in childhood, it is difficult if not impossible to bring about major alterations in the behavioral repertoire of adults, unless intensive and long-term individual treatment is undertaken. Social and cultural change, then, cannot be expected to occur rapidly, and major changes may be expected to require several generations (especially in Hagen's theory).

3. The importance of childhood in shaping man's internal state reduces the influence of the contemporary environment on the individual's behavior. The social context may be expected to "trigger" motives, anxiety, rage, and various other forces, but it is in the operation of these forces themselves that the determinants of action are to be found. The social context plays the additional role of serving as the object of behavior, that is, of providing the human and material environment with

41. McClelland (1961).

which the individual interacts, although on the whole the social context is a relatively passive phenomenon, not an important causal agent.

4. Attempts to alter behavior must concentrate first and foremost on changing man's internal state. According to McClelland, for example, industrialization depends on men with high need-achievement, and thus any program designed to increase the rate of economic development must include procedures for changing this aspect of the internal state. According to Hagen, innovating personalities, which produce entrepreneurs, are created by decreasing men's anxieties, rage, and feelings of guilt to such a low level that innovating behavior is no longer blocked by these characteristics.

5. Present knowledge concerning ways of altering man's internal state is quite limited. Furthermore, since it is postulated that personality or needs cannot be significantly changed after childhood, there is little point in even attempting to bring about changes in the mental states and consequent behavior patterns of adults.

Evaluation. Psychodynamic models of man at first glance seem quite reasonable, but on closer examination many of the underlying postulates and assumptions appear to have only limited empirical support. The data marshalled in support of propositions concerning the nature and operation of the internal state are open to question, and many of the foregoing implications, especially the last, do not seem to be in accord with reality or experience. Psychodynamic models generally, and the two examples under discussion specifically, may be questionsd on the following grounds:

1. The internal state cannot be studied directly, most of its components have doubtful empirical referents, and many of the internal processes cannot be measured with presently available procedures. For example, there is very little empirical support for the events which Hagen assumes occur within the boy's mind described in the above quotation. McClelland attempts to measure need-achievement objectively, but he basically infers it from carefully measured examples of overt behavior in stories, on pottery, etc. It can be argued, therefore, that he does not actually measure the internal state itself but only its behavioral manifestations.

2. The causal relationships between observed behavior and postulated characteristics of man's internal state at present are almost impossible to demonstrate or validate. The demonstration of such a causal sequence is especially difficult because the various elements making up

the internal state are usually inferred from the behavior itself. Students who write achievement-oriented stories, for example, are thereby assumed to have high need-achievement, and it is this high need-achievement which presumably causes them to write achievement-oriented stories. A major element of any causal hypothesis is inference, and since much of the internal state is expressed only through behavior, it is difficult to validate the causal relationships and inferences in terms of independent criteria.

3. The model cannot account for data such as the Cornell-Peru project or the spectacular rise of entrepreneurs in Pakistan. In the first instance, fundamental changes in the behavior of Indians occurred over a five-year period,[42] and in the second, entrepreneurial activities increased severalfold in the span of only ten years.[43] Rapid changes in behavior are difficult to explain in terms of a psychodynamic model of man. Hagen, for example, attempts to account for the Pakistan case by assuming that a society's social structure sets up barriers to the overt manifestation of innovating personalities, but this is not an entirely satisfactory answer.[44] At the very least, the operation of these barriers and their specific effects on the behavioral manifestations of personality are not indicated.

Any model of man which emphasizes the internal state as the major determinant of action must confront the foregoing criticisms which raise doubts concerning the validity of many propositions contained in the model and its applications. While future work may reduce these difficulties, present methodological limitations necessitate the search for other models.

BEHAVIORAL MODELS

A major alternative to psychodynamic models is a group of "behavioral" models based on the various learning theories that have emerged in experimental psychology during the last fifty years.[45] While the assumptions concerning the process of learning differ from one theory to the next, there are enough similarities to justify the formulation of general propositions that are relevant for sociological analyses: [46]

42. Holmberg (1960a).
43. Papanek (1967).
44. Hagen (1963).
45. For brief descriptions and evaluations of the major theories, see Hilgard (1956).
46. The major sources of these propositions are Bandura (1969), Staats and Staats (1963).

1. Individuals are subject to conditions of physiological deprivation and satiation.

2. Some types of deprivation and satiation are learned and have a cultural origin.

3. The effectiveness of action varies directly with the level of deprivation and inversely with the level of satiation of the individual.

4. If in the past, in a certain context, a behavior pattern has been rewarded (reinforced), the probability that the same behavior patterns will be emitted in the future, under similar circumstances, is increased.

5. If in the past, in a certain context, a behavior pattern has been punished (not reinforced), the probability that the same behavior pattern will be emitted in the future, under similar circumstances, is decreased.

6. The specific components of rewarding and punishing consequences of actions are functions of the social context and may be expected to vary among individuals and over time.

It is apparent from these propositions that man's internal state—consisting mainly of his learning history, culturally determined deprivations, and learned expectations of particular consequences for specific activities—is little more than an intervening variable. The major implication for development analysis, and especially for the formulation of action programs, is that *behavior can be changed at any time.* By judiciously altering those aspects of the social environment which constitute rewarding or punishing consequences for specific activities, it is possible to alter these behavior patterns and to initiate and accelerate social change.

During the last few years, a large number of social scientists have employed one or another explicitly behavioral model of man.[47] The vast

47. Thibaut and Kelley (1959) have extended the behavioral model to the analysis of dyadic, triadic, and more complex relationships. Homans (1961) has attempted to explain certain findings of social psychology in terms of the behavioral model, while Blau (1964b) and Yinger (1965) have employed it in their analysis of large-scale social phenomena. De Lamater (1968), Akers (1968), and Akers and Burgess (1967), finally, have employed it in the analysis of deviance. DeFleur and Westie (1963), along with Adler (1956), have indicated some of the advantages which accrue to sociologists when concepts such as "value" and "attitude" are considered from the behavioral point of view. Among anthropologists, Goldschmidt has recently come to the conclusion that functional analysis may have to rely on the "understanding of reward and punishment in learning, the importance or reinforcement and the like," (1966:46) and Adams and Romney (1959) have shown that authority can be analyzed in terms of these principles. Erasmus's (1961) theory of culture change is based on a behavioral model of

amount of empirical evidence that has been accumulated in support of learning principles,[48] and their utility which has been amply demonstrated in the study of individual and social phenomena, leads to the conclusion that behavioral models are more promising than are psychodynamic conceptions of man.

There is, unfortunately, some confusion concerning both the term "behavioral" and the human applicability of this perspective. Duncan and Schnore,[49] for example, speak of the "behavioralistic" approach when they actually mean the psychodynamic point of view. "Behavioral model," then, should refer only to those models which are based on one or another learning theory. An additional problem is that the word "behavioral" evokes in many men visions of rats and pigeons. As the works of Bachrach,[50] Bandura and Walters,[51] Staats and Staats,[52] Ullmann and Krasner,[53] and others indicate, however, there is a rapidly growing emphasis on work with human beings, and the increasingly sophisticated conceptualization and analysis of learning have made early and narrow interpretations somewhat irrelevant.

Since the systematic analysis of social processes requires specific statements concerning the determinants of behavior and the role of the social context, the general behavioral model discussed above has to be phrased in terms of more specific propositions. The question arises, then, as to which behavioral model of man, which learning theory or approach, should be employed in the analysis of social change. The model that has received most attention in recent years, and in terms of which most research has been done, will be described in the following chapter.

---

man, specifically the importance of individuals' predictions concerning their actions' consequences, and Harris (1964) has devoted an entire book to the proposition that anthropology can benefit from learning principles and the minute analysis of behavior.

48. As illustrated, for example, by Ayllon and Azrin (1968), Krasner and Ullmann (1965).

49. Duncan and Schnore (1959).

50. Bachrach (1962).

51. Bandura and Walters (1963).

52. Staats and Staats (1963).

53. Ullmann and Krasner (1965).

iii *An Outline of*

Behavioral Analysis

A Behavioral Model of Man

During the past few years, an increasing number of psychologists have concentrated their efforts on the analysis of the relationship between individuals' behavior and the past and present social context.[1] These experiments—usually performed under carefully controlled conditions and subjected to validation procedures involving objective, verifiable measurements— have made it possible to formulate a number of learning principles.[2] The resulting model of man, described below, continues to receive support from a large number of studies involving many different subjects and behavior patterns.[3] The great heterogeneity of circumstances in which studies of learning have been performed, the variety of procedures which have been employed, and the fact that in spite of these differences the basic conclusions concerning the learning of behav-

1. For examples of these efforts, see the studies collected in Staats (1964) and in Ullmann and Krasner (1965).

2. The term "learning principle" is still a subject of debate. Some researchers hold that present knowledge is too limited to justify the use of "principle," and others prefer to speak of "procedures" rather than of principles.

3. Good examples of the methods that can be employed to solve various behavior problems in more or less "free" environments are found in the *Journal of Applied Behavior Analysis*.

ior are the same, provide a relatively secure basis for the present behavioral model of man.[4] This is not to say that further work by psychologists will have no effect on the model; rather, as more information becomes available, the relatively simple descriptions available today will be replaced by more complex, though not basically different, formulations. The present model, then, while tentative, reflects the best and most reliable available evidence.

Until a few years ago, the vast majority of learning studies had animals as their subjects. In recent years, however, an increasing number of psychologists have investigated the principles involved in human learning, and today there is a large body of respectable evidence concerning the shaping, maintenance, and extinction of human behavior patterns. The propositions which constitute the present model of man, for example, are all derived from studies with human beings. A comparison of the present model—based on results of human studies—with models based on animal studies shows no essential differences. More specifically, the relationships indicated below apparently do not differ substantially from relationships established by work with animals. While it is beyond the scope of this book to draw philosophical conclusions from this state of affairs, it must be remembered that the behavioral model of man presented in this chapter has *independent* empirical support, and that similarities with the results of animal studies are merely coincidental. Such similarities of human and animal studies are irrelevant from the point of view of sociologists, for the analysis of social phenomena does not require the acceptance or rejection of assumptions concerning the phylogenetic continuity of man and animal. However, it may be useful to remember Lorenz' admonition that "only the person who knows animals, including the highest and most nearly related to ourselves, and who has gained insight into evolution, will be able to apprehend the unique position of man." [5]

The components of the behavioral model of man, considered in terms of the requirements of sociological analysis, are as follows.

THE PSYCHOLOGICAL DETERMINANTS OF BEHAVIOR

The basic postulate of the model is that the great majority of behavior patterns are established and maintained by means of the differential rein-

4. See Staats (1964), Ullmann and Krasner (1965).
5. Lorenz (1966:220).

forcement of activities after they have been performed. That is, not all possible activities, but only those deemed "desirable" by a group or society are rewarded, others are not, and still others may be punished. When an activity is rewarded after it has been performed, the probability of repetition in similar circumstances is increased and eventually approaches certainty. Conversely, when an activity is punished or not rewarded, the probability of repetition under similar conditions declines and eventually approaches zero.

The term "activity" here refers to the vast majority of behavior patterns which constitute daily life, be they verbal, symbolic, or corporal. The activities collectively known as "language," for example, are shaped and maintained in ways which are not essentially different from those involved in driving an automobile—one *learns* to be proficient in both.[6] The range of rewards and punishment is equally wide, including material objects, behavioral elements such as caresses, and symbolic expressions such as "good" or "terrible."

The specific factors involved in the learning of verbal, symbolic, and corporal behavior patterns may be summarized as follows: [7]

1. Behavior (R) is established and maintained or weakened by its consequences, usually called *contingent stimuli,* which may be either *reinforcing* (S^r) or *aversive* (S^a). More accurately, the presentation of reinforcing stimuli (loosely speaking, rewards) or the removal of aversive stimuli increases the probability that the behavior pattern will be repeated, whereas the presentation of an aversive stimulus (loosely speaking, punishment) or the removal of an S^r decreases the probability that the behavior pattern will be repeated in the future. The absence of contingencies (S^o) also decreases the probability that the activity will be repeated, and the extinction of behavior is the usual result.

There are many varieties of both reinforcing and aversive contingencies. While *primary* stimuli—with a largely physiological basis—influence behavior to some extent, most daily and extraordinary actions are associated with *secondary* contingent stimuli. Secondary contingencies

6. For present purposes it is enough to recognize that men *learn* to speak and comprehend an existing language. The *nature* of language and the controversy surrounding this topic (Chomsky, 1959), are of little interest in development analysis.

7. The major sources of the following statements are Bandura (1969), Gagné (1965), Staats and Staats (1963), Ullmann and Krasner (1965), Krasner and Ullman (1965).

are learned—for example smiles—and thus have a social or cultural origin. Finally, there are *generalized reinforcers*—such as money or prestige—which may be exchanged for a wide variety of other more specific primary or secondary reinforcers. Food is probably the most important primary (or unconditioned) reinforcer, while the number of secondary (or conditioned) reinforcers is very large indeed—including such phenomena as popularity, clothing, hair styles, and certain verbal expressions. Similarly, the number of primary aversive stimuli such as physical punishment is much smaller than that of secondary S^a—such as frowns, verbal expressions, and various evidences of failure.

Primary contingent stimuli are quite similar from one culture to another, but secondary contingencies may be expected to vary greatly from one society to another and even among subcultures within a nation. For example, tousling someone else's hair is generally considered a reinforcer in American society, but among the Melanesians it is considered an aversive contingency.[8] Problems associated with the use of "silent languages" provide good illustrations of variations in cultural definitions of what constitutes "rewarding" and "punishing" behavior in human interaction.[9] Most contingent stimuli are basically the actions of men—simple acts such as smiles, complex sets such as "deference," or intermediaries leading to primary reinforcers such as the serving of food or the payment of wages that can be exchanged for basic necessities.

In summary, the "reinforcement" of an action is not necessarily equivalent to the presentation of a reward; at times the removal of an aversive stimulus may be rewarding, while the withdrawal of an S^r may be considered as punishment. The contingencies of action may therefore be formulated as in Figure 3–1.

2. The *schedules of presentation* of contingencies affect especially the maintenance of behavior and its smoothness. If reinforcement is continuous, behavior is easily maintained while reinforcement lasts, but when rewards are terminated the extinction of behavior is quite rapid. If reinforcement is intermittent (i.e. on a discontinuous schedule), behavior will be equally well maintained, and after the termination of rewards behavior patterns will be more resistant to extinction. Most schedules of daily life are discontinuous and a combination of fixed

8. Spicer (1952:Case 9). For a discussion of social and cultural factors in perception, see Tajfel (1969).
9. Hall (1959).

	Reinforcing Stimulus (S^r)	Aversive Stimulus (S^a)
Presented	(positive) reinforcement	punishment
Withdrawn	punishment	(negative) reinforcement

FIGURE 3–1: Variations in Contingencies
From: Holland and Skinner (1961:245).

and variable ratios and intervals. Men must learn the schedules to which they are subject, but not all persons necessarily learn all of the schedules found in life. Thus the "short range point of view," so characteristic of some subcultures, reflects the learning of short-interval schedules, while the "long-range point of view" is a reflection of long-interval schedules in which reinforcers may not be presented for years. Alterations in schedules, especially the lengthening of intervals, affect performance and often involve emotional reactions such as anger. For example, men who have learned to live with long interval or low ratio schedules are said to have a high "frustration tolerance," whereas persons used to frequent reinforcement have a low frustration tolerance—that is, they exhibit emotional reactions when reinforcers are not presented at the accustomed rate or time.

3. The effectiveness of any reinforcing stimulus for the shaping and maintenance of behavior depends in large part on the *state variables* (SV), the individual's characteristics of deprivation and satiation in a large number of areas. Deprivation, which makes reinforcing stimuli effective by their capacity to reduce it, may be primary (i.e. largely physiological) or secondary (i.e. largely learned), such as the culturally determined emphasis on proper dress or popularity. Under conditions of satiation, previously operating reinforcers cease to be effective; consequently, the repetition of most activities depends on the degree to which at least some kind of deprivation can be maintained. Deprivation is facilitated by generalized reinforcers such as money which, since they can be exchanged for many things, bring a wide range of deprivations into operation. It may be concluded, then, that in noncash societies the range

of reinforcers is quite narrow, and that it may thus be more difficult to shape new behavior patterns there than in communities in which the cash nexus is well established.

There is a close relationship between state variables and contingencies; in fact, one may well be considered in terms of the other. Satiation makes reinforcers less effective, and the most powerful rewards are those which tend to decrease the greatest or most important deprivations. Human beings are characterized by a large variety of possible secondary deprivations, acquired in childhood and newly learned throughout life. Since deprivations vary among societies and subcultures, the student of social behavior must expect to find that even the most "impossible" elements may serve as reinforcers, and that men may learn to be deprived of the "craziest" things.

Reactions to deprivation conditions, like any behavior patterns, are learned. Men who have learned to accept low rates of reinforcement, for example, may act "normally" in spite of great deprivations. Conversely, children who are used to high rates of reinforcement and who have not learned to live with deprivation, are characterized as "spoiled brats"— the term referring to a particular repertoire of activities.

4. Heretofore the term "reinforcer" has been used as if it were one discrete entity. The complexities of human life are such, however, that few activities are followed by simple consequences. Rather, men act in terms of total contingencies which often involve a complex arrangement of long- and short-range consequences. In addition, it is postulated that, generally speaking, men attempt to *maximize the totality of contingencies.* That is, men are assumed to sum up the various consequences of activities and to select that behavior pattern which promises to result in the most beneficial total contingency. The usual consideration of costs and profits, however, while applicable, is too restricted for the explanation of behavior patterns in a complex social system. Among the major *components of the total contingency* are:

a) the time period, which limits the contingencies that are to be included in the summation;

b) the state variables, which determine not only whether a particular contingency will be "positive" or "negative," but also its weight;

c) the schedules on which the various contingencies are presented;

d) the individual's learning history (and by implication the norms and values to which he has been subjected).

e) the individual's awareness of the contingencies and their schedules;

f) the individual's knowledge of the relationship between action and various contingencies;

g) the individual's ability to predict, evaluate, and combine all of the relevant contingencies of an action;

h) the individual's ability to behave in a manner consistent with his judgment of the optimum totality of contingencies, that is, to select and perform the activity that has the predicted consequences.

Two major problems are immediately apparent: first, perfect maximization is infrequent. Limitations of knowledge, restrictions of experience, and the narrow parameters presented by short-range points of view, not to mention the social changes which make long-range predictions hazardous, would indicate that *maximization is a matter of degree.* Second, an outside observer is likely to have information which is substantially different from that of a participating member of a group or society. Hence it is to be expected that there will be several different judgments of the "optimum consequences" of any activity. In short, *maximization is a matter of perspective.*[10]

From these considerations it follows that behavior may be changed even when the individual's surroundings remain objectively the same. For example, literacy may expand his horizon to include more consequences, his time perspective may shift, or he may learn new deprivations; as a result the total contingencies of his present activities and alternative actions may change sufficiently to lead to an alteration of behavior. Conversely, it is possible for the environment to change while behavior is maintained, because the individual may not be able to perform the activities that would lead to the improved consequences in the new setting. The postulate of maximization, then, does not lead to the conclusion that behavior change necessarily follows from environmental changes, or that an individual's objective social context must be changed in order for behavior to be altered. While there is abundant clinical and

10. The concepts of "maximization" and "rationality" have presented social scientists with thorny issues (Ball, 1968). For a treatment of the philosophical and methodological problems of these concepts, and of the dangers that attend their use, see Hempel (1965:463ff). Rapoport (1966) provides an example of how these concepts are employed in game theory, while Luce and Raiffa (1957: 275ff) present a mathematical view of decision-making under conditions of partial ignorance and uncertainty.

experimental evidence that behavior change results from alterations in the individual's social environment, the contingencies in these cases are relatively simple and straightforward. Behavior change is much more difficult to bring about in an open, free, and complex society, where the contingencies are complicated, often difficult to predict, and where the relationships between behavior and consequences are somewhat nebulous and subject to the intervention of intermediary agents.

5. When a reinforcing stimulus is presented after an activity has been performed in a particular context (for example telling a joke in a group of men), the behavior will be repeated in the same or a similar context, or in a specific aspect of it (a group of *men*), eventually even without immediate reinforcement. Those elements of the context in whose presence a behavior pattern was reinforced, called *discriminative stimuli* (S^D), eventually come to "control" the behavior; that is, the probability of their presence being followed by a particular behavior pattern increases and approaches certainty. If another part of the context (S^Δ), if present, is not followed by the reinforcement of an activity, or is followed by aversive consequences (for example, telling the same joke in mixed company), then the probability of the activity being performed in the presence of that element (*mixed* company) will decline and approach zero. Since an S^D is established by the reinforcement of an activity, there is a close relationship between S^r and S^D, and between S^a and S^Δ. In addition, since contingencies are closely associated with state variables, it follows that it would be quite difficult to establish discriminative stimuli without the existence of some degree of deprivation.

Most discriminative stimuli of daily life are men or behavior. These range from simple verbal expression—"come here"—to highly complex phenomena such as a man's "status." In all instances, however, the referent of S^D is behavior, for it is only through action that it is possible to know what constitutes a discriminative stimulus.

6. It is evident that not all elements of a person's context affect his behavior, because not all are directly associated with discriminative or contingent stimuli. The rest of the environment, which usually plays an important role only when it changes drastically, is referred to as *constant stimuli* (SS^c).

7. An important question of behavioral analysis concerns the extent to which any activity needs to be dissected. A finger movement, for example, will probably be irrelevant, but co-operation in slash-and-burn agri-

culture will be important. For present purposes it will be sufficient to combine muscle movements into *behavior patterns,* ranging from relatively simple ones like walking or tending a machine to rather complex patterns such as co-operative hunting. It is only by means of such shorthand notation that the millions of actions in which an individual engages in the course of a year can become part of development analysis. Any number of activities which occur over time but form a theoretically relevant and distinct unit may be considered as a behavior pattern, be it "harvesting" or "working in a factory." Investigators of small groups, for example, have a distinct focus of analysis and definition of pattern, while students of bureaucracies have another. It must be remembered, however, that complex patterns may have to be dissected into their constituent elements when a detailed behavioral analysis is to be performed.

8. Every activity is related to one or several preceding S^D and subsequent contingencies, and thus any behavior should be conceptualized in terms of these three basic components:

$$S^D \text{————} R \text{————} \rightarrow \underset{S^o}{\overset{S^r \quad S^a}{\bigvee\limits_{or}}}$$

Most activities of daily life do not form such independent units, however, and few behavior patterns are directly followed by primary or even secondary reinforcers. Rather, the basic units are combined to form *chains,* and only at the end of a series of activities—at times lasting several years—can reinforcement be said to occur. Not all chains are that long, of course, and daily life may be viewed as a complex arrangement of concurrent chains of varying lengths, with many chains ending in some kind of reinforcement at quite frequent intervals. A month's labor is followed by a paycheck, courtship by marriage, or a man may work hard for a number of years—such as acquiring a college education—in order to eventually reap the rewards of a good position. It is proper, then, to speak of *behavior chains* in which a person's activity at any one moment is a discriminative stimulus for further action, while this activity is also, at the same time, a conditioned reinforcer for preceding actions. The links of a chain need not be restricted to one person, however, for the activities of several individuals may influence each other. Any person's actions may be considered as being "tied" to the actions of others in the sense that one person's behavior may be another person's (conditioned) reinforcer and a third person's discriminative stimulus for further action. In fact, it is only in rare instances that the behavior chains which make up an individual's daily life do not include other people's activities as both discriminative stimuli and conditioned reinforcers.

The distinction between patterns and chains is usually one of methodological convenience, for very complex behavior patterns obviously consist of a number of chains involving several people. Harvesting, for example, involves the actions of many men in the cutting, bundling, transporting, and storing of grain. Thus, the decision as to the use of "chains" or "patterns" in an analysis, along with the definition of these units, will depend on the nature of the study and the theoretical requirements of the particular case.

9. While most activities of daily life are patterned, and preceded and followed by discriminative and contingent stimuli, *random behavior* is also possible and does occur. However, precisely because it is random, the action is not likely to be relevant for sociological analysis. Random behavior is important only insofar as it is a source of "new" behavior patterns.

10. In order to learn, a person need not himself experience the consequences of his actions, nor must differential reinforcement directly affect the individual. Recent studies, especially those of Bandura and his associates, have indicated that direct, personal experience is not necessary for shaping or maintaining behavior.[11] It has been shown, for example, that the individual may learn new behavior patterns by observing other people and especially the consequences of their actions. Thus, if a child observes another person's actions and if these actions are rewarded, the child will, under similar circumstances, act the way the other person did. This procedure, called *modeling,* is assumed to play a major part in the learning of behavior, not only among children but also among adults. The basic learning principles discussed above are assumed to operate in modeling, but they operate indirectly, so to speak. Thus, Bandura and Walters hypothesize that most learning occurs through the "vicarious experiences" of many activities and the establishment of "vicarious reinforcement." The modeling approach to learning indicates the importance of communication, and especially of information concern-

11. Bandura and Walters (1963), Bandura (1969:118–216).

ing other people's activities and their consequences. Thus communication among individuals becomes an important variable in any analysis involving the behavioral model of man.

11. From these considerations it is apparent that behavior patterns will not change as long as the factors maintaining them remain constant. That is, the *probability of behavior replication* is high as long as the state variables, discriminative stimuli, and contingencies remain constant. Conversely, behavior patterns will be altered when the relevant factors (again SV, contingencies, and S^D) change. When an activity is no longer rewarded it will eventually be extinguished, the length of time being a function of the schedule of reinforcement and the number of times the activity has been rewarded in the past. For example, when reinforcement is consistent and intermittent, when mild deprivation is maintained, and when the discriminative stimuli are firmly established and do not change, behavior will be maintained. However, when contingencies change or reinforcement ceases, when deprivations disappear or new ones come into being, when the schedule of rewards is changed drastically, or when old discriminative stimuli no longer appear, the probability of behavior replication will decline and eventually approach zero.

12. Presently available information leads to the conclusion that the same learning principles operate in all cultures, races, and stages of the life cycle. It is true, of course, that what is rewarding in one culture may be aversive in another, and that the rewards of childhood are rarely those which affect the lives of adults. The basic principles or procedures, however, are the same, and thus may be taken as the *constants* of any sociological analysis. Some individuals learn more slowly than others, and genetic and physiological factors may influence the rate of learning and limit the activities that can be shaped.[12] The rate or "ease" of learning is also affected by the number of other activities, and especially of incompatible behavior patterns, in the person's repertoire. Old people, with an extensive repertoire, may thus have difficulty learning new activities. The basic principles seem to be the same, however. The fact that behavior patterns have been shaped and extinguished by means of operant conditioning procedures in normal individuals, neurotics, and inmates of mental institutions lends support to the view that learning principles appear to be equally applicable to all men, no matter what their other psychological characteristics.

12. Franks (1964).

THE INTERNAL STATE

Neither the learning approach to human action nor the resulting behavioral model of man denies the existence of an internal state. Rather, they represent attempts to reduce the importance of presently unmeasurable variables and processes in the causal analysis of social phenomena and to substitute for such variables clearly defined procedures. The assumptions which are made concerning man's internal state are grounded as much as possible in experimental and other empirical evidence. When learning is viewed as a set of procedures for the shaping and maintenance of behavior, the explanation of behavior may be based on either these procedures or on certain characteristics of the individual which are assumed to have been established in the course of the successful application of these procedures. Prominent among these characteristics are the individual's deprivation or satiation, his perception of discriminative stimuli, and his conception of reinforcement probabilities. These components of the internal state have clearly delineated procedural referents, and it is these referents which distinguish them from the elements or mental states which are prominent in the various psychodynamic theories.

It may be concluded from both experiments and the application of learning principles in clinical and other situations, that these internal states and processes can be quite accurately predicted when the learning history of the individual is known, and that they may therefore be considered as "constant" or given factors.[13] Consequently, the explanation and prediction of behavior is possible without an exhaustive analysis or careful investigation of these states. The investigator's knowledge of an individual's past and present social environment—that is, his learning history—is usually sufficient for the prediction of most actions in which sociologists are interested.

Since the present tools of the social and behavioral sciences are not able to measure man's internal state directly, or at least independently of behavior, postulates concerning internal characteristics must be approached with caution. However, while it is impossible to definitely indicate the elements of the internal state and their interrelationships, there is insufficient information for the denial of the existence or operation of an internal state. The nature of the internal state, its operation and its

13. For a discussion of the internal state in behavioral models of man, see Bachrach (1962), Marx (1963), Bandura (1969:32–45).

effects on the behavior of men remains largely a mystery today. *The behavioral approach outlined in this chapter is designed to circumvent the mystery, rather than to deny its existence or to make it an integral part of the analysis of social phenomena.*

AN ILLUSTRATION OF THE MODEL: LANGUAGE LEARNING [14]

Babies and young children, in the course of their random babbling, make many of the sounds which are contained in the world's languages. Some of the noises are made in the presence of other people, usually the mother, who rewards certain types of sounds—depending on the language of the society. For example, the sound "ma" (R) may be reinforced by smiles, fondling, or rocking, (S^r), and thus the probability of the sound's being repeated increases. The child soon learns that "ma" is not always rewarded, however. Only when a large hulk looms over the crib (S^D) is "ma" followed by fondling—when the hulk is absent (S^Δ), there are few pleasurable consequences (except hearing one's own sounds). Soon the mother is likely to reward only upon the repetition of sounds "mamamama," and eventually only when the child makes specific sequences—"mama" and not "mamama." Later, the child learns that the sounds "mama" are reinforced in the presence of one hulk but not in that of another—the other giant rewards only sounds such as "papa." The child thus learns to discriminate among a variety of S^D and, by means of modeling and the reinforcement of successively more specific sound combinations, he learns to speak. In one culture, sounds such as "the" are reinforced, in another such sounds as "öl," while large categories of sounds are extinguished since they are not rewarded. Eventually, then, children in different societies acquire different languages because different sounds are reinforced by the different social environments. Parents, siblings, and, later, peers and the "rest of the population" reinforce by means of smiles or simply by responding (S^r) only those speech patterns (R) which are "intelligible" in the particular society or subculture. People do not reinforce, for example by ignoring (S^o), the sound combinations which are "unintelligible," and they are likely to punish (S^a) those which are "intelligible" but "undesirable." Much of the rest of the child's environment, for example the physical context, has little influence on the learning of language (SS^c). A smile, fondling, or a "treat" will be reinforcing only to the extent to which the child has previously been de-

14. This illustration is based on Staats and Staats (1963).

prived of attention, sweets, etc. (SV), and to the degree to which smiles have been learned to be considered as "rewards." If parents continually fondle a child or supply him with ample sweets, neither attention nor candy is likely to become an effective reinforcer. In later life, finally, the members of one's own society (S^D) will provide occasion for speaking (R), and the granting of requests, responding to questions, etc. will be ample rewards (S^r). In a group of foreigners (S^Δ), however, few attempts at speaking will be made—but gestures may be tried out, to be repeated if "rewarded" by successful communication.

A NOTE OF CAUTION

A major criticism of the behavioral model of man outlined above is that some of its components appear to be tautological. For example, if "reinforcer" is defined as a "consequence of behavior that increases the frequency with which an activity occurs," then the proposition that "the presentation of a reinforcer increases the frequency with which the preceding activity occurs" is tautological. Two major solutions have been proposed, neither completely satisfactory. First, reinforcers can be defined in terms of the reduction of deprivations, be they physiological or cultural. In many societies, for example, money is a reinforcer since it can be used to reduce a wide variety of deprivations. In most cases it is not necessary to investigate individuals' specific deprivation characteristics in order to hypothesize that cash is a reinforcer and will help to maintain behavior. Second, reinforcers may be defined in terms of their effects on *specific preceding* activities, but once they have been defined their presentation may be hypothesized to influence the probability of *quite different future* events. For example, smiles are learned reinforcers that are established early in childhood, mainly by parents. Later on, however, smiles continue to operate as rewards, and the smiles of people in general will affect the probability of behavior replication in many areas of life.[15]

The variety of activities that have been shaped, maintained, extinguished, and altered by means of differential reinforcement is great indeed. Words, gestures, a large number of skills, and practically all of the actions involved in daily life and required by special occasions, are known to be subject to the learning principles sketched above. Yet it is too early

15. For an example of how the problem might be solved, see Burgess and Akers (1966).

to generalize that *all* behavior can be explained in terms of operant conditioning procedures. Present knowledge leads to the conclusion that *most behavior patterns of interest to sociologists* can be explained in this fashion, but the limitations of research and the relative youth of experimental psychology require that any efforts to extend generalizations beyond available evidence proceed with caution. As long as sociologists are interested in regularities of behavior or the conditions underlying deviance, the behavioral perspective will be useful. The explanation of individual genius, however, for example that of the *Grosse Fuge,* is presently beyond the pale of the behavioral approach. The uncertainties of available information and interpretations are well illustrated in the case of aggression. Lorenz [16] suggests that activities generally viewed as "aggression" are phlyogenetically adapted behavior patterns, but other studies show that aggression is subject to alteration by changing its contingencies.[17] Thomas and others,[18] for example, report that aggressive behavior in children is markedly reduced when it is no longer rewarded by the often inappropriate "attention" of well-meaning teachers and parents.

This illustration points to a further problem, that of confusing activities with their labels. While some of the activities described by Lorenz and Thomas are the same—for example "hitting others"—it is very easy to speak simply of aggression and to forget that different investigators may have different empirical referents for the same behavioral label. Whenever possible, then, the activities themselves, rather than commonly applied labels, should be employed in an analysis.

The components of the behavioral model outlined above are purposely stated in quite general terms. Much more research is required before more specific relationships—for example between particular types of punishment and specific behavior characteristics—can be incorporated into the model. It follows that the sociological implications of the behavioral model can also be stated in only general terms, and that care must be taken when learning principles are extended to the structure and operation of social phenomena. All that can be done at present is to provide an outline and some of the ways in which the behavioral perspective contributes to the conceptualization and analysis of social processes; the task of specifying procedures must be reserved for the future.

16. Lorenz (1966:chapter 3).
17. Montagu (1968), Bandura (1969:378 ff).
18. Thomas *et al.* (1968), and Zeilberger *et al.* (1968).

So far, very little has been said concerning the actual process of learning, that is, what occurs within the individual while he learns or while behavior patterns are being established or maintained. The major reason for this neglect is that any statements concerning the actual process of learning would have to be based largely on inferences or assumptions which are not yet amenable to objective verification. The reinforcement of an activity results in an increased probability that the particular action will be repeated in similar circumstances, but the process that takes place within the individual between input (for example, the visual perception of a smile) and output (the probability of the recurrence of behavior), is relatively unknown.[19] A number of theories have attempted to solve this problem but so far it has been impossible to determine their validity. Connections of neurons within the brain, the contiguity of various stimuli, or the creation of specific conditions in the person's internal characteristics—such as a state of readiness or a predisposition to respond—have been postulated to be responsible for the learning of behavior. Present knowledge is insufficient, in both quantity and quality, for the acceptance or rejection of any of these theories. Instead of burdening students of economic development with the continuing controversy and debate concerning the nature and mechanisms of learning, which are of major interest only to psychologists, it is sufficient to recognize that *there are specific relationships between certain stimuli emanating in the past and present environment and the observable actions of individuals.* The question of which explanation of these experimentally verified relationships will ultimately turn out to be correct is of concern to psychologists but need not detain the sociologist.

The question arises whether it is advisable to make use of a model of man—such as the behavioral approach based on learning principles—which contains a number of unresolved problems and unanswered questions. To psychologists, these problems and questions are important—in fact, many psychologists have made them their life's work.[20] But sociologists cannot wait until these issues have been settled, for indications are

19. Numerous psychologists have investigated the nature of the internal processes that operate between the perception of a stimulus and eventual behavior. A sample of the more important work that has been done in this area would include Allport (1955), Harvey, Hunt, and Schroder (1961), Hebb (1949), Maltzman (1967), and Miller *et al.* (1960).

20. For a comprehensive discussion of these issues and problems, see Marx (1963, 1969).

that this is likely to take at least several years. Instead, sociologists may find it advisable to select from among the available tentative models those which involve the fewest inferences, the most solid empirical evidence, and the smallest number of untestable or as yet unsupported postulates and assumptions. When these criteria are employed, behavioral models based on learning principles appear to be quite acceptable in spite of the fact that much more research is required before the formation of specific principles can be said to be complete. It is evident, however, that behavioral models must be employed with caution and that their components have the status of hypotheses, subject to change as additional empirical evidence becomes available.

THE SOCIAL DETERMINANTS OF BEHAVIOR

The components of the model described above indicate the constant "psychological" determinants of behavior in general. Since sociologists usually are not interested in activities as such but rather in the specific actions of particular people, additional factors are required in order to account for specific social phenomena. The discussion of learning principles has centered, so far, on the rather abstract relationships among various procedures and phenomena. In everyday life, these general learning principles operate within a specific context, and what have been called reinforcement, discriminative stimuli, etc., and simply particular aspects of continuing social life.

A person's social environment consists of at least three major components: other individuals, their activities, and the "rules" which summarize the regularities of others' reactions to an individual's behavior. Most discriminative stimuli, for example, are people and their actions with whom an individual comes into contact in the course of his daily life. The contingent stimuli, be they rewards or punishment, usually consist, again, of the actions of people who smile, frown, provide material goods, etc. Finally, it is from the consistency of others' reactions that the "rules" of behavior are usually inferred. A rule or norm is an abstraction which becomes significant only upon its behavioral manifestation—one "knows" that a norm exists only because of consistent reactions of others, and a norm is "apparent" only when persons behave consistently over time.

According to the behavioral approach sketched above, the social context of an individual, including his immediate family, the various groups and subcultures to which he belongs and has belonged, and the society of which he is a part, plays an important role in the shaping, maintenance, and alteration of behavior (Figure 3–2). The immediate and wider social context, especially the value system and the normative structure arising from it, determine:

1. *The contingent stimuli.* The rewards and punishments of a man's behavior are largely determined by the social context within which the individual operates, on both the immediate level—the group to which he belongs at any moment—and the wider societal level. While the values and norms of a society or subculture thus may be said to perform functions analogous to those performed by the experimenter in the laboratory, a distinction must be made between "ideal values" which indicate the behavior that *should* be reinforced, and "operating norms" which determine what behavior *is* in actuality reinforced. Values and norms need not be consistent, and some degree of discrepancy appears to be common in most societies; an activity rewarded by "society," for example, may be punished by the individual's subculture. The arrows emanating from "norms" and "values" in Figure 3–2, therefore, should be considered as being more diverse than is indicated.

2. *The schedule of reinforcement.* Whether reinforcers are presented continuously or intermittently, on a ratio or interval schedule, on a fixed or variable basis, is largely a function of the social context, such as customary payment for work or periodic festivals.

3. *The state variables.* The efficacy of particular rewards and punishment is dependent upon the set of deprivations characteristic of a particular society, its communities, subcultures, and various other groups. The influence of the social context is most direct in the establishment of secondary or learned deprivations, for example social isolation in a society which emphasizes fellowship and togetherness, but it is also apparent in the operation of primary or physiological state variables, as in the cultural determination of appropriate clothing, "decent" housing, or the kinds of food permissible for the reduction of hunger. The set of effective deprivations, and the appropriate and acceptable procedures for their reduction, may be expected to vary among subcultures, thus giving rise to a variety of behavior patterns even within the same society.

4. *The discriminative stimuli.* By reinforcing particular behavior patterns when they appear in a specific context, the normative system of a society or subculture determines which aspects of an individual's context

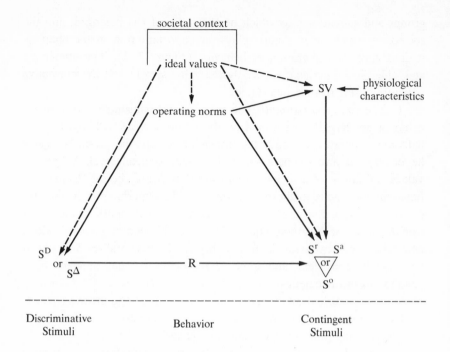

FIGURE 3–2: A Behavioral Model of Man

Glossary of Important Terms:

R = any activity
S^r = reinforcing stimulus (loosely speaking, rewards)
S^a = aversive stimulus (loosely speaking, punishment)
S^o = absence of any consequences
S^D = stimulus in whose presence R has been reinforced
S^Δ = stimulus in whose presence R has not been reinforced
SV = state variables (i.e. conditions of deprivation and satisfaction)
Ideal Values = theoretical determinants of state variables, discrim-
     inative and contingent stimuli
Operating Norms = actual determinants of state variables, discrim-
     inative and contingent stimuli

Source: Kunkel (1966:50).

will eventually take on controlling properties. Honesty in social relations, for example, will usually be rewarded except in special circumstances, when customs of politeness may indicate that "white lies" are not only appropriate but required. Inconsistencies and ambiguities in the norma- tive structure regarding appropriate behavior and circumstances usually result in incompletely established discriminative stimuli, leading to individuals' uncertainty as to how to behave.

5. *The behavior of individuals.* By playing a direct part in the determination of deprivation variables, by assigning reinforcing stimuli and the schedules of their presentation contingent upon specific activities, and by the creation of discriminative stimuli, the societal context indirectly determines the behavior patterns and chains of individuals. By defining the specific components of the operant conditioning procedures in the various groups to which men belong, the values and norms of any society or subculture become an integral part of any explanation of behavior.

This discussion of the role of social factors has been carried out from the point of view of the individual. As far as observers are concerned, however, it is not entirely accurate to say that the "norms define" discriminative stimuli, or to speak of the "social context" as a more or less undifferentiated entity. "Norm" actually refers to certain abstracted characteristics of consistently observed behavior patterns in a population. For example, activities and speech patterns directed by young people toward the old, and old people's reactions, may be summarized as the norm of "deference toward the aged." The *norm* would refer to both the children's *consistent actions* toward a *specific* class of persons and the *consistent reactions* of these and other persons. Thus a "norm" is difficult to conceptualize without the attendant definitions of appropriate circumstances and contingencies.[21]

When a particular person is the frame of reference, "social context" refers to the more or less consistent activities of other people. However, when an observer is the frame of reference, it may be best to speak of "social structure" as the shorthand term for the myriad activities which constitute the operation of any community, subculture, or society. Both terms, in short, are methodological conveniences, and no existence apart from men's actions, no dimension or other characteristic, can be ascribed to them.

Any individual, while acting in accordance with contingency probabilities and his experience, is himself part of the social environment of others. That is, his activities are likely to constitute discriminative and

21. This view of norms is consistent with current sociological usage and has been discussed at some length by Homans (1961) and by Blake and Davis (1964).

contingent stimuli for others' behavior, and the societal norms in terms of which he acts (in the sense that they define behavior patterns appropriate for the dispensing of rewards) are *expressed* by him as he selectively reinforces the behavior of others with whom he deliberately interacts or who simply come into contact with him. The explanation of an individual's behavior, then, includes not only learning principles, but also the systematic activities and reactions of other people (including verbal expressions) summarized as the norms (and values) of a subculture or society. The behavioral analysis of any individual, group, or subculture assumes the relevant context as "given" and concentrates on the relationship between the context and the men and activities that are the focus of the study. The various components of the context itself, be they individuals, groups, or subcultures, may be of interest in another study, and the context of these individuals or groups will then be assumed as "given." The definition of "context," in short, is arbitrary and depends on the focus of the study.

So far, the individual's social environment has been treated as if it were quite independent of the person's behavior. Actually, however, many components of the environment are amenable to modification and control by the behaving individual, and it is therefore proper to speak of the reciprocal influence of individual and social context. A society's or subculture's values and norms determine the parameters of the social environment's variability, but it is the person who in large measure creates the specific characteristics of his context. The norm of "friendliness," for example, means that men are likely to smile and to exchange greetings, but if a person is gruff and never greets anyone, few if any of his associates will continue to act friendly toward him. Norms and values thus indicate the range of possible responses, but in order for these activities to occur, the individual has to provide the people in his environment with the proper discriminative stimuli, i.e. a set of specific actions. As the psychological literature amply demonstrates, men have succeeded in creating for themselves social environments that range from pleasant to unbearable, by in effect inviting their fellows to be delightful companions or repellent bores.

While some aspects of the social environment are subject to modification and control, others are quite impervious to the individual's influence. Peasants in many developing nations, for example, are confronted by social contexts that include self-serving politicians, reactionary landowners, narrow-minded officials, short-sighted elites, and fellow villagers with many of these same characteristics. The malleability of the environment, then, has to be delineated anew in every study of social change and economic growth, and generalizations even within nations are dangerous; what faces the urban middle class professional man is not what confronts the peasant in the hinterland. In general, the more educated a person is, the more he knows about the operation of the social system, and the higher his position in the class structure, the greater the probability that he can influence his social environment and the greater the latitude presented by societal values and norms.

THE BEHAVIORAL PERSPECTIVE AND CURRENT SOCIOLOGY

It is part of the conventional wisdom that behavior is affected by rewards and by punishment, and no careful observer of social life can avoid the recognition that behavior is learned. One may expect, therefore, that both early sociologists and current literature show considerable familiarity with the basic aspects of the behavioral perspective. However, since careful experimental research with human beings and of relevance to sociologists has flourished only in the last few years, and since the transmission of information from one field to another often involves a considerable time lag, the specific components of a more or less complete behavioral "model of man" have not been available. As such a model is being developed, it may be expected that much current sociological thought will not only be congruent with it, but may indeed benefit from the specification of the relationships among men and among activities. The following discussion presents several examples of well-known sociological concepts viewed from the behavioral perspective.

Sociologists, and especially social psychologists, have long been interested in the major components of an individual's social context. Most members of a society are able to predict rather well how others will react, and to behave accordingly. Thus it may be advantageous to speak of the "generalized other" as the set of responses which a person expects from his fellows and in terms of which he acts.[22] The "generalized other," then, is a product of experience and refers to the abstracted elements of other people's reactions, without necessarily specifying the exact behavior patterns that particular persons in an individual's environment will exhibit.

22. For a slightly different use of this famous term, see Mead (1934).

Not all individuals who constitute a person's social context will be providers of (or be themselves) discriminative and contingent stimuli. The frown of a stranger, for example, is not likely to be an aversive stimulus, but that of a friend, relative, or superior, is likely to take on the property of "punishment." The social environment may therefore be conceived as a set of "significant others," those individuals whose activities affect the shaping and maintenance of behavior, and one of insignificant persons whose presence and/or actions do not constitute discriminative or contingent stimuli.[23] The definition of "significant others" is, of course, a social phenomenon, a reflection of a subculture's or society's values and norms, and thus is a result of learning. This is not to say that all members of a society, or even all members of a subculture, can be expected to have identical definitions of "significant others." It is possible, then, for two individuals to act quite differently in similar situations— for example in a small peasant community when there is an opportunity for trade—because one person's definition of "significant other" (such as men in other villages) is not shared by another person whose frame of reference is restricted to his native community. The accurate prediction of behavior, then, requires knowledge of an individual's definition of "significant others" in a large variety of circumstances and with respect to a multitude of specific activities. While the person's membership in a community or subculture provides much of this information, it cannot be assumed that the learning experiences of all members will be identical. Here again it is likely that cultural factors will be significant, for example by restricting the contacts and hence information which various groups within a community are "allowed" or "expected" to have.

The term "reference group" has been widely employed to indicate the source of an individual's behavioral standards and the agency for their enforcement.[24] For example, while a peasant belongs to a number of groups such as his family and village, much of his behavior may be congruent with the activities of men who live "in town." As far as he is concerned, it is *these* men who are the sources of discriminative and contingent stimuli, and thus the determinants of his behavior.

Rose's "Systematic Summary of Symbolic Interaction Theory" pro-

23. For an extended treatment of these ideas, see Mead (1934).
24. For example by Kelley (1952), Kemper (1968), Merton (1957a), and Newcomb (1950, 1952).

vides a further illustration of the behavioral perspective's congruence with existing sociological knowledge. His first three assumptions, except for terminology, arise directly from the behavioral model of man: [25] "Man lives in a symbolic environment as well as a physical environment and can be 'stimulated' to act by symbols as well as by physical stimuli"; "Through symbols, man has the capacity to stimulate others in ways other than those in which he is himself stimulated;" and "Through communication of symbols, man can learn huge numbers of meanings and values—and hence ways of acting—from other men." Some of the other assumptions, for example concerning the stages of socialization or the process of thinking, while not inconsistent with the behavioral model, are attempts to formulate some of the variables which may intervene between symbols and action and at present are difficult to substantiate.

The congruence of social systems analysis and the behavioral perspective is much less evident, though still discernible. For example, Parsons speaks of the actor's "gratificational" and "orientational" aspects; "the first concerns the 'content' of his interchange with the object world, 'what' he gets out of his interaction with it, and what its 'costs' to him are. The second concerns the 'how' of his relation to the object world, the patterns or ways in which his relations to it are organized." [26] It is only with the later additions, such as "cathectic attachments" and "internalized value-patterns" that Parsons goes beyond the limitations of the behavioral perspective.

The preceding treatment of "values" and "norms," and the discussion of "generalized other," reference groups, symbolic interaction theory, and the social action approach, indicate that *the behavioral model of man does not require the elimination of existing sociological concepts and propositions; rather, it provides many of them with additional, and hopefully more specific, observable referents.* This does not mean, of course, that *all* areas of sociological inquiry will benefit from a behavioral perspective. The behavioral model, for example, may not be applicable to certain problems and theoretical concerns, such as social movements or collective behavior. As far as the analysis of social aspects of economic development is concerned, however, existing sociological approaches may well benefit from the incorporation of the behavioral model of man.

25. Rose (1962:5, 7, 9); italics have been eliminated.
26. Parsons (1951:7).

Other Behavioral Models of Man

The more or less nontheoretical bent of experimental psychologists interested in operant conditioning is not widely shared. It is much more common for psychologists to either adhere to one or another learning theory or to construct their own. However, since the experimental evidence is quite straightforward, most learning theories have as their foundation almost identical observations and other data, and differ mainly in the postulates and assumptions employed in their explanation. For example, the basic proposition of the present model of man, that behavior is greatly influenced by its consequences, here crudely labeled reward and punishment, is not new and has been widely recognized by a number of scholars. Thorndike's "law of effect," Guthrie's emphasis on the contiguity of stimulus and response, and the major propositions of Hull's theory reflect the results of many experiments which indicate the great importance of an action's outcome in the learning of that action. Differences among theorists, and even among experimenters reflect, in the main, different postulates and assumptions concerning the processes which occur between the original stimulus and eventual behavior, between contingency and the later repetition of behavior.

The consequences of action are such an obvious part of learning that the psychologist has not been the only one impressed by this relationship. For example, as long as forty years ago, the anthropologist Malinowski wrote that primitive law is not obeyed because of some group spirit, but because "the fulfillment of . . . obligations is usually rewarded according to the measure of its perfection, while non-compliance is [punished in a variety of ways]." [27] The behavioral models which social scientists have employed are to a large extent based on the learning principles outlined above but usually include several additional elements.[28] For example, individuals' thoughts, needs, expectations, evaluations, and predictions have been considered to be essential components and important determinants of behavior. For present purposes it is not necessary to examine the differences among the various behavioral mod-

27. Malinowski (1959:12).
28. Feibleman (1963), Hull (1951), Jessor (1962), Miller and Dollard (1941), Rotter (1954), Whiting and Child (1953). For a summary, see Berkowitz (1969).

els except to point out that the added components are designed to explain or describe the learning process itself. Hull's discussion of drive reduction and reaction potential, for example, elaborates the processes which occur as the individual learns and as he behaves.

Only two other models of man will be described in detail, for only they have had an impact on sociology or are relevant for the analysis of economic development. Their essential features do not differ from the basic components of the behavioral model presented above, but since they emphasize different aspects of man's relation to the social environment, they illustrate the ease with which learning principles can be adapted to serve a variety of theoretical and empirical interests.

HOMANS

In his discussion of the elementary forms of social behavior, Homans presents a model of man in the form of five propositions:

1. "If in the past the occurrence of a particular stimulus-situation has been the occasion on which a man's activity has been rewarded, then the more similar the present stimulus-situation is to the past one, the more likely he is to emit the activity, or some similar activity, now." [29]

2. "The more often within a given period of time a man's activity rewards the activity of another, the more often the other will emit the activity." [30]

3. "The more valuable to a man a unit of the activity another gives him, the more often he will emit activity rewarded by the activity of the other." [31]

4. "The more often a man has in the recent past received a rewarding activity from another, the less valuable any further unit of that activity becomes to him." [32]

5. "The more to a man's disadvantage the rule of distributive justice fails of realization, the more likely he is to display the emotional behavior we call anger." [33]

It is clear from these propositions and Homans' detailed analysis of costs, profits, and sentiments that behavior is postulated to be learned

29. Homans (1961:53).
30. Ibid. p. 54.
31. Ibid. p. 55.

32. Ibid. p. 55.
33. Ibid. p. 75.

and maintained by means of differential reinforcement. Homans' model of man therefore is essentially the same as that presented earlier in this chapter. The differences are more apparent than real and reflect mainly a difference in emphasis and courage. Homans is concerned with the explanation of small-group phenomena and the more or less *direct* exchanges occurring in daily life, and is courageous enough to distill the results of experimental research. This admirable first step in the development of theory leads to propositions that are quite specific but hold only within narrow parameters. Proposition 4, for example, would lead to the hypothesis that, upon the presentation of rewards, the frequency of activities will decline. While this is at times true, the effect is only temporary and by no means universal; deprivation characteristics and the differential effects of primary, cultural, and generalized reinforcers also have to be taken into account. Homans shows in numerous illustrations that these propositions contribute substantially to the explanation of social psychological studies and experiments, but as Blau,[34] Coleman,[35] and others have suggested, the explanation of even elementary social behavior may require additional factors and more refined and complex propositions. When the focus of an analysis is the type of large-scale social phenomenon and indirect roundabout exchange involved in economic development, it may be advantageous—especially for the faint-hearted—to retain the more general statements outlined earlier in the chapter.

ERASMUS

The model of man which the anthropologist Erasmus [36] employs in his study of development projects and economic growth postulates that behavior is shaped and maintained through differential reinforcement, but the components of the model are not indicated as clearly or specifically as in the work of Homans. Behavior is postulated to be largely a function of a person's "frequency prediction," that is, his prediction of the future on the basis of his observations and experiences of the past. Individuals attempting to maximize rewards and minimize costs act according to their frequency interpretation of likely consequences of action. Such frequency interpretations need not be personally experi-

34. Blau (1964a).
35. Coleman (1964).
36. Erasmus (1961).

enced but can be performed vicariously, so to speak, by means of statistics collected by specialists. Another important factor affecting behavior is a person's probable knowledge, defined as the interpretation of one's experience and therefore in need of continual correction and revision. Erasmus hypothesizes that "people choose new alternatives (of behavior) when frequency interpretations make possible a clear connection with reward," [37] and he shows with numerous examples from developing nations that the structure and operation of peasant communities influence the contingencies of the villager's behavior patterns and through them his *frequency interpretation* and *probable knowledge*. Such a focus on individuals' cognition and consequences of action is quite compatible with the behavioral model of man outlined earlier, for a society's structure and the resulting discriminative and contingent stimuli are the major determinants of a person's frequency interpretations and probable knowledge. An important component of industrialization, therefore, is the alteration of contingencies of behavior. The consequences of men's actions, rather than the elements of men's internal states, appear to the crucial variables that inhibit or foster economic growth.

INTERVENING VARIABLES

A number of behavioral models place considerable emphasis on the individual's conception of the consequences of various activities and on his definition and evaluation of goals or effects. These essentially internal elements are postulated to be the intermediary links between previous experiences—and thus the social environment—and present activities. These links may be relatively simple, as in the case of Rotter, but in some theories they are very complex. Feibleman, for example, includes neurological components and philosophical needs, such as "the need to be," in his discussion of the determinants of behavior. When it is postulated that men act in terms of perceived probabilities of reinforcement, and that various consequences are evaluated in terms of a value hierarchy, it is reasonable to assume that such perceptions and hierarchies have been learned previously. Models which employ such intervening variables, then, are not basically incompatible with the learning model outlined in the previous section. Hull's, Rotter's, and Feibleman's models are somewhat more complex, include more so-called "internal"

37. Ibid. p. 54.

variables, and thus rely more on inferences, but the basic principles postulated to underly behavior are quite similar.

One may ask, however, whether intervening variables such as individuals' reinforcement expectations and probability predictions are necessary components of a model of man. Men do have nervous systems, they no doubt evaluate contingencies, and they often engage in philosophical speculations, attempt to measure probabilities, and try to predict the effects of their actions. But it is not equally certain that such variables must always be included in the analysis of behavior patterns of interest to sociologists. If the learning history of a person is reasonably well known, and if the relevant aspects of the past and present social environment are known—especially in terms of S^r probabilities and S^D—the behavior of a person can be predicted quite accurately without recourse to such internal variables.

According to the model of man outlined in this chapter, the alteration of the social context within which a person lives—especially in terms of discriminative and contingent stimuli—should result in the alteration of the activities which are associated with those stimuli. This hypothesis has been supported by a large number of case studies, carried out by a variety of experimenters and by therapists employing a variety of learning theories.[38] In behavior therapy—as differentiated from psychotherapy—the environment of the individual is altered, and the behavior patterns associated with the "old" context are subsequently altered. Intervening variables such as the above are not given a prominent role in this process of behavior modification, and yet people's actions *are* changed. The successes of behavior therapy do not imply, of course, that there are no intervening variables; but they *do* indicate that the social context and its changes play the dominant role in the determination of behavior and its alteration.

At the same time, however, it is true that there are circumstances in which a person's expectations, perceptions, etc., may become components of behavioral analysis. For example, when a person's learning history is unknown, or when there is insufficient knowledge of the previous operation of the social context, verbal statements about a person's expectations, conception of the past, and perceived probabilities of rein-

38. Krasner and Ullmann (1965), Ullmann and Krasner (1965), Wolpe (1964).

forcement, may have to become part of the explanation and prediction of behavior. But since such analyses can be no more accurate than the verbal statements incorporated into them, great care must be taken when they are incorporated into theories, action programs, etc.

The Individual's Point of View

The discussion of the behavioral model of man and the operation of the social context so far has proceeded from the point of view of an observer who describes and analyzes an individual's actions and his context. While the resulting type of analysis is empirically sound, and popular among those social scientists who wish to reduce the number of inferences they must make, it is not the only procedure.

The fundamental requirement of this type of analysis is the availability of long-term observations of the behavior of individuals and the operation of their social context. The nature of individuals' behavior patterns and the associated stimuli, the reinforcers in terms of which they act, the S^D related to various activities, and the deprivations which are operative, can be abstracted only from a series of careful observations of all the complexities of daily life. Such observations and the determination of a group's or society's norms and values is a difficult and long drawn-out process, however, and the expense in terms of time and effort may not always be justified or possible. A different point of view, involving different procedures and leading to another type of analysis, may at times be preferable or even necessary.

Learning principles and the operation of the social context may also be considered from the point of view of the individual who is learning and behaving in a family, community, subculture, or nation. The behavioral paradigm (Figure 3–2) would then involve the following components:

1. The individual's *perception* of previously established S^D, and his perception of the difference between the previously established S^D and the present environment.

2. The individual's *conception* of contingencies, especially of the probability that rewards or punishment will follow a specific activity; this would include his prediction of the rate at which contingencies will be presented.

3. The individual's *summation* and *evaluation* of contingencies.

4. The individual's *feelings* of deprivation and satiation, including his resulting definitions of what constitute reinforcing and aversive stimuli.

5. The individual's *remembrance* of previous experiences and their consequences.

From the point of view of the individual, then, a person's behavior is a function of: the previously learned S^D and the perceived similarity between the S^D and the present context; the perceived probability of reinforcement; the present state variables and the perceived probability of reducing them; and of the behavior patterns learned in the past. In other words, an individual acts in terms of his perceptions of the norms and values which operate in the social environments, including the reference groups, that are relevant to him. For example, it is possible for individuals who live in the same neighborhood and have had similar upbringing and experiences to still act differently, either because their perceptions of the normative system are different, or because they operate in terms of the normative systems of different subcultures and reference groups.

In an earlier section it was suggested that intervening variables such as a person's perception need not be included in a behavioral model of man, since men learn to perceive contingencies, etc. The analytical *procedure* under discussion, in relying on perception and other internal phenomena, does not contradict the behavioral model. Rather, it provides a means of analyzing behavior in terms of intervening variables when the original determinants of these factors, such as the operation of the previous social context, are unknown or inaccessible to the investigator. As was mentioned before, this type of analysis requires caution and cannot be preferred to the direct study of the social determinants of behavior.

An Outline of Propitious Circumstances

From the work of experimental psychologists and from the application of learning principles to behavior modification in clinical settings, "ideal circumstances" for the learning of behavior may be deduced. Since the circumstances differ somewhat, depending on whether behavior is to be established, maintained, extinguished or altered, four sets of characteristics will be briefly discussed. It should be remembered that these factors are derived from a limited number of experiments and the application of learning principles in an as yet small variety of settings, such as clinical situations, mental institutions, and education.[39] It may be expected, therefore, that as more experience is accumulated, the factors presently enumerated may be changed and new elements may have to be added. The sets of characteristics discussed below, although they are in accord with the best available evidence, are therefore to be considered provisional.

THE SHAPING OF BEHAVIOR

In order to shape behavior most efficiently, a logical system of successive approximation should be employed. That is, the behavior pattern which is to be established must be shaped by means of a series of *related steps,* each step consisting of activities which are either part of the final pattern or lead up to it. Secondly, contingencies must be applied *consistently,* with rewards associated with one activity, and punishment with another action. Thirdly, *stable* discriminative stimuli must be established. The discriminating ability of the individual depends on the consistency with which a specific component of the social context becomes associated with particular contingencies, and thus the consistency of contingencies is doubly important. As in the case of successive approximation, gross discrimination will have to be established before fine discriminations can be learned. Fourth, in order for reinforcers to be effective, some *deprivation* must be maintained. Fifth, the shaping of behavior should include initially *continuous and immediate* reinforcement. That is, in the early stages of learning, any act which approaches the pattern that is to be established, and also the final act itself, should be rewarded. Finally, men must be given *opportunities* to learn new activities, for example by exposure to models, and there must be occasions for actually performing the newly learned behavior patterns successfully.

The length of the shaping process depends on the complexity of the pattern which is to be established, the degree to which the factors mentioned above are present, the learning experiences of the individual (for example, the presence of possibly incompatible behavior patterns), and the availability of models. When complex patterns are to be established, such as the saving of money, learning will be facilitated by the existence

39. Staats (1964), Krasner and Ullmann (1965).

of models, that is, individuals who have saved money successfully (without aversive consequences).

It goes without saying that these elements of the shaping process not only are greatly influenced by, but also reflect the operation of, the social context. In an ambiguous, inconsistent, or rapidly changing social environment, it will be very difficult to shape complex activities, for reinforcers are likely to be applied inconsistently, discriminative stimuli will not become clearly established, and deprivations may well change from one month to the next. A rather common consequence of such a situation is a decline in the rate of any activity and the resulting apathy of men. In short, confused environments produce confused individuals, while stable environments are likely to produce stable individuals and behavior patterns. The implications for economic development, especially in terms of creating the behavioral prerequisites of industrialization, will be discussed in later chapters.

THE MAINTENANCE OF BEHAVIOR

The ideal conditions for maintaining behavior patterns once they have been established are quite similar to those found in the shaping of activities. First, contingencies must be applied *consistently,* so that an activity is either rewarded *or* punished, but not both in the same circumstances. Discriminative stimuli, once established, should be maintained, an end that is most easily accomplished by maintaining a consistent system of contingencies. In addition, some degree of *deprivation* must be maintained in order to keep reinforcers operative. Since many deprivations to which the human organism is subjected are relatively easily satisfied, secondary or cultural deprivations will be most important for members of social systems. *Generalized reinforcers* such as money, which can be exchanged for means of satisfying a large number of primary and secondary deprivations, will usually be most effective. Finally, *intermittent reinforcement* is best for maintaining behavior. In everyday life, most contingencies to which men are subject operate in terms of a combination of ratio and interval schedules.

The factors which maintain behavior are direct reflections of the social environment. When the context forms a stable, consistent system, behavior patterns will be easily and well maintained; conversely, when the context is unstable and ambiguous—as reflected, for example, in inconsistently applied contingencies—behavior patterns will be maintained only with difficulty.

THE EXTINCTION OF BEHAVIOR

Probably the best procedure for extinguishing behavior is to *cease rewarding* it. Generally speaking, when activities have been rewarded on a continuous schedule, the cessation of reinforcement brings about a rapid decline in the rate at which the activity was performed. When the reinforcement schedule has been intermittent, the halting of reinforcement results in a much more gradual reduction of the activity rate. The role of punishment in the extinction of behavior is as yet unclear. There is general agreement that *punishment* reduces the rate of behavior, but there are indications that this reduction is only temporary. After punishment ceases, the rate often returns to almost its previous level ("spontaneous recovery"). *Satiation* is another procedure for extinguishing behavior, but its effect is no different from ceasing to reinforce activities, for satiation implies that a previously effective reward is no longer reinforcing—since there no longer is any deprivation. Finally, *incompatible behavior* patterns may be reinforced, thus leading to the eventual extinction of previously learned actions.

Some of these procedures, or all of them, may be employed in order to reduce the rate with which an activity is performed. The specific method used will depend on the opportunities and limitations inherent in various situations and will thus depend on the nature and operation of the social environment.

THE ALTERATION OF BEHAVIOR

Behavior modification usually involves two components—the *extinction* of certain patterns and the *establishment* of others—and thus may be considered as a combination of the relevant characteristics discussed above. If activities are to be deliberately altered, the change agent's control over the relevant variables of the social context—such as the reinforcers, their schedules, and the stability of S^D—must be great enough so that they can be sufficiently—and consistently—altered. Furthermore, the agent's knowledge of deprivation characteristics, available reinforcers, and the steps involved in successive approximation, will affect the success with which behavior is modified. Finally, the agent's goals and the clarity with which they are expressed will affect the alteration of behavior in terms of both the rate and the difficulties which are encountered. An important complicating factor is the degree of interdependence among behavior patterns. When a number of actions (of one or several persons) are interrelated, the modification of one activity will have repercussions for other activities. The "new" behavior patterns, for example, may be incompatible with other actions, thus necessitating their alteration or an end to the relationship.

These difficulties are largely responsible for the fact that at present most experiences of successful behavior change are found in clinical settings where emphasis is on the individual. Here behavior modification in neurotics and psychotics is *clearly desirable,* there usually are *few "contaminating" influences* from the larger social context, and the therapist usually has *sufficient control* over the relevant variables—such as the operation of the hospital routine—to produce a successful change in the patient's behavior.[40]

Outside the hospital or the clinician's office, there have been so far relatively few instances of deliberate, successful, systematic behavior modification. Holmberg's program for Vicos [41] and Pakistan's encouragement of entrepreneurs are examples of attempts blessed with some success.[42] Examples of failures, resulting from the use of inappropriate procedures, incorrect information, and ignorance, are legion, thus leading to the suspicion that deliberate large-scale behavior change is not only very difficult but perhaps almost impossible in the open society. "Natural" changes in behavior, independent of anyone's deliberate efforts, are likely to occur at a low rate, for most of the ideal conditions outlined above will not be present. The absence of plans will reduce especially the consistency with which new activities are rewarded, thus preventing the systematic successive approximation of complex activities.

As will be shown in later chapters, most failures of behavior modification can be best explained in terms of the use of inappropriate procedures and lack of control on the part of the change agents, rather than in terms of the stability of personalities or the immutability of need structures. The fact that behavior patterns of individuals *have* been

40. For an excellent example of successful behavior modification, see Bachrach *et al.* (1965).
41. Holmberg (1960a).
42. Papanek (1967).

grossly changed, often in a very short time with no adverse consequences, would seem to indicate that the major hurdles which face the extension of learning principles to large-scale social phenomena and the formulation of action programs consist of the limitations of methodology and the lack of control over the relevant components of the social context.

iv *Social Behavior and*

Economic Development

The rather abstract discussion of learning principles contained in the last chapter raises two questions concerning the analysis of economic development: what is the relationship between the men who participate in industrialization and the social environment, and what is the relationship between the behavior patterns associated with economic growth and the operation of the social system. This chapter is devoted to a discussion of these questions.

Behavioral, Psychological, and Social Factors

It was pointed out in the last chapter that, as far as is known today, learning principles operate throughout a person's lifetime and affect men in all groups, subcultures, nations, and societies. The implications of this for sociological investigations are fourfold: first, learning principles are the *constants* of any analysis: they do not change over time. Second, learning principles affect *all men* and thus are essential components of every analysis. Third, learning principles explain the shaping, maintenance and extinction of behavior *in general,* but they cannot, by themselves, account for the specific actions of particular men in various societies and situations. Fourth, in order to explain specific activities, a *combination* of psychological and sociological factors is required. That is, the role of reinforcement must be recognized, but *which* activities are rewarded and by *what* are topics of equal significance.

Those who restrict their attention to the first three implications are open to accusations of psychological reductionism, for they necessarily emphasize psychological propositions concerning the learning of behavior by individuals. Those who perform their analyses in terms of the fourth implication, in emphasizing social and cultural factors, are likely to neglect an important component of the explanation of human behavior, i.e. how behavior is learned. Students of social change and economic development, in order not to restrict their perspective, should be cognizant of all four implications. Specific behavior patterns, which form the focus of sociological analysis, must be explained in terms of *constant* learning principles which operate in continuously *changing* social systems and subsystems. Instead of being interested simply in "behavior," then, sociologists are interested in "social behavior," which is learned *from others* and performed within the context *of others*. As Martindale says, "The form of society is not a product of natural conditions and of biological instincts but of learning." [1]

The behaviorally-oriented analysis of social change and economic development involves the study of activities associated with industrialization. Since it is people who save and invest, who innovate or thwart deviants, who work in factories or disdain manual labor, it is logical to speak of the *behavioral components* of both the process and its analysis. As was pointed out in Chapter Two, an interest in behavior requires the study of its determinants; and since learning principles underlie most of men's activities, it is proper to speak of *psychological components* of industrialization. The specifics of what men learn are largely determined by the social context in which they move, and thus it is logical, finally, to speak of the *social components* of economic development and its analysis.

Great variations in the behavior patterns associated with industrialization are possible, and the parameters within which social systems may vary are similarly wide. Both topics have received much attention in the literature, but it is not always clear how these two sets of factors are related. Learning principles, while they have received less attention, may be considered as a major link between these sets. However, since the

1. Martindale (1962:38).

principles are invariant, comparatively little attention needs to be paid them beyond the recognition of their existence and operation. In short, the behavioral approach to economic development may be envisaged in terms of the following schema:

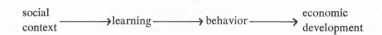

social context ——————→ learning ——————→ behavior ——————→ economic development

Behavior patterns are seen as the intermediary between societal factors and economic development, while learning principles are viewed as the major link between social and individual characteristics. Such a conception reduces and obscures the division of factors into economic and noneconomic, individualistic and social categories. Many so-called economic variables, for example interest rates, play an important role in the shaping and maintenance of behavior patterns such as investing or innovation, for they provide important reinforcers. Industrial labor force, an economic term, refers to the activities of individuals who work in factories, but these activities are being maintained by a variety of social contingencies, such as status associated with the expenditure of cash. The behavioral approach, then, contributes to the bridging of academic divisions and articulates the individualistic and societal levels of analysis.

The behavioral model of man suggests that economic development is not so much a function of man's internal state or of various mental phenomena, as it is of the activities of men. For example, the hypothesis that a positive attitude toward work and saving is a prerequisite for economic development means actually that men must work diligently, perhaps in factories, and save money, or that the probability of working hard and saving must be high. It is useful, therefore, to investigate the relationship between psychological and behavioral factors, and to indicate the effects of social and cultural characteristics on both.

Some Components of Development Analysis

Concepts such as value, attitude, and personality are being employed with increasing frequency in both empirical and theoretical studies of social change and economic development. At the same time, comparatively little attention has been devoted to an analysis of these concepts and their implications for theory and practice, beyond the rais-

ing of some questions. For example, in his summary of a recent confer-
ence on economic development, Moore mentions a controversy concerning the "psychological or institutional primacy in [the] determination
of behavior, and the minimal significance attached to the possibility of
adult personality transformation or attitudinal change." [2] In order to
evaluate the adequacy, utility, and implications of these concepts, a few
hopefully representative samples from extant definitions will be discussed. The questions and problems to which these definitions give rise
will be outlined, and alternative conceptions and their implications will
be presented. The utility of both conceptualizations will be evaluated in
terms of five "cases" from the development literature.

VALUES

The concept "value" is one of the most important in development
analysis, but, as Adler has shown, there is little agreement in the sociological literature on the definition of the term.[3] Parsons, for example,
views values as an element of a "shared symbolic system which serves
as a criterion or standard for selection of the alternatives" of action.[4]
Williams writes that "values are thus 'things' in which people are interested—things that they want, desire to be or become"; but he also sees
values as "modes of organizing conduct—meaningful affectively invested
pattern principles that guide human action." [5] Newcomb defines values
as "goals which are objects of inclusive attitudes," [6] and Kluckhohn
speaks of "a conception, explicit or implicit, distinctive of an individual
or characteristic of a group, of the desirable which influences the selection from available modes, means, and ends of action," [7] or "that aspect
of motivation which is referable to standards, personal or cultural, that
do not arise solely out of immediate tensions or immediate situations." [8]
The term value "implies a code or standard . . . which organizes a system of action" [9] that the individual has internalized, and which has thus

2. Moore (1963a:361).
3. Adler (1956).
4. Parsons (1951:12).
5. Williams (1951); both quotations are on page 375, italics have been eliminated.
6. Newcomb (1950:130).
7. Kluckhohn (1951:395).
8. Ibid. p. 425.
9. Ibid. p. 430.

become part of his internal state. A complex set of values forms a value orientation which has been defined as

> a generalized and organized conception, influencing behavior, of nature, of man's place in it, of man's relation to man and of the desirable and undesirable as they may relate to man, environment and interhuman relations.[10]

In studies not explicitly concerned with the elucidation of concepts, the definitions of value are usually more vague, such as the conception of value system as "the syndrome of general rules, sanction, and goals underlying the activities of society." [11]

In everyday life the variety and confusion of meanings may be overlooked, but in any serious attempt to explain and predict behavior a concept such as value presents severe limitations. The major problems are that it must be inferred from behavior, and that these inferences usually cannot be validated with presently available means since there are no ways of defining or measuring values independent of inferences based on behavior. As Blake and Davis put it, "by virtue of their subjective, emotional, and ethical character, norms, and especially values, are among the world's most difficult objects to identify with certainty." [12] Procedural limitations set the stage for the capricious use of "reaction-formation" to support any theory by either taking phenomena at face value or considering them in terms of their opposites. Since reaction-formation must be inferred, any theory employing the concept can be supported by any data. Consequently, it is problematical, to say the least, whether characteristics such as values can be considered as causes of action which are useful in the explanation and prediction of behavior associated with economic development.

One method of reducing the difficulties encountered in the definition and measurement of values is based on the simple question of how one knows what a person's values are. Knowledge of a man's values is based either on observations of his activities or on his verbal statements that he values, for example honesty. But what are the dimensions of the value of honesty? One may say that a man values honesty highly, and

10. Ibid. p. 411.
11. Ayal (1963:35).
12. Blake and Davis (1964:463).

that this internalized value determines his behavior. But what are the empirical referents for this statement? In reality one is saying something about certain activities and the probability of their expression. When one speaks of a man's values, or when one infers his value orientation, one is in actuality only summarizing in shorthand form certain features of many of his activities. One is abstracting, from a great variety of behavior patterns, certain manifestations or elements labeled "honest" or "honesty" by members of a society. One is able to predict a man's actions on the basis of his past activities in a particular situation, but instead of saying anything about the determinants of behavior one is only commenting on the consistency of behavior.

According to the behavioral perspective, a man acts honestly if honesty leads to success, for example in terms of reducing deprivations or avoiding noxious consequences. The determinants of activities called "honest," then, are to be found in the learning history of the individual, in the course of which he has learned both societal definitions of "reward" and that particular behavior patterns, namely those defined by his society as honest, are usually rewarded, whereas their opposites usually are not. Along this line of reasoning Homans has defined value as "the degree of reinforcement and punishment [a person] gets from [behavior]." [13] Additional conceptions of "value," emphasizing the individual's experiences of the past and expectations of the future within the dynamic social context, would be the following:

1. From the point of view of the *observer*. An individual's value refers to the probability that a particular behavior pattern will occur under specific conditions. When it is said, for example, that honesty is a strongly held value, a well-internalized value, or that it is deeply ingrained in an individual or group, it means simply that the probability of the occurrence of particular activities is high; conversely, if a value is lightly held, the probability of the occurrence is low. The value "integrity" indicates that certain activities—defined by a society as indicating integrity—are prevalent in a group or are commonly observed in an individual.

2. From the point of view of the *individual*. Probably the most common conception equates "value" with reinforcer. A person who values money, for example, may be expected to act so as to receive money. Value may also refer to the perceived set of probabilities that certain

13. Homans (1961:40).

rewards will be obtained if particular activities are performed. When a person is said to value honesty, for example, it means that he believes that activities defined as honest by his society will be rewarded—and thus he will be honest quite often. These rewards may exist on earth or they may be conceived as being found only in heaven; if the latter is the case, a man may be honest even without material rewards, and he may be regarded as "irrational" by those who do not share the same definition of reward or who are not aware of the schedule of reinforcement.

3. From the point of view of the *sociologist*. Values are constructs which refer to the theoretical regularities of behavior patterns over time and, more specifically, to the relationships which exist—ideally—between the actions of one man and the behavior of others. These regularities and relationships are often summarized in terms of "standards" which ideally determine state variables and discriminative and contingent stimuli. This conception, which was discussed in greater detail in the last chapter, is quite compatible with the definitions of value from the point of view of observers and individuals, for it differs from them mainly in terms of the inferences and ascriptions which the sociologist is willing to make.

From these considerations it may be concluded that the concept "value" has at least five different meanings:

1. the probability that a behavior pattern will occur;
2. the reinforcer itself (with implications for the nature of state variables);
3. the probability that a behavior pattern will be reinforced;
4. the theoretically existing relationships among activities;
5. the ideal "standards" of behavior, as verbal expressions.

In order to increase the specificity of development analysis, it is probably best to disregard the first three meanings. Probabilities and reinforcers are important characteristics in their own right, and specific enough to require no further elaboration. When "value" is restricted to the last two meanings, many of the problems and ambiguities, such as those discussed by Adler,[14] tend to disappear. For example, instead of using "individuals' values" one might speak of specific reinforcers or of the "probabilities of an action's occurrence." The term "value orientation," for example, would then refer to nothing more than the often

14. Adler (1956).

complicated set of probabilities that a system of behavior patterns and chains has occurred or will occur with great frequency, implying thereby a complex set of discriminative and contingent stimuli and a particular learning history.

ATTITUDES

The large number of conceptions of "attitude" in the sociological and psychological literature may be divided into two major groups. According to DeFleur and Westie,[15] "latent process conceptions" require inferences concerning the internal state, while "probability conceptions" rely more on observations of behavior.

The latent process conception postulates that "attitude is a process which occurs inside an individual which determines more or less immediately and directly the way in which he [behaves]." [16] The problems that are encountered in describing and measuring these internal processes and their effects on behavior have not yet been solved.[17] One of the best known attempts at specification is Allport's definition of attitude as "a mental and neural state of readiness to respond, organized through experience, exerting a directive or dynamic influence upon the individual's response to all objects and situations with which it is related." [18] Newcomb admits that the concept of attitude is simply a theoretical device referring to "the state of readiness for motive arousal. It is the individual's susceptibility to stimulation capable of arousing the motive in him . . . . Attitudes thus represent persistent, general orientations of the individual toward his environment." [19] Doob, finally, holds that "attitude refers to an implicit response that is both *anticipatory* and *mediating* in reference to patterns of overt responses." [20]

These definitions of attitude present the student of economic development and social change with a number of difficulties. The major problem revolves around the inferences which must be made in order to determine a person's attitude. "States of readiness" and "implicit responses" can be ascertained in one of two ways: verbal statements are

15. DeFleur and Westie (1963).
16. Ibid. p. 24.
17. For a careful analysis of the concept of attitude, see Ehrlich (1969) and McGuire (1969). Scott (1968) presents an overview of measurement problems.
18. Quoted by McGuire (1969: 142ff), who also analyzes its implications.
19. Newcomb (1950:118–19); italics have been eliminated.
20. Quoted in Green (1954:335); italics in the original.

taken as reflections of attitudes, or attitudes are inferred from actual behavior.

However, as Lindesmith, Strauss, and many others have pointed out, a man's verbal statements are "not an altogether reliable index of attitude, because the person expressing [them] can be concealing true attitudes, or may honestly say one thing but do another when the time comes to act." [21] In short, the correlation between words and deeds is far from perfect. The second procedure is also open to question, for behavior is not always consistent. If a process such as attitude "were in fact operative within the individual, it should at least show internal consistency within itself . . . . The behavior of an individual *within a given dimension of attitude behavior* should show consistency from one time to another, from one social situation to another." [22] However, as DeFleur and Westie show, high consistency is more an exception than the rule.

The question of what an attitude really is can again be approached best by asking what the referents of the term are. How does one know what a person's attitudes are? One determines them by observing his behavior or by asking him directly, and one usually will not be content with his word but will try to observe his actions. For example, it may be said that a person has a particular attitude toward an object, person, event, or someone's actions, if he behaves in specified ways toward the object and if his behavior is somewhat consistent and persists over time. A "negative attitude" toward saving, for example, refers to certain elements of behavior which are common to his actions towards money, banks, and goods. Attitude, thus, is simply a shorthand term for certain abstracted characteristics common to a number of behavior patterns which are frequently repeated whenever certain conditions prevail. According to the probability conception, then, attitude "is an inferred property of the responses, namely, their consistency. Stated in another way, attitude is equated with the *probability of recurrence of behavior forms of a given type or direction*." [23] When attitudes are considered as summary measures of behavior, or as convenient labels for specific components of actions, they are no longer conceptualized as causes of any activity. When the common elements of a large group of activities

21. Lindesmith and Strauss (1956:494), DeFleur and Westie (1958).
22. DeFleur and Westie (1963:26); italics in the original.
23. Ibid. p. 21, italics in the original.

are known—for example, "thrift"—it is possible to predict how a person is likely to act when his behavior falls into the same group—for example, actions related to money—or when he is exposed to the appropriate discriminative stimuli, but nothing is said thereby about the causes of his actions.

The behavioral conception of attitude as the common element of a number of activities leads to the conclusion that attitude-change is equivalent to behavior-change, and that both are the result of alterations in state variables, discriminative and/or contingent stimuli. Attitude-change, therefore, will demand not the manipulation of a man's internal state, but rather the systematic and consistent alteration of parts of his social environment.[24] The alteration may proceed by supplying the individual with new information concerning the environment,[25] by changing his reference groups,[26] or by changing the contingencies of behavior.[27] Most studies of attitude-change employ a psychodynamic perspective, but yet the important role of environmental alteration is clearly indicated.[28] The complexity of procedures—for example the credibility of the communicator or the effects of coercion—cannot be detailed here; suffice it to say that development analysis will benefit from the utilization of social psychological research efforts in this area.

PERSONALITY

Another important term which appears in discussions of economic development is personality. The conception, measurement, and analysis of personality are reflections of the investigator's model of man and thus should be closely scrutinized in order to eliminate doubtful assumptions.[29] Psychodynamic models treat personality as part of the internal state; Lerner, for example, speaks of the "mobile personality" characterized by empathy, and emphasizes the personality transformations that occur during the process of modernization.[30] Newcomb defines person-

24. For examples of this position, see Cohen (1964), and Newcomb (1950: 194ff).
25. For example Festinger and Kelley (1951), McGuire (1969).
26. For example Lieberman (1956), Siegel and Siegel (1957).
27. For example most of the studies discussed by Cohen (1964).
28. For example Kelman (1958), Sarnoff *et al.* (1965), and Kelley and Volkart (1952).
29. For recent discussions of problems of personality, see Ullman (1965); Marlowe and Gergen (1969).
30. Lerner (1958).

ality as "the individual's organization of predisposition to behavior . . . .
That which 'holds together' all his motive patterns—that which determines that all his behavior, both attitudinal and expressive, shall be
just what it is." [31] According to Allport, "personality is the dynamic
organization within the individual of those psychophysical systems that
determine his unique adjustments to his environment." [32] In general,
sociologists have considered personality as the totality of values, attitudes, needs, and motivations of a person, and thus equivalent to the
individual's internal state itself.

The major difficulty with the psychodynamic conception of personality lies in the fact that "personality is something that must be inferred
from facts. Hence, in actual practice, the personality is an abstract formulation composed by the psychologist." [33] The components of personality, its genesis and operation, and its effects on the individual and his
behavior, may therefore be expected to vary with the theoretical repertoire of the investigator. The validation of inferences and the lack of
objective procedures, already discussed, present additional difficulties
to those who include "personality" in their study of social phenomena
and processes.

The definition of this concept can be made more specific by considering the referents of personality: how does one know what the personality of a man is? Again the answer is his behavior—only by looking at
his activities can one know a man's personality. A "pleasant personality," for example, usually turns out to be no more than a set of behavior patterns which is similar to one's own or which one judges to be
pleasant on the basis of some standard. The problem of the referent of
personality has been implicitly recognized by some writers, for example
Parsons and Shils, who define personality as "the organized system of
the orientation and motivation of action of one individual actor" and
then again as simply the "relatively ordered system of resultant actions
in one actor." [34]

According to the behavioral perspective, personality refers to the
set of behavior patterns which an individual has acquired under the
special circumstances of his development and as a member of his soci-

31. Newcomb (1950:344).
32. Allport (1937:48).
33. Kluckhohn and Murray (1953:6).
34. Parsons and Shils (1951:7,38).

ety and the several groups to which he belongs and has belonged.[35] Personality, then, is not inferred from behavior or considered to be a cause of it but, rather, *is* the sum of a man's activities which show some durability. Just as in the psychodynamic model the term personality includes all of a person's values and attitudes, so it includes in the behavioral model the behavior of individuals and the probabilities that various patterns of behavior will occur under specific circumstances. Changes in personality, then, do not refer to changes in the internal components of man but to the altered behavior patterns themselves and to the changed probabilities of their expression. The determinants of behavior modification, therefore, are not alterations in a man's personality but, rather, the changes of the social context which determine the probabilities of reinforcement in terms of which the individual acts, that is, the contingent stimuli, their schedules, and the associated discriminative stimuli which are provided by a society and by the various groups of which the individual is at all times a part.

INTERNALIZATION

An important component of personality formation is the process of internalizing a society's or subculture's values and norms. The importance assigned to the process, however, has not resulted in a general understanding of it; as Kluckhohn says, "most acquired or derived drives are dependent upon group values which the individual has *somehow* interiorized as part of himself." [36] According to the behavioral perspective, the internalization or interiorization of values refers to the learning of behavior and of various sets of probabilities that certain actions under specific cirumstances will be rewarded or punished. This is not to imply that the individual is necessarily able to explicitly state these probabilities or their determinants. Internalization—or the learning of behavior, reinforcement probabilities, and discriminative stimuli—is the result of communication and experience and depends upon both the consistency of reinforcement, the number of occasions on which particular behavior patterns have been rewarded under specific circumstances, and the reinforcement schedule in effect durnig the learning process.

35. Lundin (1961), Berlyne (1968). Doob (1968) discusses economic development in terms of both personality and learning.
36. Kluckhohn (1951:429); italics added. For an extensive discussion of socialization, see Aronfreed (1968).

IMPLICATIONS OF THESE CONCEPTS

The major function of "values," "attitudes," and "personality" in sociological literature and development analysis today is the provision of determinants of behavior. However, when these concepts are viewed in terms of their empirical referents, it is apparent that their major function is the communication of probabilities and descriptions of behavior. The statement "Joseph has a pleasant personality, values of honesty have been well internalized, and he never lets his attitude toward success interfere with these values," serves the major purpose of increasing the accuracy of an observer's predictions of behavior. There can be no doubt that the statement does, in fact, make the prediction of action possible. But although one can predict with some confidence how Joseph is likely to act under certain circumstances, one cannot say *why* such actions occur. The prediction is based on the assumption of behavioral consistency, and causal analysis would require additional information such as Joseph's learning history.

Concepts such as values are useful in the language of everyday life, but they cannot be considered as explanations of behavior since these terms have, as their ultimate referents, the observed behavior of individuals and nothing else. Causal qualities have been *assigned* to these essentially internal or mental states, but these elements have not yet been *demonstrated* to be the determinants of behavior. According to Blake and Davis, it is probably best to "abandon [values] as causal agents and to recognize them frankly as sheer constructs by which we attempt to fill the subjective linkages in the analysis of social causation." [37] As will be shown below, even those who employ these concepts in their causal analyses usually do not rise above what amounts to the specification of the behavioral referents of attitude, etc. In terms of the behavioral perspective, the major differences among these concepts are essentially differences in the abstractions which are made, in the point of view of the observer, and in the temporal context within which the activities are considered. If one is interested in the simple description of behavior, these concepts may be useful, but *if one is engaged in a causal analysis it is not necessary that these concepts be part of it or that they be considered as part of any causal nexus.* The analysis of social phenomena and processes will be inadequate as long as poorly defined concepts are

37. Blake and Davis (1964:461).

given great weight, especially as integral parts of causal chains when in fact these concepts refer to the "end products" of such chains.[38] The essential characteristic of attitude, value, and personality is the probability that a particular set of behavior patterns will occur in specific situations and under certain conditions of deprivation.

The psychological and social prerequisites of economic development cannot be established by changing the internal determinants of behavior, that is, the values, attitudes, or personalities of individuals in developing countries, as has been argued so often and so eloquently in recent years.[39] For *to say that values, attitudes, and personalities must be changed is to say nothing more than that changes in behavior patterns must occur.* There is general agreement on this point, that behavioral alterations are part of the process of development, but the question now is: how can these changes be brought about? The belief that values, attitudes, and personality determine behavior, that behavior will change once attitudes or values are altered, and that one must consequently concentrate on the alteration of these elements, leads into several blind alleys of theory and action. First, there is no generally recognized definition of these terms which includes elements other than behavior or inference based upon it. Second, the components of these concepts are often unclear (e.g. state of readiness). Third, there are no generally recognized procedures for deliberately altering what are said to be individual values, attitudes, or personalities, except psychotherapy or the systematic alteration of a person's social environment.

The behavioral perspective with its emphasis on the shaping of behavior by means of differential reinforcement, opens a way not only to the testable explanation and prediction of behavior, but also to its alteration. The behavioral model of man leads to the conclusion that, if behavior is to be modified, changes must *first* occur in the contingent stimuli, in their presentation and schedule, and in the discriminative stimuli. This can be accomplished only through the alteration of those aspects of the social context which influence these components of the learning process. Changes in personality or individuals' values, rather than being the prerequisite of economic development, now come to be considered as concomitants and consequences; economic development means, for the average individual, changed contingencies, changed sched-

38. For a recent discussion of this problem, see Fendrich (1967).
39. For example by Ayal (1963), McClelland (1963), and Pareek (1968).

ules, and new behavior patterns, newly reinforced under new circumstances. It may be hypothesized, then, that *the major problem of economic development is not the alteration of character, values, or attitudes, but the change of those selected aspects of man's social environment which are relevant to the learning of new behavior patterns.*

The difficulties which are encountered when values, attitudes, and personalities are considered as causal factors, and the advantages of considering these concepts from the behavioral point of view, i.e. as various manifestations and summaries of action, will now be illustrated.

Some Examples of Behavioral Analysis

Many empirical and theoretical investigations of economic development have made extensive use of "values," "attitudes," and "personality." It is appropriate, therefore, that both types of studies be reviewed in terms of the problems that are encountered and the solutions that can be derived from a learning approach. In addition, the behavioral reinterpretation of major development theories contributes to the relevance of theory in an action-oriented world.

VALUES AND BEHAVIOR IN THAILAND AND JAPAN

A comparison of Thailand and Japan shows that although the latter is economically more developed than the former, the differences exist in the face of important similarities. Exposure to the West, traditions of borrowing, political independence, a respected central government, and ample foreign markets were common to both nations and thus cannot account for the different rates of industrialization. Ayal hypothesizes that "without the appropriate value system, a favorable environment [will] not bring about development. The appropriate value system is then a necessary though not a sufficient condition for development." [40] The different rates of development, therefore, must be due to differences in the value systems of the two nations. A further hypothesis is that, "in order for economic development to come about, it is essential that the value system fulfill two functions. First, it has to provide goals, either public or private, which can be promoted by increased production . . . . Second, the value system must generate, include, or at least sanction

40. Ayal (1963:39). Weber (1958) has presented the best-known statement of this type of hypothesis.

the means—namely, the propensities and the activities associated with them." [41]

The major procedure for the testing of these hypotheses "is to try and find some causal relationship between the value system and modes of behavior associated with economic development. The transmission of the general orientation of the value system into action is conceived here as being materialized through the intermediary of propensities. This shorthand term stands for internalized behavioristic and instrumental values, or predispositions to action, which have their origin in the value system." [42] The major relevant propensities are: "to accumulate capital, to work systematically and diligently, to cooperate in organizing effort in pursuance of goals, and to innovate." [43] The independent variable, "the components of the value system, may be identified primarily from religious (defined broadly) and ethical teachings. . . . The social values of established traditional society can be identified, for the most part, within the body of prevailing religious teaching." [44]

Ayal's analysis indicates that the value systems of the two nations differ greatly in the formulation of goals and means of attaining them, and thus the two hypotheses are supported by the data. The value system of Japan, for example, includes such elements as "*active* fulfillment of obligations of class status and loyalty, asceticism and frugality, development of expertise in carrying out one's tasks, and diligence in performing these tasks"; in addition, "behavior consistent with the prevailing values became a means for acquiring religious merit." [45] The value system of Thailand, conversely, emphasizes individualism, personal values, merit-making (e.g. becoming a monk), noninvolvement, passive obedience, the enjoyment of the here and now and little concern with the future. [46]

Ayal comes to the conclusion that "changes in political and social institutions, or investments by foreigners, will not, by themselves, bring about sustained economic development, unless the fundamental human values in the society are conducive to development . . . [and] that devel-

41. Ayal (1963:39).
42. Ibid. pp. 38–39.
43. Ibid. p. 39.
44. Ibid. pp. 39–40.
45. This and the previous quotation are from Ayal (1963:41); italics in the original.
46. Ibid. pp. 44–50.

opment programs which do not entail changes in values, when such are required, are bound to be frustrated." [47]

The study may be summarized by the following schema:

$$
\begin{array}{c}
\text{religious} \\
\text{\& ethical} \\
\text{teachings}
\end{array}
\longrightarrow
\begin{array}{c}
\text{societal} \\
\text{values}
\end{array}
\longrightarrow \text{propensities} \longrightarrow \text{action} \longrightarrow
\begin{array}{c}
\text{economic} \\
\text{development}
\end{array}
$$

A number of problems are immediately apparent. Both values and propensities are essentially inferred, mainly from religious and ethical teachings, i.e. writings. The nature and operation of values and propensities are not clear, for while propensities are conceived as being internal to individuals, and values the characteristics of nations, the descriptions which are provided obviously refer to the overt activities of men. For example, *both* values (e.g. frugality) and propensities (e.g. to accumulate capital) refer basically to behavior. Furthermore, the development of propensities from societal values, and the transformation of propensities into actions, are processes which are quite unclear. The relationship between ethical teachings and behavior, then, remains somewhat mysterious. The data show that such a relationship indeed exists, but Ayal's analysis throws little light on the nature of this link.

According to the behavioral perspective, certain activities such as hard work or the fulfillment of obligations, are part of economic development. In addition, certain abstracted common elements of a number of actions—such as asceticism or frugality—are part of the process. In short, what Ayal calls "propensities" and "values" are simply considered in terms of their behavioral referents. These activities, in turn, are shaped and maintained by the state variables and discriminative and contingent stimuli determined by the societal values as defined above, that is, the ideal standards reflected in religious and ethical writings.[48] In Japan, for example, "the successful accumulation of wealth through commercial endeavor became, in *Shin,* an index of religious merit in somewhat the same sense as in the 'Protestant Ethic'." [49] Conversely, the Thai concern with merit-making to improve one's *karma* reinforces behavior patterns such as noninvolvement, concern with the present, and various religious

47. Ibid. p. 35, p. 51.
48. Berkovitz (1969).
49. Ayal (1963:42).

activities. In one case capital accumulation is reinforced by religious merit, while in the other case religious merit is a contingency for *not* accumulating capital.

In a recent work Fillol hypothesizes that "the basically passive, apathetic value-orientation profile of the Argentine society must be regarded as the *critical* factor limiting the possibilities of steady, long-run economic development." [50] From this it follows that "only a transformation of Argentina's value-orientation profile towards higher degrees of activity can insure that economic gains achieved during one period will not be wiped out in a following one by social and political dislocations." [51]

The starting point of Fillol's analysis is the assumption that behavior is determined by personality and the environment. Personality, in turn, is postulated as consisting of value orientations and a need structure. These elements are interrelated, for "in the process of personality formation, needs which have been acquired help to determine value orientations, and acquired value orientations help to determine needs." [52] A society's basic personality type, which operates as a major determinant of the behavior of groups, is ascertained "by defining those dominant value orientations shared by the bulk of the society's members as a result of the early experiences which they have had in common." [53] Fillol's major source for ascertaining the Argentine value orientation consists of the writings of Ortega y Gasset, Jorge Luis Borges, and North American social scientists.[54]

For example, Argentines are suspicious and consider men to be easily corruptible and dominated by nature. In addition, the individual is thought to be perfectible only "through charity and devotion, never by means of his works, enterprise, or material achievements." [55] There is much individualism and little co-operation or concern with the future because, in the words of Ortega y Gasset, "the Argentine lives what I

50. Fillol (1961:3); italics in the original.   53. Ibid. p. 6.
51. Ibid. p. 110.   54. Ibid. pp. 8–26.
52. Ibid. p. 7.   55. Ibid. p. 9.

would call his *individual concrete future*. This is not the shared future of a common ideal, of a collective Utopia; each individual lives *his own illusions* as if they had already come true." [56] One of the basic conclusions of the study is that the Argentine "value-orientation profile is inimical to the emergence of social relationships which would enable individuals to act concertedly in the pursuit of common goals." [57]

While much of Fillol's study makes sense, the resulting knowledge has more of an intuitive than an intellectual foundation. The elements of the Argentine value orientation, such as "suspiciousness," appear to be summaries of behavior rather than determinants of action. In addition, the discussion of needs is at times circular and often weak. Need aggression, for example, is defined as "a characteristic of the individual's personality which makes [him] feel satisfaction from the act of being aggressive in thought or action, from attacking others and overcoming real or imaginary opposition forcefully." [58] Such a need leads to various actions—but it is also inferred from these actions. Many of Fillol's assumptions receive theoretical underpinning from psychodynamic theories. If the theories are not supported by behavioral data, reaction formation is assumed to have taken place—for no other reason than that the data do not fit the theory. An Argentine's "apathy is actually a means of suppressing his 'need aggression,' a cover for the anxiety and intense rage which must arise in a society built on authoritarian values." [59] At this point it is not unreasonable to ask: what objectively validated proof is there for the existence of a great variety of needs, the repression of some and the expression of others, and for the proposition that anxiety and rage *must* be created in certain societies? If such necessity follows from a theory, and if such a theory can be supported only by the capriciously applied concept of reaction-formation, it is perhaps better to investigate alternative procedures of analysis.

The behavioral model of man permits a simpler explanation of the Argentine data—assuming that Argentines act the way Fillol says they do—without amorphous concepts such as need structures or value orientations. These terms are unnecessary and cumbersome abstractions from behavior which may be made but can play no role in explaining behav-

56. Quoted in Fillol (1961:10); italics in the original.   58. Ibid. p. 23.
57. Ibid. p. 22.   59. Ibid. p. 24.

ior since they *are* aspects of behavior. Men learn to be suspicious, to be fatalistic (that is, to behave in ways defined as fatalistic), or to concern themselves only with the present, just as they learn to behave in opposite fashion. It all depends on *which* behavior patterns are reinforced and on *what* types of chains are slowly established over the years. Little is gained by postulating an intervening variable, such as value orientation, which explains nothing and only clutters up the analysis. Fillol's and especially Hagen's elaborate analysis of why people do not engage in manual labor, for example, rests on status and self-conceptions, feelings of superiority, and justification of individual worth.[60] According to the behavioral perspective, manual labor is not engaged in because it is followed by aversive stimuli, for example derision, and because in the past many who worked hard often gained little or lost the fruits of their labor. It would follow that, if the circumstances of work were altered, manual labor would occur more frequently; as will be shown in a later chapter, this is precisely what happens.

The fact that the concepts used by Fillol in his analysis of the Argentine problem contribute little to the explanation of behavior and its modification is illustrated by his discussion of the modification of work habits. Fillol's suggestions for the solution of Argentina's problems are essentially concerned with changes in the presently operating discriminative and contingent stimuli. For example, new incentives for both workers and managers, worker participation in management, explanations of decisions to those affected by them, the encouragement of co-operation, and the hands-off attitude of government, are all aspects of attempts to shape new behavior patterns through a new system of differential reinforcement. Fillol's theoretical foundation for proposing the above changes is that parental rage will no longer be directed against children, and that therefore children will be less authoritarian and will thus bring about, in two or three generations, value orientations in harmony with economic development. It is not clear, however, how the proposed alterations would affect parental rage. In addition, the relationship between managerial policy changes and alterations in needs and value orientations is not spelled out, and the process of the formation of values is unclear. Indeed, it seems as if in the last section of his work Fillol pays verbal tribute to his earlier concepts but disregards them in his concrete de-

60. Ibid. pp. 16–17, Hagen (1962:76–81).

scriptions of possible solutions. The behavioral analysis of the Argentine situation would arrive at similar specific recommendations for the amelioration of the problem—that is, the changing of behavior patterns—as does Fillol. The behavioral alternative would be simpler, however, and would have as its theoretical foundation a smaller number of principles and a minimum of inferences.

THE ROLE OF VALUES IN INDIA

One of the basic procedural assumptions of the previous two cases is that religious, ethical, or philosophical writings contain, so to speak, the values—ideal rewards or standards of behavior—of a group or nation. The question of *where* values are "located" cannot be answered so easily, however, if only because it is men who *write* philosophical treatises and it is men who *interpret* religious teachings.

The uncertainties which are involved in the meaning, measurement, and analysis of "value" as a component of economic development are well illustrated in a recent discussion concerning the role of Indian values in the process of industrialization. The question which has faced social scientists for a number of years is: are Hindu values detrimental or conducive to India's economic development? The answers are by no means clear.

India's ideals of asceticism and a spiritual life, together with the philosophy of renunciation, are usually considered to present almost insurmountable obstacles to economic development. Upon close examination, however, it appears that there is a difference between ideal prescriptions—as inferred by Westerners from Eastern scriptures—and the realities of everyday life. As Singer points out,[61] Indians in their everyday activities are as materialistically oriented as Western men; "this-worldly asceticism" is quite widespread; and the philosophy of renunciation is just that: a philosophy to which many men pay lip service—perhaps an ideal, but an ideal which attracts few practitioners in everyday life. In Singer's words, "the Indian world view encompasses both material and spiritual values, and these can be found in the behavior of the ordinary Indian existing side by side and in functional interdependence . . . . Overspecialization on the spiritual, the sacred, and the life-denying [is] to be found [mainly] in the interpretations of some Western scholars." [62]

61. Singer (1956).
62. Ibid. p. 83.

The backwardness and stagnation of India's economic system thus cannot be explained in terms of other-worldly religious values. As Singer and Srinivas point out, Indian peasants are eminently practical in their approach to the physical and social world. Why then the backwardness? According to Srinivas and Lambert, social and political institutions such as the caste system, together with a long colonial history, are the major causal factors. Srinivas, in fact, hypothesizes that "it is possible that popular interpretations or misinterpretations of *maya, samsara,* and *karma* were the aftermath of defeat—rather than its cause." [63] Karve, too, mentions that it is "not necessary to go into the early economic and social history of industrially developed nations to show that the tempo of work is more often the reflection of opportunities of progress than a prime cause." [64] It has been pointed out, for example, that "Christianity too is other-worldly, and it glorifies poverty and humility. Yet it is in the Christian countries that the Industrial Revolution was born and developed." [65] According to Singer,

> . . . a society dominated by a philosophy of renunciation need not be a society of ascetics. In India, ascetics and holy men have never constituted more than a tiny fraction of the population. There have always been a sufficient number of householders willing and able to do the world's work. And while the ideals of asceticism may indirectly influence the general population, not all of these influences oppose social reform and economic development.[66]

The reasoning of many western observers and interpreters of India seems to be as follows: the sacred literature of India contains certain values which are internalized by the people who then act in accordance with these values. Consequently, India is economically stagnant, and there is little hope of economic growth until the values—basically the religion and philosophy—are changed. This argument is based on a number of inferences and assumptions which have not yet been supported by evidence obtained by replicatable procedures based on objective criteria of measurement. The major assumptions are that the sacred literature contains a particular set of values and no other; that this set

63. Srinivas (1958:6).
64. Karve (1958:7).
65. Srinvas (1958:6).
66. Singer (1958:11).

is internalized by a majority of the population; that the values internalized by the Indians are precisely those which the Westerner "sees" in the sacred literature; that men's actions are a function of internalized values; and that the immediate circumstances in which the individual finds himself play a relatively insignificant role in the determination of his behavior.

It is apparent from the work of Singer and others,[67] however, that the values "contained" in the Bhagavad-Gita and other religious writings are merely interpretations of words which men choose to make; Westerners interpret the work as "teaching" certain values, whereas Gandhi thought that quite different values were being "taught." Hence, there arise at least two interesting questions: what values *are* contained in the Bhagavad-Gita; and are there any procedures for discovering which values *are* taught? The second question leads to the analysis of child-raising practices, but the specificity required is seldom achieved.[68] The first question, however, is difficult to answer objectively. It may be argued, fortunately, that answering the second question obviates the first—but only if emphasis is shifted from values to the behavior patterns which are being established through socialization.

The as yet unresolved controversy centering on the suitability of Indian values for economic development leads to the conclusion that, as long as definitions of values are vague, as long as proof of their existence and criteria for their measurement are absent, and as long as it is difficult to delineate with any certainty the role of values in the determination of behavior, extreme caution is required in any analysis of societal values and economic development. The need for caution is especially evident in complex *theories* of development, as illustrated in the following discussion.

HOW ECONOMIC GROWTH BEGINS

Hagen's Theory. Improvements in technology, the availability of capital, the diffusion of cultural elements, and adequate markets are not as important for the beginning of economic growth as are individuals who act as leaders in innovation. In general, these

> leaders in the transition to economic growth were neither randomly distributed throughout the population nor drawn from

67. Singer (1956), Nash (1963).
68. For an excellent example of detailed descriptions, see Whiting (1963).

the group that was most elite or had the greatest wealth or greatest opportunity for access to foreign knowledge and capital. Instead, they came disproportionately from some one or more less elite groups whose members had traditionally had a secure place in the social order but had lost the status they felt a right to expect and were now disparaged by the leading social group.[69]

Traditional societies produce authoritarian, noninnovating personalities, and thus the social and economic organization of this type of society is characterized by great stability. There may be no social change for centuries, since "the interrelationships between personality and social structure are such as to make it clear that social change will not occur without change in personalities." [70]

The process of personality formation in children produces new character types when alterations in the social organization of a society change the values and needs of certain adults. More specifically,

the basic cause of [these changes] is the perception on the part of the members of some social group that their purposes and values in life are not respected by groups in the society whom they respect and whose esteem they value.[71]

Such "withdrawal of status respect" leads to retreatism among those groups who have lost status. But

. . . retreatism is not a dead end. As retreatism deepens in successive generations, it creates circumstances of home life and social environment that are conducive to the development of innovational personality. The historical sequence seems to be: authoritarianism, withdrawal of status respect, retreatism, creativity.[72]

And thus economic development begins.

The most important element in the theory, personality, is "defined as the complex of qualities other than purely bodily ones which deter-

69. Hagen (1962:30).   71. Ibid. p. 185.
70. Ibid. p. 86.   72. Ibid. p. 217.

mine how an individual will behave in any given situation." [73] The static nature of traditional society is due to the authoritarian personality of the peasant, who "by independent decision, even in petty matters, arouses anxiety within [himself]." [74] This anxiety can be avoided only by reliance on tradition or authority. "The use of initiative . . . creates anxiety in the members of the elite as well," [75] who also feel a deep moral imperative to uphold their position. The authoritarian person does not innovate because

> . . . the painful experiences which gave rise to these perceptions [of an arbitrary, capricious world] must have created hatreds in him which shocked those around him . . . . He presses these fears and unacceptable urges out of his conscious mind and seals over his unconscious processes as best he can because he is uneasy about what thoughts and fears they include . . . . But rage and pain, though repressed, are still within him. He dared not express his rage against the superior authorities [in his youth] . . . . As he moves to successive positions of authority at successive stages in his life the anxiety he feels in ambiguous situations causes him to insist that his own authority not be questioned.[76]

Citing evidence from Burma and Java, Hagen notes that "in both cultures the child must react with rage to the anxiety and terror repeatedly created in him during infancy and early childhood." [77] This rage is converted into aggression, but

> . . . against this aggressiveness which unconsciously he fears in himself a Burmese individual erects defenses of various kinds. One of these is the very characteristic which causes casual visitors to reject as ridiculous the suggestion that the Burmese are aggressive: a merry, happy-go-lucky, friendly cast of behavior. This, I suggest, is an attitude the Burmese individual adopts as a part of the process of repressing his dangerous rage.[78]

73. Ibid. p. 99.
74. Ibid. p. 73.
75. Ibid. p. 79.

76. Ibid. p. 98.
77. Ibid. p. 172.
78. Ibid. p. 174.

The withdrawal of status respect from some groups "undoubtedly resulted in anxiety [and a] sense of lack of equilibrium or of emotional incompleteness." [79] Resentment, rage, and anxiety become part of the home life and thus of the childhood environment of youths who will emerge from it with personalities that differ from those of their parents. The son

> . . . must satisfy his need [for] dependence by valuing highly the regard of groups in authority, [but] he expects that they will not give that regard unqualifiedly and anticipates pain. As a result, he hates the members of the superior groups. He also probably envies them in a way in which his father did not. [80]

The resulting retreatism may give rise to considerate parenthood, which consists of a "mother or mother-surrogate [who] responds to [the child's] rages with composure and love." [81] The innovating individual, characterized in part by creative imagination (the ability to let one's unconscious processes work on one's behalf), is likely to come into being if the boy's

> . . . experiences of infancy and early childhood give him a firm and satisfying impression of the loving nurturance of his mother, but that repeatedly he is unable to achieve as she seems to wish him to. He may then feel that the fault must lie in him, and there may become built into him anxiety that he may not accomplish enough, anxiety that drives him all his life to achieve in order to regain fleetingly that temporary feeling of security conveyed by his mother's praise and caresses. In this case, little rage and hatred may be provoked in him, and his unconscious processes will remain accessible to him. [82]

Difficulties in Hagen's Theory. Several problems involved in Hagen's use of psychodynamic concepts and theories are immediately apparent. They may be briefly summarized as follows:

1. Hagen makes much use of personality as an internal state of indi-

---

79. Ibid. p. 187.
80. Ibid. p. 208.

81. Ibid. p. 135.
82. Ibid. p. 94.

viduals. The characteristics of the internal state are derived from psychoanalytic theory, and interpretations utilizing the internal state of individuals are then used to support the theory and the hypothesized relations among observed facts and inferred characteristics. However, since the characteristics of an individual's internal state can be ascertained only through inferences from and interpretation of his behavior, it is difficult to determine the validity of conclusions concerning the internal state. Man's behavior is assumed to be determined by several components of the internal state, but none of these components and causal relations can at present be studied directly, by means of objective measurements and replicatable procedures. Hence, it is impossible to determine which of the many hypothesized elements and relationships of the internal state are necessary, sufficient, or irrelevant for the explanation and prediction of particular behavior patterns.

The components of man's internal state usually are poorly defined (e.g. guilt, anxiety, unconscious rage), and their interrelations are usually unclear (e.g. repression, reaction-formation). In addition, the conditions under which hypothesized regularities supposedly hold are not stated (e.g. the context of the Oedipus complex). Consequently, the prediction of behavior is quite difficult. As Hagen himself notes:

> Analysis of this sequence of personality change must be speculative, or, to use the term loosely, intuitive. Sequences of action and of reaction within individuals are difficult to analyze, at least with the tools yet devised by social scientists. In the main, the analysis must be by introspective examination and rearrangement of elements of behavior within oneself until one feels that one has arrived at a sequence that accounts for certain outer manifestations in other individuals.[83]

If the utilization of the internal state and of psychodynamic concepts and relations is wrought with such hazards to replicatable, objective analysis as the researcher's introspective examination, rearrangement of elements within himself, and his feelings, it is best to disregard the presently unmeasurable components and interrelations of the internal state until their study can be independently validated by replicatable procedures.

2. The causal analysis is inadequate. Hagen infers causes from effects, but little evidence is presented to validate these inferences. The capricious

83. Ibid. p. 201.

use of reaction-formation is a good illustration of the inadequacy of hypothesized casual relations based on inferences made from an effect. If an observation does not fit into one's theory, one holds that the fact is really the opposite of what it appears to be (for instance, the Burmese may appear to be friendly, but in reality they are only trying to cover up their rage and aggression). If the observation does fit into one's theory then the concept of reaction-formation is not used. The validity of the reversal procedure seems to rest simply on the fact that only certain interpretations of phenomena fit into the theory.

The absence of validating data and replicatable procedures leads either to the use of words such as "must," "obviously," and "undoubtedly" as indications of proof, or to references to other psychoanalytic concepts and relations equally subject to doubt. Lack of precise knowledge concerning the elements and dynamics of the internal state, combined with reliance on causal chains of which only the effects are definitely known, make any test as to the nature of necessary causes impossible and are of little use in further theory-building. For example, the hypothesis—"At the beginning of [the Oedipal] period the boy may feel free to react to his new sexuality and to reach out to his mother" [84]— can be neither tested nor rejected. The word "may" indicates that, although some phenomena occur at roughly the same time, the necessary causes are unknown; the existence of causal factors and irrelevant conditions is indicated, but what these could be is not apparent. What is important is not whether the boy *may* feel free to reach out to his mother, but rather those factors which do or do not *make* the boy free to reach out to his mother, and under what specified conditions he *does* reach out.

These shortcomings, of course, are not restricted to Hagen's analysis only. They are responsible, in large part, for the variety of psychoanalytic "schools," each one emphasizing different "crucial" elements and relationships among phenomena. Anxiety, sex, birth trauma, and inferiority feelings have all been considered as *the* most important determinant of human behavior. The history of the psychoanalytic movement shows that even in the early days the lack of validating procedures and objective measurement, together with emphasis on investigators' "internal states" resulted in the theoretical divergence of Freud's first adherents.[85]

3. Finally, Hagen disregards evidence which indicates that the psy-

84. Ibid. p. 146.
85. Jones (1953–1957).

choanalytic theory he employs is culture-bound. Evidence that many psychodynamic concepts and theories are not necessarily applicable to all cultures has come from anthropologists who did not find in primitive tribes and other cultures what was expected on the basis of psychoanalytic theories of European origin. Malinowski,[86] for example, in his analysis of Trobriand society, came to the conclusion that there is no such thing as the Oedipus complex among the islanders. Instead, aggression is directed against the maternal uncle who controls the boy while the real father exerts little or no control and is always affectionate and kind. Any causal analysis of social change, then, which rests heavily upon the Oedipus complex in primitive societies, has an insecure foundation. The explanation of certain behavior patterns of middle class Europeans who lived during the late nineteenth century may be phrased in terms of the Oedipus complex, sexual repression, etc., but the indiscriminate cross-cultural application of psychoanalytic concepts is not compatible with Malinowski's data.

These problems involved in the use of psychodynamic concepts and theories lead to a search for alternative explanations of the historical and sociological data presented by Hagen.

The Behavioral Perspective.[87] The low rate of social change in traditional societies, the much higher rate in transitional societies, and the implications of the "withdrawal or status respect" for the rise of entrepreneurs and economic development can be explained without recourse to inferred causes and major assumptions concerning the internal state of individuals and investigators.

Traditional Society. Hagen, Redfield,[88] Rostow, and others begin their theories of social change and economic development with almost identical descriptions of the traditional society whose normative structure has the following characteristics:

1. Norms (expected behavior patterns and associated discriminative and contingent stimuli) are universally applicable and accepted, with only a few known, accepted, and institutionalized exceptions (e.g. shamans);

2. Norms are consistent, mutually supporting, and form a coherent, inflexible system;

86. Malinowski (1959).
87. This section is based on Kunkel (1963).
88. Redfield (1941).

3. All of the behavior patterns required for daily life are "covered" by norms;

4. Positive and negative sanctions are attached to all norms and enforced.

Several additional elements of the traditional society affect the learning of behavior by its members. The small size of either the society or the communities in which men live makes possible the quick dissemination of information that transgressions against norms have occurred, and thus mearningful sanctions—for example, immediate punishment—can be put into action. The traditionalism of the society, the respect for a sacred past, and isolation with the consequent absence of new ideas and other elements from the outside mean that both the discriminative and contingent stimuli remain the same over long periods of time. The definition and reinforcement of "accepted" behavior is therefore consistent and frequent. The very act of behaving in accordance with the norms often takes on reinforcing properties, and the transgressions themselves often elicit punishment, for example the fear of gods and their wrath, in accordance with the unquestioned traditions of the culture. In short, the characteristics of traditional society approach the "ideal" circumstances for both the shaping and maintenance of behavior outlined in the previous chapter. It is to be expected, therefore, that the establishment of behavior patterns will be relatively easy, swift, thorough, and quite complete. Furthermore, the probability that activities will be replicated—both during the lifetime of an individual and also over generations—will be high. Deviation, unlikely to occur because of incompatibility with previously established activities, is likely to be quickly found out and punished. The result is a very low rate of behavioral, and thus social, change.

These circumstances influencing the shaping and maintenance of behavior prevail especially in primitive tribes of the past and present. Similar characteristics of the normative structure of a society, leading to similar consequences, probably existed in ancient nations as long as they were relatively isolated or ethnocentric and consisted mainly of small communities.

The Introduction of New Elements. The normative structure of a society does not remain constant, however. Loss of isolation and the influx of new ideas, improvements in technology, and other elements usually bring about changes in the normative structure and create new rules and reinforcers. Ecological changes such as the depletion of the soil, droughts, etc. result in the establishment of new discriminative and contingent stimuli—leading to new behavior patterns. Traditional farming methods, for example, become inefficient or useless through soil erosion, developments in technology, or the introduction of cash crops. Old norms become inapplicable or invalid, sanctions are altered, and thus old behavior patterns, no longer reinforced, are extinguished and replaced by new ones, newly reinforced, and related to new S^D.

While new behavior patterns and alterations in discriminative and contingent stimuli present problems to the adults of a society, the shaping of behavior involved in childhood socialization will be affected to a much greater degree. The rate of learning depends in part on the degree to which adaptation to the environment has occurred, that is, on the degree to which the individual is familiar with his surroundings. The presence of incompatible chains—behavior patterns which are in conflict with what is being reinforced at present—also influences the rate of shaping, as does the consistency of reinforcement and the reinforcement schedule itself. The intrusion of new elements into a culture, especially as these affect the normative structure of a society, creates an ever-changing environment for the socialization process and thus decreases the consistency of reinforcement. Both phenomena lead to a lower rate of learning and an increasing probability that new behavior patterns will be established, especially among the young.

Transitional Society. With the wholesale introduction of new elements, the transitional society comes into being. As described by Hagen, it is equivalent to the middle of Redfield's folk-urban continuum and the second stage of Rostow's conceptualization, and has a normative structure with these characteristics:

1. There are few universally applicable or accepted norms;
2. Norms are often inconsistent, or in actual conflict with each other, and do not form a coherent system;
3. Norms do not "cover" all of the possible new behavior patterns;
4. Many sanctions are weak, or no longer applied or have been removed altogether.

Other important characteristics are the lack of isolation and the increasing size of communities and of the society. The introduction of new ideas presents alternatives to old norms and the sanctions attached to them; normative homogeneity is replaced by normative heterogeneity. A

larger population increases the probability that divergence from the expected behavior patterns will occur, and that these deviations will go
unpunished or even unknown. The growing secularity of the culture (in
Redfield's sense) means that many sanctions which formerly were perhaps largely covert (e.g. belief in a revengeful thunder god) are now
disregarded or disappear as man's sophistication regarding the nature
and origin of natural phenomena increases and as he begins to question
the past. In short, the characteristics of transitional (and later) societies
are quite different from the ideal circumstances for the shaping and
maintenance of behavior.

It is to be expected, therefore, that the shaping of behavior will be
relatively slow and difficult, and that the transmission of the behavioral
heritage will be incomplete. Furthermore, since many activities will be
only poorly established, it is to be expected that the probability of behavior replication will be comparatively low. Conversely, since behavior
in accord with norms is often not reinforced, and behavior contrary to
old norms often is not punished and sometimes is even reinforced, the
probability of the establishment of new behavior patterns is much greater
than in the traditional society, resulting in a higher rate of behavioral
and thus social change.

Withdrawal of Status Respect and Its Consequences. In a transitional
society where peasants have lived under nearly constant conditions for a
long time, few changes in behavior will occur unless the contingencies
are altered. The old and established elite will not change its behavior
patterns much either since the contingencies, though different from those
of the peasants, have also remained nearly stable for some time. New
elites, newly reinforced for new behavior patterns, will have no reason
to change if the present reinforcers are more adequate—in the sense of
satisfying deprivations—than the old ones; thus their behavior patterns
will also be stable.

But the characteristics of daily life for groups recently deprived of
old contingencies—status or respect—are radically altered. Circumstances and actions which once were followed by respectful behavior
on the part of others no longer have this result, and old patterns which
were once reinforced no longer are. The behavioral chains associated
with the S^D of high social position and the S^r of respect are no longer
reinforced and thus begin to be extinguished. Possible new behavior
patterns, which might be reinforced under the new status conditions,

will be exhibited only if they are compatible with the old behavioral chains or if these are sufficiently weakened.

Work with one's hands and many types of business activity are usually proscribed by the elite; that is, aversive stimuli (for example, derision) follow manual labor and entrepreneurial activity. Only when these negative consequences are terminated does entrepreneurial activity become possible. The probability of termination varies from family to family, depending on the tenacity with which the "old way of life" is held up as a paragon (i.e. verbally reinforced) and the perceived possibility of re-entering the old elite status in the forseeable future. As long as the old patterns are not extinguished no new incompatible behavior can be established, and thus it follows that the longer the period necessary for the weakening or extinction, the longer will be the conflict resulting from the simultaneous presence (at least in potential) of opposing behavior patterns. Since the existence of incompatible activities leads to vacillation or inactivity and apathy, the retreatism which Hagen mentions can be explained in terms of the long period of extinction required by some chains, the growing possibility of new behavior patterns, the resulting conflict among them, and the slow learning of new activities. The conflict among incompatible behavior patterns is resolved when the old actions have been extinguished to such an extent that new patterns with new reinforcers become strong enough to replace them. The important elements here are the length of time necessary for extinction, the reinforcement schedule of new behavior patterns, and the degree of incompatibility between the old and the new.

NEED ACHIEVEMENT AND ECONOMIC GROWTH

McClelland's Theory. The major hypothesis of McClelland's book *The Achieving Society* is that a nation "with a generally high level of n-Achievement will produce more energetic entrepreneurs who, in turn, produce more rapid economic development." [89] Need for achievement is one of a constellation of needs which characterizes man and determines much of human behavior; like other motives it is created through a person's childhood experiences, and thus the link between society and the individual is the family. Societal characteristics, such as class and religion, and historical events "affect motivational levels primarily as they

89. McClelland (1961:205).

affect the family, or more specifically the values and child-rearing practices of the parents."[90] McClelland, after analyzing the child-raising practices of many countries, comes to the conclusion that major sources of high *n*-Achievement are parents who teach their children to be independent early, who are interested in their offspring and their activities, and who expect much of them. More specifically, the sources of high *n*-Achievement are:

1. "Early mastery training . . . provided it does not reflect generalized restrictiveness, authoritarianism, or 'rejection' by the parents."[91]
2. "Motive intensity is acquired as a function of the 'amplitude of affective change' associated with the achievement situation."[92]
3. "Mothers of the [high *n*-Achievement] boys also show more authoritarianism toward their sons, just as they showed more 'warmth.' They appeared to be much more actively involved [in their sons' lives]."[93]
4. The best environment for high *n*-Achievement consists of "reasonably high standards of excellence imposed at a time when the sons can attain them, a willingness to let him attain them without interference, and real emotional pleasure in his achievements short of over-protection and indulgence."[94]

Low need-achievement, conversely, is likely to develop under one or more of the following conditions:

1. Extreme father dominance, "because the father makes the decisions and little pressure is put on the son to work out high standards for himself."[95]
2. "Low standards of excellence and an indulgent attitude toward the son,"[96] because careless and indulgent parents usually have low expectations regarding their children.
3. Premature achievement demands also lead to low *n*-Achievement, for the son cannot meet them successfully and thus becomes discouraged.

90. Ibid. p. 387. For a general discussion of the relationship between parental characteristics, child-raising practices, and children's personality and behavior, see Whiting and Child (1953).
91. McClelland (1961:345).   94. Ibid. p. 356.
92. Ibid. p. 352.   95. Ibid. p. 356.
93. Ibid. p. 352.   96. Ibid. p. 356.

Need-achievement, as a major component of the internal state, is inferred from a large variety of behavior patterns. Stories written for TAT pictures, many children's games, decorations on pottery, literature, performance in laboratory tasks, etc. all contain some achievement imagery. These images can be counted, and thus achievement scores can be assigned to the elementary school readers of France in 1925,[97] Spanish, English, and Classical literature,[98] and Athenian pottery.[99] When achievement scores of a nation or subculture are compared with subsequent economic development, as measured in terms of a variety of criteria—for example, achievement imagery of children's stories in 1925 and per-capita electricity production in 1950—a high correlation is evident.[100] McClelland's hypothesis—that high need-achievement is *a major* (but not the only) determinant of economic development—is supported by data drawn from a large number of nations and historical periods.[101] The argument is summarized in Figure 4–1.

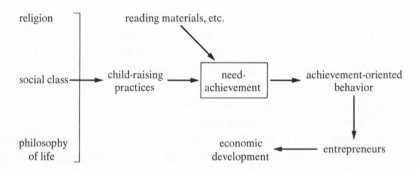

FIGURE 4–1: Diagram of McClelland's Theory

The major problem of this type of analysis is that only behavior—verbal and other types—is observed and counted. Need-achievement, as a characteristic of a person's internal state, is *inferred* from a large variety of actions. This leads to some circularity in the argument, for if

97. Ibid. p. 90.
98. Cortes (1961), Bradburn and Berlew (1961).
99. McClelland (1961:108ff).
100. Ibid. p. 100.
101. Aldaba—Lim and Javillonar (1968), for example, point out that high need-achievement is not sufficient to assure success for Filipino entrepreneurs. For additional examples, see Morgan (1964).

high *n*-Achievement is inferred from certain actions, and if other actions are assumed to be the consequence of high *n*-Achievement, all that is said is that the two types of action have certain characteristics in common. For example, high performance at difficult laboratory tasks and expressions such as "he tries to do well" in TAT stories, are both assumed to be reflections of high need-achievement. All that is known, however, is that both activities have certain abstracted characteristics—labeled "achievement"—in common. A major methodological difficulty is our present inability to validate the required inferences by the use of independent, objective procedures. A high level of agreement indicates merely that the several critics of literature, for example, were trained well enough to make the same inferences.

A related difficulty concerns the linkages between child-raising practices and need-achievement, and between need-achievement and subsequent behavior. Little is said—perhaps little *can* be said at present—about the nature and operation of these links.

Finally, there is some confusion of levels of analysis. Need-achievement, while an individual characteristic, is also treated as a national phenomenon, as when an achievement "score" is assigned to medieval Spain, ancient Greece, and modern Britain. The assumptions involved in measuring the need-achievement of Athens in Pericles' times, and linking this with the behavior of men dead these 2,400 years, are of necessity bold.

The Behavioral Perspective. Since studies dealing with need-achievement appear to be concerned, basically, with overt actions rather than with internal states, the behavioral approach should be able to account for much of McClellend's data.[102] This is indeed the case, as illustrated especially well by McClelland's discussion of the socialization procedures leading to high and low need-achievement. In effect, these procedures shape and maintain behavior patterns with certain specific characteristics —labeled "high" or "low" need-achievement.

The lists of child-raising methods mentioned above reveal that parents in various societies and subcultures shape certain behavior patterns— those with the abstracted element "achievement"—and extinguish others by means of differential reinforcement. Boys' activities involving the striving for excellence, for example, are reinforced by parental pleasure

102. For a more extensive discussion, see Kunkel (1963, 1965).

as expressed in smiles, words, etc. The consistency of contingencies is made possible by high expectations, for only those activities which meet the parental standards are rewarded. When in later life other situations with striving potential occur, behavior patterns involving "achievement" will again be exhibited.

Conversely, if a father is authoritarian, or if parents are careless and indulgent and do not expect great things of their children, then the sons are likely to learn—and perform—a different class of activities, because such an environment does not shape or consistently reinforce the class of activities which includes the element of "achievement." When parents are indulgent or overly restrictive, situations with "achievement" potential do not become discriminative stimuli, and thus striving is not often exhibited even when opportunities are present.

The achievement potential of a situation is not so much an inherent characteristic of the particular circumstances as it is the result of the individual's previous learning history and present reference group.[103] If striving for success or excellence has never been reinforced, no discriminative stimuli for "achievement" behavior will have been established. Conversely, when striving for excellence has been reinforced in a wide variety of contexts (e.g. language learning, toilet training, examinations), then the stimulus class associated with achievement behavior will be very large, and even ambiguous stimuli such as TAT pictures are likely to lead to the expression of "achievement," for example in the content of stories.

THE FOSTERING OF ACHIEVEMENT MOTIVATION

The preceding behavioral interpretation of n-Achievement and its determinants has received significant support from the description of various attempts to deliberately increase the motivation of business men. McClelland has recently modified his views of the achievement motive in an attempt to incorporate the behavioral perspective.[104] The new conception and treatment of n-Achievement amounts to a significant advancement in at least three major areas: the nature of n-Achievement, the possibility of its alteration in later life, and the implications of such alteration for development programs.

103. Kemper (1968).
104. McClelland and Winter (1969).

The Nature of n-Achievement. While *n*-Achievement is at times considered to be a motive—that is, an "affectively toned associative network"[105] which determines behavior—it is usually viewed as being equivalent to behavior as such. For example, McClelland sees the "need to achieve . . . as an index reflecting various habits or thoughts and actions"[106] and concludes that "*n*-Achievement is a term that refers to particular qualities of a person's actions, perceptions, and experience."[107] More specifically, the "*n*-Achievement behavior syndrome" is described in terms of the individual's interest in success, his relatively long time perspective, his realistic appraisal of the environment and belief that he exerts some control over it, and his strategy of maximizing the beneficial consequences of the various activities open to him.[108]

The conception of *n*-Achievement as *activity,* an *index* of behavior, or as a *cluster of expectancies* concerning the future, leads McClellend to support the learning theorist's proposition that *n*-Achievement is subject to alteration throughout a person's life. According to the behavioral model of man outlined in the previous chapters, the "achievement behavior syndrome" is likely to be shaped (or increased in frequency) upon the alteration of real and/or imagined contingencies—or in the language of economists, new incentives—that are attached to achievement-oriented activities in developing nations. In a similar vein McClelland concludes that the hope of economic growth lies to a large extent "in achievement motivation training—that is, in changing the structure of response to these new incentives."[109]

The Fostering of n-Achievement. The training programs described by McClelland and Winter are concerned primarily with the creation of achievement-oriented behavior patterns.[110] While there are variations among programs in different countries, the common elements may be summarized in the following general steps. First, the trainees are acquainted with motivation theory and the results of achievement motivation research. They are led to recognize achievement imagery in themselves and in others, and are taught to have achievement-oriented thoughts. Next, illustrations of achievement behavior patterns and their consequences in the business world are presented, and trainees are en-

105. Ibid. p. 43.
106. Ibid. p. 10.
107. Ibid. pp. 26–27.

108. Ibid. p. 23.
109. Ibid. p. 28.
110. Ibid. chapters 2 and 5.

couraged to discuss similar examples from their own and others' experiences. After the individual has learned to think, talk, and act like other men with high n-Achievement, there is a period of self-study, designed to clarify his life goals and to determine whether or not high n-Achievement and being an achievement-oriented entrepreneur are consistent with his self-image. If the answer is negative, the individual is free to leave the program (and welcome to remain). The final step is the delineation of reasonable short- and long-term business goals and the outlining of effective, specific procedures for their attainment. In order to increase the probability that the newly established thoughts and behavior patterns will be maintained, rewards in the form of "success" should be attainable, and the elimination of unreasonable goals and inappropriate methods goes a long way toward avoiding failure. However, since the environment (in the form of limited markets, governmental regulations, etc.) usually cannot be altered, the reinforcement of achievement-oriented behavior cannot be guaranteed. Throughout the training programs great efforts were made to establish a warm and friendly atmosphere so that the participants would feel free to talk, to discuss their problems and desires, and to encourage one another in the expression of achievement-oriented thoughts and actions. Ideally, the "students" of any program should become an important reference group for the individual trainee, and a source of continued support and reinforcement after the termination of the two-week program.

Results and Implications. When the economic performance of trainees subsequent to the programs was evaluated, it appeared that changes in behavior were especially prevalent for two types of individuals, regardless of their personal or religious values: owners or high-level managers, and those men who during the course perceived discrepancies between their ideal self and actual accomplishments (i.e. those who were initially dissatisfied).[111] In terms of the behavioral model of man, new activities are likely to be exhibited only when there are opportunities and rewards (and, by implication, deprivations); these elements exist for business men who can control their own actions, while those who must follow orders operate in a much more restricted, and restrictive, environment. In evaluating the overall effectiveness of training programs in general, McClelland concludes that "the courses do not so much affect goals as

111. Ibid. chapters 9 and 11.

they do the means of attaining them, [and that] opportunity plays a major role in determining whether increased *n*-Achievement leads to greater activity." [112] His major and recurrent theme—that "changes in opportunity structure ought to be combined with an attempt to change man's response to them" [113]—is precisely the gist of the behavioral perspective and the crux of development problems all over the world.

Conclusion

Many of the problems encountered in studies of economic development—as illustrated by Ayal, Fillol, and Singer—and many of the questions which arise in theoretical efforts—for example those by Hagen and the original McClelland—can be substantially reduced by the employment of a behavioral model of man. In the course of reinterpreting data and reformulating explanations, however, a number of problems have become apparent. Chief among them is the fact that while the activities of men constitute the essence of economic growth, the social system structures both the opportunities and contingencies of these activities. Education programs, extension services, training institutes, and similar limited efforts to change men's actions will not be very effective as long as there are few opportunities and rewards for the expression of the new behavior patterns that are introduced. Widespread behavior modification is not likely until significant changes occur in the social context of individuals. This does not necessarily mean that wholesale and fundamental social changes are always required. Rather, it means that the specific aspects of a person's environment which affect the new behavior patterns—for example job opportunities and pay scales for engineering graduates—must be changed so as to reinforce the new patterns of activity.

Throughout this chapter, individuals' activities have been viewed within the social context, but neither the nature of the link nor the operation of the context has been discussed in detail. The following chapter is devoted to this task.

112. Ibid. pp. 334–35.   113. Ibid. p. 368.

V *An Outline of*

Structural Analysis

The concept "social structure" is an important element in the analysis of social change and economic development, for these processes do not occur in a vacuum but are influenced by a large variety of diverse characteristics, such as a society's religious institutions, a nation's political organization, and the norms common to various population segments.[1] The utility of the concept "social structure" at present is rather limited, however, for the term is usually restricted to the description of behavior patterns and institutions, and while a considerable number of investigators employ the phrase, there is as yet no agreement on the meaning or referents of the concept. Students of economic development may ask, therefore, what the role of social structure in the development process is, and whether the concept is a useful component of the analysis of industrialization. This chapter is designed to provide at least a foundation for answers.

Social Aspects of the Behavioral Approach

THE ROLE OF SOCIAL FACTORS

The postulate that learning principles are invariant leads to the conclusion that their role in the explanation of social phenomena and pro-

1. For a good description, see Hoselitz (1960b).

102

cesses is rather limited. They cannot, by themselves, account for two of the major and most obvious facts of interest to sociologists: behavior and social relations change over time, and men in different groups, subcultures, and societies exhibit different behavior patterns. In other words, it is apparent that *psychological (learning) principles are necessary but not sufficient causes of social phenomena and processes.*

The behavioral model of man outlined in Chapter Three described certain relationships among events—for example, between behavior and contingent stimuli—and indicated that activities may be partially explained in terms of these relations. But learning principles cannot account for the specific activities which are established, the particular rewards which are effective in a society, or the nature of discriminative stimuli. Even the simple observation that people usually eat three times a day and that the evening meal is the largest, cannot be explained in terms of learning principles alone. It is true, of course, that men *learn* to eat three times a day. But the question of why there are *three* meals, with the last the *largest,* cannot be answered in terms of differential reinforcement alone. In short, learning principles indicate *how* behavior patterns are established, but the question of *what* activities are learned, and *why* these and not others, require different sets of answers.

Social phenomena such as "customs," "norms," "sanctions," and "institutions" are generally employed in attempts to account for specific behavior patterns. It may be said, for example, that the norm of three meals, or customs of "cocktails and dinner" are part of the sociological explanation. A large variety of basically *social* phenomena—that is, phenomena arising outside the individual(s) on whose behavior the analysis focuses—determine *which* behavior patterns are established, under *what* circumstances they will be exhibited, and in terms of *which* contingent stimuli men are likely to act. However, these social factors cannot, by themselves, account for behavior, because they do not indicate the nature or operation of the link between a person's social environment and his behavior. To put it differently, *social characteristics are necessary but not sufficient causes of behavior patterns and changes. The explanation of specific actions, behavior change, and behavior differences, requires both learning principles and social factors.*

Such explanations are as yet fragmentary, for much of the required information is absent or incomplete. As was pointed out in Chapter Three, for example, little is known about the actual *process* of learning, that is, what occurs within the individual as he "learns." Similarly, knowledge of the structure and operation of large-scale social systems and processes is as yet incomplete. While questions associated with the first topic are not of interest to sociologists, questions involving the second are treated below.

PSYCHOLOGICAL REDUCTIONISM

The best-known and most eloquent spokesman for the behavioral perspective, George C. Homans, has been suspected of psychological reductionism, and any behavioral model of man is subject to the same suspicion. The label "psychological reductionism" has been attached to Homans' position for at least two reasons: he has called himself a reductionist, and some of his writings are open to reductionist interpretation.[2] It is possible, however, that the label is undeserved; the first reason for it is merely unfortunate, and the second is based on selective perception. In his article on "Contemporary Theory in Sociology," [3] for example, he speaks of psychological theories as alternatives to presently popular structural and functional theories. Psychological theories, according to Homans, are those "in which the highest-order propositions are statements about the behavior of men as members of a species," [4] for example the procedures involved in the establishment of behavior. He comes to the conclusion, later on, that "the only type of theory in sociology that stands any chance of becoming a general one is a psychological theory, in the sense that the deductive systems by which we explain social behavior would, if completed, contain among their highest-order propositions one or more of those I call psychological." [5] However, the latter quotation seems to indicate that few if any such highest-order propositions have so far been developed, and one might therefore conclude that it is at present impossible to state categorically how many, or what proportion of these propositions are psychological. Statements to the effect that the behavioral approach is equivalent to psychological reductionism—or that it has nothing to do with reductionism—are evidently premature. As was shown above, the fact that specific actions and behavior change cannot be explained in terms of learning principles alone

2. Homans (1964b).   4. Ibid. p. 967.
3. Homans (1964a).   5. Ibid. p. 968.

would indicate that the behavioral approach outlined in the previous two chapters does not automatically, or necessarily, lead to psychological reductionism. Not only can it not be said that behavior is due *only* to psychological principles, or that *all* actions can be explained in terms of them, but there is in addition little empirical evidence at present for the contention that *most* of the highest-order propositions of sociological explanations contain psychological elements. It may be concluded, therefore, that useful discussions concerning psychological reductionism must await the accumulation of additional evidence.

SOCIAL STRUCTURE AND CONTEXT

The social aspects of the behavioral approach so far have been couched mainly in terms of individuals' "social context." Since sociologists usually speak of social structure, a brief discussion of these topics may be in order. The term "social context" implies that the investigator is concerned not only with *social* phenomena as such, but also with the persons for whom these are the context, and with the relationship between men and their environment. The concept, "Social Structure," however, disregards individuals in the sense that they are not considered an important focus of the investigation. For example, a subculture or community can be analyzed in terms of either social context or social structure. The former implies that, sooner or later, specific individuals and their characteristics will be a significant facet of the study, whereas emphasis on "structure" would indicate that the analysis will remain on the level of social and collective phenomena.

In the last two chapters, emphasis on learning by individuals has resulted in the use of the term "social context." The present concern with the nature and operation of this context, however, leads to an interest in "social structure."

Problems of Structural Analysis

Much space could be devoted to the exhaustive description of the problems associated with the concept and utilization of "social structure" in development analysis. However, since the present focus is on constructive solutions, the problems themselves will be only briefly outlined on the basis of a sample of writers.

DEFINITIONS

There are many definitions of "social structure" in both the socio-logical and anthropological literature, and when implicit definitions are included it almost seems as if there are as many conceptions as there are writers. The diversity of meanings as well as the direction of the apparent convergence of conceptions will be illustrated by some of the better-known students of the subject.

Among sociologists, the concept usually refers to a broad range of phenomena. Parsons, for example, views social structure as "a patterned system of social relationships of actors in their capacity of playing roles relative to one another." [6] Blau speaks of "patterned social relations among individuals and groups, including the recurrent conduct in which these relations find expression." [7] Levy, to give a final illustration, defines social structure as "a pattern, i.e., an observable uniformity, of action or operation," [8] and further distinguishes "concrete" and "analytic" structures. The first are "those patterns [of action] that define the character of units that are at least in theory capable of physical separation [in time and/or space] from other units of the same sort," [9] for example the family or business firms. Analytic structures are "patterned aspects of action that are not even theoretically capable of concrete separation from other patterned aspects of action," [10] for example economic or political aspects of action.

Anthropologists have generally devoted more attention to the method-ological and theoretical problems associated with "social structure" than have sociologists, and their literature contains somewhat more specific treatments. Firth, for example, defines social structure as the "major patterns of relationship . . . which form a systematic arrangement and which as such serve to regulate further action along the same lines." [11] An earlier, slightly different view is that social structure consists of "those social relations which seem to be of critical importance for the behavior of members of the society, so that if such relations were not in operation,

6. Parsons (1954:230). For a recent discussion of sociological definitions, see Moore (1967:171–219).
7. Blau (1964b:283).
8. Levy (1952:57).
9. Ibid. p. 88.
10. Ibid. p. 89.
11. Firth (1964:35).

the society could not be said to exist in that form." [12] This conception is similar to Radcliffe-Brown's, according to which social structure is the "network of actually existing relations . . . the set of relations, at a given moment of time, which link together certain human beings." [13] Nadel,[14] finally quotes and uses Parsons' definition. The question which arises from these definitions is how relations, or links, are to be observed, measured, and analyzed. The activities of individuals and mutual influences (as measured, for example, by changes in action) are the components of relationships, according to both Firth and Radcliffe-Brown, but a specific treatment of behavior has not been attempted by them. A rather different view is expressed by Levi-Strauss,[15] who considers social structure as the model (either conscious or unconscious, statistical or mechanical) which may be abstracted from existing, observable social relations. A similar position has been taken by Leach.[16] The diversity of explicit conceptions of social structure may be further illustrated by citing Wilson and Wilson, who define social structure as "the systematic form of limitation by which eccentricities are checked and complementary diversities are preserved; it is the inherent, negative condition of human relations. . . . It is a form of order, coherence and harmony." [17]

Not all writers who employ the term take the trouble of defining it, consequently there are a number of implicit definitions of social structure. The most common of these—as is apparent from books and articles not specifically concerned with the nature and meaning of social structure—seems to equate social structure with institutions in general, or a specific institution, or all institutions, i.e. society as a whole. Spiro, for example, writes "Since social structure consists of institutions . . ." [18] Other authors have discussed government, economic systems, and especially kinship, in works ostensibly dealing with social structure.[19] The relationship between behavior, institution, and social structure is well described by Gerth and Mills, who note that "role is the unit with which

---

12. Firth (1951:31).
13. Radcliffe-Brown (1952:190, 192).
14. Nadel (1957:12).
15. Levi-Strauss (1963).
16. Leach (1961, 1964).
17. Wilson and Wilson (1945:49).
18. Spiro (1965:1098).
19. For example, Anderson and Anderson (1962), the essays in Fortes (1949), Leach (1964), Murdock (1949), Needham (1960).

we build our conception of institutions, [and] institution is the unit with which we build our conception of social structure. There is more to a social structure than the interrelations of its institutions, but these institutions . . . do make up its basic framework." [20]

The different conceptions of "social structure" mentioned so far appear to have enough common elements to indicate the direction of convergence of meanings and the probable area of eventual agreement: "social structure" consists of behavior and social relationships. At present, however, it is not clear which types of activities are included, what the constituent elements of "social relations" are, and what the generally acceptable empirical referents of both might be. One particular aspect of the diversity of meanings, the question of the ontological status of "social structure," is important enough to merit some specific comments.

ABSTRACTION OR REALITY

According to Radcliffe-Brown, social structure is "an actually existing concrete reality, to be directly observed." [21] Firth, however, conceives of "social structure as a set of ideal patterns" [22] which must be inferred from observations and abstracted from reality. This view is similar to that of Levi-Strauss, who maintains that "the term 'social structure' has nothing to do with empirical reality but with models which are built up after it. . . . Social relations consist of the raw materials out of which models making up social structure are built." [23] Leach echoes this position when he holds that "the structures which the anthropologist describes are models which exist only as logical constructions in his own mind." [24]

The major difference which is apparent here at first glance does not seem to be crucial; after all, what difference does it make whether "social structure" refers to observed facts or to inferences abstracted from them, as long as writers indicate on which level of abstraction they are moving? The difficulty is that the two levels are often fused into one. In most works dealing with social structure—be it considered as social relations,

20. Gerth and Mills (1953:23).
21. Radcliffe-Brown (1952:192).
22. Firth (1964:38).
23. Levi-Strauss (1963:279).
24. Leach (1964:5).

institutions, or society itself, and emphasizing descriptions of kinship, tribal political systems, etc.—it is not clear whether actual behavior patterns are described, whether the abstracted rules are illustrated, or whether reality and inferences are fused to produce a more "coherent" and complete picture. This problem is especially acute when implicit conceptions of social structure form the basis of descriptions; for an institution or a community may be described without reference to any divergence between inferred rules and actual behavior.

SOCIAL "STRUCTURE" AND "ORGANIZATION"

A closely related problem is whether social structure refers to actual behavior or ideal behavior. The discrepancy between ideal and actuality is most apparent when actual behavior is compared with the theoretical rules. Does "social structure" refer, then, to the actual behavior of people—as reflected, for example, in social relationships— or does it refer to the more or less theoretical rules of ideal conduct? Most sociologists simply recognize that there are "ideal and actual structures" [25] and endeavor to specify which type is used in a particular analysis. Many anthropologists, however, attempt to emphasize the differences in their terminology. Thus Firth [26] speaks of social "structure" as referring to the ideal rules of behavior, the social relations which *should* exist, and the behavior patterns which one *should* be able to observe. Actual rules, existing social relations, and observed actions are the components of social "organization." In a similar vein, Levi-Strauss [27] proposes two types of models of social structure. "Statistical models" are those in which variations of action are possible and may be expected; they are based on actual behavior patterns, as illustrated by the fact that ideal marriage rules are not always followed. "Mechanical models," conversely, indicate ideal relationships and behavior patterns, and may be quite different from what can be observed. [28]

A structural analysis should be clearly focused on either observed reality or ideal conceptions, abstracted either from observations of action or from verbal statements. When the distinction is not made, when ideal

25. Levy (1966:26).
26. Firth (1951).
27. Levi-Strauss (1963).
28. Leach (1961) makes the same point in his discussion of "statistical norms" and "jural rules."

and reality are combined or fused in order to "round out" the picture of an institution, community, or society, the resulting description will be of little use in any further study and will contribute little to development analysis.

THE PROBLEM OF COMPONENTS

It is clearly impossible to describe completely, in every detail, the actions and social relations of even small and relatively simple societies. "Social structure," therefore, cannot help but refer to incomplete descriptions of, or abstractions from, social reality. Neither do those who employ structural analysis explain how the behavior patterns which constitute social relations affect one another, how social relations are combined into larger units, and what the boundaries and components of particular social structures are. Terms such as "links" among men, "patterns" of behavior, "systems" of action, and "relations," abound, but these are mainly descriptive and provide a largely intuitive understanding of observations. Leach,[29] Nadel,[30] and Levi-Strauss,[31] for example, although they speak of schemata and models, provide little more than descriptions of tribal life.

The inadequate or incomplete conceptualization of "social structure," and especially of its components and their interrelations, often leads to the view that social structure is something quite concrete, with almost physical properties, a more or less solid, undifferentiated unit. Such reification may provide the reader with pictures or models of social phenomena, including "forces" which act upon the "equilibrium" of structures, "stresses" in social systems, or "strains" toward consistency, but one cannot be sure that they are a valid reflection of reality. The resulting holistic conception of social structure makes it difficult to investigate the independent operation and dynamics of the various components of a structure, their different reactions to similar influences, and their differential effects on "outside" elements. Finally, it leads the student of social change and economic development to the study of similarly large-scale and amorphous processes, such as institutionalization, evolution, integration, or modernization.

29. Ibid.
30. Nadel (1947).
31. Levi-Strauss (1963).

STATIC IMPLICATIONS

When social structure is described in terms of behavior (or roles) and of relations among men (again mainly in terms of action) it is natural that emphasis should be placed on that which exists rather than on the possibility of change or the factors that might lead to structural alterations. For this reason many writers have contended that structural analysis is static.[32] Levi-Strauss, for example, holds that changes in social structure can be explained only in terms of external causes,[33] and Firth says flately that "a structural analysis cannot interpret social change." [34]

It is questionable, however, whether any structural analysis *must* be static.[35] Both Firth and Vogt,[36] among others, maintain that it is the researcher's conception of social structure as an undifferentiated unit that leads him to disregard the possibility of internal dynamics. A behaviorist would add that another important factor is the researcher's model of man. For example, when behavior is assumed to be determined largely by personality, and when it is postulated that personality is formed in childhood and is not likely to change much in later life, it must be concluded that the social structures incorporating these actions will be equally slow to change. A different model of man, with different assumptions concerning the determinants of behavior and the nature of social relations, may have quite different effects on both the conceptualization and analysis of social structure. As Moore[37] has pointed out, there are characteristics of the social system and of men which create change-producing elements and tensions. A behavioral model of man, with its emphasis on the individual's contemporary social context and the malleability of activities, is especially useful in describing the internal dynamics of social structures. It may be premature, therefore, to say that structural analysis is static; rather, *present* structural analysis often has static overtones. The future may bring different procedures and new

---

32. For a good examination of this problem, see Moore (1967: chapters 1, 2, 11).

33. Levi-Strauss (1963:309).

34. Firth (1951:35).

35. For a discussion of this topic, see Moore (1967).

36. Vogt (1960).

37. Moore (1960).

conceptions of man, which may enable students of social structure to account for social change.

A Behavioral Approach to Structural Analysis

Not all of the problems that have been described above can be solved by the employment of a behavioral perspective. For example, questions of whether one should concentrate on actually observed social relations or on ideal ones, and whether social structure consists of observed behavior patterns or of abstractions derived from observations, depend for their answers on the researcher's inclination and theoretical interests. However, a model of man based on learning principles does make it possible to describe and account for relationships among activities and among men. The basic elements of social structure, then, become amenable to analysis, and as a result it is no longer necessary to view social structure as a static, undifferentiated unit.

ELEMENTS OF SOCIAL STRUCTURE

A basic conclusion of the behavioral model of man outlined in Chapter Three is that the great majority of activities are preceded by one or more discriminative stimuli and followed by one or more contingent stimuli. Any behavioral analysis, then, begins by determining the S^D or S^Δ and S^r or S^a of the activity which provides the initial focus of interest. Such observations may be diagrammed as follows:

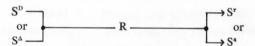

Since most discriminative and contingent stimuli consist of behavior, the next step is the specification of S^D and S^r (Figure 5–1).

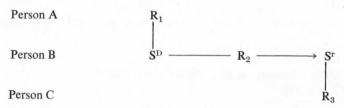

FIGURE 5–1: A Schema of Social Relations

Here R_1 is equivalent to an S^D for B's activity R_2, while C's behavior, R_3, serves as an S^r for B. The simple schema presented here is the basic building block of a behavioral conception of social structure, which may be viewed as a complex lattice arrangement of many activities. Ideally, such a behavioral lattice represents the S^D for all activities of interest in a particular investigation, indicates all important contingencies of these activities, and thus describes the interrelations of men and of actions. Finally the lattice shows how activities are being maintained by being reinforced, and suggests ways and means of modifying behavior by the judicious alteration of specific discriminative and contingent stimuli. Such a lattice arrangement of activities will be especially relevant in the analysis of economic development, for it enables the investigator to pinpoint the best or easiest locations and procedures for altering activities, if that should be required.

In order to present a more detailed discussion of certain aspects and problems of structural analysis, a lattice based on the observation of a simple event appears below (Figure 5–2).

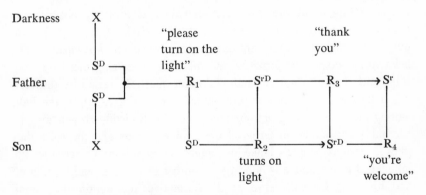

FIGURE 5–2: A Simple Behavior Lattice

Darkness and the presence of the son are discriminative stimuli for the father's saying: "please turn on the light." These words (and the associated gestures) are the S^D for the son's turning on the light. This action is a reinforcer for the father and at the same time an S^D for thanking the boy (hence S^{rD}). The expression of gratitude (R_3), in turn, reinforces the son and serves as an S^D for the conventional "you're welcome."

The horizontal lines indicate a succession of activities on the part of one person and may be termed "sequences." Vertical lines relate one person's actions to the behavior of another and indicate the role which one individual's behavior plays in the shaping and maintenance of someone else's activities. These lines may be termed "equivalences" since they indicate that the father's action, for example, is equivalent to a reinforcing and/or discriminative stimulus for the son.

The actions of one person influence the behavior of another mainly in terms of their roles as discriminative and contingent stimuli. Thus, a relationship among activities may be said to exist if one action is a discriminative or contingent stimulus for another action (of either the same or different persons). Similarly, a relationship may be said to exist between individuals if one person (and his behavior) is a discriminative or contingent stimulus for another person (and his action). The term "social relation," therefore, is a summary statement of the actions of several persons, which is abstracted from repeatedly observed behavior and the interdependence and covariation of the activities of a number of individuals.

According to Moore, "if social behavior is properly observed as organized into systems, as it clearly is, then analysis of such systems requires attention to the relevant elements *and their relationships.*" [38] The behavioral perspective provides one means of analyzing these relationships and of answering the methodological questions raised by the various definitions of social structure quoted above. For example, the links among men and among actions mentioned by Radcliffe-Brown may be profitably considered in terms of observable actions and the roles they play in various people's behavior chains. Since any man's activities are influenced in the above fashion by a number of persons, and he himself and his behavior will serve as discriminative and contingent stimuli for the actions of several other individuals, Firth's "systematic arrangement" and Parsons' "patterns of social relations" may be viewed in terms of a number of individuals whose activities influence one another's behavior by providing S^D and S^r for one another. The term "social structure" refers, then, to the more or less systematic behavior patterns of people in the roles of both discriminative and contingent stimuli. "Structure" is not something monolithic, solid, or necessarily enduring, for behavior modification is always possible.

38. Moore (1967:190); italics in the original.

The actions indicated in Figure 5–2 have been greatly simplified in order to show how a number of activities are chained together to form one more or less coherent unit within a certain time span. Peripheral elements (at least for purposes of this discussion) such as gestures, smiles, or the movements associated with turning on the light, have been disregarded for the sake of clarity. Preceding activities, for example those which established the boy's obedience to his father and the "polite" verbal responses, have not been included even though present behavior cannot be understood without knowledge of the preceding chains which shaped presently operating discriminative and contigent stimuli.

The behavioral diagram shown in Figure 5–2 consists, essentially, of a set of "squares" as illustrated by Figure 5–3. Each "square," re-

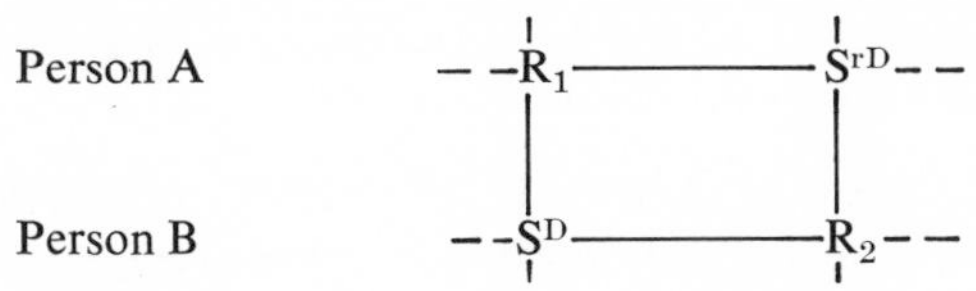

Person A $\quad\quad\quad - -R_1 \text{———} S^{rD} - -$

Person B $\quad\quad\quad - -S^D \text{———} R_2 - -$

FIGURE 5–3: The Basic "Square"

flecting the basic unit of interaction, may be conveniently designated by its two observable elements, the activities, in this case R_1 and R_2. Since sociologists are not interested in the simple, isolated interactions of two individuals, they are usually concerned with an often complex arrangement of "squares." Many of these complex series at times may be considered as units, or may be referred to by one term. For example, squares may sometimes be summarized as "norms" or reflections of general rules. In Figure 5–2, the "square" R_1–R_2 may be thought of as exemplifying the norm "obedience to parents," while R_2–R_3 and R_3–R_4 reflect the rules of "common courtesy."

From these considerations it is evident that the behavioral model of man makes it possible to integrate the actions of individuals into structural analysis, to define the position and role of the individual in large-scale social phenomena, and to investigate the mutual influences of activity and social context. The behavioral model not only indicates the "ties" between the individual and the social context, however; it also shows that an individual's behavior cannot be explained except in terms of the operation of the social context, and that the context is, in essence, the systematic behavior of other individuals. The question posed by Leach: "Why should I be looking for some social entity other than the individuals of the community itself?"[39] makes good sense to behaviorists, and his answer, that one need not, is echoed by those who use the behavioral model of man. Opler's[40] position, that the human being is (or should be) an integral part of culture theory is now provided with a procedure for realization. For example, Opler's point that "the focus of sanctions is still human beings and not the external rule they are enforcing"[41] is elaborated and supported by the behavioral approach. And his contention that culture "is the story, not of impersonal forces of prime movers and shakers, but of countless millions, each of whom has left a trace"[42] is made meaningful. It is now possible to indicate what the "traces" of individuals are—behavior and its effects on others—and how they are combined into social and cultural systems.

PROBLEMS OF STRUCTURAL ANALYSIS

The arrangement of observations into a lattice of activities illustrated in Figure 5–2 assumes the solution of a number of problems. Since these problems are basic to any behavioral analysis, the procedures employed for their reduction must be briefly described.

The Problem of Units. In the dyad shown in Figure 5–2, the units were individuals and the time span was relatively short. The analysis of large-scale phenomena, were it to be carried out in the same manner, would result in an exceedingly complicated lattice arrangement of individuals' activities. Such a complex picture, although it would correspond to reality, would make any comparative analysis extremely difficult, thus it often is advisable to simplify the lattice by treating several individuals as one unit. The definition of unit will depend on the purpose of the analysis, of course, and thus units will vary in size, composition, etc. from one study to the next. For example, a unit could be a large group of individuals performing similar roles (e.g. the electorate), or a few men engaged in similar specific tasks (e.g. factory workers). Since units vary with the analysis, they must be specifically defined, and throughout the study the same definition should be maintained in order to prevent distortion. No matter how the units are defined, it must be remembered that any multi-person unit could be dissected into individuals, and that

39. Leach (1961:300). 41. Ibid. p. 523.
40. Opler (1964). 42. Ibid. p. 525.

the combinations of men into larger units is a procedure of methodological and analytical convenience.

The Problem of R. The activities which constitute a behavioral lattice may vary from simple movements to complex behavior patterns, depending on the purpose of the analysis. In the above example, R_3 is adequate and need not be dissected further. R_2 is a much more complex set of activities which consists, actually, of a series of movements such as going to the switch and lifting the hand. It is evident, then, that each R could be dissected into a chain of actions of various lengths and specificity, or could be combined with others. The problem of defining and limiting an R in a behavioral analysis is difficult to solve satisfactorily or summarily, for just as the definition of "unit" depends on the focus of the study, so the definition of "R" is dependent on the questions which give rise to a particular investigation and on the other methodological requirements of the analysis. In the case of the subject covered in Figure 5–2, for example, it would be unreasonable to dissect the various R any further. However, if the subject under investigation had been "respect for parents," it would have been important to know how the boy reacted to his father's request—i.e. R_2 would have been dissected—and if the family's evening social life had been the focus, some of the R probably would have been combined. The complexity of R is a procedural matter, then, and varies from one study to the next. It is important to remember only that any R *could* be further dissected, and that several R *could* be combined into more complex sets.

Another aspect of this problem is the omission of activities which—presumably or definitely—intervene among the actions shown in a lattice. For example, the boy may do a number of things before he finally turns on the light, and it may be expected that the father performs a number of actions between R_1 and R_3. These activities do not appear, however, because they are irrelevant for the analysis at hand, concerned as it is with the illustration of the norm that "sons obey their fathers." Furthermore, words other than R_3 and R_4 may well be spoken, but again they are irrelevant. However, if the focus of the study were the "degree of respect" that sons have for fathers, the son's grumblings and other comments would be significant components of the lattice, as well as the speed with which the father's request is carried out. The focus of the study, then, defines "relevant" R and indicates which activities may be omitted from the lattice.

The Problem of S^r and S^D. It is evident that only activities can be observed and that their role as S^r and/or S^D for other actions must be inferred. In Figure 5–2, for example, R_3 can be easily observed, but its role as an S^{rD} for the son is more difficult to determine. If societal norms, the learning histories of the participants, and the language are known, one can declare with confidence that R^2 is *both* a reinforcer for preceding actions and a discriminative stimulus for later activities. When this information is not available, however, inferences will have to be based on experimentation or observations. Since the former procedure is in most cases impossible, only the second method remains. A *number* of observations are required, and slight variation from one to the next would be ideal. For example, the reinforcing character of R_3 will be especially evident when its absence produces some sign of disappointment on the part of the son. Furthermore, such absence would not be followed by R_4, thus indicating the role of R_3 as an S^D. It should be concluded that, in view of the great difficulties encountered in experimentation, any statement concerning the role of R as an S^r and/or S^D is basically a hypothesis whose provisional and inferential character should not be forgotten.

The Problem of Time. The time span in Figure 5–2 is quite short, but this is not apparent in the diagram. The complexity of the various R partly reflects the time interval, but it is not shown how much time elapsed between the father's request and the son's action. The actions of the father are quite short, for example, whereas R_2 is probably longer, especially if movements toward the light switch are involved. Since diagrams usually do not indicate *all* actions, and include only those which are relevant to the analysis at hand, it may be useful to show the passage of time—thus indicating other possible behavioral elements which could have been included but were not.

Preliminary Solution. As a first step toward the solution of these problems, the purpose of the study should be stated clearly and early, for the focus of the analysis defines the units, the "relevant" and "irrelevant" activities, the degree of complexity required for each R, and outlines the time span. When observations are made without a specific focus, a mass of activities is likely to be noted, but since observations can never be complete, unsystematic omissions are likely to occur. When a focus is later supplied, much relevant and necessary information may be missing. Secondly, a number of observations should be made, for it is next to impossible to know on the basis of one instance whether an activity is an D^D or S^r. While it is easy to infer that "thank you" is an S^r, such inference is based on the observer's knowledge of the language and customs of the people involved. In the absence of such knowledge, the accurate assignment of an S^r role to a particular R depends upon repeated, careful observations, preferably by more than one person.

AN EXAMPLE OF STRUCTURAL ANALYSIS

The dyadic relationships in Figure 5–2 may be considered as a two-unit system whose basic operation and underlying principles can be logically expanded into multi-unit systems. In these larger and more complex systems, any R, however it may be defined, can be an S^D or S^r or S^a for another unit (however defined) or it may be all of these to different units. Furthermore, every R is preceded by an S^D (except at the essentially arbitrary beginning of a diagram), and is followed by a contingency (except at the end of a diagram). Most of these discriminative and contingent stimuli will be the actions (or mere presence) of men, for even primary reinforcers such as affection or food usually involve the behavior of other people. ~~Robert F.~~

The material of the following illustration is based on Murphy's [43] description of the Mundurucu, a tribe in central Brazil. Only a small part of daily life can be portrayed in this chapter, and even this fragment has been abstracted from a large number of observations. Hunting and the consequent sharing of food were selected because these important aspects of social structure illustrate not only the role of values and norms but also indicate the operation of ecological factors in social organization.

According to Murphy, the hunting of game is the major food-producing activity of the Savannah Mundurucu. Although most hunting is performed in groups, there are also individual hunters, and one of these is shown in Figure 5–4. Regardless of how the game is obtained, the meat is shared by other members of the community, and especially by the extended family. Those who share game are accepted as regular members of the tribe, and their actions are met by approval. Those men who refuse to share (so rare that Murphy did not know of any) are shamed and ostracized.

43. Murphy (1960).

The various specific activities and relationships involved in the sharing of game are shown in Figure 5–4. In this diagram the units of analysis vary in complexity from individuals (the two hunters and their wives) to larger groups (the rest of the villagers) in order to illustrate the relationships between the actions of one person and the behavior of both another person and larger groups, i.e. the social context. The activities, too, vary in complexity, ranging from rather simple actions such as "shares food" to complex sets of activities collectively labeled "acceptance." The units of analysis and the various types of activities have been chosen for purposes of illustration and would be defined differently if the diagram reflected a different focus.

After a successful hunt (actually a complex series of actions here shown as R_1), the hunter gives the meat to his wife (R_2). She presents most of the meat to others (R_3) and keeps the rest for her own family (R_4). Other women use the meat for the preparation of meals (R_5). The food is both a reinforcer for preceding activities and a discriminative stimulus for the villagers' various expressions of approval (R_7). The term "acceptance" (R_7) refers to a complex series of behavior patterns which occurs over time and includes such actions as friendly conversations with the hunter and his wife, full membership in the community, participation in village affairs, and religious rites. The sharing and consumption of meat, together with a later successful hunt, are discriminative stimuli for another hunter's eventual sharing of his game (R_9). This sharing—which actually operates through the second hunter's wife (R_{10})—reinforces the first hunter and his wife's sharing of their meat and is also an S^D for sharing food after later hunts (R_{16}). At the same time, this action (R_{10}) is an S^D for various expressions of "acceptance" on the part of the rest of the villagers (R_{14}).

The activities incorporated into the behavioral lattice have been greatly simplified in order to emphasize those elements which would be essential in the discussion of general structural characteristics such as social cohesion. According to Murphy,[44] one of the most important aspects of Mundurucu social structure is the high degree of cohesion which characterizes the Savannah villages. In a behavioral lattice such as this, "cohesion" would be inferred from the number of equivalences which relate the activities of the individual members, and it would be

44. Ibid. pp. 55ff.

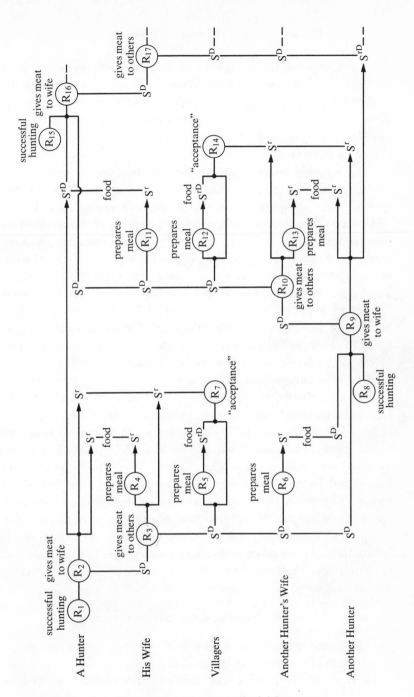

FIGURE 5–4: An Aspect of Mundurucu Social Structure

possible to say that the greater the number of equivalences, the greater the "cohesion." Among the River villages, for example, sharing of food is absent, and there is little co-operation in the preparation of gardens. Thus there are relatively few equivalences in the diagrams of river dwellers' activities, and Murphy speaks of the "few cohesive bonds" among the river Mundurucu.[45]

The activities and relationships among them shown in Figure 5–4 reflect the norm of sharing which prevails among the Savannah Mundurucu. Since people's verbal statements concerning ideal behavior and its consequences also emphasize the sharing of game, the lattice may be assumed to reflect the society's values as well. Besides being a reflection of norms, however, the structure of behavior is also the result of ecological limitations. Game is scarce and relatively large, the hot and humid climate leads to the rapid spoiling of meat, and the hunting technology is primitive—bow and arrow, a few muskets. Since not all hunters are successful every day, the sharing of game leads to an adequate food supply for all villagers. In short, *ecological conditions may be envisioned as limiting the variety of activities which will be reinforced in a particular environment.*

Not all activities and relationships involved in the sharing of game have been indicated, and no consequences of sharing for other aspects of Mundurucu life have been shown, for to do justice to these topics would require too much space. R_2, for example, actually is reinforced by more than three contingencies, and R_9, which is the same activity carried out by another hunter, is similarly followed by several reinforcers. Enough of the activities are shown, however, to indicate the operation of norms, the relationships among the activities of various groups and individuals, and the form of ecological limitations. The lattice, then, may be taken to represent a small part of Mundurucu social structure: social relations are outlined, and the determinants and consequences of behavior are indicated.

SOCIAL AND PSYCHOLOGICAL CHARACTERISTICS

The lattice arrangement shown in Figure 5–4 reflects the form in which the components of social structure—behavior and social relations —are typically found. Since any complex lattice consists, actually, of a

45. Ibid. chapter 7; see also Kunkel (1967).

number of "squares" such as R_3–R_7, it may be useful to further investigate the form of these basic units. The "square" R_3–R_7 is shown again in Figure 5–5—but in this simplified form R_5 has been eliminated, just as activities intervening between R_5 and R_7 were disregarded in Figure 5–4.

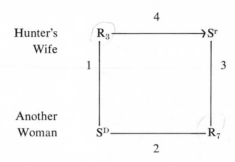

Figure 5–5: Components of the Basic "Square"

Figure 5–5 shows two behavior patterns (R_3 and R_7) which together constitute one of many social relations which make up Mundurucu social structure. The hunter's wife also appears in Figure 5–4, while the second person is typical of other women in the community. The wife's sharing of meat (R_3) is a discriminative stimulus for the other woman's smiles, conversation, etc. (R_7), which may be summarized as "acceptance" or "friendliness." R_7, in turn, serves as a contingency for the hunter's wife, in this case an S^r. The result of the interaction is that the original behavior pattern R_3 is likely to be repeated by both the same woman and by other women observing this event.

The lines connecting the various elements of Figure 5–5 have both psychological and sociological characteristics. Line 1 reflects the largely sociological phenomenon that a particular action (R_3) serves as an S^D for another individual's specific reaction (R_7). Line 2 indicates a largely psychological relationship, for it reflects the fact that a discriminative stimulus, once it has been established, is likely to be followed by the associated activity. This line, then, reflects the operation of learning principles. There are, however, some sociological overtones, for the line indicates that a specific S^D is likely to be followed by a specific R—both defined by the group to which the person belongs. Line 3 shows that R_7 has the property of an S^r—again a sociological phenomenon which reflects the definition of aversive and reinforcing stimuli prevalent in the community. However, the line also has some psychological overtones since the wife must *learn* what is reinforcing and what is not (for example, she learns various secondary deprivations). Line 4, finally, indicates that R_3 is in this case reinforced (by R_7). The fact that specified contingencies follow a particular action is a sociological phenomenon and reflects one aspect of Mundurucu culture.

While it is true that men *learn* to behave, and that learning principles are psychological and operate in individuals, the fact that R_3 is reinforced, followed by particular actions, R_7, expressed by a specific person, cannot be explained in terms of psychological principles alone. Rather, social phenomena, specifically the systematic behavior patterns of a number of persons both at present and in the past, are an important part of the explanation. Repeated observations that R_3 is followed by R_7, and that the rate at which R_3 is expressed remains more or less constant, may be summarized by the term "norm." The "square" R_3-R_7 reflects the Mundurucu norm that the wives of successful hunters share their meat with the wives of other villagers. This conception of "norm" is consistent with the generally accepted view that norms include not only expected behavior patterns but also sanctions. In fact, it is apparent that norms cannot be established or maintained in a population except through contingencies, and that norms are changed when, in effect, contingencies are altered. At the same time, this conception of norm differs slightly from that of Homans,[46] for example, who considers norms as statements that people make concerning expected activities. Since such statements are usually reflections of or abstractions from observed actions and their contingencies, little is lost when analysis centers on the observable phenomena themselves.

The "square" described in Figure 5–5 is greatly oversimplified, for any person's action may produce several different contingencies, as illustrated in Figure 5–6.

Work with one's hands (R_1) may lead to behavior patterns characterized as "avoidance" (R_2) on the part of one person, verbal expressions of "scorn" (R_3) by another, and various activities summarized as "respect" (R_4) by a third. This situation is represented by three

46. Homans (1961:116).

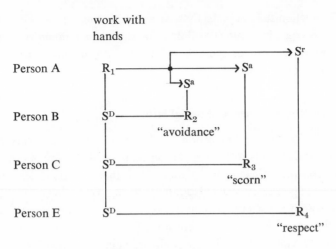

FIGURE 5–6. Complex Contingencies

overlapping "squares," R_1–R_2, R_1–R_3, and R_1–R_4, which may be viewed as representing the norms of different subcultures. In the group of which B and C are members, manual labor is unacceptable, while in the group to which E belongs manual labor is expected. It is evident that in the presence of person B or C, R_1 is not likely to be repeated, or to appear frequently. When person E is present, the probability of R_1 being repeated is higher. When all three people are present, the probability that R_1 will occur will depend on A's "frame of reference," that is, on whether B or E, and R_2 or R_4, are more important to him. More specifically, if person B is part of A's reference group, it means that B's actions will be significant contingencies—in this case aversive—for A's actions and E's behavior will be largely irrelevant. In effect, then, R_1 would be followed by two S^a and no S^r, thus making the repetition of R_1 unlikely. Here again, while the individual *learns* that B or E is important (and thus R_2 or R_4), the definition of importance and whether B or E is part of A's frame of reference are *social* phenomena, amenable to and requiring a *sociological* analysis.

Some of the activities in Figure 5–6 are speech patterns (R_3) in order to illustrate the fact that words, symbols such as smiles, and ordinary activities such as work may be understood in terms of identical principles. For example, S^D of daily life, and many contingencies such as expressions of approval or scorn, are essentially symbols. The symbolic interactionist approach, thus, is not only compatible with the behavioral perspective, but contributes to the understanding of behavior by analyzing the role of symbols in the shaping, maintenance, and extinction of grosser forms of action.

The Persistence of Social Structure

The conceptualization of social structure in terms of behavioral lattices leads to the conclusion that social structures will persist if their constituent elements—actions and their relationships—remain the same. This usually results from two conditions: a) behavioral homogeneity within a society, subculture, or community; and b) behavioral replication over time. When there are no "deviants" and activities are repeated, "social relationships" will also remain the same.

The learning principles outlined in Chapter Three lead to the conclusion that all members of a society, subculture, community, or incumbents of a particular status are likely to exhibit the same behavior patterns "appropriate" to specific circumstances if:

a) the same relevant S^D have been learned by all;

b) the same contingency probabilities operate for all;

c) the same SV exist for all;

d) all have identical (or at least very similar) perceptions of the S^D which are presented;

e) all have similar conceptions of contingency probabilities;

f) the normative system is a consistent set of activities and associated discriminative and contingent stimuli; that is, a member of several subcultures will not be presented by inconsistent S^D, R, and contingencies at any one moment.

Furthermore, behavior patterns will be replicated over time, by all members of successive cohorts, if, in addition to the above elements, the following exist:

a) the S^D remain the same;

b) the contingency probabilities remain the same;

c) the state variables remain the same;

d) the perceptions of S^D remain the same;

e) the conceptions of contingency probabilities remain the same;

f) the system of S^D, R, and contingencies retains its form and consistency.

The behavioral approach enables the sociologist to specify the conditions under which any particular social structure will persist. When these ideal conditions are sought in the operation of viable social units, however, disappointment is likely. Even in the remote tribes studied by modern, competent anthropologists the prerequisites of persistence are met to only a degree.[47] Physiological and intellectual differences even within the same subculture or tribe, the variations apparent in even the humdrum daily life of small, isolated communities, and the vagaries of the physical environment play havoc with the conditions just outlined. It may be concluded, then, that the long-range persistence of any social structure is unlikely.

The Alteration of Social Structure

The behavioral conception of social structure is essentially neutral, for learning principles are neutral in that they have no static or dynamic implications. Under certain conditions behavior is likely to be repeated, under other conditions behavior is likely to be modified, and thus the study of social change involves the analysis of how these various conditions arise in the social system and what their repercussions are. In most social systems—even in folk societies—it would be difficult to observe, or explain, the existence of even a few of the above conditions required for behavior replication. Improvements in technology, changes in the ecological limitations, variations in the behavioral parameters presented by new markets, new tools, new resources, or contacts with other societies, reduce the probability that behavior will be perfectly replicated even within one generation. In addition, it would be difficult to assume or demonstrate that, within a cohort or any group, there are identical physiological characteristics, learning procedures, or life experiences. Even minor variations, such as those reflected in a population's genetic makeup, in being a younger or an older sibling, in the unequal distribution of journeys and books, or in differential contacts with wise men or ignorant parents, will affect the probability of behavior replication within a cohort. The probability of deviant activities and behavioral heterogeneity is therefore rarely zero. In fact, the conditions leading to the perfect replication of activities and to behavioral homogeneity are so rare that the absence of behavior change, rather than change itself,

47. For example Levi-Strauss (1963).

becomes the topic of primary interest. Moore's[48] hypothesis that imperfect socialization is one of the most important indigenous sources of social change is thus elaborated by the behavioral perspective's emphasis on the past and present context of learning.

The behavioral conception of social structure makes it possible to indicate what general and specific factors are likely to result in the alteration of activities and relationships both within a cohort and over generations. In general, it may be said that *alterations in only a few aspects—and by no means most—of the social and physical environment of individuals will result in behavior modification.* Evidence for the validity of this proposition is provided by a large number of well-documented cases of behavioral therapy and by a smaller number of observations of rapid social change. The specific factors leading to behavior modification can be determined by the analysis of particular situations, such as the contingencies of existing activities and the possible contingencies of activities which are to be shaped. The variety of specific factors is almost unlimited, as illustrated by the work of Holmberg[49] and Erasmus,[50] and as described by Spicer,[51] Niehoff,[52] and others, and as will be shown in the following chapters. Since most activities serve as discriminative and/or contingent stimuli for other actions (of either the same or different individuals), it is to be expected that changes in one activity will have repercussions throughout the social structure of which it is a part.

Procedures of Structural Analysis

THE CONSTRUCTION OF BEHAVIOR LATTICES

The analysis of social structure in terms of the behavior of individuals and relationships among actions and among men requires procedures which are designed to accumulate information concerning these specific phenomena. A number of different methods are available, with the final selection depending on the focus of the study and the availability of data. Three major procedures for gathering and ordering be-

48. Moore (1963c).
49. Holmberg (1960a).
50. Erasmus (1961).
51. Spicer (1952).
52. Niehoff (1966).

havioral data are discussed below, in descending order of importance and adequacy.

A. *Observations of Behavior.* The most common procedure consists of observing the activities of men and of arranging these actions into lattices, where each R is part of a chain and most R are equivalent to S^D and/or S^r. Observational diagrams, such as those presented in this chapter, require relatively few inferences and can be validated by additional observations. Consequently, they are to be preferred to others discussed below. The three major types of lattices that are constructed on the basis of observations differ mainly in terms of levels of abstraction.

1. Single observations of a particular event, or of actions performed during a certain span of time, may be arranged into a *simple lattice*. Figure 5–2, for example, shows the activities and relationships that are observed on a particular evening. However, the observed event may be unique, or it may be specific to a particular circumstance or time span. Thus there is no assurance that the particular observation would be a good foundation for predictions or generalizations. Furthermore, the specification of discriminative and contingent stimuli requires repeated observations. For this reason the assignment of discriminative or contingent properties to activities which have been observed only once cannot help but be somewhat speculative.

2. Observations of several repetitions of an event, after each has been arranged into a simple lattice, may be combined into a *composite lattice*. Figure 5–4, an example of such a lattice, is based on Murphy's many observations of the sharing of game. Unique events, special circumstances, the initial presence of the observer, or a particularly successful or meager hunt, would be expected to have little influence on the lattice. In addition, the inferences required for the establishment of S^D and contingencies will have a firmer base.

3. On an even more general level, composite lattices may be combined into a *summary lattice* in order to indicate the usual activities and general relationships which characterize particular events, institutions, or communities. While summary lattices present an overall picture, they are usually so general that they are of limited use in the prediction or explanation of behavior.

B. *Verbal Statements of Behavior.* When activities cannot be observed in sufficient detail for the construction of observational lattices, another set of procedures must be employed. Participants' verbal formulations of what people do, what they would do, or what they should do, may be the only information available. The activities and relationships with which such verbal statements are concerned—for example, "sons do obey their fathers"—can be arranged in lattice form, to yield diagrams which do not differ, in their essential form, from those based on observations. However, since their foundation consists of what people *say,* there is the danger that the respondent may not tell the truth, that he may not tell all there is, or that he may embellish his descriptions. The resulting diagrams, then, must be treated with extreme caution. At least three types of verbal descriptions (and resulting lattices) may be distinguished:

1. *What does happen.*

a) A person describes how people behave in particular circumstances, and what the consequences of these actions are. The danger that the respondent may be unique, marginal, or of a special status, and that his statements may reflect specialized or idiosyncratic conceptions of social life, may be reduced by reliance on several informants.

b) Statements from a number of respondents may be combined to produce a lattice of activities. However, even when a number of persons agree on how people act there is room for error and misconception.

2. *What would happen.* Some events, experiences, or situations are so rare that respondents cannot describe people's behavior. In such a case only hypothetical statements may be available.

a) A person describes what people would do, in particular circumstances, and what the consequences would be.

b) In order to reduce the danger of idiosyncratic conceptions, statements from a number of individuals may be combined to yield a composite lattice of what people would do.

3. *What should happen.* For some purposes, as shown below, it is useful to have information concerning people's conceptions of ideal activities and consequences.

a) A person describes how men should act, under certain conditions, and what the consequences should be.

b) Statements from a number of individuals may be used to construct a lattice of ideal behavior patterns.

C. *Idealistic Formulations of Behavior.* Religious prescriptions, philosophical precepts, and idealistic statements of activities and their associated discriminative and contingent stimuli can also be used for the construction of behavioral lattices. The dangers presented by investigators' inferences and misinterpretations, as discussed in the last chapter, give such formulations an extremely tentative character.

THE UTILITY OF BEHAVIORAL LATTICES

The procedures outlined above lead to ten different behavior lattices or descriptions of social structure. A short stay in a community or nation can produce a number of different and perhaps inconsistent or contradictory accounts of social structure, and it is easy for travellers to disagree in their descriptions of even routine aspects of daily life. Unless the sources of descriptions are specified in detail, therefore, the integrity of the investigator or the sanity of the inhabitants may be questioned, and the work will be of little use. The lattice arrangement of activities, combined with the source of the formulation, should go far to reduce inconsistent or contradictory reports and analyses of social structures. For example, procedures A2, B3a, and C may generally be *expected* to yield different views of social structure, but this would not necessarily indicate any social "disorganization" of the community.

The sources of behavioral lattices are especially important for the outlining of development programs. Generally speaking, when such programs are formulated on the basis of a social structure involving procedures C, failure is the likely result. Conversely, programs based on structures developed with procedures A2 and B2b will probably succeed best.

While lattices constructed on the basis of A have the best empirical foundation, lattices based on B and C may also be useful. For example, procedure B2 would indicate the range of acceptable variations of behavior more clearly than the procedures under A, especially if the number of observations is limited. If behavior is to be changed by the alteration of contingencies, procedure A may be used to discover the actual contingencies, while the procedures under B may be used to determine possible changes in contingencies and to evaluate the difficulties involved in these changes. For example, the alteration of behavior within the limits of acceptable variation is usually easier and faster than the establishment of activities outside these parameters.

Procedures in categories B and C are especially useful in determining the *probabilities* inherent in social life. If three observations of an event show that a particular activity is rewarded, it may appear to the uninitiated observer that *all* such activities are *always* reinforced, that consequently the probability of behavior replication approaches 1.0, and that it would be extremely difficult to modify the behavior. Procedures B and C may show, however, that there are other possible contingencies, that the observations do not provide a random sample of events, and that the probability of reinforcement is far from 1.0.

Discrepancies between the results based on procedures A and B, and especially A and B1, and B1 and B3, to mention some common examples, are often summarized as "stress" and "strain" in a social system. In behavioral terms, such discrepancies reflect inconsistent contingencies and weakly established discriminative stimuli. Discrepancies which become apparent in the construction of behavioral lattices therefore become an integral part of the analysis.

VI *Social Structure and*

Economic Development

Students of economic development have long recognized that industrialization cannot be separated from changes in the other facets of social life, and that a nation's political arrangements, class system, religious and educational institutions, family organization, etc. influence the rise, course, and probable success of economic growth.

Two major topics are involved in the analysis of social structure and economic development. First, since social structures are not undifferentiated entities but rather sets of elements, it is these elements and various combinations of them that affect the various components of the industrialization process. As long as a study centers on "political institutions," for example, only very general statements can be made, and it is not until the constituent elements of "political institutions" are analyzed in their relationships with specific aspects of economic development that the formulation of meaningful and practical hypotheses becomes possible. Second, the nature of the links between social structures and economic development must be carefully specified, for they vary among nations and from one historical period to another. The experiences of western Europe, for example, show that social structures created the foundation and preconditions for economic change, while in today's Third World social structures present barriers to development that are

133

often difficult to overcome.[1] This chapter is devoted to an examination of these two topics.

The Behavioral Perspective of Social Structure and Economic Development

The study of behavior and social relations, including the specification of conditions for the shaping, maintenance, and alteration of particular activities, enables the investigator to recognize the multivariate character of both social structure and industrialization, and to analyze the relationships among their components. Behavior is not immediately categorized into sets such as institutions; instead, the determinants and consequences of specific activities are outlined, and their roles in the establishment of industry are indicated. The need for behavior modification can then be assessed, and the procedures that might be employed can be evaluated. The following simplified example of behavioral analysis is designed to provide an outline of basic principles and general procedures rather than to reflect current understanding of a specific topic; later sections of this chapter will provide illustrations from actual cases.

The example focuses on two behavior patterns that occur in small agricultural villages characteristic of much of the Third World and on their hypothetical roles in economic development. One pattern, "wasting of cash," is assumed to be detrimental to economic growth, while the other, "purchase of consumer goods," is assumed to contribute to industrialization. In the course of development analysis, the formulation of answers to four major questions would be emphasized:

1. What are the detrimental roles of various behavior patterns—for example, "spending money on fiestas and religious rites" which often amounts to a waste of scarce individual and community resources?

2. What are the supporting roles of various behavior patterns—for example, "purchasing (manufactured) consumer goods"?

3. What are the determinants of the existing activities, be they detrimental or supporting?

4. What are the possible methods for extinguishing the detrimental

1. Hoselitz (1960b). For specific examples, see Hauser (1959b) and Kahl (1959).

activities, e.g. "wasting," and for establishing or maintaining the supporting activities, e.g. "purchasing"?

The behavioral conception of social structure and the analytical procedures outlined in the previous chapter not only contribute theoretical answers but also indicate which practical measures might be useful and how they might be employed.

1. *The detrimental role of particular activities.* As a first step, the constellation of behavior patterns associated with secondary industry—that is, the behavioral referents of industrialization—are specified in as great detail as possible. This is no easy task, and the list is likely to be incomplete and ambiguous. Next, the activities observed in a community or nation—for example, the wasting of cash—are compared with those associated with economic growth. If the observed activities appear to be incompatible, it may be concluded that their alteration is necessary. This conclusion is tentative, however, because "incompatibility" is difficult to establish and measure. At the very least it must be recognized that the short-run consequences of an action may be significantly different from long-run effects; if a peasant saves his coins in order to make a substantial purchase in the future, for example, incompatibility is at least in part a matter of perspective. An additional consideration is the frequency with which the activity occurs; if one villager hoards cash it matters little, but when vast population segments bury coins systematically, the market for manufactured goods is greatly affected. Activities summarized by the term "individualism," for example, may be detrimental to industrialization when they are expressed too frequently, yet some men must engage in these actions if economic innovation is to occur. At present, not even experts are agreed on the frequency of individualism and other activities that are required for economic development.[2] Finally, incompatibility may be indirect, as when an activity reinforces another action that is detrimental to modernization. The evaluation and labeling of activities are hazardous undertakings, then, and in the present context of limited knowledge the results must always be considered hypothetical.

2. *The supporting role of particular activities.* The basic procedures and difficulties are similar to those just outlined. Economic development is fostered and supported by a large variety of activities, ranging from very direct contributions to indirect support. On one extreme are

2. Levy (1962).

actions which are part of industrialization itself, such as work in factories or investment. On the other are activities that are parts of chains whose later links affect industrialization, or actions which reinforce other activities that are integral components of economic growth. The example under discussion—the purchase of manufactured consumer goods—falls into the second category since these activities contribute mainly to the expansion of a market for industrial products. The evaluation of "contribution" is made difficult because an activity may appear to be supportive in the short run but turn out to be detrimental in the long run. In addition, at times it is the frequency of occurrence that is the crucial variable. For example, activities subsumed under the label "consumption of manufactured goods" support economic growth by expanding the market, by helping to establish a mobile and willing labor force, and by providing pressure for changes in the structure and operation of communities. When these activities are expressed too frequently or too strongly, however, they may no longer play a supporting role because they may force governments to adopt policies that are incompatible with the requirements of solid, stable, self-sustaining economic growth.

3. *The determinants of existing activities.* No matter whether an observed activity is detrimental or supporting, an analysis of its determinants is required for any program that is intended to a) eliminate the detrimental action, b) shape a supporting action in its place, or c) maintain existing supporting activities in the face of projects designed to bring about large-scale changes.

The first step is the careful, repeated observation of the relevant activities and their contexts, usually including much of the daily life in a community. By means of the procedures outlined in Chapter Five, the observations are summarized in the form of behavioral lattices. Generally speaking, the more careful and extended the observations, the more specific the information concerning behavioral determinants is likely to be, and the greater the probability of developing a successful program.

Figure 6–1 is a composite lattice that combines several observations; since its major function is the illustration of analytical procedures, only one activity is labeled while other actions are arranged so as to show a variety of relationships among them. The lattice is centered on R_7—the wasting of cash—which is assumed to be detrimental to economic development. It is further assumed that another activity—the purchase of

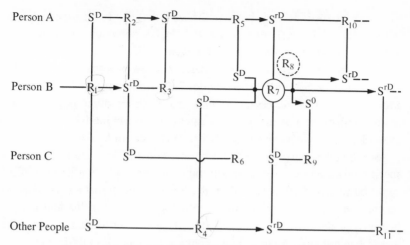

FIGURE 6–1: Structural Diagram Required for Changing R_7 into R_8

manufactured consumer goods (R_8)—should be substituted for it. Ideally, a causal analysis of R_7 should indicate the factors which presently maintain the activity and the conditions under which it is likely to be altered. In addition, it should outline the requirements for "natural" changes in R_7, the probability of the occurrence of such changes, and the steps involved in a successful program of behavior modification. According to the structural diagram of Figure 6–1, the major determinants of R_7 are:

a) The *total contingency,* as expressed by the combination of R_9, R_{10}, and R_{11}—in that order. The probability of reinforcement is established by either past experience or knowledge of the social structure's operation. Here it is important to remember that both the individual's and the observer's experience and knowledge are required, and that it is the events of the *past* which provide this information.

b) The *probability* of others' activities. Both Person A and Other People behave in certain ways (R_{10} and R_{11}) upon the presentation of the appropriate S^D, in this case R_7. This implies, among other things, that these individuals have specific learning histories and that both R_{10} and R_{11} have been reinforced in the past (by events not shown in the lattice).

c) The *specific sequences of activities.* In this illustration—as in most aspects of daily life—there is a certain order of activities (R_3, R_4, and then R_5) and each can serve as an S^D only when it is part of a specific sequence. It may be hypothesized that R_3 is an especially important factor, for it is not only a link in B's behavior chain that culminates in R_7 but it serves as an S^D for R_5 as well.

d) *Previous activities.* Past experiences are necessary not only for the learning of S^D and the prediction of reinforcing contingencies; in addition it may be necessary to take into account other preceding activities which are not immediately apparent discriminative stimuli. For example, R_1 serves as an S^D for R_4 which is itself an S^D for R_7.

Some additional points should be mentioned. First, the limits of any specific analysis are essentially arbitrary. For example, the present effort could be carried farther back than R_1, but how much farther will depend on the purpose of the study, the eventual use of the results, and the experience of the investigator. Consequently it is often difficult to indicate at the beginning of a study how complex the causal analysis will eventually become.

Second, not all activities which are observed and incorporated into a behavioral lattice are necessarily part of the causal complex under investigation. For example, R_6 is irrelevant, for it does not appear to serve as a discriminative or contingent stimulus for another action, and R_9 turns out to be quite unimportant. It is relevant, in the sense that it is a contingency for R_7, but it is a contingency which is simply "there" —it is equivalent to S^o. In other words, person B probably takes cognizance of R_9 but is not really concerned with it. Since both R_6 and R_9 are unimportant, it may be concluded that person C need not be included in the causal analysis. However, just because person C is unimportant in this particular lattice does not mean that his actions will be unimportant components in other events.

Finally, it is only upon repeated observations, the careful construction of behavioral lattices, and the constant checking of causal hypotheses derived from them, that the determinants of particular behavior patterns can be ascertained. For example, even though R_3 and R_4 are not connected by a direct relationship, R_3 is a determinant of R_4. The latter activity is reinforced—and thus maintained—by R_7, and this action depends on a previous link, R_3, which is also responsible for the provision of an S^D for R_7 in the form of R_5.

4. *The outline of procedures for changing particular activities.* When it has been determined that "wasting of cash" is detrimental to industrialization and that it should be replaced by "purchase of consumer

goods," R_7 must be extinguished and R_8 must be shaped. The first goal can be achieved in one or both of two major ways: the contingencies of R_7 can be changed, or the S^D associated with R_7 can be eliminated. Since the latter would involve the elimination of R_4 and R_5, the former procedure in this case will be preferable. The behavioral lattice indicates the steps appropriate for the termination of reinforcement and/or the punishment of R_7. For example, person B's reference group might be changed to remove the influence of A. Or the actions of other people, such as R_{11}, might be eliminated so as to no longer reward R_7. It may also be possible to establish R_7 as an S^D for activities on the part of others which are aversive to B. For example, R_9 which is now an S^o might be changed to S^a by intensifying it. The selection of steps and the specification of procedures depends on the particular situation, of course, and the examples provided below can only illustrate the range of possibilities.

By means of instruction, modeling, and/or successive approximation involving differential reinforcement, the new behavior pattern R_8 (and its associated S^D) is gradually established and replaces R_7 in the diagram. This will include the "attaching" of reinforcers to the new activity, for it is they which make learning possible and maintain the new activity. The reinforcers may be new or old, depending on the parameters presented by the particular situation. For example, words of praise which once followed R_7 could now follow R_8, or R_8 may be reinforced by the comforts and advantages provided by certain consumer goods such as sewing machines. The problem of new reinforcers, of course, is that they will not be effective unless they are associated with new deprivations, or until the individual has learned that old deprivations can be reduced in new ways.

From the discussion of learning principles in Chapter Three it is apparent that the shaping of R_8 will be easiest and most rapid if the new contingencies are presented consistently and if R_7 is consistently punished or at least no longer rewarded. Such consistency, together with the systematic alteration of the various S^D and S^r required for successive approximation, are not commonly found in "natural" situations, and thus it is likely that the substitution of R_8 for R_7 will slow. But if the two activities have some similar elements, or if the environment can be controlled to increase the consistency of contingencies, the rate of behavior modification can be increased.

While the changes required for the shaping of R_8 can be specified on the basis of a behavioral lattice such as appears in Figure 6–1, the diagram does not indicate the wider repercussions of these changes. The modification of R_{10} and R_{11}, for example, will involve certain efforts to produce these alterations. These efforts themselves may have repercussions on other facets of a community's social structure, and the consequences of these efforts—R_8, the elimination of R_{10}, etc.—can also be expected to affect activities not shown in the lattice. One should not conclude that all of a community's organization will necessarily be altered by attempts to modify a few behavior patterns, but at the same time it is unlikely that any small segment of life—designated and circumscribed by the investigator—can be changed without regard for other facets of social structure.

The general procedures which have been described here in terms of the limited and very abstract schema sketched in Figure 6–1 will now be illustrated by concrete examples. Two well-known studies of deliberate behavior modification on a large scale will be followed by a discussion of two important components of the development process.

The Vicos Project

One of the most successful and best-known programs of deliberate large-scale social change is the Vicos Project. Organized by the anthropologist Allan R. Holmberg, it accomplished more in the space of five or six years than other programs have produced in decades. Since much of the information is as yet fragmentary, a full-scale discussion and behavioral representation is not possible. However, the sketch that follows illustrates the major procedures of the project and reasons for its success.[3]

VICOS

The Vicos hacienda is situated in an Andean valley about 250 miles northeast of Lima. It consists of 35,000 acres, varying in altitude from 9,000 to 14,000 feet. Most of its area is mountainous and rocky; only about 5,000 acres are suitable for grazing cattle and sheep, and

3. Among the most important sources are Collier and Collier (1957), Fried (1959, 1962), Holmberg (1960a, 1960b), Mangin (1957), Whyte and Holmberg (1956).

2,500 for the growing of maize, potatoes, barley, and wheat. More than 300 Indian families, about 1,850 individuals, live on the property. They own no land and cultivate 90 per cent of the arable land in the form of subsistence farmsteads. The other 10 per cent of the good land is used to provide for the need of the patrón. Vicos has been in the hands of a Mutual Benefit Society for a number of decades; every ten years the hacienda is leased to the highest bidder, and the rent is used to support hospitals and other services.

The study of life in Callejón de Huaylas was initiated in 1949; and in 1952 the so-called Cornell-Peru project began by leasing the hacienda for a five-year period.

LIFE BEFORE 1952

Like many other peasant communities in Latin America and much of the rest of the world, Vicos was characterized by hostility to the outside world, conservatism, and great poverty. Life had changed little in the previous 400 years.

The patrón controlled the land and people, and had complete economic, political, and judicial powers. There were a few elected village officials, but their influence was restricted mainly to religious events. In return for his plot of land, the Indian had to fulfill certain obligations toward the patrón:

a) from each household, the labor of one adult member for three days a week;

b) unpaid use of the Indians' animals;

c) additional unpaid services to the hacienda, whenever needed, in the form of cooks, grooms, watchmen, shepherds, and general servants.

In short, life in Vicos approached the conditions of feudalism. The major social characteristics have been summarized by Holmberg as follows:

> Positions of responsibility in public affairs were lacking in the life of Vicos, adequate leadership did not develop, almost no public services were maintained, and the community was in a highly disorganized state. Apart from alliances with immediate kinship groups and a common devotion to religious practices, particularly the fiesta of the local saint, there were almost no values that were widely shared among the

members of the Vicos community. At the same time standards of living were at a bare minimum. Health and nutrition levels were extremely low. Educational facilities and consequent skills were almost completely lacking. Cooperation within the community was the exception rather than the rule, and resistance to the outside world was high. Attitudes toward life were static and pessimistic.[4]

GOALS AND METHODS OF THE PROJECT

The Vicos Project was designed as a broad and integrated attempt to produce "higher standards of living, social respect, and a self-reliant and enlightened community which can eventually take responsibility for the direction of its own affairs as a functioning part of the nation." [5] In addition, Holmberg hoped to develop "within the community independent and dynamic problem-solving and decision-making organizations which could gradually assume the responsibilities of leadership in public affairs in a rational and humane manner and along democratic lines." [6]

A third major goal was to increase the productivity of the Indians' efforts, for it was recognized that under the existing conditions of poverty

> . . . it would not be possible to support the institutions necessary for the adjustment of Vicos to modern life except on a welfare or gift basis, and this is not a likely prospect in Peru, considering the state of its economy and the nature of its power structure. Nor would a welfare approach lead to a solid type of development, rooted in the desires and responsibilities of the community itself.[7]

The basic methodological principle of the Vicos Project was

> . . . to find out first what the community aspired to achieve and then, through the formation or strengthening of local groups . . . to place these goals in a broader setting, so that in achieving them the community would also be building a

4. Holmberg (1960a:80–81).   6. Ibid. p. 83.
5. Ibid. p. 82.   7. Ibid. p. 84.

body of knowledge, skills, and attitudes which would in turn foster in it a solid and self-reliant growth. In the long run this kind of growth can only take place through education in the broad sense of the word.[8]

In addition to education, attention was directed toward the improvement of technology, nutrition and health, and community organization. All of the specific programs of the Project were based on the assumption that success would be achieved only if the Indians became actively involved, and thus community participation was a significant component—and goal—of every program. In line with these considerations, outside personnel was kept at a minimum, and at no time were more than two North Americans and two Peruvians at the hacienda.

In behavioral terms, the major goal of the Project was the alteration of a constellation of activities. In order to maintain the new behavior patterns, new contingencies had to be attached to these activities, contingencies which would follow more or less "naturally," without the continued interference or direction of Project personnel.

PROGRAMS

The various programs which constitute the Vicos Project have been described in some detail. However, while these descriptions indicate *what* was done, and what the results were, they do not present a theoretical basis for the action. That is, while the Project was an unqualified success, it often is not clear *why* it was a success, or how the various programs contributed to it. In this section, three major programs will be described, and a behavioral analysis will be presented. The initial behavior patterns and their contingencies will be outlined, and the new activities, together with their associated reinforcers, will be delineated. Information is not sufficiently detailed to construct many behavioral lattices, but the influence of the social structure on both the old and new behavior patterns is clearly evident in the descriptions.

Economics and Technology. In most situations Indians did not work hard, or perform their duties well. Those who cultivated the hacienda lands, collected tolls at the mountain pass, or helped the patrón in other ways, did only a minimum of labor. Good work habits had never been established, for there was no pay, and those who produced more never

8. Ibid. p. 89.

saw the fruits of their efforts. For example, agricultural production, especially that of potatoes, had always been low. A poor and rocky soil, bad seeds, lack of fertilizer, old and inefficient techniques, and the philosophy "plant and pray" were major reasons. The most important cause, however, was that Indians did not care about the patrón's crop and were not interested in producing more. However, while the Vicoseños did not labor hard or long, hard work was respected in the community. For example, the kinship factor

> . . . is of little or no significance in assigning positions of prestige in the social structure. To accumulate wealth in an agrarian society like Vicos . . . the peasant must work hard and also be frugal. It is through physical labor that he gains dignity and it is through frugality that he accumulates wealth.[9]

Thus it was the *operation* of the hacienda which was not conducive to hard work, for the patrón neither expected nor rewarded it, and the Indian's labor provided no benefits for his own family. According to Holmberg, an Indian is not

> . . . willing to labor long and well under all conditions. In most instances he will do so only when he is working for himself or within his own culture. When working outside this framework, under conditions in which he is held in disrespect and generally receives little in the way of reward, he usually tries to get by with as little effort as he can. This was true under the traditional hacienda system at Vicos, and labor productivity was much lower on hacienda fields than on the Indians' individual plots.[10]

One of the first steps of the Project was to eliminate unpaid services to the patrón. Indians began to be paid for their labor. For example, the toll collector was allowed to keep the money he received from travellers, in return for guarding the hacienda's stock. This cut the livestock loss, and the money thus saved was greater than the tolls collected

9. Ibid. p. 85.   10. Ibid. p. 85.

by the Indian. Gradually, work habits improved and the productivity of labor increased, in large part because the contingencies of work were changed.

The most successful economic program centered on the improvement of the hacienda's major crop. Holmberg offered the peasants new seed potatoes, fertilizer, insecticides, and instructions concerning the preparation and fertilization of the soil, proper weeding, and cultivation. However, the Indians were poor, or had no land, and were quite suspicious. It was not until materials were offered on credit, with repayment in the form of a specified part of the crop, that a few peasants tried the new methods and seeds.

During the first year the yields more than doubled, and the new patrón kept his word by taking only the prearranged amount as repayment. New behavior patterns and hard work, in other words, were strongly reinforced. As expected, the following year more men used the new methods, and within two years almost everyone had accepted the new practices. Yields increased greatly, in some cases more than 400 per cent, and potatoes now could be exported. New behavior patterns were shaped and maintained not only because adequate instructions and demonstrations assured success. In addition, Indians kept most of what they produced, and since "wealth is held in high esteem in the Indian community," [11] money served as an effective, generalized reinforcer.

Community Organization. Behavior patterns labeled "leadership" were absent since they had never been shaped while the patrón made all secular decisions. Six *mayorales* or foremen used to be appointed by the patrón to supervise the operation of the hacienda. Since these men were highly respected, having passed through the religious hierarchy of the community, Holmberg used them as the nucleus for new leadership groups.

Beginning very early in the Project, some decision-making powers were gradually given to the *mayorales.* As these learned to organize activities and to lead men, more responsibilities were given to them, especially in the solution of cattle and land conflicts. All major decisions of the *mayorales* were discussed with the whole labor force, and thus all could see *how* decisions were arrived at and that the "people's will"

11. Ibid. p. 85.

was actually carried out. Additional leadership groups were established to help initiate—and later run—organizations designed to solve community problems of health and education. As the various leaders learned to organize and direct the work of others they also developed the ability to work together.

The crucial procedures in the successful transfer of power from the Project staff to elected community leaders consisted of giving leaders control over the contingencies of their own and others' actions, and of gradually increasing this control as men learned to successfully direct others. More specifically, successful leadership means that other men do follow orders, and that the following of orders leads to some kind of improvement (or solution to problems). The basic requirement for these two characteristics is that there be a logical, consistent, natural relationship between action and consequence. As long as the patrón controlled all contingencies, the basic requirement was not met, and there were no leaders. Toward the end of the Project, however, the relevant aspect of the Vicos social structure could be sketched as follows (Figure 6–2). A complex set of actions labeled "giving orders" was reinforced by others' following them and by the successful completion of work; Indians began to obey their leaders because these actions were reinforced by the successful solution of problems.

Education. The problem of education and its solution has received the most careful attention in descriptions of the Vicos Project, and thus the utility of the behavioral perspective and the successful application of learning principles is most apparent in this area. Consequently, somewhat more space will be devoted to this program.

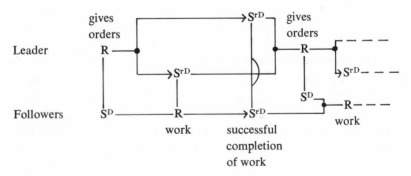

FIGURE 6–2: Leadership in Vicos

Although there had been a school in Vicos since about 1940, ten years later no child could read and write well, and there were only five literates in the community. "In a single year the total school population had never exceeded fifteen to twenty pupils out of a possible 350, and none of them had ever had more than a year or two of the poorest possible training." [12] The reasons for this state of affairs fall into four categories:

a) The patrón, concerned mainly with the maintenance of the status quo, did not support education since illiterate Indians were considered to be tractable and easy to handle.

b) Teachers were of very low quality and often absent; living and working facilities were poor.

c) Children saw no benefits in "education." In addition, they were treated as inferiors by teachers, and had to perform servant and gardening chores for them.

d) Parents were aware of these abuses, saw no benefits in having literate children, and, most importantly, needed children at home to help around the house and garden.

The two behavior patterns associated with education were evidently followed by definitely aversive contingencies (Figure 6–3). The major features of the Project's education program consisted of a) eliminating the aversive contingencies and b) attaching reinforcing stimuli to both

FIGURE 6–3: Contingencies of Education

From the parent's point of view:

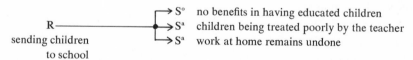

From the children's point of view:

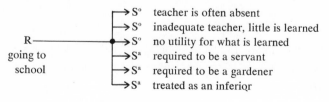

12. Ibid. p. 90.

the parents' sending of their children and the children's attending of classes. While some of the new contingencies were deliberately applied, others became apparent in the course of other programs, especially the production of a cash crop.

Most of the aversive stimuli were removed by the hiring of better qualified teachers who were interested in Indian children. This eliminated both absenteeism and the exploitation of pupils as laborers. In addition, the physical facilities were improved so that effective teaching became a possibility. In this connection Holmberg assumed that

> . . . unless most members of the community made some contribution to the construction of the new school, few of them would have any interest in putting it to use. The more members who pitched in to help build it, the more who would feel entitled to a return on their investment in the form of sending their children to school.[13]

On the positive side, teachers not only *taught,* but the subjects were also relevant to the daily life of the village: technical training in agriculture and industrial arts. A school lunch program was started (and Holmberg suspected that this was a major incentive in the early days). Further reinforcement was provided by the increasingly evident utility of learning. The new cash crop brought Vicoseños into increasing contact with the outside, and those who were skilled in reading and algebra were more successful in dealing with merchants. Finally, the fact that Vicos soon had the best school in the area became a source of pride for the whole community.

As a result of these changed contingencies—which ultimately derived from changes in the actions of the patrón—"going to school" became an increasingly common activity, not only for boys but for girls as well. Attendance, which had fluctuated between 14 and 18 in 1951, increased to 200–250 by 1957.

LIFE AFTER 1957

In October, 1956, the people of Vicos elected delegates to direct and manage the affairs of the hacienda, and a year later complete control was transferred to the community. During the first year "after inde-

13. Ibid. p. 92.

pendence" the production of cash crops doubled, even with a reduced labor force, and marketing procedures were greatly improved. Since then, substantial payments toward the purchase of Vicos from the state have been made. In addition, Vicoseños have improved access roads and their water supply. The community now serves as an inspiration for the surrounding area, and the Peruvian government has launched five similar projects in other parts of the country.

SUMMARY

The modification of a large number of behavior patterns was accomplished by means of alterations in the relevant contingencies. While the early observations of base line behavior were not arranged into lattice form, the discriminative and contingent stimuli of every action that was to be changed were specified. In other words, it was on the basis of a careful structural analysis that the various programs were formulated and carried out.

IMPLICATIONS OF THE PROJECT

Holmberg's conclusions for Peru and indeed Latin America are quite optimistic:

> The Vicos experience indicates so far that dramatic results can be achieved at a relatively small cost. They can be attained, however, only if careful attention is given, not only to the problem of modern techniques, but also to the people and their culture. For this reason, from the very start the Cornell-Peru project has given careful thought to the problem of developing a spirit of independence, responsibility, and leadership in community affairs. . . . The experience of the Cornell-Peru project clearly indicates that the people of the sierra, once given proper encouragement, advice, and respect, can do much by themselves to better their lot. . . . Moreover, the process of modernization within this long-isolated population can take place without the loss of certain fundamental and positive values that are deeply ingrained in Indian society; respect for work, frugality, co-operation. Our experience at Vicos indicates that, if granted respect, the Indian will give respect. If allowed to share in the making of de-

cisions, he will take responsibility and pride in making and carrying them out.[14]

The question arises of how these general prescriptions—for example, encouragement and respect—can be translated into specific procedures. Developing nations are full of ruins of idealistic programs dreamed up by dedicated men. It is apparent from both the Vicos project and the fact that man *learns,* that ideals and dedication must be tempered with the application of behavioral principles. By changing contingencies, behavior can be changed; but first ideals have to define the behavior that is to be shaped, and dedication has to underlie the program of action.

REASONS FOR THE SUCCESS

In the face of so many failures of development programs, it is natural to ask why Vicos was such a conspicuous success. A number of answers may be suggested.

While Holmberg speaks of "changing community attitudes and values in Peru" [15] and treats these concepts as if they were characteristics of the internal state, his procedures bear evidence that a behavioral model of man served as a foundation for his actions. No "discriminative stimuli" appear in his writings on Vicos, and no one needs to know an S^r before he can understand the meaning of the Project. Only those who would replicate these programs need recognize the technical details underneath the well-turned phrases and exciting implications of the various descriptions.

More specifically, it is evident that the procedures employed in Vicos were congruent with the model of man outlined in previous chapters. For example, Holmberg knew which behavior patterns had to be extinguished and which had to be established. He employed differential reinforcement by rewarding certain activities and not others. Consistent contingencies were attached to those activities that were to be shaped, and no social welfare approach was employed. All relevant aspects of the environment were taken into account, which meant that an activity's contingencies emanating from various facets of the community were analyzed and changed if necessary. Finally, successive approximation

14. Ibid. pp. 87, 96, 97.
15. Holmberg (1960b:63).

was employed in shaping complex activity sets such as community leadership.

These procedures for the selective extinction, shaping and maintenance of activities were effective because the Vicos hacienda presented an almost perfect laboratory situation. The community was relatively small and quite isolated, behavior was carefully observed, and consistent contingencies could be presented with relative ease. Incompatible and new behavior patterns were not likely to be introduced haphazardly from the outside. Holmberg, as the patrón, had complete control over all relevant variables, especially contingencies and their schedules. In addition, he could alter discriminative stimuli almost at will, for example he changed the image of the patrón from exploiter to helper. Finally, deprivation already existed—in the form of poverty and malnutrition—and thus it was quite easy to find and employ effective reinforcers.

It may be concluded that *all* of these conditions contribute to the success of a development program; behavioral principles by themselves, in a large open society, will not lead to another Vicos, and the social welfare approach in small, isolated villages is not likely to foster independence and responsibility.

CONCLUSION

The Vicos Project is useful not only as an illustration of the application of behavioral principles; it also serves as a means of evaluating the various approaches to development analysis based on psychodynamic models of man.

According to Hagen's theory, the static conditions of Vicos before 1952 would be the result of either the authoritaritan personality created in traditional societies, or the retreatism which characterized the displaced elite. In the latter explanation the Indian population would be assumed to have developed retreatism since the time that Pizarro repressed the former rulers. While the situation prior to 1952 can be explained rather well, the successes of the actual Project would be difficult to account for. Not only did fundamental changes in behavior and social organization occur in the space of five years, but in addition it is evident that these changes occurred not so much in children as they did in adults. Finally, Holmberg did not concern himself with child-raising methods or the manipulation of personalities and other internal characteristics of the Indians; all he did was change certain aspects of individuals' environment. Hagen's theory has difficulty in explaining fundamental changes that occur rapidly, in adults with previously established personalities, and by means of relatively simple alterations in the social environment. When confronted by the fact of a rapid increase in the number of entrepreneurs in Pakistan in a relatively short time, Hagen proposed that "new personality may not cause a conspicuous change in behavior until it has burst through external barriers. Where institutional change suddenly eliminates former barriers and creates new economic opportunities, a slow budding process may suddenly burst into bloom." [16] The hypothesis raises more questions than it answers, however, both in the case of Pakistan and of Vicos. For example, there is little evidence that innovating personalities existed "beneath the surface," so to speak. It addition, it might be asked: What structural characteristics suppressed the expression of these personalities, and how did this suppression operate? In order to answer these and other questions, a number of additional assumptions would have to be introduced into the model of man, including mechanisms for the "rapid flowering" of personalities.

According to McClelland's theory, the static conditions of Vicos before 1952 would be due mainly to the prevalence of people with low need-achievement. Such a characteristic would have to be inferred from the behavior at that time, however, and from the then-prevalent child-raising practices, and this information is difficult to procure. However, while the explanatory hypothesis is impossible to test, it cannot be rejected, for there is no information to the contrary. McClelland probably would explain the rapid changes in behavior and social organization, and especially the great alterations in agriculture and education, in terms of a raise in need-achievement. The question then becomes how need achievement was increased, at such a rapid rate and especially in adults, when there is no evidence of a concerted effort to alter the villagers' need-achievement. According to the theory, need-achievement is created especially in childhood, in school and through socialization, but the need is not expressed in socially significant actions until the children become adults—that is, roughly two decades later. It might be argued that need achievement had been high but had been repressed by the social structure, or that it can be increased rapidly, even in adults. However, there is little evidence for this, and such reasoning would require the addition of several assumptions to the model of man. Holmberg did not introduce

16. Hagen (1962:60).

achievement-oriented literature into the school—and if he had the effects would not be evident until 1970. He did not alter the child-raising methods—and if he had the effects would again not yet be evident. Finally, he did not set out to manipulate the Indians' internal state; rather, he altered the operation of their social environment, and especially the context of the adult population. While it is evident that the Vicos success could be explained more easily by McClelland than by Hagen, both explanations would require not only a modification of the original theory and its model of man, but also the introduction of additional elements, propositions, and concepts—such as repression by social structure—for which it might be difficult to find empirical referents.

The Zande Scheme

The list of development programs that have failed is long, and a perusal of the literature produces both smiles and tears. In terms of their human implications, it seems that these projects fall into a continuum ranging from triviality to tragedy. The East African peanut project, for example, reminds one of an exquisite Alec Guinness comedy, while the Zande Scheme produced confusion and ill will among the "natives." Since the major ingredients of failure appear to be white men's narrow "good intentions" laced with ignorance and ethnocentrism, the examination of a failure with these features will be useful.[17]

ZANDE DISTRICT

The Zande district is an area of approximately 21,000 square miles in the southern part of the Sudan Republic. Climate, soil, and topography are favorable to agriculture, and most of the 170,000 people are farmers. There are additional Azande in the neighboring Central African Republic and in the Congo, who lead a life similar to that of their brothers in the Sudan. Roads are scarce, and transportation and communication are difficult (at least during the time of the Scheme).

The Zande Scheme was outlined and planned during the early 1940's; it began operations in 1946 and was an evident failure by 1955.

LIFE BEFORE 1946

Major changes in family structure and social and political organization had been occurring since the advent of Europeans, and thus it is

17. The material of this section is based on Reining (1966).

difficult to draw a base line. The major features relevant to the Zande Scheme, however, may be briefly described.

The Azande were agriculturalists but had hardly any livestock. Most families were practically self-sufficient, and cash played only a minor role in their daily lives. Money was considered simply another commodity, which could be exchanged for a variety of goods. Related families lived close together, and upon death the homestead was abandoned.

While kinship was relatively unimportant, patron-client relationships, based upon unspecified mutual reciprocity, was a significant element of social organization. When chiefs became less powerful upon loss of many of their functions, and when the people no longer followed them, the patron-client relationship was transferred, to some extent, upon the British.

During the 1920's, the population was moved away from the streams and resettled along the roads. This first resettlement was occasioned by a tsetse fly eradication program which was so successful that by 1940 the people were allowed to return to their original habitat, the banks of streams. In 1946 a third resettlement was instituted in order to facilitate the supervision of cotton production. In each of these moves, little regard was shown for the kinship system or political structure of the Azande.

Until the development scheme began there were few Europeans in the area. The district commissioner, two physicians, and a few traders and missionaries were the only whites with whom the Azande came into regular contact.

GOALS AND METHODS OF THE SCHEME

The major goal, delineated in 1943, was "the complete social emergence and the social economic stability of the Zande people." [18] Economic self-sufficiency was seen as the basis for the development of "happy, prosperous, literate communities, based on agriculture and participating in the benefits of civilization." [19] Social emergence and development, while never defined, were thought to include literacy, education, and protection against exploitation. Economic stability was to be gained by the growing of cash crops, especially cotton, by the manufacture of cloth, and by the production of other goods needed in everyday life, such

18. Quoted in Reining (1966:143).
19. Quoted in Reining (1966:143).

as shingles. Each family was to grow one acre of cotton and receive high prices, and the rewards were to make the cultivation of cotton an integral part of the Azande way of life.

Even before the Scheme began operation, however, these original goals were modified. For example, only one cash crop was to be grown, and compulsion rather than high price was to be the motivating force. Education was eliminated as a goal, and it was decided that the Azande should have no voice in the planning or execution of the Scheme. Economic self-sufficiency was de-emphasized, but the industrial aspects of the Scheme remained (thus leading to a costly industrial experiment in an uneconomic region). Finally, the resettlement of the population became part of the project.

The methods employed in the Zande Scheme can be described best in terms of the various programs. Since cotton was the major cash crop, only this program will be analyzed in detail.

Cotton Production. In order to facilitate the supervision of cotton growing, Azande families were resettled along "lines," or roads. Each family was arbitrarily assigned a strip 300 feet wide and about a mile long, without regard to kinship or other considerations. It was thought that the people would settle near the roads, so that transportation, communication, and supervision would be easy. However, most people built their courtyards away from the roads, leading to isolation and difficulties in supervision. Thus, the original purpose of "villagization" was not realized, and cotton production was hindered from the very beginning. Matters were not helped any by the fact that strips of land were laid out without regard to ecological or climatic conditions, leaving many families with land that could not produce cotton. Furthermore, since the whole strip was considered as being "owned," it had to be abandoned upon death of a family member.

Families were forced to grow half an acre of cotton each year. Those who did not were fined a month's labor for the government. The price paid for cotton was very low, at times appearing to be approximately half of that paid the Azande in the Belgian Congo. While most families *grew* cotton, as was required, not all *harvested* or *marketed* cotton, since this was not required and seemed a waste of time in view of low prices.

The ginning and weaving enterprises, rather than being modern as originally envisioned, consisted of antiquated machinery. The major product, gray cloth, was superior in quality to imported cloth; however, it could be bought in only a few stores and carried a high price, and therefore little was sold in the Zande District. As a solution to bulging warehouses, the Scheme administrators decided to export the cloth to the northern Sudan and Khartoum. In order to meet the competition there, however, the exported cloth had to be offered at a low price; it was common knowledge that Azande cloth was sold in Khartoum at a lower price than in the District, in spite of duties and transportation costs.

OPERATION OF THE ZANDE SCHEME

During the first two years of operation, cotton production was high. In 1947-48 the yield amounted to four million pounds, and in 1950-51 eight million. Then, however, production began to decline; in 1954-55 only 2.7 million pounds were produced, and by 1955 the Scheme was judged to be a failure. The total cost of the Scheme was estimated at more than $2.4 million, but since the administrators had paid various taxes and other costs equal to half that amount, the British government was out only a little more than one million dollars. The lives of the Azande had not been materially altered, except for re-settlement along the "lines," but their distrust of Europeans had greatly increased.

IMPLICATIONS

According to Reining,

> The Zande Scheme proved that it is possible to establish an industrial community in the center of Africa, if cost is no object, and that the Azande could adjust to industrial procedures with aplomb and could produce large amounts of cotton when interested in doing so. But the Zande Scheme also proved that many things cannot be done. Some of its weaknesses—especially those in ecology, social organization, and communication [between whites and blacks]—will be found, in one form or another, in other widespread attempts at economic aid and commuity development. [20]

The original human and other ingredients of the Scheme could only lead to an optimistic appraisal of the future. The Europeans were sin-

20. Reining (1966:231).

cere and had good intentions, and the Azande were "tractable" and in the past had amply demonstrated their willingness to work. In addition,

> The Europeans had brought to the Zande District certain valuable ingredients for development: stable administration, contact with the world economy, benevolent ideas, technical knowledge, and capital investment. The Azande possessed equally valuable ingredients: interest in their own development, and productive potential of their labor, and detailed knowledge of their environment. [21]

The eventual fate of the Zande Scheme therefore must be explained in terms of an unfortunate *combination* of these two sets of factors, or by the absence of a crucial element. Since many of the above characteristics—good will, sincerity, technical expertise, etc.—are found in programs all over the world, it will be useful to make a careful examination of the superficially positive elements and their apparently deadly combination.

REASONS FOR THE FAILURE

The behavioral analysis of the Zande Scheme pinpoints a number of important errors which were built into the project, at least in its revised form. Since the largest and most important program of the Scheme was the development of a cotton industry, the production of cotton will serve as the major example.

The "growing of cotton" involves the shaping of a complex series of behavior patters. Since these were often not in the repertoire of individuals, instructions and demonstrations, along with adequate and initially frequent reinforcement, would be the best procedures. Actual procedures, however, had almost the opposite characteristics. The resettlement of families, for example, which actually had no agricultural rationale, meant that families had to adjust to new situations and neighbors. Since the fields were often far from the roads, little instruction and demonstration, if any, were available. Most important, the contingencies for growing cotton were aversive rather than reinforcing. First, the use of compulsion and fines meant that growing cotton came to be viewed as a means of avoiding punishment. Second, the very low prices paid by the

21. Ibid. pp. 219–20.

government (or the Scheme's administration) represented inadequate rewards. The Azande knew the payment was low because they knew the price of goods in stores, and they were familiar with the price that people in the Belgian Congo rceived for their cotton. Third, since cash payments were viewed by the Azande as reflecting the personal worth in which they were held by the patrón, low price was doubly aversive. Fourth, the system of bonuses had effects opposite from those intended, for a low bonus or none— the most common situation—was viewed as a personal affront or a gift, both leading to confusion and irritation. Finally, the high price charged for cotton cloth manufactured with cotton grown by the people themselves indicated to them that there were no local and real benefits associated with the production of cotton. As a result, cotton was still planted—in order to avoid punishment—but since there was no reward for the harvesting or selling of cotton, little reached the market. Rather than becoming part of the Zande way of life, "the cultivation and marketing of cotton was [placed] in the same class as taxes or conscript labor for administrative projects." [22]

During the first two years, the Azande worked hard and produced and marketed respectable amounts of cotton (around 400 pounds per acre). Their expectations of high payments were not met, but the people were willing to wait.

> After the first crop they were disappointed but thought that an adjustment would be made later. After the second poor payment they began to suspect that there might never be greater rewards. . . . . Their final reaction to what they considered inadequate rewards was delayed because they believed the British to be good patrons who would, in time, make amends. [23]

The administrators attached inadequate rewards to the cultivation of cotton for several reasons. First, they pointed out that wages and payments under the Zande Scheme were *higher* than before (but their comparison was with *conscript* payments!). Secondly, "most Europeans believed, implicitly if not explicitly, that a low monetary income was really desirable for the Azande. Money was a potential source of harm,

---

22. Ibid. p. 179. 23. Ibid. pp. 180–81.

particularly if the Azande got too much too quickly." [24] Third, some Europeans thought that the Azande had no need for money, as illustrated by the "misery of the man in a white shirt, a hat, and with a pack of cigarettes compared to the happy wearer of bark cloth." [25] Finally, many Europeans believed that the Azande did not value money and had no "money sense." For example, it was pointed out that Azande did not like to work for wages, and that they did not know how to deal with money. Yet the empirical referents of these statements were simply that the people were unwilling to work for abysmally low wages, and that Azande bought things that Europeans did not. A logical extension of this view, of course, was that money could not be used as a reward and that compulsion was therefore the best means of getting people to grow cotton.

The major source of failure, implied in the above, was the Europeans' lack of knowledge concerning practically all aspects of Azande life. Social distance and the language barrier produced almost complete ignorance concerning the feelings, ideas, and desires of the Azande. For example, the British assumed that the Azande

> . . . did not have the ability to make proper decisions for themselves and hence had to be protected from their own erroneous desires. The European official's tendency was to disregard whatever the Azande said, rather as a matter of principle, assuming that they were not capable of making valid decisions. The Azande were often likened to children, unable to reason adequately, and behaving in strange ways. The notion of the Zande as the "happy-go-lucky child of nature" was a prevalent one, whereas the Azande of course considered themselves to be fully capable adults.[26]

As a consequence, there was thought to be little point in studying the Azande, their thoughts and desires, their views of money, cotton, or of anything else, for that matter. Most of the everyday activities of the Azande were known, of course, but the contingencies which maintained them, and the state variables, were not. Administrators, therefore, would have been unable to construct behavioral lattices and to devise programs based upon them. The thought would not have occurred to the Europeans

24. Ibid. p. 190.
25. Quoted in Reining (1966:191).
26. Reining (1966:194).

in the first place, however, for since they thought the Azande to be immature, procedures effective with English children were presumed to be sufficient.

Since the state variables were not known, it was impossible to attach effective reinforcers to the new behavior patterns that were being established by means of the somewhat haphazard instruction and demonstation program. Furthermore, the reinforcers which were effective in a European context—the bonuses—were applied in a population which considered cash "gifts" as insulting and "bonuses" as reflecting the employer's esteem of the worker. Since most bonuses were small, the recipients viewed them as indicating low esteem. What the Europeans considered to be a reward, in short, was seen by the Azande as considerably aversive—with behavioral consequences that were opposite of the intended ones.

The absence of effective reinforcers was in part the result of deep divisions over policy within the administration of the Zande Scheme. The rapid turnover of officials restricted their time perspective, and the lack of knowledge of even basic facts—for example, the evaluation of dietary changes—made it difficult to establish or change specific procedures consonant with the goals of the Scheme. Consistent contingencies, thus, were almost impossible to even outline, let alone specify and apply.

Finally, the original goals were at times in conflict with the basic view that most Europeans had of the Azande. The British assumed that the Azande were unable to make proper and rational decisions, and thus the very basis of the application of a learning approach to behavior change was absent.

CONCLUSION

It is evident that the ideal conditions for shaping and maintaining behavior, outlined in Chapter Three, were far from being met. The Europeans had only a very vague and general idea of what behavior patterns were to be shaped, and had developed no specific procedures. The area and population were large, and thus it was practically impossible to attach consistent contingencies to behavior—except at the ends of very long chains, such as fining men or paying them for their cotton. While some deprivation existed, the fact that most families were subsistence producers meant that reinforcing contingencies would have to be carefully established and systematically provided. Adequate contingencies, however, conflicted with the Europeans' view of the Azande. Finally, Europeans' belief that the Azande did not behave in terms of their evaluation of contingencies removed the basis for the hope that behavior *could* be fundamentally changed by means of differential *reinforcement*—rather than mere punishment.

In short, while the Vicos hacienda approached the characteristics of an ideal laboratory, and Holmberg those of a wise experimenter, the Zande District had no laboratory characteristics except isolation, and the men in charge often appeared to show limited wisdom.

Saving

The Vicos Project and the Zande Scheme illustrate the effects of changes in social structure on a wide range of behavior patterns. The behavioral perspective of social structure makes it possible not only to investigate the successes and failures of specific development programs, but also to analyze the role of various social characteristics in the activities associated with economic development. Only one of these actions, saving, will be studied here. The analysis of other activities, for example investing or hard and systematic work, would follow similar patterns.

One of the most important prerequisites of economic development is adequate capital, for the rise and growth of industry as well as the creation of social overhead require vast amounts of cash. The major sources of money in the early stages of industrialization are taxes, foreign trade, foreign aid, and saving; only later do profits become important. Each of these involves a number of problems, and no one source is likely to provide an adequate amount. For example, taxation presupposes a reasonably well organized and respected government—characteristics which are often lacking in new or developing nations. The foreign trade of underdeveloped countries usually consists of the exportation of raw materials and the importation of manufactured goods, resulting in little if any trade surplus. Foreign aid, even when it is in a form that is relevant to the development problem of a particular nation, is usually insufficient. Savings, finally, are not likely to amount to much, for in most of the Third World the average per capita income is less than one hundred dollars a year.

The development literature contains a large number of technical and detailed studies of the various problems encountered in capital formation.[27] Taxes, trade, and aid, especially, have received the attention of a number of economists. Saving, and particularly the social and psychological aspects of saving, have received relatively little attention, and thus will be emphasized here. An additional reason for the analysis of saving is that the behavioral approach is more relevant to saving—a clearly individual activity—than to foreign trade or aid, which are subject to national and international policies.

In this section, emphasis will be on voluntary saving (rather than forced saving or taxation), and especially on saving in the household sector of the economy (rather than in the industrial sector). It is in the voluntary saving by men that the operation of social and cultural factors is most clearly evident, and it is here that a significant proporation of a developing nation's capital formation takes place.[28] By itself, however, saving will have little impact on the development process. In order to affect industrialization directly, savings must be discouraged from being invested in the household sector, savings must be transformed into money, and the money must find its way into the industrial sector. In the following discussion, the later links of the chain will receive only superficial treatment.

THE SAVING SET

It is necessary to speak of saving as a *set of elements* since it involves not only a number of activities but also other social and individualistic characteristics which must be present if saving is to occur. The most important behavioral elements of the saving set consist of accumulating goods, money, or other resources, of retaining them in a variety of ways, and of postponing consumption.[29] Since this can be accomplished by means of many different activities, the term "saving" must be considered as referring to a host of diverse action, or as the common element abstracted from these actions.

The behavior patterns involved in "saving" do not exist in isolation, of course. They are related to preceding and concomitant actions, as described in the preceding chapter, and thus an adequate understanding of

27. For example Nurkse (1953), Tangri and Gray (1967). For a recent summary, see Higgins (1968).
28. Lambert (1963:117); for an example of statistical studies of saving in rural areas, see Panikar (1961).
29. Swift (1957).

"saving" requires the analysis of these related elements as well.[30] The additional elements of the set may be viewed from the perspective of the observer and that of the individual who does the saving; both will be outlined below.

The Observer's Perspective. The behavior patterns labeled "saving" are usually evident only when basic physiological necessities have been met. That is, existing deprivations must be on such a moderate level that they do not endanger the continued existence of the individual and his family. Basic necessities and moderate deprivation are defined in terms of both physiological requirements and cultural criteria, and thus may be expected to vary among subcultures, communities, and societies.

An additional element is the presence of limited obligations to others —that is, little if any reinforcement for periodically sharing one's resources with others. Further, there must be no aversive consequences when one does not spend all of one's income. As an alternative, there must be mechanisms for avoiding or escaping the aversive contingencies of saving, for example by great secrecy, or there must be ways in which obligations to friends and relatives can be circumvented. Here it is to be remembered that the limits of a person's obligations to others are defined by his and/or others' overt actions and not by the theoretical standards which may be verbally expressed in the community but may be largely ineffectual in daily life.

The rewarding of saving is one of the most important elements of the set. Reinforcement may consist of avoidance of real or imagined future deprivations, the promise or high probability of future gains, or various expressions of approval on the part of other men. Which of these contingencies operate depends largely on the previous operations of the social context, for example the experiences of fellow villagers. If saving has in the past been followed by inconsistent contingencies—such as occasional scorn by one's fellows and inadequate protection against emergencies—it is not likely that saving will become a significant part of a person's behavioral repertoire. Furthermore, since the reinforcement of saving usually is not presented or at least evident until some time has passed, the consistent and systematic operation of the social structure is imperative for the establishment and maintenance of saving.

The Individual's Perspective. The set of behavior patterns character-

30. For numerous cases from all over the world, see Firth and Yamey (1964).

ized as "saving" may also be viewed in terms of individualistic elements. A person's conception of contingencies, and especially of the probabilities of reinforcement, plays a major role in determining his behavior. If a man believes that the various components of a society operate systematically and will continue to do so, and if he believes that the future operation of the social system can therefore be predicted, the probability of saving is increased. In addition, the conception of a lawful universe should include the belief that it is possible to influence the operation of the constituent parts so as to correct the errors which might occur in certain parts of the system. For example, the saving of money for a rainy day or for investment makes sense only if one believes that man *can* control his fate.

A further element of the saving set is rational decision-making. This refers to the making of choices after all relevant alternatives have been evaluated in terms of their actual consequences and according to consistent criteria. Such choices are based on the individual's ability to sum the actual costs and rewards of every alternative. The summation, in turn, presupposes the person's ability to accurately predict the behavior of others and the operation of the wider social structure of which he and they are a part. Although much of this knowledge—especially concerning the world outside the immediate community—is acquired by means of formal education, the experiences of daily life are also important. A few years of education, for example, designed to create the conception of a lawful universe, will have little effect on the establishment of rational decision-making if the rest of the individual's life is spent in an essentially capricious social environment.

The final component of the saving set is the length of the individual's time perspective. Since the rewards of saving usually lie in the somewhat distant future, it is essential that the person be ready and willing to wait until the advantages of saving become apparent.

It may be hypothesized that *all* of the elements of the saving set must be present if saving is to occur, and that an incomplete set will not result in saving. A peasant may be able to accurately predict the behavior of others, and contingencies may be systematically applied, but this alone is not sufficient. What if he can predict that other villagers will be resentful if he does not spend money on a fiesta, or if the major consequence of saving is the "evil eye"? The points raised in this rather abstract discussion of the saving set will be illustrated by two cases in which saving does not occur on a large scale.

SAVING IN SOUTHEAST ASIA

Figure 6-4 presents a summary of Lambert's [31] discussion of the "saving" set in the social structures of many peasant communities in Southeast Asia. The activities which constitute the lattice are arranged in terms of what people say *would* happen and, according to Lambert, usually *does* happen in rural communities. The diagram, thus, is based on two of the procedures outlined in the previous chapter.

It should be noted that the basic unit of the lattice is, again, the "square," such as R_1–R_8. Furthermore, there are a number of overlapping "squares," such as R_7–R_{11} and R_7–R_{14}, indicating that activities have a number of consequences. The behavior patterns that constitute the lattice, many of which are complex and occur over long periods of time—for example, acceptance (R_{10})—are not shown in sequence, of course, and not all relevant actions and relationships are delineated. Clarity of presentation required the elimination of some reactions to the wealthy man's alternatives, and a complex series of behavior was combined into "deference" (R_{12}). A person who has cash and/or other resources above the requirements of the average (low) standard of living faces a number of possible actions, seven of which are represented (R_{1-7}). Each of these activities—or ways of using the cash and resources —is a discriminative stimulus for one or more actions on the part of members of the extended family, fellow villagers, or spirit beings. These reactions, in turn, are equivalent to reinforcing or aversive stimuli, thus producing a high or low probability that the activity preceding them will be performed. The relationships among activities shown are reflections of customs, societal values, and religious beliefs. Since the latter include actions which are, so to speak, "performed" by nonhumans, some additional comments are in order.

Religious beliefs, values, and conceptions of the universe usually can be fitted easily into behavioral lattices. All that is required is that the presumed activities of religious beings—water nymphs, evil spirits, gods, etc.—be viewed as operating in a systematic fashion. For example, if people believe that cheap rituals performed by men who can afford more

31. Lambert (1963).

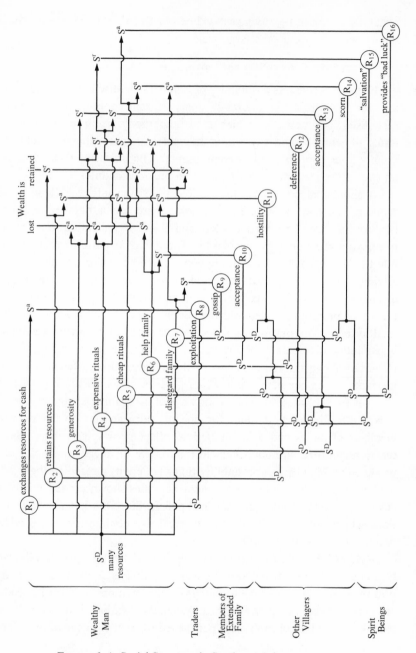

FIGURE 6–4: Social Structure in Southeast Asia

166

expensive ones will result in "bad luck," that is, certain activities of spirit beings which are equivalent to bad luck, then these relationships can be indicated by the square R_5–R_{16}. Conversely, if it is believed that the sponsoring of expensive rituals (R_4) leads to expressions of benign interest on the part of spirit beings that may be expressed as "salvation" (R_{15}), the relationship expressed by this belief can also be indicated.

Any wealthy man is part of such a lattice arrangement of activities. On the basis of his past experiences, observations of the fate of others, and the verbal expressions of his neighbors, he can predict rather well the consequences of the various alternative actions. The alternatives are not mutually exclusive, of course, and he may perform several of these actions, not all of them necessarily consistent. For example, it is possible for a man to sponsor cheap rituals (R_5) and to help his family (R_6), thus inviting both positive and negative reactions. Any single activity, in fact, may be followed by reinforcing and aversive stimuli: R_4 leads to one S^a and three S^r, while R_5 leads to three S^a and one S^r. While the diagram does not indicate the weight or magnitude of the various contingencies, an approximation of the *total* consequence of an action is indicated by the summation of S^r and S^a. Thus, R_4 is more likely to occur than R_5.

When the various contingencies of a wealthy man's behavior patterns are examined, the lattice presentation leads to the hypothesis that most individuals will not convert their resources into cash but rather will consume them in one way or another, especially on rituals and the extended family, leaving little for saving, the purchase of manufactured goods, or investment.

Those who do not share the beliefs of their fellows would be subject to only a part of the relationships shown in the lattice. For example, a man who does not believe in these particular spirit beings would be part of a structure that lacks, in this case, R_{15} and R_{16} and the contingencies they represent. Consequently, those who do not hold the community's religious beliefs are likely to keep at least part of their resources, but only those who are somewhat isolated from the rest of the village—and thus less subject to the aversive contingencies of R_{11} or the reinforcement qualities of R_{12}—are likely to retain a significant part of their wealth. Lambert's finding is precisely this, for isolates and outsiders are the most likely candidates for the exchanging of resources for cash and the saving and investing of money.

The sociological concept of marginality—often considered as an important element in deviation, innovation, and entrepreneurship—can now be viewed from the behavioral perspective. If the wealthy man in Figure 6-4 is well integrated into the community, he is part of the structure shown. If, however, he is a marginal man (but with a family), he would care little about R_{12}, or worry much about R_{11}, R_{13}, and R_{14}. Thus he would not be subject to the S^a associated with R_{14}, or with the several S^r provided by R_{12} and R_{13}. He is not likely to sponsor expensive rituals (R_4) since all of the S^r have been "removed," leaving only the S^a of less money. In some cases, then, it may be possible to measure marginality in terms of the number of vertical lines (equivalences) which relate a person to others, be they individuals or groups.

The complexity of the Third World and the multivariate nature of economic development make it necessary to guard against a partial view based on a small area or a limited perspective of social change. While the behavioral alternatives facing a peasant usually are as described above, some saving *does* occur and men *do* spend some of their resources in economically productive ways. Panikar's analysis of peasant families' budgets, for example, shows that significant proportions of rural Indians' income is saved or spent on real estate improvements.[32] A more general concern with systematic (indirect) saving and the expenditure of cash on larger projects is found in the operation of "rotating credit associations." Individuals form an association which meets at regular intervals, often for overtly "social" purposes. In the simplest case each member contributes a certain amount of cash, and the sum is given to the person who requests it or who is chosen by lot. When every member has received the sum collected at the various meetings, the informal association disbands or is continued for those who are interested. The rotating credit associations described by Geertz[33] and Anderson,[34] found especially in Asia and Africa, enable individuals to acquire significant amounts of money without having to worry about the safety of a slowly growing amount of cash. Furthermore, since familial, friendship, and other social ties are the major basis of many of these associations, the future "return" of one's savings (or investments) is practically guaranteed.[35] In short, the

---

32. Panikar (1961).
33. Geertz (1962).
34. Anderson (1966).
35. For an example of the importance of social aspects of saving, see Mahony (1960).

contingencies of saving are much less aversive than they would be for an individual operating alone.

SAVING IN MIDDLE AMERICA

Nash [36] has provided detailed descriptions of social structures which are inimical to the accumulation of cash in many peasant villages of Guatemala and Mexico. Since the lattice arrangement of relevant activities would be similar to that presented in Figure 6-4, a short description of the behavioral alternatives and their contingencies facing the relatively well-to-do in these villages will be sufficient.

In the community of Amatenango (Mexico), for example, a "democracy of poverty" is maintained by two major wealth-equalization devices. First, *all* men must serve in a hierarchy of twelve religious and civil offices. The duties take time and some resources of the family are used up, thus reducing the wealth not only of individuals but of their extended families as well. Second, certain men may be selected to serve in the ritual and sacred office of *Alférez*. Duties include the feasting of neighbors, relatives, and officials, the provision of liquor on various occasions, and the renting of special costumes at festivals. The total cost is greater than the annual income of the richest man in the village, and thus the family of the *Alférez* is reduced to near-poverty. Only the rich are selected for the post, and since it is impossible to conceal wealth—animals, land, and the health of children are the criteria—it is almost impossible to be wealthy for very long.

Those who do not perform their duties are subject to expulsion and/or sacred retribution, especially witchcraft. As Nash says, witchcraft befalls those "who are rich but not generous, who refuse communal obligations, who become outstanding in some dimension which violates the corporate nature of the community or upsets its tendency to economic homogeneity. . . . Witchcraft as a working means of sanctioning behavior is not an easy thing to live with, and at least one man is killed every two months for being a practitioner of witchcraft." [37]

The accumulation of resources, in short, is followed by very definite aversive consequences, and thus little if any saving occurs. A further result of the operation of this type of social structure is that there are no incentives for any kind of innovation or hard work. These activities, to the extent to which they would lead to more goods, would only expose

36. Nash (1961, 1964a).
37. Nash (1961:191).

the individual to onerous and expensive obligations, or the threat of being exposed to—or being accused of—witchcraft.

A similar situation exists in the Guatemalan village of Cantel. Again, there is a hierarchy of religious-political offices through which all male heads of households must move and which involves the expenditure of time and resources. In addition, rich men are expected to maintain a saint for a year and to sponsor the related festivals—an expensive undertaking. These characteristics of the social structure, together with the low level of technology and the custom of bilateral inheritance, make capital accumulation highly unlikely.

Only those who are willing to leave the Indian community—physically, or culturally by becoming a ladino ("Indian" in appearance only) —can accumulate resources or expand enterprises. "Anybody who begins to orient his activity to economic self-interest begins to detach himself and his family from the local community. . . . . People who run enterprises, on however small a scale, tend to get ladinoized, and if they are very successful tend to become ladinos." [38] It is only by such detachment—by becoming a "marginal man" as far as the community is concerned—that the aversive consequences of capital accumulation can be avoided. Since the negative consequences make up a large portion of daily life, however, the probability of many individuals' abandoning the community is low.

CONCLUSION

A behavioral analysis of "saving," when performed for a particular community, indicates the specific changes which are required for the establishment or increase of "saving" activities. Since many of these alterations—such as the modification of *alférez* obligations or the reduction of belief in witchcraft—would not only be difficult to institute but also have additional repercussions, the rate of change is likely to be low. However, it does not follow that *all* of a community's or nation's social structure, or *most* of a village's way of life, must be fundamentally altered if specific actions conducive to economic development, such as saving, are to be established. As the studies of "rotating credit associations" have shown, the foundation for extensive saving already exist in many areas and only needs to be improved by the judicious alteration of the relevant aspects of the social structure. The time required for the success of such

38. Nash (1964a:295).

efforts is considerably less than might be expected on the basis of psycho-dynamic theories; Schuman has shown, for example, that the psychological and behavioral consequences of the Comilla Project in Pakistan were measurable after only five years.[39]

The term "saving" refers to relatively simple behavior patterns, and neither their determinants nor their contingencies are overly complex. The utility of the behavioral perspective in the analysis of economic development receives a more severe test when it is applied to complex constellations of activities and determinants. One such constellation, often thought to represent one of the most important problems of development, will be discussed below.

Demographic Factors

Saving and other means of capital formation, investment in industry, hard work, and increased productivity do not necessarily lead to rapid economic development, for population increases may absorb the benefits of these efforts. Demographic characteristics, and especially the vital rates of developing nations, have therefore received considerable attention.[40] In this section, only three major aspects of the "population problem" will be discussed, for the behavioral perspective's contribution to demographic analysis is limited to those elements that are directly concerned with individual's activities.

POPULATION AND ECONOMIC DEVELOPMENT

The relationship between population growth and industrialization has been widely discussed, especially in recent years, and it has generally been concluded that high rates of population increase are detrimental to economic development. Stockwell, for example, shows on the basis of careful statistical analysis that "with only a few exceptions, those countries which have experienced the highest annual rates of population growth since 1952 have realized the smallest gains as far as per capita income is concerned"; [41] nations whose population grew at a rate of less than one per cent had an average rate of income growth approaching six

39. Schuman (1967).
40. For example Coale (1963), Coale and Hoover (1958), Enke (1963), Glass (1963), Jaffe (1959), Krishnamurti (1967), Leibenstein (1957: chapters 10, 14), Spengler (1960, 1961).
41. Stockwell (1962:252).

per cent, but countries whose population increased more than two per cent a year increased their per capita income by only 1.7 per cent per year. The major reason for such an inverse correlation of population growth and economic development is the generally limited capacity of poor nations to accumulate sufficient capital for the expansion of industry and the increase of per capita productivity. As Spengler [42] points out, a nation must save (and invest) between four and five per cent of its national income in order to counterbalance a one per cent increase in population. Consequently, a national savings rate of "eight to ten per cent is required to enable a population to grow one per cent per year and at the same time experience an increase of one per cent per year in per capita income. If each of these growth rates is doubled, the required saving rate becomes sixteen to twenty per cent per year." [43] The population problem of developing nations follows from the fact that population increase in many nations is greater than two per cent, that a two per cent increment in per capita real income is insignificant (unless it occurs for several years), and that an eighteen per cent rate of saving is an unrealistic goal for most nations of the Third World.

While there is general agreement on the negative consequences of rapid population growth, there are some dissenters. Hirschman,[44] for example, hypothesizes that population pressure spurs a nation to find new methods for maintaining living standards by exploiting new opportunities for economic growth. And Ness argues that there is no consistent relationship between the rate of population growth and the rate of economic development; [45] the rate of population increase can be either an obstacle or a stimulant, depending on the specific historical, cultural, and economic characteristics of a particular nation.

The two major factors responsible for a high rate of population growth are a) a falling or low death rate and b) a high birth rate. Death rates are declining rapidly all over the world, due especially to the miracles of modern medicine, and thus attention has centered on the problem of high birth rates that show no similar rapid alteration in rates. Since the rate of population increase cannot be reduced by increasing the death rate, the only morally acceptable alternative is the reduction of the

42. Spengler (1956).
43. Ibid. p. 318.
44. Hirschman (1958:176ff.).
45. Ness (1962).

birth rate. The factors responsible for a high fertility rate, and the possibility of changing these factors have received considerable attention and will now be viewed from the behavioral perspective.

THE DETERMINANTS OF FERTILITY

In line with the procedures employed previously, the phenomenon of "fertility" is first dissected into its behavioral constituents. Davis and Blake have proposed a list of eleven "intermediate variables" through which social and cultural factors affect fertility.[46] It is evident that both actual and prevented births are the results of different combinations of these variables, and that both the explanation of high birth rates and programs to lower them are likely to be complex since all variables have to be taken into account. The clearly behavioral determinants of fertility rates are a) the frequency of intercourse (including, at one extreme, voluntary abstinence), b) the use of contraceptives, c) voluntary infecundity, and c) voluntary foetal mortality (e.g. abortion). While a high fertility rate is the result of a specific constellation of these variables or behavior patterns—for example, high frequency of intercourse *plus* nonuse of contraceptives *plus* nonuse of abortion—a low fertility rate may be achieved by any one of them—for example, contraception *or* abstinence *or* abortion.

According to the behavioral model of man, activities resulting in high (or low) fertility rates are maintained by their actual and perceived total contingencies. The consequences of "saving" discussed in the previous section are relatively simple, involve a limited time perspective, and concern basically inanimate factors such as cash. Thus they can be easily and correctly evaluated by any individual confronted with a choice of saving or not saving, and the behavioral analysis of "saving" activities is correspondingly simple. But the activities resulting in fertility rates have essentially different consequences. The total contingency is made up of complex elements including, for example, the "costs" of raising children and the "benefits" of parental security in old age; the time perspective must cover several decades and their unpredictable events; and many of the consequences involve human beings, such as the quality of a child's life or the family's living standards. The individual's perception of reality, his knowledge of the world, his visions of the future, and his

46. Davis and Blake (1956). For a description of the Latin American case, see Stycos (1968).

evaluations of consequences are therefore not only much more important but also more likely to be subjective (and different from objective facts of life).

Before industrialization, the total contingency of activities leading to high fertility rates usually was clearly reinforcing. Among the "benefits" were the children's labor contributions, the parents' old age security, the strength and power of the (extended) family, and high status in the community. For most families the costs were relatively low, for there was little beyond the satisfaction of the children's basic physiological needs, clothing, shelter, and whatever was required for a "good" marriage. In addition, members of the extended family usually could be called upon to provide assistance. With economic development, and especially as the conditions of life were altered and mortality rates declined, the *actual* consequences changed, resulting in a new *objective total contingency*. But the consequences *perceived* by the individual changed more slowly, often leading to a perpetuation of the old *subjective total contingency*. Yet behavior change will not occur until the perceived or subjective total contingency changes.

This conclusion, usually phrased in terms of "rationality" when that term is broadly interpreted, is congruent with both theoretical and empirical studies. Leibenstein, for example, assumes "that motivations with respect to family size are, to a considerable extent, rational; that, on the whole, parents will want an extra child if the satisfactions to be derived from that child are greater than the 'costs' that are involved." [47] On a more abstract level, Spengler hypothesizes that "changes in a household's aspirations may greatly modify its disposition to control fertility," [48] and Keyfitz cautions that "the provision of land to peasants may, in some circumstances, be nothing but a signal to them to have children—as they will interpret it, in the absence of contrary messages." [49]

The hypothesis that contingencies affect behavior leading to fertility is also supported by empirical evidence. On one extreme is the type of general investigation performed by Adelman and Morris.[50] A factor analysis of social and political determinants of fertility, based on a sample of fifty-five developing nations, was summarized in the hypothesis that

47. Leibenstein (1957:159).
48. Spengler (1961:263).
49. Keyfitz (1963:229).
50. Adelman and Morris (1966).

the basic element of the social and political transformations associated with fertility decline "is the development of the spirit of rationalist individualism. . . . The spread of thought patterns which encourage the application of individual rationality to everyday decisions seems to be both a prerequisite and a concomitant of the socio-cultural and technological revolution associated with industrialization and urbanization." [51] The question now arises whether the ordinary individual, barely literate and often unfamiliar with the ways of the world, can accurately perceive the new objective total contingency—and act accordingly. A survey of fertility attitudes in Ghana suggests that altered contingencies are widely known.[52] For example, a majority of the respondents recognized that large families were likely to lead to impoverishment, and only five per cent pointed out that children provided for a secure old age. In addition, many parents recognized that children were not as productive now (in cash farming) as they had been in the past (in subsistence agriculture), that children now *had* to be educated, and that education was costly. Finally, parents were acutely aware that children *expected* more from parents, and that the total cost of having children had increased greatly even within a very few years. The survey revealed that in the northern, less developed part of the nation, the traditional contingencies still operated and that the major sources were social, that is, the opinions and good will of fellow villagers. In the more industrialized southern part of Ghana, however, the new total contingency was being increasingly recognized, and economic—or material—considerations were replacing the old social reinforcers. For example, the number of children "recommended" by northern families was thirteen, while southern families "recommended" only eight. Customs, philosophical precepts, and religious ideas provide only a segment of the total contingency, while the economic realities confronting the citizens of developing nations provide another—and increasingly important—segment. Thus Caldwell comes to the conclusion that "the arrival of the cash economy and education can strengthen desires for relatively small families even amongst people with such deeply entrenched high-fertility traditions as the Ashanti." [53]

The analysis of fertility determinants is an interesting endeavor, but it does not become relevant for the modern world until the resulting knowl-

51. Ibid. p. 142.
52. Caldwell (1967).
53. Ibid. pp. 236, 237.

edge can be applied in development programs. The morality of death control has never been subject to discussion, but the widespread concern with a similar control of births had only recently gained acceptance. Just as the behavioral perspective contributes to the analysis of high birth rates, so it plays a part in programs designed to reduce these rates.

IMPLICATIONS FOR ACTION

The behavioral model of man cannot answer the essentially philosophical question of whether births *should* be controlled, and it does not contribute to discussions of whether developed (white) nations should offer either medicine *or* contraceptives, or *both,* to developing (nonwhite) nations. However, once it has been decided to balance death control programs with birth control programs, *then* the behavioral perspective can contribute to the delineation and implementation of efficient procedures.

According to the behavioral model, activities resulting in a high fertility rate will be changed when the (perceived) total contingency is sufficiently altered. Any action program, therefore, must be concerned with both the alteration of the total contingency and the shaping *and* reinforcement of new behavior patterns. Concern with only one aspect will lead to failure, for either contraceptives will be given to "nonmotivated" individuals, or people who "want" to limit the number of their children will not know how to do it.

The alteration of total contingencies. Any developing nation almost by definition presents new total contingencies to a significant proportion of the population. It is not certain, however, whether these new contingencies—or at least the circumstances giving rise to them—are recognized, and thus it is possible that old activities leading to a high birth rate are replicated in the face of new conditions such as a lower infant mortality rate. At the same time it is quite possible that people in new nations are more aware of the changes occurring around them than outside observers give them credit for. As a first step in any action program, then, the variety of perceived contingencies prevalent in the various subsultures of a nation must be ascertained. This knowledge can then be used to either change old contingencies or to strengthen the perception of new conditions, if this should be necessary.

At present it is not possible to make *a priori* assumptions concerning men's awareness of new contingencies. The previously mentioned survey of fertility attitudes in Ghana, for example, indicated that large segments of the population have rather accurate perceptions of the new contingencies of "fertility behavior," and similar evidence is accumulating in other nations.[54] Furthermore, it must not be forgotten that the "total contingency" is made up of several elements. Contingencies presented by religious organizations, for example, are only *part* of the total, and this part varies from one person to another. Knowledge of a person's religious affiliation, for example, does not enable the observer to predict whether the individual does or is likely to use contraceptives. Thus it is not at all surprising that Catholic nations such as Chile, Honduras, and Mexico should have state-supported birth control programs.[55] It is not necessary, in short, for *all* elements of the total contingency to be altered; rather, a few new elements may be all that is required.

If individuals are *not* aware of new contingencies, a program must be designed to either educate the population or provide more or less artificial new contingencies. Freedman and his associates [56] have described a program built around education and the dissemination of contraceptive information and techniques on Taiwan. In effect they assumed that many women were ready to limit their families but lacked sufficient knowledge of proper and easy methods. Enke,[57] however, assumed that old contingencies were still operating, especially in India, and thus outlined a program of government payments for prevented births. He assumed that new reinforcers—money—were required to shape new activities such as the use of IUDs.

The shaping of new behavior patterns. Although an individual may be aware of new contingencies, he cannot act in terms of them until he has an opportunity or the ability to do so. As those who enjoy a regular smoke or drink know, information concerning cancer and cirrhosis is not very aversive, especially if one has only two or three cigarettes or drinks a week. New behavior patterns must not only be learned, but *there must also be opportunities and means for performing them.* Few husbands or wives, aware of the great "costs" of another child, are able to simply abstain from intercourse; yet knowledge of these "costs" may well be sufficient for the continued use of IUDs or other contraceptives when these are available.

The Taiwan fertility study has shown that large numbers of women ac-

54. As described, for example, by Kirk and Nortman (1967).
55. Ibid.
56. Berelson and Freedman (1964), Freedman and Takeshita (1969).
57. Enke (1960, 1962, 1963).

cepted the use of contraceptives without monetary or other incentives, and that even minimal educational efforts such as posters were effective. In addition, many women not subject to the direct efforts of the program received information concerning the possibilities of contraceptives by word of mouth, and voluntarily contacted the program. In behavioral terms, it may be concluded that once the new activities were introduced or made available, they were being maintained by already existing "new" total contingencies. The Indian program of payments for prevented births has also been effective, but as yet it is unclear what role the added contingency of cash has played.

Conclusion. The shaping and maintenance of behavior patterns leading to low fertility rates can be left to "natural processes" only if large amounts of time are available. Those who argue that industrialization will eventually reduce birth rates are able to point to historical events for support, but at least during the early stages of economic growth, when cottage industries predominate, the effects on birth rates are small.[58] Today an increasing number of developing nations, both old and new, are establishing programs to reduce the rate of population increase. Their successes indicate that there is widespread awareness of new total contingencies, and that the importance of some of the old contingencies— associated with ethical and religious assumptions—are being discarded by an increasing number of people in all walks of life.[59]

The Complexity of Social Reality

This chapter has concentrated on relatively simple social aspects of economic development, and each factor under consideration has been related to only a small number of other elements. While education in Vicos, cotton production among the Azande, saving in Middle America, and birth rates are part of industrialization, the *relationships* among these and other elements are equally important aspects of development analysis. The behavioral approach to the study of these relationships begins with activities and earning principles and works "upward" to the operation of institutions, national policies, etc. Knowledge gained by means of these procedures may then be used to explain how and why

58. Jaffe and Azumi (1960).
59. Kirk and Nortman (1967).

particular institutions, policies, programs, laws etc.—as commonly described in the development literature—did or did not contribute to industrialization.

For example, Moore's [60] discussions of institutions, order, and predictability gain significance when the role of these characteristics in the shaping and maintaining of behavior is delineated. And specific historical phenomena—such as patent laws, guilds, and the establishment of universal education—become important explanations of the presence and/or absence of specific activities involved in economic development. Historical descriptions of various aspects of industrialization, such as those found in the works of Gerschenkron,[61] can provide no more than a very general and often superficial statement of *how* a particular event influenced behavior. The behavioral perspective of structural analysis, as illustrated by the case studies of this chapter, contributes to the specification of the relationships between *social* or *historical* phenomena and the *behavior of men,* and between the *behavior of men* and eventual *industrialization.*

Historical descriptions and present-day observations of the development process indicate that an adequate analysis of noneconomic aspects of industrialization cannot be performed as long as the focus is limited to one element or behavior pattern, or when the context of these is considered as "given." At the very least, it must be recognized that each element is likely to have some influence on its context. Furthermore, many of the more important and more complex factors—such as innovation or entrepreneurs—are related, through their components, to so many other variables that much of a society and culture eventually becomes part of the analysis. When the focus remains on only one element, and when only a few characteristics of the immediate context are emphasized—that is, when behavioral analysis does not proceed beyond the necessarily limited initial steps—the result will be a distorted view of reality. In order to do justice to the complexity of elements and their relationships, much larger portions of the social system need to be included, or at least the investigator must be ready to follow the requirements of his analysis farther than the immediate discriminative and contingent stimuli that have provided the focus of this chapter. Such an expansion of view is presented in the following chapters.

60. Moore (1963a).
61. Gerschenkron (1962).

VII *An Outline of*

Systems Analysis

Systems and Economic Development

The varius aspects of economic development discussed in the last chapter illustrate the complexity of the process and the myriad activities and relationships of any society or community which are involved. Economic "backwardness" is always the result of several factors, and each of these, such as low productivity or lack of adequate capital, results from the operation of a number of elements. Programs designed to initiate or accelerate development, therefore, even when they are focused on only one element—such as the fostering of etrepreneurship—must take into consideration the wider social and cultural context for example as it affects both the present lack and future rise of entrepreneurs.

The study of development requires the simultaneous analysis of a large number of variables and relationships, on both the individual and the social level, and in the several major institutions of any community or nation. To focus on only one aspect is to invite distortion, and to propose a single-purpose program is to court failure. Unfortunately, while it is easy to advocate a multivariate approach to the analysis of economic development, it is difficult to outline and employ the required procedures.

As was pointed out in Chapter Five, it is conceptually and metho-

180

dologically impossible to consider social life simply in terms of its constituent elements—that is, men and their actions—for there are too many of them in even small communities. The combination of these elements into social structures and institutions facilitates the study of large-scale phenomena and processes such as nations and the development of communities, but new problems of analyzing these structures and their interrelations then arise. Structural analysis, whether performed on the level of microanalysis as in the preceding chapter, or on the level of macroanalysis, as in the work of Horowitz [1] and Levy,[2] sooner or later confronts at least two important sets of questions:

1) What are the sources of change in a social structure, what determines the course of these changes, and what factors affect the rate of change and the eventual "state" of the new social structure? The principles which appear to be involved in the extinction and establishment of behavior are rather well known, but knowledge concerning the sources of the factors responsible for extinction, the elements governing the selection of "new" activities, and the parameters which affect the eventual shaping of these actions, is still fragmentary. As was pointed out in Chapter Five, structural analysis has no static overtones because behavior and social relations can change at any time, but structural analysis by itself usually can provide only rather limited and descriptive answers to these questions.

2) It is one of the truisms of sociology that social phenomena usually are more than simply the sums of their parts. According to Buckley, for example, "the 'more than' points to the fact of *organization,* which imparts to the aggregate characteristics that are not only *different* from, but often *not found in* the components above; and the 'sum of the parts' must be taken to mean, not their numerical addition, but their unorganized aggregation." [3] This position leads to a number of questions which must be answered before "organization" can become a meaningful component of social analysis: what are the characteristics of organization, how does organization affect the components of a social phenomenon, and what is the role of organization in the alteration of these phenomena and their constituent elements? In all of these questions the term "organization" is to be understood in a broad sense, for there obviously are different kinds

1. Horowitz (1966)
2. Levy (1966).
3. Buckley (1967:42); italics are in the original.

of "organization." Some peasant communities change rapidly, for example, while others change hardly at all; some institutions and groups resist change and others do not. Further questions, crucial for economic development therefore would be: what type of organization is conducive to social change, and what type of organization resists alteration or produces a low rate of change?

These two sets of questions may be answered, at least in part, by general systems theory. Since the systems approach in sociology has not been employed extensively, there are a number of as yet uresolved problems which are encountered in the systems analysis of social phenomena. These will be briefly indicated after an outline of the systems approach has been provided. In the following discussion, the word "systemic" will refer to the systems approach, while the word "systematic" will retain its common meaning of "regular" and "orderly."

The Systems Approach

Since the focus of this book is on the *social* aspects of economic development, it follows that the system under analysis will be the *social system.* "Social system," while often thought of as equivalent to society, must be conceived more broadly, for it includes not only institutions, but also normative and cultural element, and the psychological characteristics of its members. Buckley has provided a good description of systems as they are viewed by sociologists: "A complex of elements or components directly or indirectly related in a causal network, such that each component is related to at least some others in a more or less stable way within any particular period of time." [4] Every system interacts with the environment, which may be physical or social. However, in the case of open social systems "with a highly flexible structure, the distinction between the boundaries and the environment becomes a more and more arbitrary matter, dependent on the purpose of the observer." [5] A society may be conceptualized as a number of interlocking systems, on different levels of generality and of varying sizes and complexity, each consisting of "interacting components with an internal source of tension, the whole engaged in continuous transaction with its varying external and internal environment." [6]

4. Ibid. p. 41. The material of this section is based on Kunkel (1969).
5. Ibid. p. 41.
6. Ibid. p. 128.

The phrase "may be conceptualized" raises the question of the nature of systems—do systems exist in nature (natural systems) or are they products of the mind (constructive systems)? Present knowledge of society is so limited and rudimentary that it is not possible to prove the existence —or absence—of natural systems. At the same time, the systems approach has proven quite useful, even when the investigator evidently "constructed" the system he analyzed. According to Easton, "we can simplify problems of analysis enormously, without violating the empirical data in any way, by postulating that any set of variables selected for description and explanation may be considered a system of behavior." [7] For present purposes, it is neccessary to add only that the variables which are included in a systems analysis should at least logically *appear* to be part of a more or less distinct, observable entity in the empirical world.

Systems analysis has not been widely used in sociology, even though the word "system" is one of the most common in the literature. In the last few years, a number of writers have outlined the nature and form of systems analysis, but the social sciences have been rather slow in making use of this analytical tool, and only very recently has there appeared an outline of general systems theory and its implications for sociology. The systems approach to social phenomena described by Buckley and others [8] raises a number of questions which must be answered if this approach is to become a significant component of development analysis. The major problems revolve around the nature and operation of systems components, the relationships among components, and the nature and operation of "feedback" in social systems. These topics are usually discussed in such general terms—for example, by Parsons [9]—that widespread sociological applications must await the specification of relevant concepts and relationships. In this chapter a behavioral foundation for such specification will be provided, and one set of solutions to these problems will be outlined. In the course of these discussions the most important characteristics of systems analysis will become apparent. Finally, a number of ways in which the systems approach to social organization and change may be useful in the analysis of economic development will be indicated.

7. Easton (1965a:30).
8. For example Deutsch (1963), Bertalanffy (1962), Nadel (1953), Parsons (1951), Easton (1965b), Boguslaw (1965), Cadwallader (1959), and Maruyama (1963).
9. Parsons (1961).

THE NATURE AND OPERATION OF SYSTEMS COMPONENTS

The components of most systems analyzed by sociologists fall into a large variety of categories. For example, individuals, groups, behavior, interaction, values, norms, self, technology, demographic characteristics, ecological parameters, money, resources, etc. have been treated as components by one or another investigator. In short, practically every phenomenon or characteristic that has been studied by sociologists seems capable of being incorporated into systems analysis.

The first step in any systems analysis is the specification of the questions the study is designed to answer. These questions—together with the nature of the system—set up the parameters of both the system and the study, determine the types and numbers of components that must be included in the analysis, and, in combination with the investigator's theoretical orientation, delineate the relevant characteristics of these necessary components. In development analysis, the relevant questions center on the characteristics of industrialization, the operation of social prerequisites and concomitants, the role of economic and psychological factors, and the conditions under which particular combinations of elements are likely to result in social change or stagnation. While these and similar questions are concerned with characteristics which are part of societal or national systems, it is methodologically advisable to restrict the systems analysis of economic development—at least initially—to smaller subsystems. Knowledge of communities or particular institutions is often more detailed and complete than knowledge of total societies, and thus the analysis is likely to have a firmer empirical base. In addition, economic development does affect individuals, villages, and institutions—and may indeed be considered as the sum of personal, communal and institutional changes within a nation. Finally, the relative isolation and independence of villages, towns, or even social classes, enables the investigator to treat these smaller units as subsystems, amenable to the same type of systems analysis as is employed in the study of nations.

As far as social scientists are concerned, there appears to be general agreement that activities are the basic components of any social system. Thus Easton writes that "all social systems are composed of the interactions among persons and that such interactions form the basic units of these systems." [10] According to Buckley, "the sociocultural pattern is

10. Easton (1965a:36).

generated by the rules . . . *and by the interactions* among normatively and purposively oriented individuals and subgroups in an ecological setting." [11] Interaction, or basically behavior, does not exist by itself, however. It is men who behave, and thus men are inescapable components of social systems. For example, Parsons writes that "a social system consists of a plurality of individual actors, interacting with each other," [12] and Homans,[13] too, has argued this position in a most persuasive manner.

It is not sufficient, however, to simply delineate components. In addition, the major characteristics of the various components of the system must be ascertained and analyzed, for these properties determine not only the parameters within which the components operate, but also the form and character of the relationships among elements. In the case of a social system, for example, the characteristics of men and behavior must be specified because their limitations place an indelible stamp on any system of which they are a part. According to Buckley, the analysis of social phenomena should also include "psycho-social dynamics, [for these,] acting as intervening variables between 'structural' forces and behavior, are beginning to provide the basis for the deeper explanation of organizational dynamics." [14] More specifically, Inkeles writes that "the human personality system . . . becomes one of the main intervening variables in any estimate of the effects of one aspect of social structure on another." [15]

Most systems analyses require more than the simple description of components, because it is the investigator's conception of components, rather than the "natural" elements themselves, which are incorporated into the system he constructs and analyzes. Thus it is not simply "men" who are part of social systems, *but the particular model of man the investigator chooses to postulate.* For example, "as Parsons formulates his conception of the social system, elements in the biological constitution and physiological functioning of man . . . are excluded. To a Malinowski it might well seem that this is a form of academic monasticism in which men are cleansed of their baser passions for sex, food, and material possessions by theoretical purification." [16] Homans, on the other

11. Buckley (1967:62); italics are in the original.
12. Parsons (1951:5–6).
13. Homans (1964a, 1964b, 1967).
14. Buckley (1967:133).
15. Inkeles (1959:251).
16. Gouldner (1959:246).

hand, admonishes: "Let us get men back in, and let us put some blood in them." [17]

Similarly, it is probably not sufficient to say simply that "behavior" is a component of systems analysis. Along with observable activity it is necessary to postulate the general determinants and consequences of action, for it is only through these that it is possible to relate one acivity to another. Here again it is *the theoretical framework of the investigator* and the general purpose of the study, rather than the requirements of systems analysis in general or the characteristics of the specific system under investigation, which is important. The investigator's assumptions concerning men, behavior, and social relations not only are instrumental in the specification of these components of systems analysis, but they also delineate additional factors and information which may be required. Any model of man will require specific items of information which then will have to be incorporated into the analysis of the system in which the model of man appears.

Since there are at least as many different types of social systems analysis as there are sets of assumptions concerning these two components, the question arises as to whether it is possible to establish criteria for determining the types of elements, information, and assumptions that are required. It has been proposed, for example by Buckley, that complex models of man and consequently complicated determinants of action are to be preferred, largely because the very complexity provides explanatory richness.[18] Such wealth, however, usually requires a large number of propositions to explain a specific action, or even activities in general, and thus an inordinate amount of effort may have to be directed toward the explanation of behavior rather than the analysis of the system.

The analysis of a *social* system centers on the system itself, its genesis, structure, operation, and change. The study of its components and their interrelations is required only to the extent to which such knowledge is relevant for the investigation of the various characteristics of the system and its operation. If the elements themselves—for example, men—are analyzed too minutely, the investigator may lose sight of his original purpose. The ease with which sociologists are carried away by studies of individual characteristics is illustrated by the popularity of such

17. Homans (1964b:816).
18. Buckley (1967:119).

topics as value orientations and need achievement. This is not to say, of course, that the systems analysis of individuals is not a legitimate enterprise. However, when individuals are the focus of analysis, social phenomena become part of the environment.

The analysis of social systems—especially with respect to economic development—would be most efficient if the number of assumptions concerning man and behavior were small, if the validity of these were well established, and if as few as possible assumptions of questionable validity were made. As long as the focus of a systems analysis is on society, then, the "explanatory richness" of a particular model of man may be largely irrelevant. When a large number of assumptions concerning man and behavior are required, and when many of these are of questionable validity, a different and more austere model of man may be more useful in the analysis of social systems. One such model, described in Chapter Three, includes propositions concerning man and behavior which are quite small in number, relatively simple, and based on significant empirical support. The utility of this behavioral model for the analysis of social systems is worth investigating in spite of the fact that this approach has not been widely employed by sociologists. Buckley's rejection of the S-R approach in general, for example, appears to be based more on older theories than on the newer works produced by experimental psychologists and behavioral therapists during the last two decades. While the behavioral perspective presented in Chapter Three ultimately may be superceded by a better one, its sociological utility as shown in the preceding chapters indicates that it may be fruitful in systems analysis as well.

An additional consideration is that some of the basic postulates of the behavioral model of man already have been employed—at least implicity—in the systemic analysis of certain social phenomena. In his discussion of social control, for example, Nadel writes that "Custom remains . . . because its routinized procedures afford maximum success with least risk." [19] He also explains the self-regulation of social systems in terms of feedback loops which include as their most important elements information concerning the contingencies of action. It will become apparent below that the behavioral perspective of systems is little more than the elaboration and specification of ideas contributed to socio-

19. Nadel (1953:266).

logical and anthropological literature by men such as Nadel, Firth, Buckley, and others.

The behavioral model of man, together with its implications for the social determinants of activities and the nature of social relations, contains little of the explanatory richness found in the work of Mead or in psychodynamic theories. It provides sufficient information for the incorporation of men and behavior into sociological analysis, however, and the rather stark picture of man which emerges does not distract the sociologist's attention from his major task, the analysis of *social* systems. In fact, this somewhat "simplistic" conception of man is congruent with the limited empirical information presently available. There are many often quite complicated theories concerning various aspects of personality,[20] but actual empirical information produced by objective procedures is scant, and especially so in the case of man's internal state. Thus, more elaborate models of man are often of limited value in systems analysis since much of the information they require is not available or must be inferred on the basis of often dubious hypotheses and procedures.[21]

RELATIONSHIPS AMONG SYSTEMS COMPONENTS

The analysis of social systems has made it increasingly evident that "we cannot make a neat division of those things that are and those that are not systems; rather, we shall have to recognize varying degrees of 'systemness.' "[22] These degrees depend largely on the *organization* of system components, and especially the types of relationships that hold among them. In addition, many of the components of social systems are themselves products of relations with other elements, and thus their very form and operation depend on present and past interrelationships. The clearest example of the importance of relationships is provided by a major component of any social system: the person. Sociologists are not interested in the physical individual, nor in the isolated one. Rather, interest centers on the person as a member of a veriety of groups. Such a person, "the behaving individual, . . . is essentially an organization that is developed and maintained only in and through a continually on-

20. Hall and Lindzey (1957).
21. Marx (1963).
22. Buckley (1967:42).

going symbolic interchange with other persons." [23] It may be concluded, then, that elements are parts of a "system" to the extent to which they are interrelated, and that relationships among men and among activities are among the most important characteristics of social systems.

The behavioral perspective enables the sociologist to analyze these relationships in terms of observable variables with a minimum of inferences. As was pointed out in Chapter Five, a relationship among activities may be said to exist if one activity is a discriminative and/or contingent stimulus for another, and a relationship among individuals may be said to exist if one person (and/or his action) is a discriminative or contingent stimulus for another person (and/or his action).

AN EXAMPLE: RECIPROCAL LABOR SYSTEMS

The utility of the behavioral perspective of systems analysis, especially as far as the relations among components are concerned, will be illustrated by a study of peasant communities in western South America. These social systems are small, somewhat removed from the larger society, and simple enough so that significant parts of life can be discussed without doing violence to their unity. One of the most important subsystems of many peasant villages is co-operative farm labor. As will be shown below, the activities involved in this practice constitute a system presently undergoing change and can therefore serve as a relevant illustration of economic development.

In many Latin American peasant communities agricultural work requirements periodically exceed the strength and speed capacities of individuals, and thus co-operation is an important part of village life. Reciprocal labor practices have been exhaustively described by Erasmus,[24] the changes which are presently occurring have been analyzed in similar detail, and thus there is sufficient information to outline the structure and operation of this particular subsystem and its alteration.

There are two basic types of reciprocal labor. In "exchange labor groups" individuals in groups of about ten help each other in various usually unspecialized tasks involved in the clearing of land, and the planting and harvesting of crops. In this way each man has his labor needs satisfied and in turn helps everyone else in the group. Obligations of reciprocity are generally recognized by all villagers, and an exchange ratio

23. Ibid. p. 44.
24. Erasmus (1956).

of one day's labor for others for one day's labor from others is the rule. On rare occasions food and drink are provided by the owner of the land, but the usual practice is for workers to bring their own. Both the quality and amount of work are usually quite high, for informal sanctions are quite effective, and in addition it is recognized that "the quantity and quality of work given is the measure of its return." [25] Most co-operative work is performed by more or less permanent groups of small farmers and sharecroppers whose livelihood depends on its smooth operation. The "rewards" for an individual's working in the fields of others consist of their helping him in his fields, but because of differences in crops, topography, and amount of land, the time which intervenes between one man's work and others' helping him may be quite long.

"Festive labor groups" are usually engaged by wealthier land owners or "hosts" who periodically require large numbers of workers. These groups are usually quite large, involve statuts differences between host and guest, and are characterized by sociability and some competition among guests. The "rewards" received by guests are immediate and consist mainly of the host's provision of a fiesta, including extraordinary food and drink. This fiesta is usually a reflection of the host's evaluation of his guests' performance, but at the same time the host's lavishness on this occasion confers status upon him and is remembered by his guests as an indicator of how hard they should work the next time they are asked. The rule appears to be that there should be a fair amount of food and drink for a fair amount of work rendered.

The men, behavior patterns, and relationships which constitute these two systems of co-operative labor may be conceptualized in terms of the lattice arrangements shown in Figures 7-1 and 7-2. These diagrams are only partial representations, of course, for they include only four persons and a few of the significant activities. For example, the line between R_3 and R_6 (Figure 7-1) disregards the many actions intervening between the two work periods. It is evident, however, that the rewards for helping others appear only at the end of behavior chains such as R_3–R_6–R_9. The presentation of a complete work group would require a much more complex lattice, but it would be little more than an expansion of the basic elements apparent in these figures.

As was the case in previous diagrams, the horizontal lines indicate sequences of action while the vertical lines indicate that a particular activity is equivalent to discriminative or contingent stimuli for another action.

25. Ibid. p. 448.

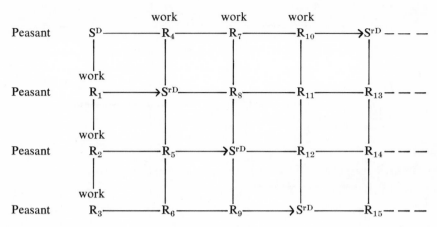

FIGURE 7–1: Exchange Labor

The basic units of the lattices consist of two activities which are related so as to form "squares" such as R_1–R_4 (Figure 7-1). In these diagrams the "squares" reflect ecological and technological requirements and indicate the operation of norms; for example, slash-and-burn agriculture usually cannot be performed by single individuals, and thus the "square" R_1–R_4 is a reflection of ecological requirements. The norm that in festive labor workers are rewarded by adequate food and drink is indicated by the "squares" R_3–R_6 and R_4–R_6 (Figure 7-2).

The larger system—such as the "economic institution" or the community as a whole—may be analyzed in similar fashion, with different units and different definitions of the relevant R. The system under discussion, for example, consists basically of individuals and their actions. "Co-operative labor," however, may itself be considered as a component of the village system, and the village may be conceived as an element of the even larger, national system. It is the focus of analysis which defines the components of the system, determines its boundaries, and indicates the degree of specificity with which the particular components themselves must be analyzed. In the analysis of the village system, for example, the various activities appearing in Figure 7-2 might well be summarized as one R, "festive labor."

INFORMATION

The characteristics of relationships among components vary from one type of system to another. In the systems studied by chemists, physicists, and astronomers, for example, exchanges of energy together with

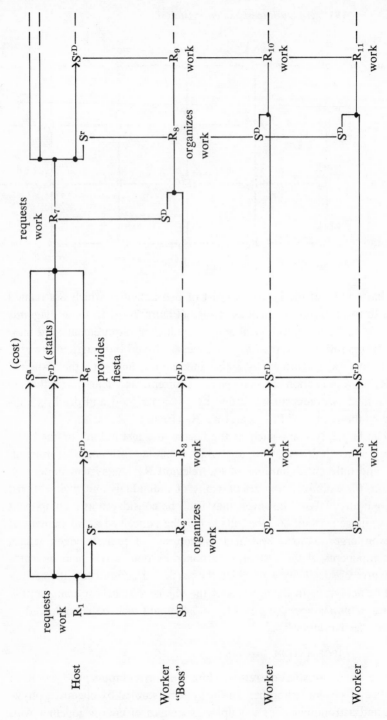

FIGURE 7-2: Festive Labor

spatial and temporal phenomena—such as gravity—constitute the major links among components. The major link among the components of any social system consists of information; and since information is the basic element of feedback, an extended discussion of this subject may be useful.

The behavioral perspective enables the systems analyst to specify the types and operation of information beyond the usually rather abstract discussion of this topic. While it is correct to say that "the sociocultural system is to be viewed as a set of elements linked almost entirely by way of the intercommunication of information," [26] "information" cannot become a meaningful part of social systems analysis until its characteristics and the nature of its ties with the various components—such as men and action—have been delineated. According to the behavioral perspective and the example outlined above, "information" as an element of systems analysis usually refers to a number of somewhat different phenomena. The following are the most important:

1. Together with other formal and informal rules, the values and norms of a society or subculture provide individuals with information concerning the probable consequences of various behavior patterns and the circumstances under which specific actions should or should not occur.

2. Discriminative stimuli provide a person with information that, if a particular action is performed, the probability of (eventual) reinforcement is high.

3. Contingent stimuli provide a person with information concerning the efficacy of a particular activity, whether it was successful or not, in accordance with values and/or norms, etc. This information affects the probability that the action will be repeated or changed in the future.

4. Finally, verbal instructions and observations of others' activities and associated contingencies represent compact information, usually abstracted from the operation of the social system, concerning the discriminative and contingent stimuli of a large variety of activities within the individual's and group's behavioral repertoire.

From these considerations it is evident that relationships among activities are based very largely on information, especially concerning the efficacy of actions and the selection of a specific behavior pattern from among those which are theoretically possible. For example, a specific dis-

26. Buckley (1967:82).

criminative stimulus provides—and perhaps should be conceived as representing—information that a particular action, and not any other, is likely to be reinforced. According to the behavioral perspective, the transmission of information is the essence of relationships among men and among activities. In Figure 7-2, for example, the horizontal line R_3–S^{rD} provides the worker "boss" with information that the work performed (R_3) was adequate, while the horizontal line S^{rD}–R_8 in effect informs the host that the fiesta he gave (R_6) was an adequate reward for his worker-guests. It is evident that the behavioral perspective supports Buckley's statement that "information is not a substance or concrete entity but rather a *relationship* between sets of ensembles of structured variety." [27] A learning approach goes further, however, by specifying the nature of these relationships and by outlining the contribution of information to the shaping, selection, maintenance, and extinction of behavior, and thus the operation of the system. It may be pointed out, finally, that so much information in social systems consists, essentially, of the actions of men—in this example, the fiesta is information—that it may be useful to concentrate on the analysis of behavior rather than on simple "information" itself.

Information is usually analyzed in terms of senders, receivers, channels, noise, and filters. Each of these elements may be viewed from the behavioral perspective. In the diagram of festive labor groups (Figure 7-2) many of the lines may be considered as part of an information network. "Information" itself refers to a wide variety of phenomena such as orders, praise, measurements of the work completed during a day, and the food provided for the guests. For example, if less work is completed than the host feels is customary, this information leads to action such as providing a smaller quantity of liquor for the fiesta. The smaller amount, in turn, provides guests with information concerning their work and indicates displeasure of the host. The channels of information are reflections of the social structure, both of the community and of the festive work group. For example, a man requiring work channels his request through the leader who informs the other members of the work group. The host watches the workers and, upon completion of the labor, pays or feasts them. The types of information that may be sent by a person are usually restricted by a community's customs. For example, the host, even when dissatisfied with the performance of his guests, cannot

27. Ibid. p. 47; italics are in the original.

indicate his displeasure directly, such as by overt criticism. Any man may be a receiver of information, but there usually are some structural or normative limitations. For example, requests for work parties are usually directed to the leader because followers customarily do not receive this information directly. There are various types of "noise" in any information system. In the above example, noise may take the form of orders and directions being lost or misunderstood, ritualized responses of the host concerning his evaluation of the workers' performance, or workers' inadequate conception of what constitutes a "fair return" for their labor. Filters, finally, are usually reflections of norms and psychological characteristics of individuals. For example, the high status which the community accords hosts of festive labor groups may make it difficult for the host to accurately assess the economic costs of co-operative work parties. The most common filter is probably a person's inability to accurately perceive discriminative stimuli or predict reinforcement probabilities, thus excluding information which is actually "there."

The discussion of relationships has so far centered on the components of a system. Of equal significance, however, is the relationship between the system (and its components) and the environment. In the case of *social* systems, the environment may be physical or social, and if the latter it may include cultural, normative, technological and other aspects, and at times the mere physical presence of men may be important. System-environment relationships and their consequences are usually analyzed in terms of open and closed systems, and since complex and dynamic social systems are "open," a short discussion of this topic is advisable.

"OPEN" AND "CLOSED" SYSTEMS

The analysis of various kinds of systems, performed by men in various disciplines, has led to the recognition of two major types of system, "open" and "closed." Mechanical systems, and most of those studied by chemists and physicists, are "closed" systems; biological systems, and especially social systems, are "open." [28] The major, and distinguishing characteristics of "open" systems are that there occurs an exchange of matter and information between the system and the environment, and that such exchanges may lead to alterations in the structure

28. Bertalanffy (1952:125ff).

and operation of the system so that it persists in spite of changed circumstances or new environmental requirements and limitations.

Closed systems, with rather limited adaptability and environmental exchanges, are not likely to persist in the face of drastic environmental changes. However, "the typical response of open systems to environmental intrusions is elaboration or change of their structure to a higher or more complex level." [29] In addition, the later state of the open system is quite independent of the initial circumstances and elements (equifinality). The eventual characteristics of the system are "not dependent on the inital conditions but only on the ratios between inflow and outflow, building-up and breaking-down. In other words, the final state does not depend on the initial condition but on the system conditions which control the ratios just mentioned." [30]

Just as there are degrees of "systemness," so there are degrees of "openness"; and "as we proceed up the system levels (i.e. from physical to social) we find the systems becoming more and more open in the sense that they become involved in a wider interchange with a greater variety of aspects of the environment." [31] In the case of social systems, the degrees of "openness" are often largely cultural phenomena. For example, Wolf [32] has described Mexican villages which, while economically related to the nation, are socially and culturally "closed." As a result, the rate of social change is low and the old way of life is maintained. While many chemical, physical, and mechanical systems are "naturally" closed, most closed social systems are "culturally" closed. That is, there is nothing in the nature of the system that makes it theoretically impossible to increase the degree of "openness," as illustrated by the Vicos Project.

Many parts of developing nations consist of more or less "closed" subsystems. Economic development, then, would consist of the conversion of closed into open systems, and development analysis would involve the study of factors which presently maintain the closed systems and of procedures for the "opening" of their subsystems. Exchanges with the environment constitute one set of factors, and the economic incorporation of isolated communities has been suggested as one means

29. Buckley (1967:50).
30. Bertalanffy (1952:143).
31. Buckley (1967:51).
32. Wolf (1957).

of increasing the probability and rate of social change.[33] A further set of factors consists of certain internal characteristics of systems, namely, feedback circuits.

"FEEDBACK" IN SOCIAL SYSTEMS

An essential characteristic of open systems—indeed the distinguishing mark of any social system which successfully adjusts to alterations in the environment—is the existence of feedback loops. These consist, essentially, of series of relationships among elements and paths of information transmission which result in a) the system's gaining information concerning the efficacy of its operation and b) the system's ability to make the necessary alterations in its structure and operation as the environment changes. Further elements of the feedback loop are "internal test parameters" (ITP) and "criterion-testing subsystems" (CTS). These terms refer to the existence of a set of criteria against which the performance of a system can be measured, and the operation of a subsystem which performs this evaluative function. There are two basic types of feedback: *negative* feedback loops operate so as to reduce the deviation from the original norm, while *positive* feedback operates to increase the original deviation. Since there usually is a time lag between the original deviation and the system's compensation, negative feedback commonly results in some degree of oscillation.

Complex social systems typically are open systems with a preponderance of positive feedback loops. Thus it is to be expected that few deviations—no matter what their origin—will engender sufficient countervailing forces to return the system to its original condition. As the environment changes, the structure and operation of the system are also likely to change, and thus the "normal" operation at one time may be quite different from the "normal" operation at another time or in different circumstances. "Normal," in other words, is defined in terms of the internal test parameters and may be expected to vary among systems and over time.

The behavioral perspective enables the sociologist to analyze the feedback loops and internal test parameters in terms of observable activities and specifiable relationships. When social phenomena are diagrammed in ways similar to the examples shown in Figures 7-1 and 7-2, it is possible not only to determine the existence of feedback loops but also to delineate the structure of a particular system and to specify the opera-

33. Kunkel (1961).

tion of its various components and the adequacy of the criterion-testing subsystem.

In the usual festive group (Figure 7-2) there are at least two feedback loops. First, the host's request for labor (R_1) results in the performance of work $(R_{3, 4, 5})$, thus reinforcing the request and increasing the probability that the request will be repeated (R_7). Second, the workers, upon being called and after completing the assigned tasks, $(R_{3, 4, 5})$ are rewarded by certain amounts of food, drink, and/or pay (R_6). The amount of liquor, especially, is considered to be a reflection of the host's satisfaction with the men's labor, thus indicating to them the efficacy of their actions. When their work has been adequately rewarded, the probability of the men's returning for another work party $(R_{9, 10, 11})$ is high. The two feedback loops, then, together lead to the continuation of the festive labor system.

As was mentioned before, feedback loops can be self-regulating—and the total system can be self-adjusting—only if there are also internal test parameters and criterion-testing subsystems. In the illustration, the internal test parameters are certain conventions regarding a "fair" day's labor and an "adequate" fiesta. In the first feedback loop, for example, the host measures the labor performed by the group against some commonly accepted standard of daily work and fiesta costs. In this case the host himself comprises the "criterion-testing subsystem," while his definitions of "fair" and "adequate" constitute the internal test parameters in terms of which he operates. If the work measures up to these definitions, customary food and/or pay are provided, and he is likely to sponsor other festive groups in the future. The internal test parameters of the second loop are the workers' definitions of "just compensation" for the "fair" work rendered, while the men or their leader constitute the criterion-testing subsystem. If the fiesta provided by the host does not measure up to these definitions, the co-operative work system is likely to change in the direction of less work in the future, thus bringing the "low" rewards into line with the amount of effort that is expended. Generally speaking, the nature of feedback loops—whether they are positive or negative—can be ascertained only by a number of observations.

For illustrative purposes, the first deviation from the "normal" operation of the festive labor group may be assumed to be a change in R_6 (Figure 7-2), such as the provision of a relatively simple fiesta. This fiesta will not meet the worker loop's internal test parameters and thus the men are likely to work less hard when they are called again. Poorer performance, however, is likely to result in a still simpler fiesta provided by the host, leading to still further reductions in work. In the short run, then, original deviations are likely to be amplified.

Normative and ecological parameters, however, may operate to make the feedback loops negative, especially in the long run. As long as the host *requires* help in his agricultural pursuits, he cannot afford to give such poor fiestas that workers will refuse to attend his work parties. And since his status in the community is tied to fiestas, he is not likely to provide such poor fiestas so as to jeopardize his status. The workers, since they depend to some extent on the goods provided by hosts, cannot afford to ignore the opportunities for work provided by the host, and thus are not likely to work so little that the host will terminate festive labor. From these considerations it may be expected that, in the long run, no matter what the original level, minimal fiestas will be provided by the host, and minimal work will be offered by the men.

Personal experiences—such as a trip to another village—may lead the host to alter his definition of how hard men should work for a given type of fiesta, or workers may decide that formerly adequate fiestas are now defined as inadequate, justifying less work in the future. In general, idiosyncratic test parameters are likely to result in altered activities or their rates, and changed systems. Conversely, amorphous internal test parameters will probably contribute to the stability of behavior patterns, feedback loops, and social systems. For example, internal test parameters in noncash economies are usually somewhat vague, and performance is often difficult to measure, as when the economic "cost" of a fiesta cannot be ascertained because the host produces his own liquor and food stuff. Consequently, there may be some difficulty in ascertaining whether the operation of the system matches the requirements, and the system is likely to be somewhat more stable. As soon as cash is introduced, however, it is possible to compare performance and test parameters relatively objectively and quickly, with a consequently higher probability that changes in the system will occur as soon as performance falls outside the parameters. With the rise of a cash crop, for example, the host may change his evaluation of the economic "cost" of co-operative work and the status "benefits" derived from such labor and fiesta. If the former is greater than the latter, the operation of the system no longer meets the internal test parameters of "profitability" and changes can be expected to occur.

It may be concluded that precise replications of behavior and thus the continuation of a social system will occur only under certain circumstances such as a stable environment which results in the continued effectiveness of the system, or test parameters which are vague or not subject to objective measurement. When the environment of a system is altered, for example, by the development of a market for cash crops, activities constituting several loops are likely to be altered as soon as a system's performance no longer matches the test parameters. Such alterations will usually involve the extinction of certain activities and the establishment of new behavior patterns, combined into new feedback loops, and the definition of new internal test parameters.

From these considerations it is evident that *feedback loops operate much the way behavioral principles do.* According to the latter, an activity will be repeated when it is reinforced, and according to the former, a system will continue when its operation is "successful." In one case "success" is conceived as reducing deprivations, and in the other as meeting the requirements of internal test parameters. It may be concluded, therefore, that the behavioral perspective presented in earlier chapters is quite compatible with systems analysis. In fact, it appears that the behavioral approach is particularly well suited for the analysis of feedback in social systems since both emphasize the importance of an activity's consequences for the future repetition or alteration of that activity.

Dynamic Aspects of Systems Analysis

While the systems approach is useful as a means of analyzing a large variety of social phenomena, it is in the study of social change that the utility of the systems perspective is especially apparent. Maruyama,[34] for example, has provided a detailed analysis of social change in terms of "deviation-amplyfying mutual causal processes," or morphogenesis, and of "deviation-counteracting mutual causal processes," or morphostasis. According to Buckley, most sociologists have conceptualized social change in terms of the latter "model" while many observed

34. Maruyama (1963).

changes actually follow the first pattern. Systems theory indicates under what conditions a social system is likely to persist in a particular structure and operation, and under what circumstances fundamental changes may be expected.

Much of the developing world, both on the level of communities and of nations, is characterized by a welter of intersecting negative feedback circuits. Economic development, therefore, means that positive feedback —which amplifies deviation from the original—is substituted for negative feedback.[35] A major focus of development analysis, consequently, consists of the determination of the social and cultural phenomena responsible for the creation and maintenance of negative feedback. On the basis of such information, procedures can be developed for the establishment of social and cultural factors which would change the feedback circuits from negative to positive.

Macroanalysis has provided much useful information on the negative feedback loops of underdeveloped nations. Myrdal [36] and Leibenstein,[37] among many others, have concentrated their attention on both the economic factors which constitute an important set of feedback loops, and on the possible procedures which might be employed to change the nature of these loops. Economists' analyses are often incomplete, however, since the social "links" in the feedback circuits are usually not considered in sufficient detail. Furthermore, the fact that largely economic and largely noneconomic feedback circuits often have common elements—as illustrated in the following chapter—leads to the conclusion that an adequate understanding of "under-developed" economic systems is not possible until all of the relevant factors, together with their structure and operation, are known. One recent attempt to introduce noneconomic elements into development analysis is that of Myrdal, which includes a detailed description of major normative, social, cultural, and psychological factors relevant to the economic development of southeast Asia.[38]

The information provided by macroanalysis is often of such an amorphous nature, however, that it cannot be easily incorporated into detailed studies of what occurs on the observational level or of what procedures might be employed in specific development programs. For

35. For an example of this position, see Myrdal (1957).
36. Ibid.
37. Leibenstein (1957).
38. Myrdal (1968).

example "traditionalism" or "unwillingness to invest" are important elements in some economic feedback circuits, but they cannot be incorporated into development analysis until the nature of these elements, their structure and operation, their determinants and consequences, are specified in sufficient detail so that they can be unambiguously related to other phenomena.

Such specification, while at times approached in the course of macroanalysis, usually requires the careful and detailed observations which ideally characterize microanalysis. The utility of the systems approach for the study of economic development depends on the adequacy of feedback circuit analysis, and this, in turn, depends on the specificity of the elements which are employed. Since *relations* among elements are crucial in any feedback circuit, and since knowledge of such relations depends on the specificity of elements, the more specific the information concerning elements, the better the analysis of feedback circuits is likely to be. The behavioral approach is especially useful in the specification of elements, relationships, and conditions conducive to the alteration of activities and feedback circuits. A behavioral analysis, for example, could be designed to indicate the various activities subsumed under the label "traditionalism," to determine the factors responsible for the shaping and maintenance of these activities, and to outline the consequences of these activities for other actions. From such information, programs for the alteration of activities—and of the feedback circuits of which they are a part—could be derived with relative ease.

The specific conditions which determine behavior replication over time, both within cohorts and over generations, may be analyzed on two levels. On the individualistic level, learning principles indicate when behavior will be maintained or altered, while on the social level systems analysis indicates when original deviations will be amplified or counteracted. The combined analysis of these conditions makes it possible to outline the internal dynamics of social systems in terms of observable activities, their interrelations, and the behavioral changes resulting from altered relations with the environment. Such an example of the behavioral perspective of systems dynamics is provided by the studies of co-operative labor cited above.

AN EXAMPLE: CHANGES IN RECIPROCAL LABOR SYSTEMS

The introduction of a cash crop, bananas, changed both the requirements of agricultural labor and the amount of cash available to farmers.

When cash became a larger and integral part of daily life, the peasants learned to evaluate various activities in terms of their cash equivalents. As a consequence, festive labor groups have been largely replaced by wage labor, but exchange labor groups still flourish, although to a lesser degree than before.

Festive labor. The poor quality of work and the difficulty of controlling worker-guests had been widely recognized, but this had been offset by the need for labor and the high status accruing to the host. The cash nexus provided another means of meeting labor needs—wages—and of providing status—consumption—and thus the problems of quality and control became both more evident and amenable to solution. In addition, the concentration on cash crops led to a decline in food production so that the fiesta ingredients now had to be bought—thus presenting a substantial direct cost. Prestige came to be measured not so much in terms of the fiesta a host provided as by the goods he consumed, and the workers themselves became more interested in money and the various goods which could be purchased than in the fiesta provided by the host. Scattered remnants of festive labor remain only because there are some peak labor requirements which may occur when cash resources are low.

Exchange labor. While exchange labor groups generally have outlasted festive labor, they are gradually declining in popularity and frequency. The major reasons for this decline are inconveniences associated with unequal land holding and the scheduling of work, and the difficulty of adequately rewarding special skills. Wages "equalize" the labor requirements of unequal land holdings, reduce the "inconvenience" of unconfortable work schedules, and provide the "most convenient type of imediate reward for special skills—one which facilitates delayed reciprocity in differential form." [39] At the same time, however, exchange labor is being maintained because "labor exchange is considered superior to wage labor both for its high quality workmanship and its low cost." [40] Workers usually provide their own food and recognize that the kind of work they "put into" a project will be returned to them by their fellows —the harder a man works for others, the harder others will work for him. Hence the new conditions—especially the cash nexus—exert relatively little influence.

The different rates of change may be explained on the behavioral and the systems level, as follows:

39. Erasmus (1956:464).
40. Ibid. p. 463.

The Behavioral Perspective. The differential substitution of one set of activities—wage labor—for two other sets—festive and exchange labor —can be explained partly in terms of behavioral principles. The market for cash crops in effect reinforced new behavior patterns associated with growing bananas, but in addition the generalized reinforcer which became available—cash—could be exchanged for a large variety of goods. In this way strong and lasting deprivations became, in effect, part of the villagers' lives. Wealthier peasants who had previously gained status through conspicuous giving were now able to gain status through conspicuous consumption. The evaluation of work in terms of money made the host's lack of control over his worker-guests more evidently aversive, and the "cost" of feeding guests not only became measurable but also increased. In terms of the behavioral lattice of Figure 7-2, the S^a associated with R_6 became greater, and the S^r associated with R_6 became relatively less important. In short, as the number and strength of aversive contingencies attached to festive labor increased or became more evident, requests for festive labor—R_1—were extinguished and replaced by wage labor.

Less affluent peasants, who in the past had relied on exchange labor since they could not afford festive labor, were less subject to the influence of the cash crop. While cash served as a generalized reinforcer and the growing of bananas became profitable, these men were able to grow only limited amounts of bananas, and thus the general lack of money— insufficient reinforcers—made it difficult to shape new activities. More importantly, exchange labor was both more profitable and lacking in major aversive consequences. Since workers provided their own food, there were few "costs" involved, aside from reciprocal obligations, and since a man's hard work was, in effect, reinforced by the hard work of others later on, sloppy work and lack of control were no problems. In short, the behavioral lattice (Figure 7-1) contiued to exist because the contingencies remained the same.

The Systems Approach. The foregoing analysis is based essentially on individualistic phenomena, men's actions and the operation of learning principles, and indicates why specific behavior patterns remained or were altered. The systems approach places these behavioral elements into the wider social context of the community.

The introduction of a cash crop introduced new internal test parameters—monetary profit—into the festive labor system. More specifically, the ITP of the host began to include the evaluation of monetary costs, the sale price of bananas, and the resulting profit. The workers' ITP began to include the evaluation of the money paid by the "host" and eventually a comparison of wages within the community and the surrounding area. The relationship between the reciprocal labor system and the environment—involving now the growing and exporting of bananas—was altered mainly in terms of the behavior patterns associated with the production of the new cash crop. The structure and operation of the old festive labor system were unable to successfully incorporate the new relationship to the environment or the new test parameters of cash profits. The old system did not "measure up" to the new internal test parameters, and the new relationship to the environment shaped and reinforced behavior patterns which were incompatible with many of the activities constituting the old system.

A new system of agricultural labor, based on wages, developed for at least three reasons. First, the internal test parameters were altered fundamentally, to cash profits, and the associated activities—work and spending—were strongly reinforced by the acquisition of a wide range of goods. Second, the criterion-testing subsystems also underwent change as landowners began to define status in terms of conspicuous consumption and workers began to define work as a means of acquiring cash. Third, the behavioral constituents of several feedback loops were altered, as just described, and new loops were established, mostly in terms of labor associated with banana plantations.

It may be hypothesized that the probability and rate of change in a social system depend in large part on the number of elements—and thus the number of feedback circuits—which are altered initially. The importance of change in several factors is illustrated by the persistence of exchange labor. Cash and the new ecological relationship exerted some influence, but they were not sufficient to bring about rapid morphogenesis. First, the feedback loops involving the exchange of labor did not include "high cost" elements such as fiestas, the internal test parameters —reciprocal hard work—could not be easily translated into cash equivalents, and the old ITP continued to be met. Second, the new ecological relationship did not produce much cash for the poorer peasants with whom exchange labor had been traditionally associated. The operation and structure of the "old" system were still relatively efficient, in terms of both the "old" and the slowly emerging "new" internal test parameters, and thus the rate of change in the system was quite low.

When systems analysis is performed on the level of individuals and their activities, the scope of the study is perforce limited to rather small systems or subsystems. Figure 7-2, for example, represents only a fraction of the reciprocal labor system, and the actually operating festive labor groups in a village would require an exceedingly complex diagram. Since reciprocal labor is only a tiny element in the life of peasant villages, it is evident that the behavioral lattice of a village's ordinary operation and extraordinary events throughout a year would require a diagram of such complexity that it might well be incomprehensible. The major solution to the problem of complexity is, of couse, the combination of activities into ever larger and more amorphous R, where "festive labor" becomes one R and "exchange labor" becomes another.

When R comes to stand for a set of complex activities performed by a variety of men, lattice diagrams such as those appearing in the last two chapters lose much of their meaning. For, while activities can still be represented, it is no longer correct to say that a specific R such as reciprocal labor is associated with a particular discriminative and contingent stimulus. Another way of conceptualizing and representing the various components and interrelations of a system must be sought. Such an alternative is easily found, fortunately, because most analyses of social systems and subsystems have been performed on relatively high levels of abstraction. A number of representations have recently appeared in the social science literature, but only one of these, illustrative of the best efforts, will be presented in detail.

Large Scale Systems Analysis

The analysis of social systems in terms of complex and somewhat amorphous elements is well illustrated by Buckley's flow chart of "stabilization of deviance in a social system," [41] Easton's diagrams of feedback loops of political systems,[42] and Maruyama's system of mutual causal influences.[43] The basic elements of Maruyama's conceptualization of macrosystems will be employed in the following analysis of a subsystem of economic development.

Figure 7-3 shows the relationships among a number of components of the industrialization process, as they have been discussed in the litera-

41. Buckley (1967:170).
42. Easton (1965a:110, 1965b:374).
43. Maruyama (1963:176).

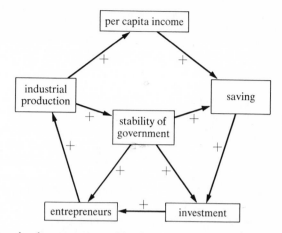

+   indicates that the elements connected by the arrow change in the same direction; i.e. both increase or both decrease.

—   indicates that the elements connected by the arrow change in the opposite direction; i.e. as one increases the other decreases.

FIGURE 7–3: A Deviation—Amplifying System

ture. Arrows indicate causal relations, for example, that increasing industrial production leads to higher per capita income and a more stable government, both of which result in a greater amount of saving, etc. The (+) on an arrow indicates a "positive influence," where as one element increases, the other also increases (or both decrease). Conversely, a (−) indicates a "negative influence" which means that as one element increases (or decreases) the other decreases (or increases). It should be noted that the elements and connecting arrows form a closed circuit in which original deviations—such as an increase *or* a decrease from the original state—will be amplified. For example, an increase in the industrial production leads to a higher per capita income, more saving, more investment, a larger number of entrepreneurs, greater industrial growth, and so forth. Conversely, a decline in industrial production leads to a lower per capita income, less saving, fewer investments, fewer entrepreneurs, and a further decline in industrial production. The major characteristic of the system, for present purposes, is the fact that all of the relationships produce loops which are deviation-amplifying. That is, initial alterations—no matter in which element or direction—will be amplified. Increases in investment, for example, will eventually produce further increases, while declines in per capita income will produce reduc-

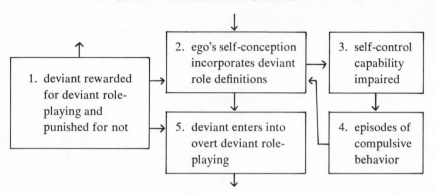

FIGURE 7–4: A Systems View of Deviance

tions in the other components and a further decline in income. In short, any change in any element will affect the system as a whole and will bring about "morphogenesis." This is due mainly to the nature of the loops (and their constituent influences between any two elements) which make up the system. In Maruyama's words, "in general, a loop with an even number of negative influences is deviation-amplifying, and a loop with an odd number of negative influences is deviation-counteracting." [44] When a system consists of several loops, as is commonly the case, the operation of the system, whether it is "deviation-amplifying or deviation-counteracting depends on the strength of each loop" [45] and, ultimately, the "sum" of positive and negative "strengths."

The elements and relations presented in Figure 7-3 include a number of characteristics and problems which are representative of other analyses of large-scale systems. Since most systems analyses of economic development have been performed on a similarly high level of abstraction, a short discussion of these characteristics and problems is in order.

THE NATURE OF COMPONENTS

The components included in most systems analyses are quite heterogeneous, often on different levels of abstraction, and representing different facets of social reality. In his analysis of deviance, for example, Buckley presents the following five components of a social system (Figure 7-4). [46]

Since this is only a segment, there are arrows to and from the rest of the system. It is evident that components 2 and 3 are characteristics of a

44. Ibid. p. 177.
45. Ibid. p. 178.
46. Buckley (1967:170).

person's internal state, and that 4 refers to behavior. While 5 also indicates action, it is clear from the discussion that the component refers to a gradually increasing *rate* or probability at which an action occurs. Component 1, finally, reflects a segment of the social environment's operation.

Figures 7-3 and 7-4 illustrate the fact that fundamentally different *types* of components may be incorporated into a large-scale systems conceptualization, and that many of the components result from the investigator's model of man. Element 2 in Figure 7-4, for example, reflects an essentially psychodynamic conception, while the above discussion of investment (Figure 7-3) reflects a behavioral model. The operation of learning principles is not precluded in the second illustration, however, for component 1 is definitely an aspect of differential reinforcement. From these considerations the question arises whether it is a legitimate and useful procedure to employ various types of components and various levels of abstraction in *one* systems analysis. On the one hand it may be argued that the representations of Figures 7-3 and 7-4 do reflect reality, and that they are useful in describing and organizing observations and inferences. In addition, since individuals are themselves systems, the incorporation of men into systems analysis may *require* the introduction of some human-system elements into social-system analysis. Finally, since most components are multivariate phenomena, their complexity has to be taken into account. Often this involves the use of different "levels," as when the component "saving" is recognized to include both behavior and psychological characteristics.

On the other hand, the free use of different types of elements, on different levels of abstraction, may facilitate the merely superficial and oversimplified description of reality. This is true especially in the case of inferred components, such as "ego's self conception" (Figure 7-4). In addition, there is the danger that dissimilar components will be treated or conceptualized as if they were similar, if only because ordinary diagrams usually do not distinguish among components that are rates, persons, behavior, internal states, social factors, etc. Finally, the use of different levels of abstractions in the same analysis or diagram raises the danger that two components may actually refer to slightly different views of the *same* phenomenon. For example, if self-conception is inferred from activities, including verbal behavior, components 5 and 2 (Figure 7-4) may well refer to the same phenomenon. Needless complexity and confusion may thus be introduced. It may be advisable, therefore, to attempt restricting large-scale systems analysis to one level, and to reduce as far as possible the number of different types of components which are included.

THE NATURE OF RELATIONSHIPS

In large-scale systems analysis the relationships among components is often stated in very general terms. Buckley, for example, speaks of "information" as an undifferentiated phenomenon, Maruyama discusses "mutual causal relationships," and others are content with the drawing of arrows in a diagram or with descriptions of the relationships involved.[47]

The lack of specificity in the discussion of relationships is due, in large part, to the amorphous nature of the systems components which are related. Only when the elements constituting two systems components are analyzed in detail can the relationship between the components be specified—mainly in terms of the relationships among the basic *elements* of the two components. Such specification is usually based on a theory, or an implicit theoretical perspective, and thus it follows that a vague theoretical conception—for example, of entrepreneurs—leads to the statement of vague relationships between entrepreneurship and various social phenomena. In Figure 7-3, for example, a positive relationship is indicated between "stability of government" and "investment," signifying that as the former increases, so will the latter. While this is usually true, it is difficult to determine why such a relationship should hold. It is only upon the dissection of these two components, and the employment of learning principles, for example, that the nature of the relationship—and especially its complexity—becomes apparent. Investment depends in part on the safety and potential profitability of this use of resources. When major control of violence rests in the state, when there is a generally agreed-upon procedure and time table for the exercise of power by one group, when there is little threat of revolution or cataclysmic alterations in basic governmental policies—in a word, when government is stable— these requirements of investments are met. Instead of there being one arrow, then, it could be argued that there should be several—but as soon as the two related components are dissected, and separate relationships between pairs of elements are established, the diagram would take on the properties of that shown in Figure 7-2. The relationships shown in Figure 7-3, then, are summaries, and serve the useful purpose of giving an overview of a complex system. When the related components have clearly

47. Easton (1965a, 1965b).

defined constituent elements, or when empirical referents can be specified, causal statements can begin to be made. Often, however, such requirements are not met, and one may have to be content with saying, simply, that one element "leads to" another. The relationships among systems components shown in Figure 7-4, for example, cannot be clearly specified since many of the elements of the components are characteristics of the internal state whose operation and relationship to other phenomena is unclear even to psychologists. The relationship between self-conception and self-control, for example, depends for its specification on the investigator's theory and cannot be tested except in terms of inferences derived from observed activities.

Descriptions of relationships and arrows in a diagram often fail to take into account what is known as "step functions," "whereby a variable has no appreciable effect on others until its value has increased or decreased by some minimal increment." [48] For example, investment may not occur until a particular degree of governmental stability has been reached. In addition, savings will probably have to have surpassed a certain proportion of annual income. The latter proportion, however, may well depend on the degree of governmental stability, so that either step function involved in these two relationships will depend on the other. All of the relationships shown in Figure 7-3 probably involve step functions; when income increases from very low levels no simultaneous rise in saving is usually observed, and a small number of entrepreneurs are not sufficient to propel a nation into the "take-off." The determination of step functions is based on empirical observations and/or theoretical requirements. Since observations usually are not sufficiently precise, major weight rests upon the theoretical considerations. Since the validity of propositions concerning the structure and operation of systems will depend in large part on the nature of step functions involved in the various relationships, the validity of theories concerning these step functions— and the components involved—will have repercussions throughout the systems analysis. Here it should be remembered that step functions may operate in *each* relationship between one system component's various elements and another component's elements, so that the arrow between "saving" and "investment" is to be conceptualized not only as a series of relationships, but each with its own (perhaps independently operating) step function. From these considerations it may be concluded that an

48. Buckley (1967:67).

investigator's systems analysis will approach reality as closely as do his theoretical preconceptions, and that it will reflect all of the strengths and shortcomings of his own theories.

The final problem of relationships among components is the variable nature of these relationships over time. Linear relationships may become curvilinear as the size of components increases or decreases, deviation-amplifying loops may become deviation-counteracting loops and vice versa, and step functions may operate only within narrow parameters of component alteration. In the early stages of industrialization, for example, sizable accumulations of capital usually lead to sizable investments in industry, which result in further increases in capital. Later this deviation-amplifying loop is likely to be changed, because when income taxes are instituted and unions are recognized, the capital-investment loop may become deviation-counteracting, leading to a stabilization of capital formation. The relationship between health services and the death rate is likely to undergo a different type of change. When modern medicine is first introduced into an underdeveloped country, the death rate declines rapidly; later on, however, similar increments in medical know-how are likely to produce less noticeable effects, and when the death rate reaches 10, the effects of additional medical efforts are hardly evident at all. The variable nature of relationships over time can be determined by observations or, more generally, on the basis of theory, or a combination of both.

COMPREHENSIVENESS

Most systems analyzed by social scientists are partial representations of reality which consist, basically, of abstractions deemed relevant for the study at hand. While the questions underlying the study, together with the concepts and theories utilized by the investigator, indicate the components that are to be included in the system, it is possible that actually relevant components and relationships among them may be excluded. Most systems analyses are limited to specific topics, and thus it is to be expected that there will be a number of relationships to other systems which cannot be studied in depth insofar as this would involve the analysis of these other systems. Since many systems are constructed by the investigator, so to speak, it is possible that significant components of the social phenomena under scrutiny are not included in the analysis, perhaps for philosophical or emotional reasons. The result of such omission is a distorted and perhaps incorrect analysis.

Figure 7-3 represents only a small portion of a social system, and its deviation-amplifying character is likely to lead to an optimistic appraisal of possible rates of industrialization. It may be argued, however, that a number of significant components have been left out, and that their inclusion is necessary for both an adequate understanding of economic development and an accurate appraisal of the probability of success. The component "stability of government," for example, is influenced not only by "industrial production" but also by the society's historical heritage, its economy, the stratification system, and so forth. In addition, the effects of governmental stability, for instance on entrepreneurs, depend also on the *type* of government. Apter, for example, describes three major types of political systems, each with its distinctive implications for entrepreneurs, saving, investing, and other aspects of economic growth: [49] the mobilization system (e.g. Guinea and Ghana), the reconciliation system (e.g. Nigeria and the U.S.), and the modernizing autocracy (e.g. Morocco and Ethiopia). Figure 7-3 may therefore be taken as the representation of a *general* system, while the representation of specific national systems would be expected to include not only additional but also different components and relationships.

Figure 7-5 represents the diagram of Figure 7-3 plus a number of demographic components. Yet even this addition does not result in an adequate systemic view of industrialization, for a number of other components, such as technology, foreign trade, and agriculture, have not been included. As shown in Figure 7-5, industrial growth leads to an improvement in health services with a consequent decline in the death rate and an increase in population. Population growth, of course, leads to a decline in per capita income or, at best, a lower rate of increase in income. A further addition in this diagram is the recognition of a relationship between per capita income and governmental stability. Here it is assumed that the increase in per capita income is not only an economic statistic but also represents an improvement in the average family's purchasing power and life style. But in nations where this assumption does not hold, the relationship may be weak or nonexistent. Since any series of causal relations with an odd number of negative influences is deviation-counteracting, a loop that includes the demographic elements, no matter whether it operates through "saving" or "government," will be deviation-counteracting. On the basis of recent experience in the Third World, it

49. Apter (1963).

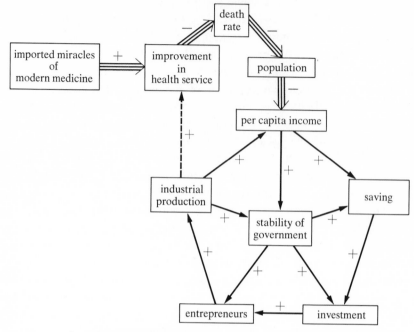

+ indicates that the elements connected by the arrow change in the same
   direction; i.e. both increase or both decrease.
— indicates that the elements connected by the arrow change in the
   opposite direction; i.e. as one increases the other decreases.

FIGURE 7–5: A Deviation—Counteracting System

may be hypothesized that the demographic relationships are usually quite
"strong," whereas the relationship between industrial growth and per
capita income has often been "weak." That is, death rates are apt to be
quickly and inevitably affected, leading to large population increases,
while per capita income is likely to rise slowly and to be unequally
distributed.

The overall picture of economic development now appears to be much
less optimistic, for the system now contains some powerful deviation-
counteracting causal processes. The strength of the demographic loops is
further increased by the fact that many improvements in health services
are in large part of external origin. Thus it might be argued that if the
system were relatively isolated, industrial growth would lead, initially, to
a slight improvement in health services and the death rate, thus produc-

ing a rather weak demographic loop. As a result the probability of successful industrialization would be markedly improved. The experience of Europe over the last two centuries illustrates the operation of a relatively isolated system in which medical inventions were made rather slowly and the death rate was not characterized by a precipitous decline. The importation of the miracles of modern medicine from urban-industrial societies, however, provides great strength for the demographic loop in developing countries and, by implication, for the deviation-counteracting sets of relationships among components significant for economic growth.

These considerations lead to a question with far-reaching implications: how can one be sure that a systems analysis includes all of the relevant components and relationships? The system presented in Figure 7-5 is more adequate than that shown in Figure 7-3, but a number of important elements and relationships remain to be added, simply on the basis of information already available. Food production, urbanization, the class structure, and job opportunities, for example, affect governmental stability and are in turn affected by the population size and the rise of industry. In addition it is clear that technology and ecological factors also play an important role in agricultural productivity and should be included. The answer, then, depends on the testing of the systems analysis. If predictions derived from systems analysis are not supported by data, the system is inadequate and additional components and relationships may have to be included.

The attempt to include *all* relevant components may also lead to the inclusion of irrelevant elements, of elements which appear to be important only at first glance, or of elements which are simply parts of a chain in which only the first and last links are important. In Figure 7-5, for example, "death rate" is introduced even though it is evident that improvements in health services would lead to an increase in population. Were "death rate" to be omitted, the line between the other two elements would be positive ($+$), thus leaving intact the "odd" number of negative influences in deviation-counteracting loops. The component "death rate" is an actual and logical link in the chain of events, but it is perhaps not a necessary one if one remembers that the major factor in population increase is a decrease in mortality rates.

In order to eliminate or at least reduce the number of irrelevant components and relationships, it may be useful to ask concerning every component of a system: is this one necessary in order to derive the next component from the preceding one? The answer will depend, of course, on the sophistication and expertise of the investigator, and thus it is to be expected that different men may construct different systems of even the same social phenomenon.

The problems encountered in the systems analysis of economic development require the cautious application, rather than the abandonment, of the systems perspective. Behavioral analysis of necessity concentrates on relatively small phenomena, such as saving or entrepreneurs, but cannot indicate how these affect the over-all process or probability of economic growth. The systems perspective, by suggesting the eventual repercussions of changes in any component of the system, indicates the direction, and at times even the amount, of change required in a component. The behavioral model of man and the systems perspective in combination thus provide both the specific steps that need to be taken in, and the broad outline of, development programs.

SYSTEMS AND SIMULATION

The testing of predictions derived from systems analysis, especially in the area of economic growth, is likely to be a complicated and drawn-out process. Not only are the required data often difficult to assemble, but the changes which may be predicted are usually long-term and thus difficult to ascertain in the short run. Another procedure for testing propositions derived from systems analysis is simulation. The components and relationships of a system are assigned various "reasonable" magnitudes and characteristics, and the structure and operation of the system are then analyzed by means of computer or game simulation.[50] The major advantage of simulation over "natural" tests is that components of systems can be dissected into various sets of constituent elements, thereby in effect testing propositions concerning the basic characteristics of a system's components and, by implication, the associated relationships. The major disadvantage is that while gross errors in systems construction and analysis are likely to be detected, it is possible for certain constellations or series of errors—such as incorrect weights—to "cancel out," thus giving the false impression that the system corresponds to reality when, in fact, it does not.

---

50. Scott *et al.* (1966), Raser (1968), Abelson (1968).

VIII *Social Systems and*

Economic Development

When communities and nations are viewed as social systems, economic development refers to specific alterations in particular components and relationships of these systems. In the words of Lerner, "modernity is an interactive behavioral system. It is a 'style of life' whose components are *interactive* in the sense that the efficient functioning of any one of them requires the efficient functioning of all the others. The components are *behavioral* in the sense that they operate only through the activity of individual human beings. They form a *system* in the sense that significant variation in the activity of one component will be associated with significant variation in the activity of all other components." [1] Within the confines of a book it is impossible to describe all components of a system, and in the course of a chapter only a few illustrations can be provided. The examples chosen here—world view, communication, and education—are designed to show how effective the learning approach can be even when the topics at first glance appear to have little to do with behavior.

1. Lerner (1963:329); italics are in the original.

217

World View

Anthropologists have long been fascinated by the relationship between a man's behavior and his conceptions of the world and universe. According to Foster, for example, "the members of every society share a common cognitive orientation which is, in effect, an unverbalized, implicit expression of their understanding of the 'rules of the game' of living imposed upon them by their social, natural, and supernatural universes. A cognitive orientation provides the members of the society it characterizes with basic premises and sets of assumptions normally neither recognized nor questioned which structure and guide behavior." [2] In recent years, especially, considerable work has gone into descriptions of the various beliefs and philosophies that are found among peasants in small agricultural villages. Since developing nations consist largely of such communities, peasants' conceptions of the world are important for both the analysis and fostering of economic growth.

A person's conception of the universe, his ideas about the ways of the world, and his assumptions concerning man's position in both, are usually summarized as his "world view." [3] The central component of any world view is a complex and not necessarily consistent set of principles in terms of which the universe is assumed to operate. World view thus includes many of a man's religious and philosophical beliefs, but is not necessarily synonymous with his religion or philosophy or congruent with empirical evidence.[4] For example, a peasant's world view may include belief in "divine justice" and the "evil eye." These two elements will be as real to him as are "scientific laws" to modern man. And just as modern man makes allowances for the laws of motion in his daily life, so does the peasant take the "evil eye" into account. While it is true that only individuals have a world view, men in the same subculture often subscribe to many similar or even identical beliefs, so that it is possible to speak of a "middle class ethic" or the "culture of poverty." It cannot be assumed, however, that all peasants share the same world view, or even that people in the same village or nation hold the same beliefs.[5]

2. Foster (1965:293).
3. For a comprehensive study of world view, see Redfield (1952).
4. For a discussion of over-simplified conceptions of peasants' world views, see Bennett (1966) and Kaplan and Saler (1966).
5. For a discussion of the problem of heterogeneity in peasant societies, see Erasmus (1967) and Piker (1966).

Students of economic development are interested in world view primarily because of its relationship with behavior, and the analysis of world view therefore revolves around three major questions: how does a man's world view affect his behavior,[6] what are the sources of his world view,[7] and how can this world view be studied? The behavioral model of man provides one set of answers.

THE BEHAVIORAL PERSPECTIVE

Since man is aware of himself and his environment, it may be assumed that he is also aware of a significant proportion of the deprivations and positive and negative consequences associated with his daily activities. In terms of the behavioral perspective, then, a man's world view consists, basically, of his perceptions of discriminative stimuli, conceptions of contingency probabilities, definitions of state variables, and impressions of the relationships among these factors and behavior. More specifically, a world view consists of a set of propositions defining and linking various classes of behavior to specific sets of discriminative stimuli and contingency probabilities. Since the characteristics associated with a number of activities may be identical or very similar, several behavior patterns may be combined, or similar consequences of different activities may be summarized by one statement or belief. As a result of such combinations, a world view is usually somewhat simpler than the great number and variety of daily behavior patterns would suggest. However, the propositions comprising world view do not necessarily reflect objective reality, for example actual contingencies, and may not form a consistent whole. Members of various subcultures, communities, and nations, and often even individuals within these groups, may be expected to subscribe to different sets of propositions, thus making generalization concerning a community's world view somewhat dangerous.

1. *World view and behavior.* The propositions which relate various activities to specific discriminative and contingent stimuli are essential components of the procedures by means of which behavior is shaped and maintained. One of the best illustrations of this is provided by the famous hypothesis that the Protestant Ethic was a major cause of European in-

6. The problem of explaining behavior in terms of world view is discussed by Kennedy (1966).

7. For a discussion of the interaction of world view and social structure, see Silverman (1968).

dustrialization.[8] According to Weber, behavior patterns associated with economic growth—for example hard work, saving, and investing—were reinforced by contingencies derived from religious precepts concerning the will and power of God. For example, the early Protestants believed that God demanded hard work, punished idleness, and required the rational acquisition of wealth for purposes other than a merry life. Both entrepreneurs and laborers behaved accordingly, for God's displeasure and the threat of damnation were very real to them. In this case hard work and the accumulation of money were not reinforced by the eventual acquisition of material goods, but rather by the individual's sense of having done his duty, of having acted in accordance with God's will. If an observer had not known the early Protestants' world view, or had not believed in it himself, it would appear to him that there were no reinforcers. The early Protestants, therefore, would appear to have behaved irrationally. It is not until the individuals' world view is known, until their assumptions concerning the existence of heavenly rewards are understood, that behavior patterns can be explained.

The behaviorist's concern with differential reinforcement rather than with theological systems enables him to account for the fact that different religions often lead to similar activities. The religious beliefs prevalent in the Japan of the nineteenth century, for example, were quite different from the beliefs of European Protestants three hundred years earlier.[9] Yet both world views contributed to the shaping and maintenance of behavior patterns associated with economic growth. The important question in development analysis, then, is not "what is the world view?" but rather "what activities does the world view maintain?"

A man's world view does not define all contingencies or deprivations, of course, nor does it affect all of his activities. *Beliefs* about the world and the *realities* of daily life exist side by side and are not necessarily congruent. Whether the significant contingencies of specific activities arise from one or the other can be determined only by careful observations of behavior in various circumstances. Furthermore, since a man's world view affects his interpretation of his environment and experiences, it is likely that the determinants of behavior must be sought in both.

8. Weber (1958). For a critical assessment of Weber's hypothesis and the data he used, see Samuelsson (1961). According to the evidence presented by Samuelsson, the economic beliefs and behavior patterns usually associated with the "Protestant Ethic" actually were part of the moral outlook of mercantilism prevalent in many European nations, including France and Italy, since the sixteenth century.
9. Ayal (1963).

2. *The sources of world view.* There are two major sources of world view. First, men learn to perceive S^D and predict contingencies by means of personal experience or observations of others' experiences. Secondly, ready-made definitions of discriminative and contingent stimuli, carefully outlined schedules of reinforcement, and state variables may be provided by others in the form of descriptions of events, proverbs, stories, or philosophical propositions. No matter what the source, however, daily life—whether directly experienced or merely observed—continues to influence world view by testing the predictions derived from it.[10] When behavior in accordance with the various propositions of a world view is reinforced, the world view is substantiated, while lack of reinforcement in effect makes some of the propositions doubtful. Most world views contain elements which explain or reduce the contradictions and inconsistencies between beliefs and daily experience, thus making it difficult to empirically test—and refute—propositions. For example, the belief that "God sees all" enables a man to continue believing that the world is just, and to behave honestly, even when there are few immediate rewards and when other men, acting dishonestly, appear to avoid punishment.

The behavioral conception of world view leads to a causal analysis which concentrates not so much on the broad categories of the environment—such as educational or religious institutions—but rather emphasizes the individual's learning of propositions and relationships regardless of source. Belief in "divine justice," for example, may be created by means of direct religious instructions or indirectly through stories and proverbs. Since the sources do not always operate in concert, conflicts and inconsistencies are not only possible but likely. Religious precepts and the operation of the social environment, especially, may well lead to different conclusions about discriminative and contingent stimuli, resulting in somewhat inconsistent components of a world view. Thus it is possible for asceticism and bribery, other-worldliness and concern with gold ornaments, to co-exist in the same community.[11]

3. *The study of world view.* Some anthropologists have doubted the average person's ability to describe the relationships he perceives between various activities and their associated discriminative and contingent stimuli. Yet Lewis's recent studies of Mexican families have shown that ordinary individuals *are* capable of describing their perceptions of the

10. Silverman (1968). For an example from urban-industrial societies, see Ball (1968).
11. As described, for example, by Singer (1956).

world around them.[12] The analysis of world view does not depend only on personal descriptions, however. Answers to indirect questions, responses to various psychological tests such as TAT pictures, and the content of proverbs, tales and philosophical principles, can also be used to formulate propositions concerning the state variables, discriminative and contingent stimuli, and behavior, which presumably have been established for individuals and, to some extent, populations. Any world view derived from such sources must be regarded as being tentative, subject to change as additional information becomes available, for it is open to considerable methodological questioning. No investigator can ever be certain, for example, whether men tell him the truth, or all they know, or that their words are accurate reflections of their world view. Furthermore, verbal statements must be interpreted, and even test scores and TAT stories are subject to misinterpretation. Religious and philosophical treatises often are not understood, especially by men from other cultures, as illustrated by Westerners' incorrect views of the Bhagavat-Ghita.[13] Finally, in the case of literature and proverbs, it is often difficult to determine whether the sample is representative, and whether it reflects—or produces—the world view under consideration.

In spite of these problems, "world view" is a useful concept, and people's philosophical assumptions and religious beliefs have been employed in several studies of economic growth.[14] From the behavioral point of view the only requirement for the use of such studies is the recognition that any description of world view is subject to continuous reassessment, and that the characteristics of daily life are usually the most important determinants of behavior.

WORLD VIEW AND SYSTEMS ANALYSIS

The propositions which comprise a world view play three major roles in the systems perspective of social phenomena and processes; they provide a description of the social system's structure and operation, indicate the discriminative and contingent stimuli that establish relationships among men and among activities, and define the internal test parameters of the social system and its various subsystems.

12. Lewis (1961, 1964). For another good example, see Guiteras-Holmes (1961).
13. Singer (1956).
14. For examples, see the articles in Braibanti and Spengler (1960).

First, certain components of a world view provide an overall description of the nature and operation of the social system and other more extensive systems—including, for example, spirit beings and supernatural forces—which affect daily life. This usually includes a description of the nature of man and of his relations to the other elements of the various systems.

Second, some components of world view delineate the subsystems in which the individual participates directly, consisting of the person, his activities, and the reactions of others in his social environment. More specifically, world view components define state variables, discriminative and contingent stimuli, and the reinforcement probabilities associated with various actions. Wolf [15] and Erasmus [16] have provided good illustrations of subsystems in peasant communities, where "institutionalized envy" and "invidious sanctions" on the part of others are predictable and contribute to the maintenance of behavior patterns that result in continued poverty and lack of innovation. The internal test parameters of these subsystems are *the efficacy of the activities* to which the world view gives rise—defined broadly enough to include the avoidance of negative reactions from other villagers. Generally speaking, a world view will persist over time if the activities which result from it are reinforced, and change is likely to occur when the activities and predictions derived from it are no longer rewarded and borne out by experience. The transition from one world view to another, or the more probable case of the selective alteration of specific components, is rarely a period of tranquility. Old definitions of "proper" behavior patterns, contingencies, and the operation of supernatural forces usually are discarded before new definitions are generally accepted; not all men discard the old at the same time or rate, and during the interim even daily life will be characterized by uncertainty.

Finally, some components of world view constitute the internal test parameters of a system and thus serve to evaluate its operation. As long as the system—that is, a particular series of activities—meets the ITP, the series is likely to be repeated. When the activities no longer match the world view component, the activities or the ITP will change, depending on the specifics of the situation, as illustrated in the previous chapter's discussion of co-operative farm labor. For example, many inhabitants of

15. Wolf (1955, 1957).
16. Erasmus (1961).

peasant villages believe that the material resources of the community cannot be expanded rapidly and should be shared equally. It does not matter whether this belief corresponds to reality—what is important is that people have defined "equality of poverty" as *one* of the community-system's internal test parameters. As long as all villagers are equally poor and perform similar activities, the requirements of the ITP are met. However, when a villager works extra hard, has an especially good harvest, or acquires wealth (except when it is of external origin), the ITP is no longer met, and a variety of sanctions begin to operate to return the system to its original condition of "equal poverty"; "improper" amounts of wealth are discouraged in various ways, and resources are distributed among villagers, perhaps through the more or less compulsory sponsoring of communal feasts.

WORLD VIEW AND ECONOMIC DEVELOPMENT

The major role of world view in the industrialization of developing countries is its contribution to the shaping and maintenance of behavior patterns which contribute—or are inimical—to economic development. Systematic hard work, factory labor, saving, investing, and such general characteristics as the "long-range perspective," are affected by the world views of both the individuals who might engage in these actions and of the people whose reactions provide the social context of these individuals. For example, the belief that all men should be equally poor is detrimental to industrialization because "capital accumulation, which might be stimulated if costly ritual could be simplified, is just what the villager wants to prevent, since he sees it as a community threat rather than as a precondition to economic improvement." [17]

Since any world view consists of a number of components, not all of which depend on one another for support, it should be conceived as a loose arrangement of elements rather than a rigid, concrete entity. And since one of the major sources of a world view is experience, i.e. the events of daily life, it may be concluded that changes in components are possible and indeed probable when the conditions of life—and especially the contingencies of behavior—are altered.

Only one of the many components of world view will be discussed in

17. Foster (1965:307).

detail: the conception of a capricious universe. It should not be supposed that this is the dominant motif in developing nations, for as yet the weights of other components—for example the "culture of poverty" [18] and religious precepts—have not been determined. The following analysis merely illustrates how the behavioral perspective can be employed and does not purport to be definitive.

A Component of World View: The "Capricious Universe"

Many descriptions of village life are very general and do not adequately reflect the differences among peasants' beliefs.[19] Additional descriptions of particular communities will therefore be necessary to provide information that is specific enough for a behavioral analysis. While it is dangerous to generalize from a few communities, the recurrence of similar activities and relationships makes it possible to formulate preliminary hypotheses concerning the causes and consequences of world view. Anthropologists who have studied peasant villages all over the world, for example, have been struck by a recurrent theme: the average villager's fatalism, dependence on "luck," and his short-range point of view.[20] One long-time student of Mexico describes life in the village of Tzintzuntzan as follows:

> Good luck, in the form of a fine harvest, freedom from robbery or sickness, finding buried treasure, or acquiring a helpful patron, is the principal hope for improvment in position and, conversely, bad luck explains failure. What happens depends on the wish—but not on the grand design—of God. People rarely speak in the future tense without qualifying proposed or hoped-for action with *Si Dios me da licencia,* if God gives me permission. . . . Divine providence, above all, is the good fortune that spells human well-being. But accepting divine providence does not imply belief in a grand design, a pattern and system, which rules the universe. Rather, the universe about one is marked by absence of law and order: it, and

18. For a discussion of the nature and implications of the "culture of poverty" see Lewis (1965).

19. For example Redfield (1956), Wolf (1966).

20. For example the studies reported in Potter *et al.* (1968).

God's plan as well, are capricious and unpredictable, quixotic and surprising. Something happens, not because of preordained regularities in the universe and in the world, but because God—or whoever the ultimate authority in the particular instance may be—has willed it. A child dies: it was part of God's plan. The highway comes to town: General Lázaro Cárdenas willed it. Since chance and accident are the mainsprings of the universe, systematic expectations and consistent behavior are seen as valueless. Western-style foresight is a positive value only within a predictable system.[21]

Studies of other peasant communities show similar characteristics. For example, in the village of Erongarícuaro, Mexico, it is generally believed that "success can come only through capricious outside intervention, and not through one's own efforts." [22] Typical responses to card 1 of the Thematic Apperception Test—which shows a boy with a violin— are: "God will help him become a good musician . . . the child likes to play, but he cannot . . . he will be able to do it because he likes to and the Virgin will help him." [23] Peasants in Montegrano, Italy, respond similarly and believe that success comes as a result of luck, achievement through fortuitous circumstances. Concerning the same TAT card, Banfield writes: "dramatic success came only as a gift of fortune: a rich gentleman gave a poor boy a violin, a rich gentlewoman adopted an abandoned child, and so on." [24]

Man's relation to nature involves similar overtones of uncertainty and subservience to nonhuman elements of the physical environment. According to Redfield, for example, "to a very large extent and in a degree that helps us to characterize the way of primitive peoples on the whole, the primitive person works within the elements, not against them." [25] And Horowitz elaborates: "The traditional orientation toward self-resignation and away from social responsibility represents a fundamental commitment to 'nature' as something to be accepted and lived with, rather than a series of hurdles to be overcome." [26] This conception of man in nature extends to even the smallest aspects of life. The villagers

21. Foster (1967:117).
22. Nelson (1967:54).
23. Ibid. p. 54.
24. Banfield (1958:66).
25. Redfield (1952:35).
26. Horowitz (1966:300).

of Khanh Hau, Vietnam, for example, believe that some people have a gift for raising pigs or chickens and that others would fail. Thus many resign themselves and forgo the raising of these animals, for "heaven" would not reward them.[27]

When a peasant is said to "depend on luck," to be "fatalistic," or to "lack foresight," these terms refer to certain of his activities and/or verbal statements. A major determinant of these behavior patterns, in turn, is the individual's conception of the universe as something that is essentially unpredictable and uncontrollable. Phillips, for example, summarizes life in a Thai village as follows: "For most Ban Chaners, all human intentions are forever set within a framework of cosmic, and particularly moral, unpredictabilities." [28] This does not mean that everything is unpredictable, but rather that much of the universe is thought to operate capriciously, with the extent of unpredictability depending on the individual's education and experiences.

BEHAVIORAL ASPECTS OF THE "CAPRICIOUS UNIVERSE"

The social environment impinges upon the individual mainly by providing the contingencies of his activities. In a systematic universe these contingencies can be predicted, and much of the individual's environment in effect can be controlled by him. Conversely, *the essence of the conception of a capricious universe is man's inability to predict and control the contingencies of his actions.* In this case the relationship between a person's behavior and the consequences originating in the environment takes one of two major forms. First, the consequences of any behavior are distributed more or less randomly and have no logical or other connection with the preceding activity. Spirits, gods, natural forces, and various agencies of "fate" intervene between action and contingency, so that any consequence—good or bad—is the result of capriciously operating phenomena rather than of the individual's preceding action:

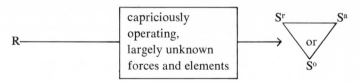

27. Hendry (1964:263).
28. Phillips (1965:80).

Second, the consequences of action are viewed as being essentially pre-determined and unchangeable, so that alterations in behavior will have little if any effect on the contingency. In this case the consequences are predictable, but since they are essentially independent of the preceding action they cannot be controlled either. Spirits, forces, etc. again may be assumed to operate, this time in conjunction with the individual; however, it is these capriciously operating forces, much more so than men, which are responsible for the contingency:

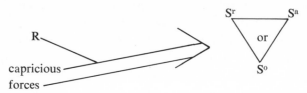

Foster, for example, notes that in many peasant villages it is commonly believed "that any kind of success and progress is due to fate, the favor of deities, to luck, but not to hard work, energy, and thrift." [29] A man realizes that he must grow crops in order to eat, but he also knows that, no matter how hard he works, it is likely that only an "average" harvest will result.

When one assumes that there is no relationship between behavior and contingency, or when the relationship is viewed as one in which changes in behavior do not result in commensurate alterations of the consequence (because of some powerful "intervening" factor), it is quite logical that one should rely on "luck" and/or the operation of these "intervening" factors. Behavior consistent with the second alternative is usually labeled "fatalism." In addition, it makes little sense to plan for the future, or even to look ahead at all.

When the individual faces an environment not amenable to control, when he cannot modify its operation by means of his behavior, and when he cannot count on many rewards emanating from his interactions with the social context, activities, words, and thoughts expressing "apathy," "hopelessness," and "despair" are among the probable results. According to Bandura, attitudes such as hopelessness, and general views of man-and-universe such as despair, are in large part the consequences of life experiences characterized by a very low rate of reinforcement. When

29. Foster (1965:307).

one encounters few rewards in life no matter how hard one tries or what one attempts to do, self-depreciation and negative definitions of life are quite logical. Such an outlook usually does not lead to behavior patterns that have a high probability of objective "success," thus reinforcing the negative outlook on life by the continuation of failures. Peasants and many other groups in developing nations, by virtue of the combination of their own behavior deficits (such as limited social and mechanical skills) with a rigid social environment and the view of a capricious universe, cannot be expected to have a future- or action-oriented philosophy. Yet, while activities associated with economic growth will not be common in these circumstances, there is hope. The behavioral model of man indicates that *self-definitions, world views, and the resulting activities will be modified if the social structure is altered so as to provide a higher rate and probability of reinforcement.*

SOURCES OF THE "CAPRICIOUS UNIVERSE" CONCEPTION

The belief that the universe is capricious is acquired in one of two major ways. First, one may learn an already articulated belief from others, in the form of stories, proverbs, or explicit propositions. Second, one may conclude from one's own and others' experiences that the universe is capricious. The first source—as a given cultural element—presents the student of economic development with little difficulty, and will not be treated here in detail. The second source—youthful and adult experiences and observations—is more difficult to analyze and therefore will be emphasized here.

In the following discussion it must be remembered that although there is mention of "peasants" and "villages," there is no implication that *all* peasants or villages necessarily have similar characteristics. The phenomena described below are likely to produce the conception of a "capricious universe," consequently it is only in villages with roughly these characteristics that the conception of a capricious universe will be prevalent. In order to determine the world view of men in a particular village, district, or nation, therefore, one should not generalize from other areas but investigate the behavior of the particular population.

For purposes of a causal analysis, man's experiences fall into three major groups: the socialization procedures together with the principles which are taught to children; daily confrontations with the physical environment, including agriculture, natural phenomena, and demographic characteristics such as infant mortality; and later experiences with others, especially men's reactions—often merely presumed—to one's behavior.

Socialization Procedures. In accordance with the behavioral perspective, it is hypothesized that the conception of a capricious universe is the result of a person's generalization from many of his experiences, especially those concerning the contingencies of his various childhood activities. Inconsistent parental reactions, described by a number of students of peasant villages, are the major source of the view that the universe is capricious. When parental actions cannot be predicted and controlled by the child, such uncertainty is likely to be generalized to other areas. In the Italian village of Montegrano for example, children are punished when they are naughty—and even when they are not. Parents and teachers believe that occasional blows lead to refinement and improve character, and thus children are often beaten regardless of what they have done.[30]

In a family where the father is considered the major authority, it is especially his behavior toward children that is likely to affect their views of the world. In Erongarícuaro, Mexico, for example, children consider both God and father as extremely powerful. "God, by His power, commands respect. Whatever His action, however capricious it may seem, He is entitled to it, because of this power. . . . In human families, the father-husband plays much the same role as God; he is remote (almost always psychologically, and often physically as well), all-powerful within the realm he dominates, capricious and owed obedience, however willful his comportment may be. . . . Both with respect to God and the father-husband, emotional security derives from submission to the superior will, through passive acceptance of what is decreed." [31]

Lewis's recording of the life stories of Jesús Sánchez's children provides a poignant illustration of how the conception of a capricious universe is established. The father gave little and inconsistent affection to his children and often browbeat his sons for no apparent reason. For example, in the words of Manuel, during a family meal "I was about to take a gulp of coffee when I turned to look at my father. 'Just to see you bastards swallow gives me pain, yes just to see you swallow.' We hadn't done anything, yet that is the way he spoke to us." [32] An isolated incident

30. Banfield (1958:155–57).
31. Nelson (1967:58).
32. Lewis (1961:28).

is not significant, of course, but when much of a person's early life consists of such events, where he cannot predict or control the reactions of others, it is likely that he will generalize from his experiences to life in general. Similar events also occurred frequently in the life of Manuel's brother, Roberto. For example, the boy was never able to understand why his sisters and step mother told his father lies about him, or why the father believed them and punished him. The boys became suspicious, trusted no one but each other and one or two friends, and found that behavior congruent with these views of man and the universe was rewarded, at least in the sense of preventing exploitation and ridicule by others.

One of the most anomic communities that has ever been described is Montegrano. Banfield's summary of child-raising practices illustrates one important cause for this state of affairs; he emphasizes

> the reliance upon blows to direct behavior and the capricious manner in which punishment is given. Punishment, it has been noted, is unrelated to any principle of "oughtness"; at one moment the parent kisses and at the next he cuffs. If gratification and deprivation—"good" and "bad"—depend upon the caprice of one who has power, no general principles can be internalized as conscience. The individual may try to propitiate the power holder, but he will not be surprised if his efforts fail and he receives ill when he deserves good. To receive ill will be "bad fortune" and to receive good will be "good fortune." Neither, of course, will have any relation to principle.[33]

It is clear from Banfield's further description that the child's peers, his relatives, and the adults with whom he comes into contact behave so as to make generalizations from his parents' capricious actions not only easy but useful.

Conceptions of the universe, usually established in childhood, do not necessarily remain the same throughout life. Whether or not childhood experiences are significant for the adult's world view depends on the events of later years. The fact that behavior patterns learned by children are usually repeated in later life does not mean that behavior is "deeply ingrained"; rather, it reflects the fact that the contingencies emanating

33. Banfield (1958:161).

from the social context have changed little over the decades, thus maintaining "old" activities.

The Social Environment. Many observers of peasants have commented upon the mutual distrust, caution, and reserve that characterize the social relations of daily life.[34] However while it appears that peasants are generally individualistic and suspicious, not all of life has such a tenor; the Thai, for example, "does not feel that distrust of this variety at all precludes reaping the rewards of relaxed and enjoyable association with the objects of his suspicion." [35] There are few if any group activities, for "traditional peasant societies are cooperative only in the sense of honoring reciprocal obligations, rather than in the sense of understanding total community welfare, and . . . mutual suspicion seriously limits cooperative approaches to village problems." [36] According to Banfield, for example, "As the Montegranesi see it, friends and neighbors are not only potentially costly but potentially dangerous as well. . . . Friends are luxuries that the Montegranesi feel they cannot afford." [37] "In Tzintzuntzan, as in the Italy and the India described by Banfield and Dube, envy is a dominant note in people's character. To see others gain an advantage reminds one of his own scant resources, his unfulfilled hopes, or his habitual bad luck." [38] Fear of others' envy, in turn, leads to secrecy as the primary means of defense; and since men are generally aware of their own and other people's secrecy, they suspect that others have more than is apparent. Thus it is that envy, fear, secrecy, and suspicion form a vicious circle which underlies much if not most of the social interaction of villagers. Finally, the actions of officials—both local and regional—are not seen as being consistent, in the interest of the community or oneself, or amenable to control.

At first glance it appears that a basic characteristic of the social environment is its predictability—often a villager can predict that his fellows are envious and hence dangerous, that they will not co-operate except in terms of strict reciprocity, and so forth. Yet the fact that some people are more successful than others, in terms of any number of criteria, indicates to the peasant not only that there is "luck," but that this

34. For good summaries, see Foster (1960), Lopreato (1967:chapter 4); a good example of an individual case is provided by Guiteras-Holmes (1961).

35. Piker (1966:1204).

36. Foster (1965:308).

37. Banfield (1958:121).

38. Foster (1967:153).

luck often involves the operation of the social environment—as when an official is favorably disposed toward his friends or when one can surreptitiously exploit one's fellow villagers.

The social environment, then, is at times predictable; but to the extent to which predictions concerning the behavior of others can be made, it is usually negative consequences, or at least the absence of reinforcing contingencies, which can be expected. It is logical, therefore, that the peasant in this type of community will attempt to avoid those actions which would involve others' (usually negative) reactions, especially in vital areas of life. Only those men who are defined as trustworthy and whose reactions are on the whole positive and can be predicted on the basis of long and intimate association—usually meaning members of the immediate family—are likely to be sought out. A low rate of interaction, except for superficial relations in association with leisure or when dire necessity requires temporary reliance on others, reinforces both the peasant's view of the community and the resulting behavior patterns, mainly by avoiding the negative contingencies presumed to follow interaction. While it is possible that the peasant's predictions of aversive contingencies might be proven incorrect by his experiences, the very predictions are likely to prevent his having these experiences. Furthermore, the general suspiciousness of the village's population—that is, the common prediction of aversive contingencies—is unlikely to produce such (positive) experiences. The villagers' conceptions of one another's intentions and of the operation of the community, their predictions of others' reactions, and their own behavior patterns, thus form a morphostatic system. Slight deviations—for example one man's freely helping another—will in all likelihood be followed by corrections and a return to the previous state. In Montegrano, for example, those who are "friendly" or act "generously" are immediately suspected of ulterior motives and are rebuffed, subjected to malicious gossip, scorned, and rejected.

The Physical Environment. The lives of most peasants in developing nations are greatly affected by the limited amount of land available, the low productivity of the soil, a primitive technology including incomplete knowledge of modern agricultural principles, and limited information concerning the operation of natural phenomena. As Foster says, "in the traditional peasant society hard work and thrift are moral qualities of only the slightest functional value. Given the limitations of land and technology, additional hard work in village productive enterprises simply does not produce a significant increment in income. It is pointless to talk of thrift in a subsistence economy in which most producers are at the economic margin; there is usually nothing to be thrifty about." [39] The farmer knows the best time for planting, of course; he is able to work the soil, and knows how much of the crop must be set aside for next year's seeds. Yet droughts parch his crops, animals invade his fields and consume his harvest, floods rage over his land, and soil washes away. None of these events can be predicted, and few if any effective measures can be taken. All in all, there is little he can do to assure a successful harvest. A peasant may do all he can to produce a good crop—and see all his efforts come to naught while his neighbor may be spared any misfortune. Even appeals to divine protection or the intervention of benevolent spirits is likely to be insufficient because these beings often are considered to be capricious themselves.

In addition, the sudden death of men and animals surrounds the peasant throughout the year. A large proportion of children die, often from one day to the next, and few men reach old age. Death cannot be predicted, and disease cannot be controlled. As Banfield so aptly says, "To be a peasant is to stand helpless before these possibilities." [40]

The nonhuman evironment, in short, reinforces the peasant's learned conception of a universe whose operation is capricious and cannot be understood, against whose forces man is essentially powerless. "When God wards off calamity, ability and initiative count for something. . . . But since one cannot know in advance whether God will intervene or not, life is no less a gamble than if He did not exist or never intervened." [41]

Conclusion. Child-raising practices and many experiences of youth, the operation of the later social context, the conception of a capricious universe, and the limitations presented by the physical environment, constitute a system whose internal test parameter is the efficacy of the behavior patterns derived from the world view (Figure 8-1). Daily life in small, relatively isolated, agricultural villages [42] is likely to verify the world view a man has acquired in youth, in the sense that predictions and behavior in accordance with it are reinforced. Consequently, when he himself raises children, he will probably pass on the information con-

39. Foster (1965:307).
40. Banfield (1958:64).
41. Ibid. p. 113.
42. As described, for example, by Lewis (1964).

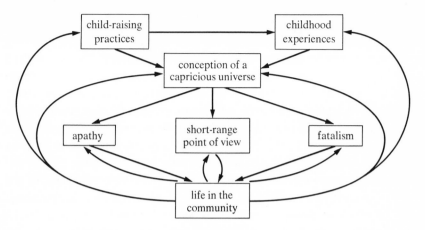

FIGURE 8–1: The Capricious Universe

cerning life and the universe which he has found to be useful and correct. He will repeat the stories, proverbs, and personal experiences which constitute his practical wisdom, leading to the replication of world view—and behavior—over the generations.

Theoretically, the subsytem formed by the individual, his world view, his behavior patterns, and the reactions of others in the community will continue its operation until external conditions change to such an extent that the internal test parameter—for example a "reasonably good life"— is no longer met. This may occur because the old activities and conceptions no longer work, or because definitions of "reasonably good" are changed as rising expectations result from the community's increasing contracts with the outside world. However, *in order for the system to change, the divergence from expectations must be obvious, consistent, and lasting*—something that is not characteristic of life in agricultural communities, as illustrated by the experiences of "Pedro Martinez." [43] The unfulfilled promises of the Mexican revolution (in his view), together with the limitations imposed by the social and ecological characteristics of the village, led him to lower his definitions of a "good life" as he grew older. Here the "old" subsystem was maintained because the internal test parameters changed until they were congruent with the system's operation.

43. Ibid. The life of "Pedro Martinez" is a perfect illustration of the interplay of world view and personal experience, the fate of ideals and dreams in the harsh realities of peasant life in Tepoztlan, and the transmission of at least the essence of a father's world view to his children.

THE "CAPRICIOUS UNIVERSE" AND ECONOMIC DEVELOPMENT

The conception of a capricious universe is involved in the shaping and maintenance of several activities associated with economic development. In this section, only two major behavior patterns will be briefly considered. Activities labelled "co-operation," and the component "long-range point of view" found in many actions, are generally considered to be among the important behavioral prerequisites and concomitants of industrialization. Conversely, their absence makes economic growth difficult; thus in communities and nations where these elements do not exist, steps may well have to be taken to create these prerequisites if development programs are to have a reasonable chance of success.

Co-operation. The term "co-operation" is the summary expression of a set of activities of a number of persons in a situation where the contingencies are structured so that the reinforcement of any one individual's behavior will depend in large part on the synchronized activities of all. Such a "structure" and "synchronized activities" may be the result of deliberate human planning—for example incentives in a factory—or they may arise from technological and ecological parameters—for example the requirements of agriculture and complex machinery.

There is general agreement not only that co-operation is necessary for economic development, but also that there is very little co-operation in most peasant communities. While villagers help each other on occasion and during emergencies, such co-operation usually has a personal basis and a specific project as its frame of reference. On the whole, villages in developing nations appear to be characterized by little identification of peasants with the community or nation; Hendry, for example, remarks on the "surprisingly individualistic cast to many attitudes, given the communal organization that has characterized village life in north and central Vietnam." [44] And Geertz writes that "what has developed, consequently, is not so much a general spirit of cooperativeness—Javanese peasants tend, like many peasants, to be rather suspicious of groups larger than the immediate family—but a set of explicit and concrete practices of exchange of labor, of capital, and of consumption goods which operate in all aspects of life." [45]

44. Hendry (1964:244).
45. Geertz (1962:244).

In terms of the behavioral perspective, the essential elements of co-operation are: a high probability that by working with and for others the individual will (eventually) be rewarded, and the individual's ability to predict the behavior of others.[46] Both elements depend on the conception of a systematic universe. In a capricious universe, the behavior of other men is predictable only to a limited extent (unless they are part of the family), and any work that is not of immediate benefit to oneself may *never* have positive consequences for the worker. Co-operation in specific periodic tasks, for example in the clearing of fields as described in the previous chapter, does provide some assurance of benefits; but nonrecurring and more amorphous projects—such as constructing a sewer system—especially when they are on such a large scale that the individual's part in them is quite small, often do not provide immediate, certain, and obvious benefits. The conception of a capricious universe, then, does not rule out all co-operation; rather, *such a world view restricts the variety, scope, and extent of co-operation and is likely to limit such endeavors to small projects and those persons whose activities are positive and can be predicted,* i.e. members of the family and a few other carefully selected individuals. As Banfield says, "The idea that one's welfare depends crucially upon conditions beyond one's control—upon luck or the caprice of a saint—and that one can at best only improve upon good fortune, not create it—this idea must certainly be a check on initiative. Its influence on economic life is obvious: one who lives in so capricious a world is not likely to save and invest in the expectation of ultimate gain. In politics, too, it must have an effect. Where everything depends upon luck or Divine intervention, there is no point in community action. The community, like the individual, may hope or pray, but it is not likely to take its destiny into its own hands."[47]

It should not be concluded, however, that co-operation in all areas of life and at all times is a prerequisite of economic growth. While *some degree* of co-operation is necessary, especially in tasks that are beyond the capacities of individuals, some degree of *individualism* is also required. Most alterations in communities and nations have been proposed and instituted by individuals who acted contrary to the ways of the rest

46. Azrin and Lindley (1956).
47. Banfield (1958:114). Such lack of control over the consequences of behavior also leads to low need achievement (McClelland and Winter, 1969).

of the population, and Levy's discussion of individualism in China and Japan [48] indicates that activities characterized as "individualism" were greatly influenced by the social structure and the contingencies it provided for men in certain positions, such as merchants.

The long-range point of view. In the discussion of saving and investing (Chapter Six) it was pointed out that the maintenance of these behavior patterns, like that of most others, requires a high probability of reinforcement. Since the wisdom of saving and the advantages of investment usually are not evident for some time, it is essential that the individual be able to accurately *predict* eventual reinforcement. Such predictions of the future rest heavily on the conception of a systematic universe, for in a capricious one the future is uncertain. Work in factories, too, depends on accurate predictions—in this case an adequate supply of food throughout the year.[49] Innovation and enterpreneurship are also dependent upon some modicum of predictability and thus regularity in the operation of the social system, for the rewards of innovation rarely accrue within a short period of time. As a final example, political stability and the legal exercise of power depend upon the conception of a regular and systematically operating political system. It is only when there is some assurance of future tests of policies and power—elections—that it makes sense to wait rather than conspire. In a capricious universe, conversely, political systems and ideologies cannot be trusted, and thus the stature and beliefs of a leader take on paramount importance—*personalismo* in Latin American politics. In short, many of the behavioral prerequisites and concomitants of economic development are based on a future-orientation and the assumption that future contingencies not only can be predicted but are also amenable to human intervention and control.

The long-range point of view, which is implicit in all of these actions, depends on the conception of a systematic universe. In a capricious universe where only a few elements are predictable or subject to human control, it makes no sense to plan for the future, or even to take the future into account beyond the basic agricultural cycle. The illustrations of various aspects of peasant life presented in the preceding sections provide abundant evidence of the peasant's emphasis on the here-and-now. This emphasis is not only the result of the conception of a capricious universe, but also of the fact that the long-range point of view must be

48. Levy (1962).
49. For a discussion of this problem, see Salz (1955).

learned. Psychological experiments indicate that behavior can be maintained even when the latency period (i.e. between behavior and contingency) is quite long, but they also show that men must *learn* to live with long latency periods, that men do not naturally or automatically operate in terms of long-term contingencies.[50] The analysis of child-raising practices, especially those involved in the creation of complex behavior patterns such as "responsibility," indicates that the community's economic organization and subsistence pattern act as important causal factors.[51] The problems encountered in shaping activities congruent with the requirements of the village economy, and by implication the activities associated with economic development but irrelevant in community life, are well described in Whiting's monumental cross-cultural study of child-rearing.[52] In addition, the characteristics of daily life, and especially the economic limitations imposed by tiny resources, make long-range planning impossible and the long-range point of view irrelevant. In Tzintzuntzan, for example, "the relative absence of planning and foresight are certainly due in part to the fact that people who normally live a hand-to-mouth existence have little opportunity to develop such skills. Yet this character trait also reflects a deep-seated feeling that the world about one is so capricious and uncertain that to plan ahead is to be presumptious, and very likely to contravene divine will. . . . Life can be lived with a minimum of foresight and since the best laid plans are apt to come to naught, this quality seems of slight value to people. Fate and chance are seen as much more significant factors determining what happens to one." [53]

The social system of small agricultural communities is maintained not only by simple technology and narrow ecological parameters, but also by the restricted perspectives and limited experiences of their inhabitants who know little of the outside world. If economic development implies the alteration of behavior, dynamic communities, and social change, it is not enough to inject money and technical knowledge into morphostatic community systems. The foregoing discussion of world view suggests that an additional requirement for social change and behavior modification is the provision of new and accurate information concerning life outside the

50. Schneider and Lysgaard (1953).
51. Barry, Child, and Bacon (1959), Kiray (1968).
52. Whiting (1963).
53. Foster (1967:115–16).

peasant village—its promises, systematic operations, and opportunities—to set the stage for new activities and contingencies.[54]

Communication

Information is the major link between social structure and the individual, and access to communications channels and availability of information reduce the uncertainties of a person's encounter with both the social and physical environments. In the small agricultural villages that are characteristic of developing nations, much of the information necessary for daily life is acquired by means of observation and personal experience. The average person who grows up in a peasant community is likely to have all the information required for the behavior patterns that constitute village life by the time he is in his teens. The problem is that much of the information concerning the nation and the world at large may be incorrect, and that it will necessarily reflect the experiences, perspectives, and beliefs of men in the community. Much of the peasant's existence, therefore, will still be characterized by uncertainty, especially when he ventures beyond the village. These uncertainties may come to be defined as normal aspects of, for example, the capricious universe, and thus the average peasant is not likely to seek additional information as long as the village and its surroundings do not change or as long as his definition of the "good life" is satisfied. To put it differently, no new information is required as long as the subsystem consisting of an individual, his behavior, and the reactions of others meets the internal test parameter of the "good life."

In the developing nations of today, however, these conditions do not exist except in the most isolated areas. Instead, additional information is likely to become available as part of national development efforts or to be required by men who struggle to adjust their lives to rapidly changing circumstances.

The spread of literacy and the development of mass media open communication channels and offer additional information to an increasing number of individuals. It is through communication that isolated villages and differentiated subcultures coalesce into nations, and that national definitions of state variables, discriminative and contingent stim-

54. Lerner and Schramm (1967).

uli replace the host of local variations.[55] As Deutsch has pointed out, nationalism is based on an efficient communications network, and it may be hypothesized that self-sustaining economic growth has the same foundation. In fact, nationalism provides individuals with new definitions of rewards and long-run schedules of reinforcement—such as temporary austerity programs—that can make significant contributions to the rate and probable success of economic development.[56]

By expanding an individual's horizon beyond the confines of his village and his own life, by establishing the city or nation as his reference group, and by providing specific information, various means of communication make it possible to add elements to, and perhaps even change, his world view.[57] Lerner has shown, for example, that mass media can produce changed contingencies and new deprivations even when the immediate social and physical environments remain the same: by acquainting young men with life in cities, the promises of the *nation,* and the opportunities in both, the frames of reference were changed from immediate village and neighborhood to distant city. Expressions of displeasure by village elders, formerly truly aversive, became much less important than the rewards of "keeping up" with national life.[58]

Communities caught up in a rapidly changing environment are usually confronted by changes in the effectiveness of "old" activities. For example, when a village becomes part of a national cash-based economy, the old ways of subsistence agriculture may no longer be reinforced as they were formerly; and when the infant mortality rate declines, the same behavior patterns which previously resulted in five teen-aged children now lead to nine. Since *new contingencies can lead to behavior modification only when information concerning behavioral alternatives is available,* developing nations must provide their people with the knowledge that is required for the performance of new activities, special skills, etc. Yet the mass media often are not concerned with such mundane matters,[59] and the alternative of special educational efforts is often inadequate. In short, the information that peasants require in order to adjust to both the

55. For some detailed discussions of this topic, see Deutsch (1953), Nash (1957), Pye (1962).

56. For a discussion of possible detrimental effects of nationalism, see Hoselitz (1956).

57. Pool (1963).

58. Lerner (1958)

59. For a summary of mass media in developing nations, see Pool (1963).

nation and its rapid rate of change is frequently insufficient in both amount and content.[60] Furthermore, the mere description of altered contingencies, the simple definition of new deprivations and reinforcers, and the possibility of new activities, usually are not enough to assure behavior modification. An additional requirement appears to be the intervention of "opinion leaders" or at least the discussion of new information among those most likely to be affected.[61] Since much of the information presented by the mass media is—in the eyes of the peasant—abstract, of doubtful validity, and provided by unknown men of unknown credibility, it is quite logical that discussions with friends, family members, and respected men in the community should be as important for the ultimate acceptance of information as the objective content of the message itself.[62]

When communication is restricted to information about new contingencies *only,* old behavior patterns are likely to be maintained because old deprivations will continue to be reduced by old contingencies. And when new deprivations are created by the mass media without the provision of new behavior patterns and information concerning the new associated reinforcers, activities characterized as anger, frustration, and unrest are the probable result. Even when communications are properly balanced in terms of goals and means, however, the problem of differential acceptance is likely to create difficulties.[63] A new definition of the "good life" apparently can be learned more easily and quickly than the often complex activities required to attain it, thus leading to the "new revolution of rising frustrations." [64] Furthermore, improved communication *among* nations has been responsible for the "demonstration effect," whereby men in developing countries become aware of certain "positive" aspects of urban-industrial life and exert pressure for the replication of these aspects in their own nations. All too often this cannot be done—given the social, political, and economic limitations—at a speed that is acceptable to those who have become aware of life beyond the sea.

The systems perspective leads to the conclusion that, while individuals may attempt to initiate change, no fundamental alterations in the village will occur unless and until the internal test parameters of the community —and not of the individual—either are not met or are defined to be

60. Dube (1967a).
61. Katz (1957).
62. Hovland and Weiss (1952), Katz and Lazarsfeld (1955). For an example of the problems and successes of communication, see Dube (1967b).
63. Schramm (1967).
64. Lerner (1963:330).

inadequate. An individual may provide the impetus for a re-evaluation of the community-system's internal test parameters, but until there is widespread dissatisfaction and a definite alternative—that is, recognition of the system's inadequate operation and the possibility of specific new procedures—it is not likely that the system will change. Rather, institutionalized envy or invidious sanctions—as experienced by those who attempted to innovate in Montegrano or Tepoztlán, for example—will be employed to bring errant individuals back into line. In fact, the tragedy of Pedro Martinez's odyssey lies in his repeated attempts and failures to live the "new good life" promised by the Mexican Revolution. The conditions leading to the widespread recognition that the old system is inadequate and that new alternatives are available depend on economic, social and cultural factors of which mass media appear to be only a small part. While individuals confronted by novel situations often can afford to experiment and to seek the right solution by trial and error, few social systems can afford these luxuries. A social system can make an adequate adjustment to a changing environment only if there is adequate information concerning behavioral, technological, and other alternatives. A communications network that provides a nation's subsystems with all of the information needed for the adjustment of these systems to the changes involved in economic development is therefore a fundamental requirement of any nation that seeks to remain a viable unit. Part of such a network consists of the mass media. Another part is made up of the many informal communication channels to which peasants are exposed as they begin to travel outside their communities. Education, finally, is increasingly being recognized as the major means for systematically providing villagers and others with the information required by life in a changing world.

Education

An individual acquires information necessary for the shaping and maintenance of activities associated with daily life in a number of ways. The most important sources of such information are:

a) the personal experiences of the individual;

b) the directly observed or otherwise known experiences of known, specific other persons;

c) the hearsay experiences of unknown others (e.g. what is reported to have happened to people in another community);

d) various proverbs, stories, myths, and fairy tales (whose "moral" concerns the probable or theoretical contingencies of various actions);

e) historical knowledge—or, more specifically, what is said to have happened in the past;

f) specific statements concerning a community's or society's ideal values and operating norms, and the deliberate presentation of specialized skills.

In isolated, small agricultural villages without educational facilities, most information will probably come from the first four sources, and little historical knowledge and few specific statements or skills will be available —or even necessary. While information will be consistent, it is likely to be rather restricted—sufficient for ordinary daily life but not enough to dispel the uncertainties confronting the individual who ventures outside the village or who faces extraordinary decisions within it.

As was pointed out above, economic development is furthered by the dissemination of accurate information concerning the required new activities and associated contingencies. The first four sources of information often result in partial and incorrect knowledge concerning the operation of social structures outside the village, because the individual not only has to interpret information and abstract "principles" from his and others' experiences, but he also has little opportunity to verify the knowledge thus gained except in the restricted context of the community. Education, by making additional information, new activities, and specialized skills available, is therefore a significant element in any attempt to foster growth.

With the coming of schools the importance of the last two sources is greatly increased. An almost built-in problem of inconsistency arises, however, for educational institutions usually present the ideal values of a society and those operating norms which, on the national level, correspond to them. Local variations, and especially the subcultural norms derived from the villagers' personal experiences, often are not taken into account. In addition, schools usually present up-to-date information while the word-of-mouth conventional wisdom of peasants represent knowledge of the past that may no longer be relevant. Finally, the specialized skills that are offered may reflect abstract administrative policies rather than concrete local requirements.[65]

Ideally, formal education is the source of accurate, direct information

65. For a description of these problems, see Anderson (1963).

concerning presently operating (and future) discriminative and contingent stimuli of specific new and old behavior patterns. Furthermore, education contributes to the creation of new secondary state variables, especially material deprivations. In this way new types of "rewards" and "punishment" are defined, and new nonlocal reference groups for the dispensing of them are established. Most important, education is the source of information and skills which may be used in relating more effectively to the environment. Knowledge and utilization of new agricultural methods are reinforced when production increases; literacy and knowledge of arithmetic are rewarded when the peasant is no longer cheated in his transactions with merchants. For the individual, *the utility of education lies in the successful manipulation of the environment,* no matter what the criteria of such success may be. Poorly trained teachers, inadequate methods, and irrelevant information cannot help but be aversive for both parents and children. Resistance to education, thus, is due more to the structure of contingencies than to "apathy," as illustrated by the rapid changes in Vicos.

The major advantages of education over the other sources of information are not only that it reduces inadequate information, uncertainty, misinformation, and the amount of time necessary to acquire *any* information or skill, but also that it makes available knowledge and behavior outside the individual's purview and experience. The conception of a capricious universe, for example, can be modified in spite of the fact that daily life in a community appears to be congruent with it, for education may provide a youth with information concerning the principles of national and regional governments, ideals of justice, the operation of economic systems, law, etc. The study of national and regional history as a series of interrelated events, with a more or less logical sequence of human activities and governmental, economic, and political forms, would help the individual gain the conception of a systematic universe and a lengthened time perspective.

Within the community-system, education is the source not only of more effective means for relating the system to its environment, but also of new internal test parameters. Either contribution can change the structure and operation of the system, and thus it is unlikely that communities with well functioning schools will remain static.

It should not be concluded that the mere introduction of a school into a peasant community, or the establishment of educational institutions in a society, will automatically bring about the shaping of behavior patterns consonant with national values and norms or economic requirements. If the major purpose of education is the shaping of such activities by establishing the associated state variables, discriminative and contingent stimuli, then the best measure of the efficacy of educational efforts is the modification of students' behavior (including verbal statements of what they know). The effectiveness of education is reduced by a number of conditions which are quite frequent in large parts of developing nations.

First, educational efforts are limited by the discrepancy between the individual's everyday experiences (including the deductions and inferences he derived from them) and the information and skills presented by education. More specifically, the effectiveness of education may be expected to vary with the magnitude of the discrepancies and the perceived utility of new skills, the frequency with which the discrepancies are apparent to a person, and the nature of the discrepancies. Of special importance are the inconsistencies which may exist within the system of abstract principles itself, for example the conflicts among national norms and values.

Since an individual may misinterpret his experiences or draw the wrong inferences from them, information presented by schools may conflict with the incorrect interpretations rather than with the experience itself. Some discrepancies may be largely imaginary, therefore, and can be eliminated with relative ease.

The efficacy of educational efforts is reduced by the empirical demonstration (or what passes for this) that information and skills presented by education are invalid or do not apply in a particular situation. Abstract, national ideals of justice, for example, may clash with daily evidence that there is considerable local injustice. The mere presentation of information and skills, then, is not enough; both must be integrated into daily life in the sense that their efficacy must be exclusively demonstrated— not to the educated teacher or administrator but to the students and their parents.

Second, the success of schools is dependent upon the actual and perceived ability to successfully manipulate the physical and social environment. If the acquistion of new information—for example literacy—is not reinforced, few children will continue to attend school and few parents will continue to send them. The major problem here is the time lag inherent in any educational effort. Although some of the information presented in schools is of immediate relevance and can be used within a short period of time, thus leading to the immediate reinforcement of the individual's efforts, many results of schooling do not become apparent until considerable time has passed. In fact, the time between the learning of abstract principles and the moment of their potentially successful use may be so long that the association between the two phenomena is lost.

The heterogeneity of developing nations is reflected in the local variants of these problems, and thus it may be hypothesized that a high degree of local autonomy in the planning and execution of curricula will be beneficial.[66] Even when this is possible and the most effective teaching methods are employed, financial limitations and political considerations are likely to reduce the effectiveness of educational efforts. Moreira points out, for example, that "to receive the minimum education required to cope with the exigencies of a modern society, children need to attend school from 7 to 14 years of age. None of the Latin American countries reaches this minimum standard." [67] The complex relationships between education and economic development have been investigated both statistically [68] and historically,[69] yet it cannot be concluded that education is a sufficient condition for economic growth. According to Vaizey, "only rarely, historically speaking, has education been concerned with developing what may very broadly be called a 'scientific' or pragmatic attitude to life." [70] In short, it is not "education" as such that is important in economic development, but rather certain *types* of education, curricula, and schools.[71]

Conclusion

When a peasant community is the frame of reference, both communication and education are external causes of change; villagers

66. Ibid.
67. Moreira (1963:308).
68. For example by McClelland (1966).
69. For examples see Anderson and Bowman (1965).
70. Vaizey (1962:41).
71. For a summary of current controversies and problems of planning education programs, see Higgins (1968:chapter 19). For illustrations of the need for specialized educational efforts and the problems associated with their implementation in particular nations, see Levine (1965) for Ethiopia, Jayasuriya (1968) for Ceylon, and McQueen (1968) for West Africa. For an example of how social structure affects educational institutions, see Harbison and Myers (1964), Moore (1963b), and the papers collected in Parnes (1962).

learn new deprivations from the mass media, for example, and new behavior patterns are taught in the schools. It should not be assumed, however, that the impetus for change is always provided by elements extraneous to the system. When the *nation* is the frame of reference in a development analysis, many aspects of economic growth, such as entrepreneurs, originate within the social system. Indeed, even in peasant villages, communication provides little more than new information. Whether the new ideas and activities are accepted or rejected, and the use to which they are put, will depend on the characteristics of the village. Internal causes of change, therefore, whether in the form of invention or the acceptance and use of outside information, are important aspects of economic development. The following chapter outlines a behavioral approach to this topic.

ix The Conditions

of Behavior Change

Economic growth does not simply "occur," and urban-industrial societies do not come into being fully-blown. Rather, industrialization has a "beginning"—though this is often difficult to specify—and urban-industrial societies can be traced back to a number of sources—though these are often difficult to ascertain. Among the elements which constitute the foundation of economic development are technological improvements and the resulting changes in ecological limitations, inventions and the diffusion of various cultural elements, the establishment and growth of secondary industry, the development of a wage labor force, and the expansion of markets for manufactured goods. All of these elements, however, *operate through men,* and in fact cannot be analyzed except in terms of human actions. It is men who use tools, make inventions, accept or reject new elements, organize and run factories, work with machines and buy their products.

Economic development implies, among other things, that certain behavior patterns and social relations are changed in a particular direction. The question of how and why activities change—not randomly but in a more or less orderly fashion culminating in self-sustaining economic *growth*—is answered best by the analysis of two related phenomena: be-

249

havioral deviation from existing patterns, and behavioral innovation that produces enduring new patterns.

Deviation

The deviation of behavior from what the average person considers to be "normal" is a significant aspect of any complex social system and has received considerable attention from a number of sociologists.[1] Economic development is not concerned with crime and drug addiction, of course, but it may be postulated that manual labor and entrepreneurship in a society where these activities are defined as deviant involve the operation of similar factors and conditions. Behavioral deviation is a matter of degree and may be conceived as being part of a continuum that ranges from conformity through temporary variants and enduring variants to deviation. Variants are *"new* forms of behavior that are well within the range of the institutionally prescribed or allowed [limitations]," [2] and while such activities are not followed by negative sanctions, less than enthusiastic approbation is usually associated with them. Behavioral deviation, however, means that activities clearly fall outside the normative limitations of "acceptability," and thus are followed by negative sanctions or would be if these activities were known. The new behavior patterns associated with economic development may be simply variants—in which case they are relatively easily established—or they may be actually deviant and consequently more difficult to shape. One of the tasks of development analysis, therefore, is to ascertain the normative parameters of activities in a community or subculture in order to establish whether the specific behavioral requisites of industrialization would fall within the limits of "acceptability" as defined in particular communities, subcultures, and nations.

DEVIATION AND ECONOMIC DEVELOPMENT

Traditional societies as described by anthropologists and others are characterized by few of the behavior patterns required for and associated with economic growth.[3] And it may be concluded from evidence presented

1. For example Becker (1963), Dubin (1959), Merton (1957b, 1959).
2. Merton (1959:181); italics are in the original.
3. For examples of descriptions, see Cottrell (1955), Foster (1965), Lerner (1958), and Redfield (1941).

in the previous chapter that many communities in developing nations are unlikely to undergo significant change until widespread behavioral alterations occur. Students of development have discussed prerequisites of industrialization and behavior patterns which form the foundation of economic growth, and while their theoretical frameworks differ, there is considerable agreement.[4] Manual labor, entrepreneurship, hard and systematic work, saving and investing, the production of surplus food, factory employment, and the acceptance of new ideas and techniques, are some of the most important specific activities. Among the more amorphous actions and general behavioral characteristics are the elimination of nepotism, and reacting to others as role performers rather than as individuals. All of these activities are initially deviant actions, and thus deviation from established behavior patterns, commonly accepted norms, and generally held beliefs is part of the foundation of economic development.

Deviation does not necessarily mean the wholesale overturning of established ideals and ways; rather, it means that there occurs a selective alteration of behavior, by certain individuals with specific characteristics, in particular circumstances and at certain times. Activities associated with entrepreneurship, for example, do not develop randomly but rather in specific groups and situations, as shown below. The question arises, therefore, under what conditions deviation is likely to occur.

BEHAVIORAL ASPECTS OF DEVIATION

When analysis focuses on one person, his behavior may be said to simply "change"; it is only when the person is considered as a member of a group, and others' actions are taken as a standard of comparison, that behavior change can be characterized as "deviation." [5] The conditions producing deviation, then, are those which lead to:

a) the extinction of some actions in certain individuals;

b) the shaping and maintenance of new activities in some persons; and

c) the maintenance of old behavior patterns in most other members of the group, community, subculture, or nation.

Part of the explanation of deviance consists of the learning principles discussed in Chapter Three. However, since these principles indicate only very general relationships, additional factors are required, chief among

4. For an example of such a list, see Moore (1963b).
5. For a discussion of this aspect of deviance, see Becker (1963).

them the contingencies of various actions. The behavioral components of deviation, then, may be considered as the following:

a) aversive contingencies, or other lack of reinforcement, associated with certain activities of particular persons;

b) the availability and reinforcement of new behavior patterns for some individuals;

c) the continued reinforcement of old activities performed by large segments of the population.

Changes in contingencies occur in two major ways: the actual and perceived reinforcing and aversive stimuli are altered, or state variables change so that "old" contingencies no longer have reinforcing or aversive properties. The reinforcement of new and initially deviant behavior patterns is complex enough to warrant additional comments. The deviant act may be rewarded directly, either by other persons or by the successful completion of the act itself. Thus, when a boy steals an apple and is not caught, the tasty fruit in effect reinforces stealing. The deviant act may also be reinforced indirectly, as when the individual's friends and relatives continue to "accept" him in spite of his new activities. DeLamater [6] describes the important role of continued primary group contacts for the deviant and points out that the occurrence of completely isolated deviants is extremely rare. It must be remembered, here, that "reinforcement" is subcultural and not necessarily defined in terms of community-wide criteria. Thus criminal activities are often rewarding for the criminal, and entrepreneurial activities may (and often do) appear to be immoral and reprehensible to tradition-oriented peasants.

When a time perspective and population cohorts are added to the analysis—as they must be in any treatment of long-term processess—it is necessary to distinguish two basic types of deviation. First, there are the individuals who learned the commonly-accepted behavior patterns of their society, but *who later altered their actions*. For these men, the original state variables, discriminative or contingent stimuli changed. But if they encounter no reinforcing contingencies in the old social context—or do not foresee any—they will either revert to the old activities or move to new environments where new reinforcers are provided or can be expected. Such a movement is especially likely when deviant behavior in one area of life leads to negative responses on the part of others to the whole spectrum of daily activities, when deviants are exposed to general strictures, or when they are shunned by most or all of their fellows. Con-

6. DeLamater (1968).

versely, when there are several deviants in the community, or when the individual has knowledge of other deviants in other places, the movement may be symbolic rather than actual, such as the establishment of closer ties with these individuals—especially in the form of mutual reinforcement for deviant activities. As yet research does not provide a firm basis for generalizations concerning the establishment of "original" deviant activities.[7] All that can be said is that the conditions giving rise to deviation are complex and involve a number of variables beyond the control of the persons concerned, such as the community's norms, the labeling of deviance by others, and systematic reactions to deviants. Since many of the contingencies of original deviation are usually considered to be aversive and are to a large extent predictable, the probability of "original deviation" is quite low, especially in peasant communities characterized by the elements described in the previous chapter.

The second type of deviant is the individual who grew up in previously deviant families or subcultures and who learned to behave in ways defined as "deviant" by other subcultures or the dominant society. For this person the state variables and the discriminative and contingent stimuli did not necessarily change over time. Furthermore, he will encounter fewer difficulties in the expression of his deviant activities since he is already part of a deviant family or subculture—in fact, he may not even see himself as a deviant. His behavior may not be reinforced by the larger society, but it will meet the approval—and perhaps even the requirement—of his reference group. As a member of a deviant group, moreover, the person is likely to be somewhat insulated from many of the aversive contingencies provided by the dominant society, and is almost guaranteed rewards for a wide range of "deviant" actions. The probability of deviant activities being learned and repeated in this context, then, is quite high.

Since the second type of deviant can occur only after some original deviants have established themselves, development analysis must concentrate on the first type. The opportunities for deviance, the consequences, and the situations in which deviance is likely, proper, or unlikely, are provided by various characteristics of the social structure.

SOCIOLOGICAL ASPECTS OF DEVIATION

Deviance implies that the contingencies of *some* actions change while those of others remain the same, and that *some* people are exposed to altered or entirely new contingencies, while others are not. Differentials

7. Rogers (1962).

in the consequences of behavior, state variables, and discriminative stimuli determine *which* actions will be maintained or replaced by "deviant" behavior, *which* new activities will be maintained, and *which* persons are likely to be involved.

Questions concerning the sources of changed and differentially operating discriminative and contingent stimuli have been investigated by a number of sociologists. The best-known exposition concerning the relationship between social structure and deviance has been provided by Merton.[8] The original formulation has been improved—for example by Dubin[9]—and various elements have been added, for example by Cloward,[10] DeLamater[11] and Merton himself.[12] Merton postulates that in any society there are goals and legitimate means for their attainment. He assumes that men direct many of their activities toward the fulfillment of goals as defined by their society within the limitations of legitimacy (also as defined by their society). In behavioral terms, goals are the reinforcers (and by implication the deprivations) in terms of which men act, while legitimate means refer to certain sets of activities which theoretically are followed by the attainment of goals, or reinforcement. While goals and means may be congruent, that is, the employment of legitimate means may lead to goals, or $R \longrightarrow S^r$, this is not always true. Especially in complex, heterogeneous societies the congruency of goals and means is a matter of degree, and for many individuals behavior patterns labeled "legitimate" are not rewarded. When this occurs frequently, the individual is likely to attempt new or different activities, depending on his knowledge of alternatives and the opportunities for their expression. While many of these may be "legitimate," other activities may be labeled "deviant." Individuals who are not aware of behavioral alternatives, or who consider "failure" to be less aversive than the punishment they predict for the expression of "illegitimate" activities, are likely to continue behaving in the old way.

The *probability of deviant behavior* is dependent upon "the extent of dissociation between, on the one hand, the cultural goals and institutional norms men accept as binding, and on the other, the social position or situation in which they find themselves, making it relatively difficult or easy for them to live in accord with these goals and norms. The greater

8. Merton (1957b).
9. Dubin (1959).
10. Cloward (1959).
11. DeLamater (1968).
12. Merton (1959).

the dissociation between cultural values and the facilities provided by a social position, the greater the pressure for deviation." [13] The lower the perceived probability of reinforcement, the smaller the probability that the "old" activities will be repeated, and the greater the probability that "new" behavior patterns (which *may* be labeled "deviant") will be tried out. In complex, heterogeneous societies such trials may be rewarded, or at least are not likely to be punished, and thus the probability of their being established is quite high. In small agricultural communities, conversely, the probability of deviant behavior occurring and being established will be relatively low. The *amount of deviant behavior* in a society depends on the number of individuals who cannot reach commonly defined and accepted success-goals through legitimate means, the number of such activities that are not reinforced by eventual success, and, most important, the probability that deviant behavior will be reinforced, or at least not be punished.

Since there are many different kinds of deviance, development analysis requires additional information concerning the selection of deviant activities. It is likely that a person's values and his subculture's norms channel deviant behavior; for example, "the 'rule-oriented' accent in middle-class socialization presumably disposes persons to handle stress by engaging in ritualistic rather than innovating behavior." [14] A further element affecting choice is the availability of illegitimate means, for the individual must not only *learn* specific deviant activities but also have occasions to *express* them. Yet the opportunities to acquire and employ various illegitimate means (successfully) are limited and depend on the individual's position in the social structure.[15]

Deviation from "normal" activities, as defined by members of various groups, subcultures, or the society at large, can take a number of different forms, such as ritualism, apathy, or various types of crime. In the analysis of economic development it is especially one kind of deviation—broadly labeled "innovation"—that is significant.

Innovation

In the elaborate typologies of deviant behavior developed by sociologists, innovation is only one—and usually a minor—aspect of

13. Merton (1959:187).
14. Cloward (1959:167).
15. Cloward (1959).

deviance. However, innovation has been postulated to be a major source of social change [16] and industrialization,[17] and thus a more detailed discussion of the topic is required.

BEHAVIORAL ASPECTS OF INNOVATION

In order to specify the role of innovation in economic development, the characteristics of the phenomenon must be indicated first. The essence of innovation is, in the area of materiél, the novel combination of existing elements and/or the invention of new elements. In the behavioral area, innovation is the extension of "old" activities into new directions, and/or the expression of new activities. Innovations are not alike, however, and it is the diversity of their characteristics that is in part responsible for the differential rates of acceptance and rejection even in superficially similar circumstances. Rogers [18] considers five aspects to be of special significance, as *perceived* by members of the group that is the frame of reference in any particular analysis: a) the *relative advantage* of the innovation when compared with existing tools or activities; b) the *compatibility* of the innovation with individuals' values and past experiences; c) the complexity of the innovation; d) the *divisibility* of the innovation which determines whether various parts can be tried out first; and e) the *communicability* of the innovation, that is, the ease with which both the essentials and the results of the novelty can be transmitted from one person to the next. New seeds are an innovation with a certain constellation of characteristics, while Protestantism is quite a different constellation. The acceptance or rejection of an innovation depends in large part on the specific combination of these perceived characteristics.

Even the terms "old" and "new" must be applied with caution, for their meaning depends on the context and the observer's perspective, and any explanation of "new" behavioral or material elements requires the prior delineation of the context. A new activity in a village, for example, may not be an innovation but simply the diffusion of patterns common in the larger society. In this case the question would not be: "what caused José to create the new activity?" but rather "why did José adopt the behavior patterns of people in the outside world?" Such specification of the context is important since both the questions and their answers are di-

16. Barnett (1953), LaPiere (1965).
17. Hagen (1962), McClelland (1961).
18. Rogers (1962:chapter 5).

rected and limited by it. Furthermore, "creativity" is as yet not well understood, while "adoption" and "rejection" can be investigated and explained much more readily.[19]

The process of creativity is usually analyzed in terms of individualistic, internal characteristics, and the hypotheses currently available raise many questions which cannot be answered by today's procedures. Hagen, for example, views creativity as consisting of: being open to novel experiences, some detachment from oneself and society, belief that the world is orderly and therefore can be understood, and the ability to let one's unconscious processes work on a problem.[20] LaPiere views creativity in terms of mental nonconformity, a strong motivation to innovate, and "the ability to ascertain all the possible permutations in the arrangement of the symbols that are being manipulated." [21] Barnett, finally, in discussing the basic processes involved in innovation, speaks of fusions that take place on a mental plane, the synthesis of existing elements, and mental configurations of cultural objects.[22]

In these and other studies the conditions which are conducive to innovation and creativity are described, but the actual procedures remain to be specified. Hypotheses abound, but undefined terms and vague psychological processes and relationships reduce them to the status of being merely "interesting." In view of the limited information available, then, it is probably best to make no theoretical commitment and to treat "creation" and "innovation" as relatively unknown processes. For purposes of development analysis it is sufficient to assume that novelties— be they symbols, tools, ideas, or behavior patterns—become available to a community or individual. The novelty may be introduced from outside the system under discussion, or it may be created within the system in some as yet largely unknown way.

SOCIOLOGICAL ASPECTS OF INNOVATION

Far more significant than the ultimate source of the novelty is its future career, for a novelty will not become a significant component of industrialization until it is used, and thus its acceptance or rejection de-

19. For a summary of a large number of studies in this area, see Rogers (1962).
20. Hagen (1962:88ff).
21. LaPiere (1965:118).
22. Barnett (1953:181ff).

termine whether it will become part of development analysis. The acceptance of a novelty may be viewed from two perspectives: that of the innovation itself and that of the adopter.

According to the data summarized by Rogers, the probability of acceptance varies with the characteristics of the innovation. Generally speaking, acceptance is likely if potential adopters *perceive* that the novelty a) has an obviously greater relative advantage over present or other alternative activities; b) is compatible with present values and experiences; c) is simple enough so that no extensive training or extraordinary efforts are required; d) is easily divisible so that the various parts can be tried out; and e) is easily communicated, so that the novelty and its consequences are easily apparent to both the adopter and his reference group.[23]

The characteristics of men who adopt innovations are not as clear cut, in part because of the fragmentary and contradictory evidence provided by psychological studies. There appears to be general agreement, however, that adopters—compared with those who reject innovations—are younger, have more dispersed reference groups, consider themselves as being deviant, are better able to deal with abstractions, and are less rigid and dogmatic.[24]

Both sets of characteristics can be integrated into the implications derived from a behavioral model of man. As was mentioned before, a new activity will be shaped (or accepted) and maintained, and a new tool will be tried out and accepted, if reinforcement follows. The total contingency that determines the acceptance or rejection of an innovation consists of two major sets of elements. First, the action itself has certain direct consequences; using improved seed potatoes and employing new methods of cultivation, for example, resulted in greatly increased harvests in Vicos. Second, the new activity is likely to produce reactions on the part of other men, and these may be aversive. Whether a new behavior pattern will be repeated, then, and whether a new material element will continue to be employed, will depend on the individual's summation of these consequences. Furthermore, the person's prediction and evaluation of possible contingencies will determine whether the "new" behavior pattern or ma-

23. Rogers (1962:chapter 5).
24. Barnett (1953:chapter 14), LaPiere (1965:chapter 6), Rogers (1962: chapter 6).

terial element will be tried out in the first place. The contingency assessment of an innovation consists of four major elements: a) the anticipated behavioral reactions of others, b) the actual behavioral reactions of others, c) the anticipated direct consequences of the novelty, and d) the actual direct consequences. The characteristics of both the innovation and the individuals confronting it influence these contingencies and their evaluation. For example, an innovation that can be divided into parts is more likely to be viewed positively, for if one part should fail, comparatively little will have been lost. And if a peasant's reference group includes men outside his village, the negative reactions of his neighbors will not be the only consequences he considers important. Each of the four elements is evaluated in terms of individualistic and subcultural criteria, and thus it is to be expected that one person's assessment may differ from that of another. Furthermore, to the extent to which men in the same community have access to different types of information, it is possible for villagers to arrive at different conclusions concerning the "advisability" of accepting a particular novelty. While the *initial* try-out involves only two elements, usually (a) and (c), the *continuation* of the novelty is based on all four. The consequences which an individual anticipates may be unrealistic and incorrect, of course, and an observer's summation may be biased and incomplete, and thus it is to be expected that the acceptance and rejection of innovations at times appears to be "irrational" or even "inexplicable" to an outsider.

Spicer [25] and Niehoff [26] have described a number of attempts to introduce new tools and behavior patterns into peasant communities. The explanations that are offered for both the successes and failures of various programs usually involve the contingencies of acceptance. For example, when the change agent uses ethnocentric criteria to define "needed" innovations, when he does not employ the proper procedures for shaping behavior, or when villagers do not perceive an innovation as markedly superior to existing conditions, it is quite logical that the novelty should be rejected. The foregoing discussion would lead to the conclusion that the *contingencies* of an innovation (including the way it fits into a culture) are at least as important as the presentation of the novelty.

The significance of the behavioral and sociological aspects of devia-

25. Spicer (1952).
26. Niehoff (1966).

tion and innovation is illustrated best by industrial entrepreneurs, the individuals who are usually considered to be the instigators of industrialization.

An Example of Deviation and Innovation: Entrepreneurs

BASIC CHARACTERISTICS

The most important "deviant" individual in economic development is the entrepreneur. Thirty years ago Joseph Schumpeter wrote of the entrepreneur as "the fundamental phenomenon of economic development. The carrying out of new combinations we call 'enterprise'; the individuals whose functions it is to carry them out we call entrepreneurs. . . . The ordinary characterization of the entrepreneur type by such expressions as 'initiative,' 'authority,' or 'foresight' points entirely in our direction." [27] Since then, entrepreneurial activities have been considered to be a major causal factor of industrialization, both in the Europe of the 18th century and in the developing world of today.[28] It is the entrepreneur who recognizes and exploits profitable opportunities in new commodities, markets, resources and organizations of production. More specifically, the entrepreneur initiates enterprises, introduces new ideas and techniques of production, management, and distribution, and assumes many of the associated risks. While some writers [29] consider capital accumulation, technological change, and entrepreneurs of roughly equal significance, others assign a special importance to entrepreneurs. In fact, the shortage of entrepreneurs in developing nations has often been cited as a major element responsible for the low rate of industrialization.[30] An important task of development analysis, therefore, is the investigation of factors that influence the existence and prevalence of entrepreneurship.

This task is complicated by the fact that while industrial entrepreneurs may be absent or exist in only small numbers, a nation may have a wealth of mercantile entrepreneurs.[31] The question, then, is not "why are there no entrepreneurs?" but "why are there no industrial entrepreneurs?" Consequently, those who are interested in designing development pro-

27. Schumpeter (1961:74–5).
28. For comprehensive examinations of this topic, see Higgins (1968), Hoselitz (1952), and Supple (1963). For a specific example, see Geertz (1963).
29. For example Morris (1967).
30. Hirschman (1958), Leibenstein (1957), Lewis (1955).
31. Lewis (1955:chapter 3).

grams need to analyze the factors which produce one type of entrepreneur and discourage another. In keeping with the theme of this book, the activities listed above and subsumed under the heading "industrial entrepreneurship" will provide the focus of the analysis. Since this category includes various types of activities—such as the abstraction of "foresight" and observables like "use of new production technique"—the causal factors may be expected to be equally heterogenous.

INDIVIDUALISTIC FACTORS

The crucial role played by entrepreneurs has provided impetus for a number of explanations based on individualistic—and often internal— characteristics. According to Hagen, the typical entrepreneur is a person with a creative personality who does not inhibit his creative urges. In McClelland's view the most important characteristic is high need achievement. These two factors are determined by the combination of original internal elements (ego, needs) and child-raising practices. Since the latter are functions of the wider social environment, societal factors are considered to play some—though necessarily limited—role.

The behavioral perspective leads to a different analytical procedure. The basic component of entrepreneurship is the class of behavior patterns labeled "entrepreneurial activities." The learning principles discussed in Chapter Three thus are parts of the causal complex, as are the deprivations which individuals have learned. In addition, the S^D and the reinforcers which have been learned for these actions, and the reward probabilities which men have learned to expect, contribute to the shaping and maintenance of entrepreneurial activities.

Learning principles, of course, are quite general and small in number, while the variety of deprivations, conceptions of S^D, and so forth is great. By themselves, then, individualistic characteristics cannot explain the presence or absence of the relatively specific behavior patterns under discussion. It is the individual's context, that is, the structure and operation of the social system, which determine the activities that will be reinforced and the reward probabilities that will be learned.

By initiating the analysis with the behavior patterns that constitute entrepreneurship, it is possible to delineate the types of social structures that are conducive to the creation of entrepreneurs and to specify the changes (if any) that must occur if the number of entrepreneurs in a particular social system is to increase. It is generally agreed that entrepreneurs are deviants, at least in the early stages of industrialization, and thus any causal analysis is concerned with the factors which produce and maintain deviance.[32] In addition, however, it is necessary to specify the factors which shape and maintain particular deviant activities, for not all types of deviation are conducive to economic development. For example, the behavior patterns involved in the organization and management of a small manufacturing business are quite different from the activities of more or less self-sufficient agriculturalists. The behavioral perspective, in this case, would lead to the following series of questions: what are the contingencies for the "old" activities, what are the reinforcers for these "new" actions, what determines the observed differences in reinforcement, and what factors were responsible for the original shaping of these new actions? Answers to these and related questions are found in large part in the operation of the social system and in the economic structure of communities and nations.

SOCIETAL FACTORS

The social and cultural context of entrepreneurship has been discussed in detail by a number of economists and historians,[33] and practically every investigator of economic development has had something to say on this topic. When entrepreneurs are viewed from a behavioral perspective, the analysis of societal factors centers not on economic, religious, or political institutions, but rather on the way in which their components shape and maintain entrepreneurial activities. The societal factors which affect the frequency with which entrepreneurial activities are expressed in a population are rarely found in isolation, and thus it is useful to speak of "structures" that influence behavior, meaning thereby a loose constellation of often interrelated elements.

Limitations Structure. In societies where entrepreneurial activities are viewed as deviant, a major determinant of deviance is a social structure which restricts the behavior patterns and reinforcers that are available to certain population segments. The rewards of "high status" in the form of material possessions and deferential behavior on the part of others, for example, may be limited to members of the religious majority, a certain race or occupation, the native born, and so forth. Or it may be that certain activity constellations—for example specific professions—are limited

32. Hoselitz (1960a:62), LaPiere (1965:130), Morris (1967:154.)
33. For example in the journal *Explorations in Entrepreneurial History*.

to members of particular subcultures. The crucial factor is that specific activities and reinforcers (and all that is implied thereby) are limited to various population segments. While this at times can be phrased in terms of "majority" and "minority," from the behavioral perspective labels are irrelevant. Furthermore, suppression, discrimination, loss of prestige, and so forth need not be part of the limitations structure (although they often are). The structure of behavioral and contingency limitations affects all members of a society, or course, although the consequences differ from one group to another. For the average person, or the member of the majority or elite in terms of any number of criteria, one set of activities (R_1) is reinforced, and a specific S^D_1—usually some membership criterion—is established in addition to the characteristic of the environment ordinarily considered as the discriminative stimulus for these actions (S^D_n). Another set of activities (R_2), however, is not reinforced and thus is not likely to be exhibited very often, if at all. (See Figure 9-1).

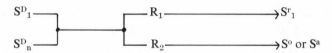

FIGURE 9–1: Contingencies for a "Majority"

Members of certain other groups, perhaps minorities but definable in terms of a large number of possible criteria, find that R_1, even when adequately performed, will not be reinforced. However, other activities (R_2) may be rewarded (S^r_2), although the reinforcer is not likely to be equivalent to S^r_1. For certain members of the society, then, the relationship shown in Figure 9-2 will hold, where S^D_2 includes as an important component the particular membership criterion.

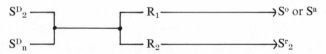

FIGURE 9–2: Contingencies for a "Minority"

In objectively identical situations (S^D_n), then, members of one group are likely to act in one way (R_1) while persons with other characteristics will behave differently (R_2). The limitations structure, in other words, limits *both* the majority and minority member's activities and reinforcers.

Students of economic history have repeatedly pointed out that entrepreneurs are not equally distributed in the population. Religious and ethnic minorities, outsiders in peasant villages, members of the displaced elite, and other relatively small groups have provided most of the entrepreneurial talent, not only in the western world but also in presently developing nations. It is equally apparent, however, that not all minorities are important sources of entrepreneurs and that marginality does not guarantee entrepreneurs. Consequently there must be additional significant factors at work.

Demand Structure. The reinforcers, and thus by implication the discriminative stimuli, which are available in any social system constitute the behaviorally significant aspects of the demand structure. The elements which determine the reinforcers and the probability of their presentation, and which limit the activities that are reinforced in specific circumstances, are population size, its rate of increase and degree of mobility, income and its distribution, foreign and domestic markets, technology, ecological characteristics and parameters, and those values which govern the consumption and production of goods. The demand structure, in short, is mainly economic, while the limitations structure is largely social and cultural. In terms of the previously employed schema, the demand structure determines what types of deviant activities (R_2, R_3, or R_4) will be reinforced, and by what.

In a society characterized by a stable population, a low per capita income, and relatively isolated agricultural villages, for example, the rewards for the production of consumer goods will be minimal, and thus the probability of the appearance of large numbers of industrial entrepreneurs is quite low. Mercantile entrepreneurs, however, will be more common. The demand structure is not static, of course, and as economic growth proceeds, an increasing number of entrepreneurial activities is likely to be rewarded with a widening array of reinforcers. In addition, governmental policies such as taxation, various incentives, and import restrictions affect the demand structure. Thus it is through the careful manipulation of *selected* components of the demand structure that the behavior of significant numbers of people can be shaped and/or maintained. While it is true that "social reinforcers" such as high status usually cannot be provided directly by the demand structure, the material rewards which are offered usually form the foundation for future social gains. Thus, when development has reached a certain (as yet unspecifiable) stage, entrepreneurship begins to be followed by social rewards, as when manufacturers become "respectable."

Opportunity Structure. In order for entrepreneurial activities to be successful they have to be reasonably adequate, complete, and competently performed. The meeting of these and other requirements—that is, the nature and quality of R_2 in the above schema—depends on the opportunity structure. Furthermore, whether R_2 rather than R_3 or R_4 will be performed depends not only on the demand structure as just described, but also on the opportunities confronting the potential entrepreneur.

The probability that entrepreneurial activities will be performed, and the selection of a particular set of actions, is influenced by the following factors: the availability of capital; management and technological skills; information concerning production methods, labor, and markets; predictions of the eventual outcome of possible ventures; and finally, the opportunity to learn, directly or through imitation, all of the activities associated with the effective planning and successful operation of industrial enterprises. The objective assessment of opportunities and the accurate prediction of contingencies depend on the kind and amount of information available to the individual, and thus a person's access to dependable information is an important component of the opportunity structure. While this does not necessarily imply literacy, a well-developed communications network of one sort or another appears to be essential for the rise and especially the *development* of an entrepreneurial group.

For the more or less isolated individual there is not likely to be much of an opportunity structure; it is only when information concerning capital, production methods, etc. becomes available that the opportunity structure begins to take shape. Solitary entrepreneurs are very rare, then, whereas the presence of a number of entrepreneurs—equivalent to accurate information—encourages the development of others. It cannot be concluded, however, that such a direct relationship will persist, because as the number of entrepreneurs increases, the opportunity structure develops just as the demand structure tends to narrow, for example in the shape of an expanding but eventually limited market.

Labor Structure. Industrial entrepreneurs depend, for the successful completion of their operations, on an adequate number of willing, competent laborers. Although the supply of labor might be viewed in similar terms as the supply of capital, that is, as part of the opportunity structure, the fact that labor means "men" and is a function of several variables makes it advisable to speak of a separate "labor structure." [34] The supply of factory labor depends largely on the existence of alternative ways of making a "reasonably" good living. Thus, when agricultural pursuits are available to all members of a village, and when the "good life" as defined by the subculture can be attained with locally available means, few if any men will seek factory jobs, for the "old" activities continue to be reinforced. Land pressure, poor harvests, rising expectations, and knowledge of life and jobs "in town" will increase the supply of factory labor, for "old" activities are no longer sufficiently rewarded. An additional factor is the uncertainty associated with future food requirements.[35] Men who work in factories must be sure that there will be food even though they themselves do not grow any, hence the conception of a capricious universe may be expected to be detrimental for the labor supply. Finally, "traditionalism" and isolation appear to be much less important than the above elements, as indicated, for example, by Moore's study of Mexican villages.[36] The more isolated and traditional of two communities provided significantly more laborers for a distant factory, mainly because the land was scarce and poor, and not all villagers were able to make a living. The "push" and "pull" required for an adequate labor supply thus can be specified in terms of the differential reinforcement of agricultural and industrial activities.

For the peasant, then, there are limitations, demand, and opportunity structures much as there are for the entrepreneur, except that the specific components of these structures are different. The general *operation* of the structures is similar, however, in that they provide reinforcers for certain activities such as factory labor, impose restrictions on possible behavior patterns, and attach different contingencies to the activities of various population segments in the community.

The Four Structures. It is apparent from these considerations that industrial entrepreneurs depend for both their existence and number on the degree to which all four of these structures are found within a society or community. It is not likely, however, that *all* components of the structures are known to *all* men. The demand structure, for example, may not be easily apparent, and information concerning the opportunity structure

34. Moore and Feldman (1960).
35. Salz (1955).
36. Moore (1951).

may be available to only a few.[37] Thus it is useful to distinguish between objective and perceived structures and to propose the hypothesis that *the incidence of entrepreneurship depends on both the objective and perceived configuration of the four structures.* Any discrepancy between objective structures and the actual incidence of entrepreneurs will be due to inadequate or incorrect perceptions of the various structures. There is probably some leeway in both the components and configurations of structures conducive to entrepreneurial activities, but the parameters within which entrepreneurs are likely to flourish have yet to be determined. It is evident, however, that entrepreneurship depends on rather specific combinations of circumstances which are difficult to create and easy to destroy.

The relative importance of the four structures varies not only among nations and over time, but also with the "stages" of industrialization. The limitations and demand structures, for example, probably are most important in the early development of entrepreneurs, but when the criteria of status shift as the economy matures, when industrial activities are no longer viewed with disdain, the opportunity structure is likely to become more significant. Thus it is the *configuration* of structures within a nation and at any one time that accounts for entrepreneurs. In southeast Asia, for example, the entrepreneurial activities of the Chinese require an explanation in which the limitations structure is significant, while in Pakistan the demand and opportunity structures were much more important elements in the fostering of entrepreneurs. No matter what the configuration, however, the common element in all situations is that entrepreneurial activities are reinforced for some individuals, while for others they are not.

Most sociologically-oriented discussions of entrepreneurs rest heavily on large-scale phenomena. Hoselitz, for example, writes that "the chances for certain forms of deviance to develop will depend, *ceteris paribus,* upon the flexibility and openness of the social structure and the degree of centralization and authoritarian control in the field of decision-making, especially of decisions relevant to economic growth." [38] The behavioral conception of social structure reduces some of the difficulties of reification apparent in this quotation, while the above discussion of the four

37. Easterbrook (1963).
38. Hoselitz (1960a:75).

structures indicates *how* "authoritarian control" affects entrepreneurial activities: it introduces an extraneous element into the link between behavior and contingencies. The behavioral treatment of entrepreneurship, in other words, does not supplant existing sociological analyses; rather, it increases the specificity of the concepts, data, and relationships which are involved in the explanation and fostering of entrepreneurial activities. Existing economic perspectives, for example those which emphasize income, capital, or infrastructure, contribute to the elaboration of the demand and opportunity structures. For example, Alexander's [39] summary of largely economic factors shows their major role in entrepreneurship to be that they provide and make possible various contingencies for industrial activities.

The major role of political and social changes in the development and supply of entrepreneurs has usually been considered to be that of prerequisite. Rostow,[40] for example, hypothesizes that social and political changes are needed to provide the foundation for a viable entrepreneurial group. The behavioral conception and the four structures discussed above indicate the procedures for specifying *which* social and political changes —*if any*—are required for the reinforcement of entrepreneurial activities. It is entirely possible, for example, that only minor political changes may be required, and that no far-reaching social alterations need be considered before programs of fostering entrepreneurship can be instituted.

The analysis of entrepreneurship in terms of the four structures also makes it possible to account for a number of historical and contemporary phenomena. The fact that a disproportionately large number of entrepreneurs come from religious and ethnic minorities has been well documented [41] and can be explained by the configuration of the four structures. Not all minorities provide entrepreneurs, however, and the reason appears to be that one or another of the structures was insufficiently developed. Lewis and others have pointed out that there are entrepreneurs in developing nations, but that their attention is directed toward mercantile endeavors. The first important step has thereby been taken, however, for the recent history of Turkey and Greece as well as of other countries shows that a disproportionately large number of entrepreneurs come

39. Alexander (1960, 1967).
40. Rostow (1960).
41. As described, for example, in Alexander (1967), Glade (1967), Hoselitz (1960a).

from the merchant class. The major factors which appear to be responsible for this fit well into the four structures. Glade,[42] for example, points out that merchants have a more accurate knowledge of emerging domestic markets than do other people, are usually tied into some wholesale and retail organization, and have easier access to both capital (especially loan capital) and knowledge of productive techniques. The limitations structure, finally, operates through the low prestige which is usually attached to both merchandising and industrial activities.

While it is true that entrepreneurs tend to come from one or another type of "minority" group, it is clear that not *all* members of a religious or ethnic minority become entrepreneurs. Individual differences may be part of the explanation, but other important elements are: differential access to the opportunity structure, varying amounts of available and adequate information, differential awareness of the limitation structure, and so forth. In short, individuals within a nation or community differ in their exposure to the four structures, and structural configurations may be expected to vary among subcultures and over time. It may be concluded, therefore, that *the factors influencing the probabilities of entrepreneurial activities must be determined anew for each subculture, every nation and decade.* A low probability for one nation at one time, then, is no cause of despair for other countries, nor for that same nation at another time. The recent experiences of Pakistan illustrate not only the operation of the four structures and the utility of the behavioral perspective, but also provide some grounds for optimism concerning the future of developing nations, at least in the economic sphere.

AN EXAMPLE: ENTREPRENEURS IN PAKISTAN [43]

When Pakistan became an independent state in 1947, the outlook for economic development—and indeed for its very existence as a nation— was dim. The country was poor, had almost no industry or readily exploitable resources, and few people were engaged in commerce or industry. Furthermore, Muslims were widely thought of as having little or no interest and aptitude for commerce and industry. Since the population was considered to be fatalistic, feudal, and poorly equipped to operate a modern society, it was expected that the government would have to play a major role in any industrialization effort. Consequently, most of the

42. Glade (1967).
43. The material of this section is based on Papanek (1967).

existing theories and hypotheses concerning economic development would predict a very low probability of success. At the very least, several years and perhaps decades would be required to establish an adequate social, and especially psychological, foundation for development.

Twenty years later, in the middle 1960's, Pakistan's "rate of economic growth was more than double the rate of population growth; investment was approaching a healthy 20 per cent, and savings exceeded 10 per cent of domestic resources. Prices were stable, foreign exchange earnings were increasing at 7.5 per cent per year, and foreign resources were being used with increasing effectiveness. Pakistan was widely regarded as one of the half dozen countries with the greatest promise of steady development. In the face of its pitiful resource and capital endowment at independence, and in comparison with other countries, Pakistan's performance was outstanding. . . . Regardless of the indicators used, there was clearly an extremely rapid development of private industry in Pakistan. This was carried out almost entirely by indigenous Muslim entrepreneurs, although there had been very few industrialists or even substantial businessmen among the Muslims before Independence. Although it is impossible to prove conclusively which particular factors were most important, there is good indirect evidence that economic incentives played a very significant role." [44]

Papanek's description of the economic incentives and social structure which contributed to the rise of entrepreneurs and private industry provides almost a textbook example of the shaping and maintenance of entrepreneurial behavior patterns by means of differential reinforcement within the context of the four structures.

Limitations Structure. Members of the traditional elite group, consisting mainly of civil servants, professionals, and the military, were quite content with their lives because the departure of British and Hindu officials greatly increased the opportunities in traditional elite occupations. Landlords maintained their prestige and steady incomes, and thus their behavior patterns, too, continued to be reinforced. Merchants and small traders, however, were in a different position, for their prestige was considerably lower than that of the other groups.

The British and Hindu enterprises which remained after partition had little confidence in Pakistan's future and did not expand, thus providing little competition for newly emerging Muslim industries. Furthermore,

44. Papanek (1967:2, 32).

since foreigners had difficulty receiving import licenses and were restricted in the transmission of profits, potential foreign investors were discouraged.

As a result of these two sets of limitations, Muslim merchants became successful in both external and internal trade, accumulated significant amounts of capital, and initiated industrial enterprises. The transition from trade to industry was affected by the shifting of limitations brought on by the Korean War. During the war, international trade was very successful, but at the end of the Korean boom severe import restrictions made such trade unattractive. Those who remained importers received markedly lower incomes, yet there were few alternatives. Land ownership offered prestige but relatively little income, and the threat of land reform made this activity somewhat uncertain of success. The market for urban real estate was small, while distribution and service activities held little promise of financial reward. The final alternative was industry, where high rewards *were* possible. Governmental restrictions on financial transactions made it difficult to export capital, pressure for austerity made the display of wealth unwise, there were few goods and services on which money could be spent in a conspicuous manner, and thus capital was available for investing in industry. In short, "traders, and especially those with heavy reliance on imports, who were pushed out of their accustomed activity by dramatically declining earnings, were therefore faced with attractive investment opportunities in industry, but with limited possibilities in other fields." [45]

Demand Structure. While there were some political and economic uncertainties, especially during the early years of independence, these were more than offset by the financial rewards which accrued first to merchants and later to astute industrialists.

Partition resulted in a ready market for goods which previously had been supplied by Indian firms, and raw materials which used to be shipped to Bombay or Calcutta now had to be processed in Pakistan. In addition, during the Korean War high prices were paid for exports, imports rose, and much of the population became accustomed to the use of manufactured goods. After the war, imports were severely restricted, yet there was an expanding market for consumer goods. Since the government made life for foreign firms difficult, a highly protected and substantial market for consumer goods existed. As a result, very high prices

45. Ibid. p. 35.

could be, and were, charged, and annual profits of 50–100 per cent of invested capital were possible and quite frequent. Since it was quite possible to recover all of one's investments in the short time of at first two years and later five years, the threat of governmental instability and a precarious future seemed at least bearable.

Information concerning profitability of manufacturing enterprises attracted numerous entrepreneurs, and internal competition gradually developed. As a consequence, prices for a wide range of manufactured goods declined, in some cases as much as 30 per cent, and profits fell. Although industrialists complained about the loss of profits, these were still substantial by western standards, ranging from 20 to 50 per cent of investment.

Early industry had been concentrated in the manufacture of goods such as matches and especially cotton cloth, but when the profitability of these enterprises declined, other industries with a higher profit—for example chemicals—began to attract entrepreneurs. The demand structure and its very high rewards, then, not only shaped and maintained "manufacturing" as such, but selectively reinforced a shifting set of industries as the country developed economically.

Opportunity Structure. In the early years, the factories abandoned by Hindus and the technical knowledge provided by Muslim immigrants and foreign assistance laid the foundation for industry. Initially modest accumulations of capital were increased substantially during the export boom of the Korean War. International trade required modern bookkeeping and management procedures, and these methods, once established, could be easily transferred to the industrial sector. The government provided not only capital but also policies which assisted the development of factories. For example, machinery and other capital goods were cheap to import because tariffs were low, and the consumer goods produced with the machinery could be sold at a high price because import restrictions protected the market from foreign competition. In addition, "the government was able to protect life and property, and to develop the infrastructure required by industry, although there were frequent delays. Corruption was never so widespread, capricious, or extortionate that it siphoned off substantial resources or created great uncertainty. Given these minimum conditions, economic incentives were strong enough to overcome the effects of an inauspicious political environment." [46] Some of the

46. Ibid. p. 51.

corruption, in fact, helped entrepreneurs, for widespread and effective tax evasion kept much of the profit intact for further investment. The high profitability, furthermore, enabled the early industrialists to disregard inefficiency, and thus initial labor, management, and production problems had few aversive consequences. In later years, the various institutions which served the industrial sector—for example finance, transportation, and education—provided substantially improved services so that industries could continue to develop in spite of lower profits.

Most industrialists came from trading communities, and more than two-thirds of the industrial investment was owned or controlled by individuals or families who had originally been merchants. According to Papanek, the major reasons were that these men were used to responding to market incentives, had financial and organizational resources necessary for such responses, often had access to ready-made sales organizations, were able to raise capital among members of the trading communities to which they belonged, and could draw on these communities for trusted men as accountants, managers, and holders of other important positions.

Labor Structure. While the needs for a stable labor force were at times greater than the availability of skilled and adequately trained workers, a high unemployment rate has been characteristic for a number of years. Much of the urban unemployment has been due to high wage rates and the inability or unwillingness of industry to employ labor-intensive machinery. On the whole, the labor structure appears to have played a neutral role in the development of entrepreneurs and industry, for the type of worker that was required was neither very scarce nor overabundant.

Conclusion. Papanek's account of "economic incentives" is no more than the description of contingencies attached to the various activities of individuals in different population segments. And his treatment of industrialists, planners, peasants, and governmental controls represents a careful elaboration of the four structures and their roles in the shaping and maintenance of entrepreneurial activities. In short, alterations in selected aspects of the social environment established new behavior patterns in many a Pakistan citizen; these persons, in turn, became part of the social context of others, and an increasing number of men became economic innovators. However, since the alterations in the social structure reinforced innovation in only these limited areas of life, many other activities remained substantially unchanged, and thus entrepreneurs often remained traditional in religion and political outlook.

Papanek concludes that, at least in Pakistan, "strong economic incentives were sufficient to develop a number of industrial entrepreneurs, given, first, a social and political environment that was not excessively hostile, though it was not favorable, and, second, some groups or individuals in touch with the market and therefore affected by economic incentives. . . . Once industrial development was well underway, weaker economic incentives were sufficient to maintain its momentum. . . . Industrial entrepreneurs were overwhelmingly drawn from the groups which were pushed most strongly out of their current occupation, which were exposed most directly to the incentives making for entrepreneurial activity, and which had the ability to exploit the opportunities in industry." [47]

The experience of Pakistan illustrates the effectiveness with which governmental policies can be employed to increase the rate and success of economic development, and there is no theoretical or practical reason to suppose that other nations cannot institute similarly effective procedures to encourage industrial entrepreneurs. But governmental structures and operations are not solely designed to foster economic growth, and while some governmental programs may be very successful, other efforts or policies—for example the maintenance of autocratic regimes—may eventually undermine the whole system. The complex role of government in economic development thus deserves some attention.

Political Institutions and Economic Development

One of the most important components of development analysis is the role of government as both a determinant and consequence of industrialization. Indeed, the term "modernization," while often considered to be synonymous with economic growth, has been employed by Black [48] and Eisenstadt,[49] among others, in the description of largely *political* processes. Such interest in the political manifestations of economic development arises from the fact that the social and economic changes which occur in the Third World today are reflected in, and often expressed by, political events. Furthermore, economic growth both influences and is affected by the structure and operation of govern-

47. Ibid. pp. 54–5.
48. Black (1966).
49. Eisenstadt (1966).

ments.[50] Any development analysis or program must therefore be considered within a nation's and region's political institutions.

Most studies of the role of political institutions in economic development concentrate on descriptions of the governmental system itself, with secondary emphasis on consequences for the large-scale social and economic aspects of industrialization. Political socialization and recruitment, interest articulation and aggregation, and the making and application of rules, for example, are among the processes that have received considerable attention.[51] Political parties, the middle class, pressure groups, the military, bureaucracies, and other components of the political system have been studied in detail, especially in the new nations.[52] Finally, nationalism, socialism, and other ideologies have been analyzed in terms of their consequences for economic growth, for example in Latin America.[53]

The behavioral approach to development, since it focuses at least initially on the activities of individuals, is concerned less with such large-scale phenomena than with their consequences for behavior. From this perspective, the major role of political institutions is the provision of contingencies and their schedules of presentation for a large number of daily and extraordinary activities. Governmental structures and their operation—for example, political parties and national integration—are of concern only insofar as these affect the activities of the population. Contingencies may be provided directly, as in the case of tax rebates for plant expansion, or legal parameters may be established within which certain activities are "acceptable" and thus free from aversive consequences. It is through such controls of contingencies that political institutions contribute to the definition of discriminative stimuli—for example "law," "tax deadline," or "signed contract"—and thus contribute to the shaping and maintenance of a wide variety of simple and complex activities on the part of both citizens and officials.

BEHAVIORAL ASPECTS OF POLITICAL INSTITUTIONS

The behavioral analysis of political institutions and economic development centers on a number of interrelated topics:

50. For excellent discussions of these complex reciprocal relationships, see Apter (1965) and some of the essays in Lipset (1960). For an example of statistical studies, see Olsen (1968).

51. Almond and Coleman (1960).

52. For examples from the Near East and North Africa, see Halpern (1963).

53. Maier and Weatherhead (1964).

1. The *activities* that are being shaped, maintained, or extinguished for a large variety and number of people.

2. The *contingencies* associated with these activities. This topic includes not only the kinds of rewards and types of punishment that are used, but also the procedures which are employed in their presentation. Mild punishment that can always be counted on, for example, may be more effective than highly aversive consequences that can be delivered only infrequently, if at all. In addition, the deprivations which are involved, and the degree of satiation (if any) that is achieved, together with the sources of these characteristics, require analysis. Fines and the publication of one's name in the back pages of a metropolitan newspaper, for example, are consequences that wealthy suburban drunken drivers may well consider unimportant. There is considerable evidence for the proposition that learning occurs more quickly and will be more permanent when rewards, rather than punishment, are used.[54] Thus a political system that relies mainly on aversive contingencies is likely to establish behavior patterns with a low probability of permanence.

3. The *consistency* with which the contingencies are presented. A national government's structural and operational characteristics, such as a slow-moving bureaucracy or conflicts among various agencies, are major sources of inconsistency. Additional factors are inadequate information concerning the behavior that is to be rewarded and the lag between the occurrence of activities and the presentation of contingencies. When much time intervenes and other actions occur during the interval, spurious reinforcement or punishment of these other activities may result.

4. The *schedule* on which contingencies are presented. When complex actions are to be shaped, reinforcement should be frequent, and during successive approximation activities which merely approach the ultimate form should be rewarded. This is especially important in communities where the conception of a capricious universe prevails, where men do not trust each other, and where the future is considered to be unpredictable, for it is largely by means of the judicious scheduling of reinforcements that such conceptions will be changed. Furthermore, since behavior is at least partly dependent upon the schedule of reinforcement, it is possible to increase adherence to governmental policies by changing these schedules.

54. For a discussion of various aspects of punishment in learning, see Krasner and Ullman (1965), Azrin and Holz (1966), Bandura (1969:chapter 5).

5. The *circumstances* in which various activities are rewarded or punished. Behavior is partly the result of the discriminative stimuli which men have learned and which governments have established through differential reinforcement, and thus noncompliance with legal prescriptions may be due to poorly established and inadequately presented S^D.

It is evident that the behavioral perspective of development includes political phenomena as important determinants of both the replication and modification of behavior. The explanation of "apathetic peasants," for example, will lead the investigator from the study of the various contingencies that maintain "apathetic" activities through community power structures, officials, and land owners to the operation of regional and national governments. How much more comfortable and inoffensive are the implications of a psychodynamic perspective! Here "apathy" is assumed to be due to some characteristics of the internal state, and the investigator is led into the study of personality and child-raising practices. While the psychodynamic approach recognizes that governments affect development, it minimizes both their positive and detrimental roles. But peasant mentality, authoritarian personalities, and innate traditionalism can serve as convenient scapegoats for the slow pace of development only as long as the psychodynamic perspective holds sway. With the rise of a behavioral perspective, a new series of often uncomfortable questions arises: "what activities in the population do governmental operations maintain?" "Why does the government not shape different behavior patterns?" and "what changes in governmental operations are required if the behavior of peasants and others is to be modified?"

THE OPERATION OF POLITICAL INSTITUTIONS

The governmental determinants of reinforcers, schedules of their presentation, and so forth, must be analyzed on two levels: *ideal* prescriptions, relationships, and operations, and their *actual* manifestations. Laws, regulations, ideals of justice, organization charts and austerity programs do not enforce themselves; agencies of one type or another—and that means, in the final analysis, men—operate to shape and maintain behavior patterns consistent with such laws and ideals. Thus it is the organization and its members who implement ideals, as well as the ideals themselves, that are part of development analysis. Students of bureaucracies and other complex organizations are quite familiar with the fact that no matter what the ideals or principles may have been originally, the actual operation of any organization is likely not only to diverge from them but to include its own preservation as a major—and at times incompatible—goal.[55] The consequences can be observed in many apparently individualistic activities, such as "disrespect" for law or the central government. Upon close examination these actions turn out to be the results of inconsistent and/or poorly applied contingencies and, insofar as this was true in the past, of ill-defined and amorphous discriminative stimuli. In order to change behavior patterns labeled "disrespect," therefore, it will be more efficient in the long run to alter the contingencies and schedules of these activities—*and of their alternatives*—than to "straighten out" the individuals concerned. In the Zande Scheme, for example, the adequate reinforcement of cotton cultivation by means of higher prices would have been better than the hapazard application of a repressive law; psychoanalytic treatment of the Vicoseños would have been a poor alternative to the course of action that was followed.

The analysis of political ideals and textbook presentations of governmental structures and operations may be interesting, but as far as development analysis and programs are concerned, observed activities, operating contingencies, and real discriminative stimuli are the major concern. Here the important question is not "what is the law?" but rather, "what behavior does it reinforce?" because the focus of interest is on the *actual* behavior patterns that are detrimental or conducive to industrialization. In Pakistan, for example, governmental policies resulted in the rewarding of native industrial entrepreneurs and the discouragement of foreign competition. In Montegrano,[56] conversely, the government of the community was so ineffective that employers could get away with failing to pay the wages owed to their workers. Many laborers had to repeatedly demand their wages and often were unable to collect them for months. Under such circumstances it is not surprising that there was relatively little wage labor in spite of the fact that jobs were available and most men led leisurely lives. The casual observer—an all too frequent occurrence—might conclude that "peasants do not like to work for others" or that "peasants do not appreciate money," but it was the difficulty of collecting wages, and thus governmental weakness, that was the major determinant of the observed action. While the description of Pakistan's government and the study of municipal administration in southern Italy (Montegrano's lo-

55. Etzioni (1964).
56. Banfield (1958).

cale) may be useful, such contributions to development analysis are not as significant as investigations of the *actual behavioral consequences* of these organizations.

THE LEVELS OF GOVERNMENT

While the description and analysis of national political institutions is a significant part of development analysis, and while many programs of action are necessarily of national scope, the behavioral perspective directs attention to the immediate determinants of an individual's activities. Not only must the ideals and operations of government be considered separately, but it is also often necessary to differentiate among local, regional, and national structures and their consequences for behavior. National policies may be designed to shape and maintain certain behavior patterns among peasants, for example, but the local manifestations of these policies—and the *only* manifestations as far as most villagers are concerned—may have a quite different effect. Thus national land reform programs do not become significant for the behavior of individuals until local landowners are affected,[57] and national wage policies are irrelevant until local employers accept them.

The often rather loose articulation of national policies and local implementations is not necessarily detrimental, however. National policies, especially in heterogeneous societies, may not be able to take into account the host of different conditions in which the policies are to be applied, and local autonomy may make it possible to alter the policy sufficiently for it to be applied more successfully. The "politics of modernization," then, includes not only the structure of national governments, but also the operation of local political institutions and the relationship between national and local policies, officials, and pressures.[58]

THE FORMS OF GOVERNMENT

Students of government have repeatedly examined the assets and liabilities of various forms of government in order to determine what kind of political system is most conducive to a high rate of economic growth.[59] While there is no consensus as yet, opinion seems to favor the position that no extreme form of dictatorship or democracy can efficiently perform

57. Erasmus (1967), Senior (1958).
58. An excellent description is provided by Apter (1965).
59. For example Worsley (1964).

the functions required for the "take-off"; that is, shape and maintain the behavior patterns involved in successful long-range planning, austerity programs, disdain for inefficient and expensive "showcase" projects, and so forth. The behavioral perspective contributes to the debate by specifying the requirements of governmental operations in terms of the activities associated with the various stages of industrialization, but it cannot answer the question of which type of government is best. In fact, if a major role of political institutions is the provision of reinforcers for specific sets of activities, then the question: "which type of government is best?" cannot be answered until it has been decided under what conditions, and with what procedures, particular behavior patterns of citizens in a particular nation can be shaped most quickly and be maintained most easily and efficiently.

Any system of government has both assets and liabilities when it comes to shaping and maintaining activities. For example, in a democratic system it is often difficult to provide consistent contingencies for any length of time, be it to encourage entrepreneurs or to operate an austerity program. In a dictatorship these procedures might be employed, but the major contingency is likely to be one or another type of punishment or at least its threat—and the use of aversive contingencies is a very poor and inefficient procedure for shaping behavior. While the interposition of political considerations may be beneficial—for example by artifically increasing the probability of reinforcement—the opposite is also possible.

Laboratory and small group studies make it possible to delineate the most efficient procedures for shaping and maintaining specific behavior patterns, but social systems are so complex and involve so many unknown factors that several different procedures are likely to be equally effective. Hence there probably is some latitude in the types of governmental structures and operations that are "best" for industrialization. Factory labor, industrial entrepreneurship, and other complex sets of behavior, for example, can be established by a number of different configurations of reinforcers and schedules, depending on a region's technological, ecological, and cultural parameters. In addition, a nation's historical heritage, popular ideologies, and existing political structure provide some limitations.[60] The requirements of behavioral procedures may not be congruent with existing historical and political parameters, and thus every nation will

60. For a discussion and illustration of these problems, see Bailey (1963), Jaguaribe (1968).

have to work out its own unique combination of specific requirements and effective procedures within constantly shifting parameters. The objectively "best" procedures may not be among those that are "possible," and thus the establishment and maintenance of behavioral requisites must be based on the careful analysis of the individual case. Furthermore, it is to be expected that the "best" procedures in the early stages of development are different from those in the later stages, and thus a wide range of governmental structures and operations may be suitable for the various members of the Third World. The type of government that is best for the economic development of one nation at one time may not represent the best choice for another, and thus it is difficult—and perhaps will prove impossible—to come up with unequivocal answers as to what kind of government should be created and fostered as part of the efficient preparation for the "take-off."

THE IDEOLOGIES OF GOVERNMENT

The ideology that underlies any government's structure and operation contributes to the definition and presentation of discriminative and contingent stimuli, and thus of the behavior patterns that are "proper" for the attainment of national goals. The ideologies of capitalism and socialism help establish slightly different sets of deprivations and rewards, and at least for some individuals there are different definitions of "proper" behavior. Yet the procedures that are employed in the shaping of behavior are the same.

A dominant element in the ideologies of most developing nations is one or another variant of socialism, and the question arises whether these ideologies are more or less conducive to economic development than are (or were) capitalistic ideologies.[61] The behavioral model of man cannot answer these questions, for both sets of ideologies can shape and have maintained some activities that contributed to economic growth—for example the fostering of entrepreneurship—and other activities that are detrimental, such as corruption. International communication, the demonstration effect, and rising expectations have produced state variables and conceptions of reinforcers that were not present during the nineteenth century, and thus it cannot be expected that ideologies which were effective in the past will be effective now or in the future.

61. For an analyses of political ideologies, see Apter (1964); for a taste of the ideologies themselves, see Sigmund (1963).

From the behavioral perspective the important question is not "which ideology is best for development?" but rather "which ideology *actually* leads to activities that are conducive to economic growth?" Thus it is not the abstract ideology itself that is of interest, but its behavioral manifestations as they are produced by governmental structures and operations. As yet there are no general answers, and each ideology and its behavioral consequences must be examined anew, for each is profoundly affected by social, political, and cultural parameters.

CONCLUSION

The foregoing discussion of political institutions leads to the conclusion that the behavioral perspective can be employed in all political settings and economic systems. No matter what the dominant ideology of a developing nation may be, the transformation of ideals into action and achievement will be furthered only by the careful and dispassionate employment of learning principles. The behavioral model of man is no more than a tool—morally, politically, and economically neutral—that may be used by anyone for the achievement of any goal. The use of this tool will be described in the following chapter.

X *A Behavioral Perspective*

of Planning and Action

Theoretical discussions of social change and economic development are not only intrinsically interesting, but they also contribute to the explanation of the various rates of industrialization that have been evident during the last two hundred years. All too often, however, one arrives at the end of the argument and can only say, "yes, that is how it is, and how it came to be."

In today's world, theories which are merely interesting and provide no more than an explanation of the past and present can be of little use or comfort. "Interest" and "explanation" by themselves are curiously irrelevant in the face of high birth and low death rates, malnutrition, and qualities of life based on a per capita income of fifty dollars a year. No theoretical discussion is worthwhile unless it provides, in addition to possible explanations, realistic and practical answers to the question, "what *can* we do *now?*" This chapter is devoted to outlining some answers based on ideas presented so far.

Summary of the Argument

When the process of economic development is dissected into its various components, a major part and perhaps its most significant element

283

turns out to be the behavior of men. Economists may speak of a labor force and sociologists may describe functional specificity, but it is men who work, and social relationships are made up of individuals who engage in various activities. Such emphasis on men raises questions concerning the determinants of behavior and the nature of social relations, and a behavioral model of man was suggested as one possible source of answers (Chapter Two). The basic proposition of the behavioral perspective is that most activities which constitute daily life are learned by means of differential reinforcement. Specific relationships between individual and social environment which are involved in various learning procedures were outlined in Chapter Three. A major implication of the behavioral perspective, illustrated in Chapter Four, is that the explanation of behavior need not be based on various inferred or assumed characteristics of man's internal state. Values, attitude, indeed "personality" itself, are shown to refer to various characteristics of action rather than its causes. It may be concluded that changes in values, attitudes, and personality will follow upon the alteration of behavior, and this usually means the alteration of the contingencies of action. The individual's social environment is the source of most contingencies, and thus the operation of social structure is an important aspect of development analysis (Chapter Five). The behavioral conception of social structure leads to the hypothesis that behavior patterns associated with economic development can be established by the careful alteration of selected components of a community's social structure, especially in terms of the contingencies of those behavior patterns which are either to be shaped or extinguished. The two cases described and analyzed in Chapter Six provide support for this hypothesis. The various activities and social relations which constitute the social structure of any community or nation are usually combined into one of two major types of systems. As described in Chapter Seven, peasant communities and many developing nations are morphostatic systems in which trends toward change produce countervailing forces, while industrial nations typically are morphogenic systems in which trends toward change produce additional changes. Chapter Eight analyzes one important component of morphostatic systems, world view, and indicates how, according to the behavioral perspective, this might be changed by means of education. The major procedure for altering social systems—deviation and innovation—is analyzed and illustrated in Chapter Nine. Entrepreneurs and the case of Pakistan provide good examples of how complex behavior patterns can be shaped and maintained by the judicious provision of reinforcers for certain activities. When the system is very large, such as a nation, the differential reinforcement procedures associated with the establishment of new activities are likely to be performed by governmental agencies, and thus political institutions become part of the behavioral analysis of economic development.

One of the most important propositions of the behavioral perspective, which first appears in Chapter Two and is considered from a variety of viewpoints in later chapters, is that *behavior is replicated when contingencies remain the same, and behavior is changed when contingencies are altered.* Some of the far-reaching implications of this proposition for planning and action will now be considered.

Indigenous Change and Development Programs

Static social systems are rare indeed. Inventions, the diffusion of technology, or the opening of markets result in changed relations with the environment; inconsistencies and conflicts among the various components of a nation produce changes in some elements; incomplete socialization leads to behavioral heterogeneity; and competition for limited resources may give rise to new activities. These and other factors, presumed to exist in almost any community or nation,[1] are responsible for social changes that are essentially unplanned. The rate of change may be low, and the direction may be difficult to discern, but no society—least of all in today's world—can be assumed to require special efforts to initiate change. As outlined in Chapter Eight, the spread of education, growing literacy, and the development of communication channels, not only produce dissatisfactions with the old and visions of the new, but also provide men with the information and skills that are required to change the structure and operation of social systems, be they communities or nations.

If economic growth were considered to be a long-term process, it would be sufficient to simply analyze the operation of "natural causes" of change, as was done with reciprocal farm labor in Chapter Seven. However, industrialization today is often viewed as a solution to many problems facing the Third World, and thus planning and deliberate action are considered to be essential. Even when it is not necessary to initiate change,

1. For a detailed discussion of these and other factors, see Moore (1963c).

planning and action programs may be required to *accelerate* and *redirect* or focus the changes that are already occurring.

The steps and procedures outlined in the following sections are applicable to both dormant and rapidly changing communities. Although the common theme is the "change agent," no theoretical or practical necessity of face-to-face interaction is thereby implied, and it is quite possible for the change agent to operate indirectly. New behavior patterns can be reinforced, for example, by technological elements such as improvements in transportation networks,[2] and by carefully structured governmental programs.

Development Programs and the Behavioral Perspective

Just as most studies of industrialization concentrate on economics and are basically macroanalyses, so most of the literature on planning focuses on economic factors and emphasizes various large-scale phenomena and processes.[3] W. Arthur Lewis,[4] for example, includes the following elements in his discussion of planning strategies: the interdependence of industrial sectors, the price system, etc., foreign trade, capital intensity, regional balance, unemployment, the distribution of income, public expenditures, taxes and savings, inflation, and foreign aid. One of the best-known books on the subject, Hirschman's *The Strategy of Economic Development*,[5] is similarly concerned with large-scale economic factors, and especially the unequal development of various sectors of an economy. On the basis of the planning experiences of several nations, Hagen proposes a list of characteristics that any good development plan *should* have.

> First, a good economic development plan both proposes government expenditure projects for development and for current purposes and indicates policies which will best influence and regulate private investment and consumption. . . . Second, each project included in a development plan should be not

2. Kunkel (1961); Young and Young (1960).
3. For example Bennis *et al.* (1969), Currie (1966), King (1967), Meier (1965), Sutton (1961). For a critical analysis of planned change, see Boguslaw (1965).
4. Lewis (1966).
5. Hirschman (1958).

only technically and economically sound but also within the country's capacity to execute—which means that the feasibility of a project must be considered in the light of all other simultaneous demands on a country's resources and talents. . . . Third, the total program of government employment and government purchases plus anticipated private demand for goods and services should be no greater than the economy can supply. . . . Fourth, an economic plan should be flexible enough to permit alterations to meet unforseen contingencies.[6] [Fifth, a plan's goals must be realistic, and finally] the provisions of the plan for stimulating and regulating private economic activity must be adapted to the institutions of the country.[7]

Descriptions of actual plans and evaluations of their operation and effectiveness usually have similar orientations. Waterston's monumental *Development Plans: The Lessons of Experience,*[8] for example, provides an overview of plans that have been proposed and instituted in various parts of the world. Again the major emphasis is on economic factors, taxes and investment, governmental structures and their operation, the characteristics of national and regional planning bodies, and so forth.

The literature on large-scale planning for economic development is extensive enough, and the contributions by experts in various fields have been of such a high quality, that there is little point in summarizing or evaluating the information presently available. The behavioral perspective outlined in previous chapters *complements* existing treatments of development planning in at least three areas: 1) it emphasizes some of the noneconomic aspects of industrialization, 2) it focuses on the men and behavior patterns that large-scale plans are designed to influence, and 3) it provides a foundation for the solution of many of the problems encountered in the planning and execution of development programs. In many respects the behavioral perspective to planning is as narrow and partial as the economic perspective; in combination, however, the two make the successful planning for development a distinct possibility.

When men and their actions are viewed as important components of industrialization, it follows that programs designed to institute—or accel-

6. Hagen (1963:328–31).
7. Ibid. p. 332.
8. Waterston (1965).

erate—economic development must necessarily be concerned with the alteration of behavior. It is not enough to simply "alter" behavior, however, for the "take-off" and self-sustaining economic growth depend on the shaping of a particular set of new activities. Thus it is often necessary to eliminate one group of activities and to replace it with another.

Psychodynamic models of man require as the first step that the internal state be changed. Consequently development programs must be concerned with the establishment of creative personalities and the increase of need-achievement, for example. Even when it is known *how* such changes can be brought about (and often it is not), a considerable amount of time is required to affect these changes. In the face of rising expectations and the demonstration effect it is questionable, to say the least, whether citizens of developing nations are willing to wait for several generations, or at least a number of years, which—according to Hagen and McClelland —will pass before significant changes in behavior and thus the growth rate become possible.

The theoretical and practical shortcomings of psychodynamic models of man cannot help but be reflected in development programs revolving around the internal state. A common alternative is the disregard of men and the concentration, instead, on purely economic factors. Neither type of development program promises success, for the activities of men are either overlooked or considered to be of secondary importance.

The behavioral perspective of economic development initially concentrates on the activities performed by individuals, but since many of the contingencies originate in the regional social structures and national institutions, the analysis soon requires the insights of sociologists and political scientists. Furthermore, as long as a considerable number of rewards (and also aversive consequences) are of a material nature, the economic organizations of community and nation play a role in shaping and maintaining behavior patterns. To put it differently, learning principles provide a means by which social, political, and economic policies and programs become articulated determinants of behavior stability and change.

Behavioral Characteristics of Development Programs

Every student of economic growth sooner or later confronts the problem of initiating or accelerating social change, or at least of redirecting the course of change. Aside from the moral questions concerning the justification for such endeavors there are practical questions of procedure. Some peasants "cling stubbornly" to their "old-fashioned" and "inefficient" ways; other villagers "joyously embrace" new customs that are not "good" for them; and some natives simply refuse to be motivated by the "benefits of civilization." What is the change agent to do?

The behavioral model of man cannot answer ethical questions or provide criteria for the moral evaluation of action. Learning principles do, however, provide answers for questions such as: why are some new techniques accepted while others, apparently so similar, are rejected? In their book *Introducing Social Change,* Arensberg and Niehoff write that, concerning this particular question, for example, "there are no set rules that can give pat answers; but there is now a considerable body of helpful information that has been gathered." [9] While the answers provided by the behavioral perspective for this and other questions are by no means "pat," the answers *are* part of a consistent, and growing, body of thought and evidence. The lessons that are to be learned from both the failure and success of development projects, as summarized by a number of authors, do not conflict with the learning approach to development programs.[10] In fact, Niehoff,[11] Spicer,[12] and others provide abundant illustrations of the behavioral perspective. Whyte and Williams,[13] drawing mainly on material from Latin America, have recently sketched the outline of an "integrated" theory of development whose implications for action are derived from the assumption that behavior is greatly affected by the consequences which men anticipate on the basis of their own and others' past experiences.

The contributions of the behavioral model of man to development programs can be described best by ordering them in terms of the various steps involved in the planning process.

1. THE SPECIFICATION OF INDUSTRIAL, AGRICULTURAL, AND OTHER ENTERPRISES

No matter how abstract or concrete the goal of a development program may be, its attainment depends in large part on the various enterprises that must be established or expanded within a community, region,

9. Arensberg and Niehoff (1964:67).
10. A partial exception is Goodenough (1963).
11. Niehoff (1966).
12. Spicer (1952).
13. Whyte and Williams (1968).

and nation. Plans vary in specificity and duration, some are designed for the whole nation while others concern only one or two sectors, and some are more idealistic than others.[14] Every plan, however, must sooner or later provide information concerning the numbers and types of enterprises that are to flourish at the end of the plan. In many nations, even this first step is difficult to perform, for the data that are required to accurately describe existing conditions—and thus provide a base line for projections —are often fragmentary and inaccurate.[15] On the national level, unrealistic projections, mistakes in judgment, and wishful thinking are often rather significant components of technical and economic plans.[16] Local and regional programs are also subject to error, and as Hirschman has recently shown, the planning of specific industrial projects is often plagued by uncertainties that produce miscalculations.[17] Even when sufficient information is available the question arises whether large or small industries should be encouraged, whether various industrial sectors should develop simultaneously or whether some disequilibrium can be permitted, whether agriculture can be temporarily neglected, whether capital-intensive or labor-intensive industries and factories should be planned, and what role the production of consumer goods should play.

It is not within the scope of this book to evaluate arguments for and against balanced growth, cottage industries, or labor-intensive machinery. These and other controversies have received considerable attention in the literature,[18] and the behavioral perspective has little to contribute toward their resolution. All that the behavioral perspective requires is the description of enterprises—for example "two breweries employing 126 workers each, including x laborers with y skills"—so that the specific behavior requirements of various regions and of the whole nation can be determined. To a very large extent, then, this first step must be performed by economists, and since the specification of enterprises has always been part of the planning process, no new procedures are required for laying this foundation of the behavioral contribution to development programs.

14. For a good discussion of the assets and liabilities of these characteristics, see Waterston (1965:Part I).

15. Ibid. Chapter 6.

16. For examples see Hirschman (1963:chapter 4) and the essays in Hagen (1963).

17. Hirschman (1967).

18. For example Aubrey (1951), Fisher (1967), Herman (1956), Hirschman (1958), Kindleberger (1964), Meier (1964), Rao (1956).

2. THE SPECIFICATION OF BEHAVIOR PATTERNS ASSOCIATED WITH THE ECONOMIC DEVELOPMENT OF A PARTICULAR COMMUNITY, REGION, OR NATION AT A CERTAIN TIME [19]

The labor requirements of any development program, including not only industry and agriculture but also various services, governmental organizations, educational institutions, and so forth, are next combined into broad categories, such as "attending simple machines," "performing complex, skilled tasks," "supervising others," and "working for long, specific periods." Within each category are then listed the specific activities associated with, for example, the machines in various enterprises or the tasks in various bureaucracies. Thus, if the manufacture of cotton cloth is to be a major industry, the different activities associated with this production must be delineated, along with the number of men who should perform these activities. The resulting list of activities and their approximate frequencies usually will be of little use when the nation is the frame of reference; it is only then the activities and frequencies are placed within the context of particular regions, and perhaps even specific communities, that this information becomes a meaningful part of behavioral analysis.

Behavior patterns included in one or another job are not the only activities that are part of development programs. "Saving" and "investing," for example, are complex sets of actions that must be dissected before they can become part of behavioral analysis, as are the "purchase" and "use" of consumer goods (Chapter Six). In this step it is also important to convert other large-scale and often amorphous phenomena commonly described in the development literature—such as "education" and "respect for government"—into strictly behavioral terms. Thus education is dissected into "going to school," "sending children to school," "attending classes for x years," "giving children 'time off' to go to school," "training teachers," "supervising teachers," "providing teaching materials," etc.

The result of such dissection should be a long list, probably containing several hundred specific activities, which describes in detail all of *the behavioral requirements for the economic development of a particular social system at a specific time.* Other nations and other times may well have similar requirements, but from the very start of any behavioral program it is well to proceed as independently as possible. This is not to say

19. For a discussion of general behavioral requirements, see Moore (1963b).

that one nation cannot or should not learn from another. However, *one can only learn how to employ procedures,* and often there is little sense in learning other people's variables.

3. THE SPECIFICATION OF EXISTING BEHAVIOR PATTERNS AND THEIR DETERMINANTS

Many of the behavior patterns on the list established in Step Two are likely to exist already, at least to some extent. For example, many parents *are* sending their children to school, some men *do* work in factories, and some industrial innovation can be observed in every nation. However, the activities associated with industrialization usually are not as prevalent as required for the take-off, and too large a segment of the population may engage in behavior patterns that are incompatible with these requirements. Every activity that appears on the list *and* is observed must be related to its several determinants, that is, the specific discriminative and contingent stimuli, state variables, and schedules of reinforcement which, together, are responsible for the maintenance of the activity.

The major source of this necessary information is the repeated observation of the behavior pattern as it occurs within the operation of a specific social structure. In the course of these investigations it will become apparent that the incidence of behavioral requisites of economic development is related to the prevalence of structural elements which may be found only in certain areas of a country, in particular population segments, occupational categories, religious groups, and so forth. Sending boys to school, for example, may be reinforced for members of the newly emerging middle classes, but sending girls probably is not.

The discriminative and contingent stimuli for many observed activities will be the same or quite similar; "deferential behavior on the part of others," for example, is likely to be a reinforcer for several different activities, while "presence of peasants" may be an S^D for a number of actions. Thus, while the number of S^D and S^r initially may be very large, it will be much smaller after appropriate combinations of similar elements have been completed.

The frame of reference is not only the nation but also, in the case of many a developing country, the various significant regions and subcultures within it. Since discriminative and contingent stimuli are learned and may be expected to vary from one group or subculture to another, the frame of reference of *each activity* must be noted in order to avoid or explain inconsistencies. For example, one of the major consequences of the activity, "sending young girls to school," is the kind of person described as a "smart young female." While this may be considered an S^r in some subcultures, such as the emerging middle class in metropolitan areas, it probably will be viewed as unnecessary or irrelevant (S^o) in other groups and as actually threatening (S^a) in some segments of the population.

4. THE SPECIFICATION OF INCOMPATIBLE BEHAVIOR PATTERNS AND THEIR DETERMINANTS

Some of the observed activities are incompatible with the behavior patterns on the list established in Step Two. For example, "keeping children at home for agricultural labor" is in conflict with "sending children to school." It is therefore necessary to ascertain for each of the existing incompatible activities the associated discriminative and contingent stimuli, the schedules of reinforcement, and the state variables which may be assumed to operate in a particular community or subculture.

Incompatibility may take the form of direct conflict, as in the above illustration, or it may be indirect in the sense that time or opportunity for the required activity may be circumscribed by a series of other actions. For example, a full day's labor that may be required for the provision of basic necessities is incompatible with "sending children to school." In this case it is impossible to point to a specific action as being responsible.

While the determination of many incompatibilities has a logical foundation, as in the first illustration, there are many which have a value-laden basis. The people of Montegrano, for example, explain the absence of community organizations and co-operative efforts at least partly in terms of lack of sufficient time. They point out that agricultural pursuits, especially, are quite time-consuming. Yet Banfield found, upon careful investigation, that the average villager spent no more than a few weeks of the year in the fields.[20] Repeated and close observations are absolutely necessary, then, and the results should always be phrased in the form of hypotheses. Just as Hirschman [21] has shown that many "obstacles" to economic development are the results of theories and do not exist in reality, so it is quite possible that many superficially "incompatible activities" may turn out to be quite compatible.

20. Banfield (1958).
21. Hirschman (1965).

When the discriminative and contingent stimuli of incompatible activities have been ascertained, it is likely that, as in Step Three, many will be identical or very similar. A relatively small number of state variables, S^D, and S^r may well account for a large number of these activities.

5. THE SHAPING, MAINTENANCE, AND EXTINCTION OF BEHAVIOR PATTERNS

The behavioral component of any development program consists of three major parts: the shaping of "new" activities associated with industrialization, the maintenance of those "old" actions which are part of the process, and the extinction of incompatible behavior patterns. While much information required for the selective treatment of activities is gathered during the steps outlined above, an important question must be answered before actual procedures can be implemented: "what proportion—and which—of the behavior patterns described in the three steps will be affected?"

No development program can be expected to shape *all* of the required activities or to extinguish *all* incompatible actions. In fact, it may be impossible to affect more than a relatively small number of behavior patterns, for the amount of control over discriminative and contingent stimuli is usually quite small. If the program is to have any chance of success, behavior patterns will have to be selected on the basis of two not necessarily consistent criteria: the actions considered to be *crucial for industrialization,* and actions whose determinants are *subject to control that is sufficient for their alteration.*

The first criterion involves value judgments based partly on economists' selections of enterprises deemed crucial for the development of a particular nation. The second criterion reflects the degree of national integration, the strength and wisdom of governmental agencies, and the time span that is available. Generally speaking, the smaller the unit, the more easily and completely both criteria are met. In Vicos, for example, the "crucial" actions could be determined quite easily, and control over contingencies was more than ample. On the regional and national levels, however, it is difficult to determine crucial activities, if only because these tend to vary from one area—and expert—to the next. And control over these activities' discriminative and contingent stimuli is likely to be insufficient, if only because more people need to be subjected to it. The problem of control is aggravated by the fact that behavior is established most easily and lastingly when rewards are the dominant (but not the only) type of contingency.[22] Rewards are difficult to provide systematically and consistently, and they are often considered to be expensive; how much simpler and cheaper, therefore—at least in the short run—to rely on aversive contingencies. In the behavioral perspective, however, "control over contingencies" refers to *both* reward and punishment; and since the former is more effective and efficient than the latter, *"control" should be concerned more with reinforcing than with aversive contingencies.*

The scarcity of reinforcers in most developing nations and the often acknowledged temptation to employ somewhat authoritarian and thus suppressive procedures, makes it imperative to select those activities whose alteration requires the provision of relatively few *reinforcing and aversive* contingencies.

Behavior modification is at the core of most development programs, and the problems that are encountered in the shaping, maintenance, and extinction of activities present major threats to the success of any project. The problems and available solutions in these three areas therefore deserve special attention and will be considered separately.

6. THE MAINTENANCE AND INCREASE OF
EXISTING BEHAVIOR PATTERNS

As was pointed out in Step Three, many of the activities which are required for economic growth can already be observed to some extent in developing nations today. Development programs therefore must be designed to maintain these activities, and to increase the prevalence of these activities by having people engage in them more often or by having more people perform them.

a) Since behavior is replicated over time if the contingencies remain the same, care must be taken that the reinforcers which maintain the "desirable" activities will continue to be presented on the old or very similar schedules. Ideally, the discriminative stimuli should also remain the same, but it is possible to gradually define new S^D *provided* that the activity continues to be rewarded in the new context. In addition, existing state variables should remain the same or, in case they are altered, the associated "new" reinforcers must replace the "old."

The significance of these considerations lies in the conclusion that

22. Staats and Staats (1963), Azrin and Holz (1966), Bandura (1969:chapter 4).

development programs must include not only designs dealing with change but also designs for the *selective retention* of existing characteristics. Since many of the activities in a community's or nation's social structure are related in that they are equivalent to discriminative or contingent stimuli for other actions (see Chapter Five), the alteration of one action may well affect another. The maintenance of an activity which is reinforced by another action that needs to be changed, for example, will therefore require the judicious substitution of a new and equally effective reinforcer. The *maintenance* of an activity, then, may require as much care and ingenuity on the part of the planner as does the alteration of behavior.

b) The prevalence of an activity may be increased in two major ways, depending on whether the *rate* of performance by individuals is to be changed, or whether the *distribution* of the activity is to be widened.

Rate. The frequency with which an action is performed can be increased by attaching rewards not only to the action but also its rate. While this operation is similar to an alteration in the schedule of reinforcement, it is not identical with it, for rewards are now contingent upon *performance per unit of time.* Whether or not the rewards themselves must be changed or presented more frequently will depend on the specific activities and situations under consideration.

Distribution. The extent to which any kind of behavior is evident in a population can be increased by establishing this behavior in people who do not now perform it. In order to accomplish this it must first be determined why some people do not exhibit this behavior, and thus many of the procedures outlined above, and especially in Steps Three and Four will be relevant. Next, the procedures described in Chapter Three and Step Eight below are employed to shape the "new" activities. Structural incompatibilities will present the major obstacles, in the sense that many "new" activities may not be consistent with the behavior patterns traditionally associated with the "upper class," "peasants," "women," etc. Role definitions may have to be altered, for example, if it is agreed in various subcultures that "gentlemen do not work with their hands," "peasants cannot be given responsibility," and "women cannot be educated." Vicos and Pakistan suggest that the judicious presentation of strong reinforcers and aversive consequences can shape new behavior in spite of old role definitions.

While there usually is little argument that the prevalence of "factory labor," "saving," and "entrepreneurship" must be increased if a nation is to develop economically, there is disagreement on *how much* saving or *how many* entrepreneurs there must be. Too much saving reduces the market for manufactured goods, and too many entrepreneurs lead to overcompetition. Where should the line be drawn, and how can the distance from it be measured?

Economists' models of regional and national economies provide rough estimates, but in the absence of adequate data and validated (rather than hypothetical) models, most answers are little more than educated guesses.[23] In the early stages of development it may be safe to conclude that "more of everything" is an adequate answer, but selectivity may need to be instituted quite soon. In short, the behavioral engineer will have to rely on the economist, for the behavioral perspective cannot answer these questions.

7. THE EXTINCTION AND DECREASE OF INCOMPATIBLE BEHAVIOR PATTERNS

As was pointed out in Step Four, some of the activities in which citizens of developing nations engage are directly incompatible with the behavioral requirements of industrialization. Development programs therefore must be designed to extinguish these activists in individuals, and/or decrease the frequency with which these actions are performed without a population. In most cases the latter goal can be accomplished best by extinguishing the activities in a significant number of individuals.

a) *Extinction.* The probability of behavior replication is reduced and will approach zero upon the application of one or more of three procedures: the cessation of reinforcement, the punishment of the activity, and the shaping (and thus reinforcement) of incompatible actions. As far as is known today, it *appears* that cessation of reinforcement is most effective, for punishment often results in "spontaneous recovery" upon the cessation of aversive contingencies. The third procedure requires considerable care. Ideally, then, an activity is extinguished by withholding reinforcement. The length of time required for this procedure is quite substantial, however, for most activities are rewarded on one or another type of intermittent schedule, and thus are quite "firmly established" (Chapter Three). The extinction time may be shortened by the occasional

23. For example Leibenstein (1957), Higgins (1968), Hunter (1961), Meier and Baldwin (1957).

punishment of these activities, but in the case of most behavior patterns, and especially of those which have been part of the individual's life for quite a few years, extinction may require a number of months and occasionally several years. Even after much time has passed it is possible that an action will occur again, but if it is not reinforced, the probability of repetition declines still further. Because of the possibility of "spontaneous recovery," then, it is useful to include in any development program the capability of punishing, or at least of not reinforcing, the occasional exhibition of activities that are to be extinguished.

b) *Reduction.* The prevalence of an activity may be reduced in two major ways, depending on whether the *rate* of performance by individuals is to be decreased, or whether the *distribution* of the activity is to be narrowed.

Rate. Sometimes it is not so much the activity itself which is incompatible with industrialization as the rate at which it occurs. The rate can be reduced by reinforcing not the activity itself but the lower rate at which it is expressed, that is, by rewarding *performance per unit of time.* This procedure is especially important when the "incompatible action" is an integral part of daily life, or when it helps maintain life or the family. "Requiring children to help at home," for example, is a set of parental actions that may be necessary for the welfare of the family. But it may not be necessary to keep *all* five teenagers at home; if two can do the required work the other three are able to attend school.

Distribution. The incompatible activities that prevail in a population can be decreased by extinguishing them in people that now perform them. The procedures outlined above will be employed, subject to three major limitations. First, it is quite possible that some incompatible activities are being reinforced by actions which are neutral or useful to development, and which therefore should not be eliminated. In this case the major alternative to the cessation of rewards is the instituting of aversive contingencies, with all the drawbacks described above.

Second, some of the behavior patterns which are incompatible with economic development may be either a part of, or required by, a community's social structure, and thus are reinforced. "Preparing for law," for example, is incompatible with "engineering training," yet the former is an integral part of the gentleman's way of life in many a developing nation. Since in this case aversive contingencies will not be available, short of revolution, the major alternative is the special reinforcement of activities that are part of the development process, such as high pay (and eventually prestige) for engineers. Hopefully, incompatible actions will decline in the population because the contingencies of *other* activities are changed.

Third, a question arises concerning the *extent* to which incompatible activities must be reduced within a population. Here again, as in Step Six, there are theoretical guide lines based on economists' models, but no definite answer can be given as yet. Furthermore, as pointed out in Step Four, it is often difficult to determine whether a behavior pattern is incompatible or not.

In practice, then, it is probably best to extinguish those actions which are *obviously* incompatible, within the limitations of *reasonable* available procedures. Since "obvious" and "reasonable" are difficult to define and tend to vary from one time and circumstance to another, it is probably most efficient to concentrate the efforts of development programs on Steps Six and Eight. A good pragmatic definition of incompatibility may then be any "old" action that interferes with the establishment of the required new behavior patterns.

Once more the experiences of Vicos and Pakistan enable the behaviorally-oriented change agent to be optimistic. For many of the activities which at one time were considered to be incompatible—"laziness" and *mercantile* entrepreneurship—quickly disappeared in the face of *new* activities reinforced by *new* contingencies.

8. THE SHAPING AND MAINTENANCE OF "NEW" BEHAVIOR PATTERNS

The activities on the list prepared in Step Two which do not exist in a community or nation can be established by the application of differential reinforcement. This will usually involve the following sequence of procedures:

a) After the activity that is to be shaped has been specified, its constituent elements must be delineated. Most behavior patterns associated with economic development are quite complex, and thus it cannot be expected that they will be exhibited from the first in their final form. Rather, the various actions that constitute the behavior pattern may have to be learned separately and later be combined in the correct sequence. Furthermore, complex activities may have to be established by means of successive approximation,and thus a sequence of actions progressing by logical steps from simple existing actions to the final complex activity, needs to be determined. The ability to engage in careful, logical analysis therefore would appear to be a basic requirement of any change agent.

b) Before the actual shaping can begin, the contingencies that should —or can—be used must be specified. This implies a knowledge of both deprivation characteristics and the kinds of reinforcers one will be able to dispense during the period of learning. When generalized reinforcers such as money are to be used, one must be certain that exchange into other rewards is possible. The major problem, as illustrated in the Zande Scheme, is that planners often are not aware of people's conceptions of reinforcers, and thus great care must be taken to insure that the *reinforcers are considered adequate by the people involved,* no matter how "strange" or "stupid" the rewards may appear to an outsider. Perspicacity, insight, and a touch of wisdom would appear to be basic requirements of any change agent.

c) Circumstances in which the activity is to be performed—that is, the associated discriminative stimuli—must also be specified before the actual shaping can begin. While it is acceptable to initially reward the activity *whenever* it appears, S^D should be established as soon as possible. This cannot be done, however, unless the S^D are carefully defined. The major problem is that the change agent's order or mere presence inadvertently may become the S^D, so that villagers, for example, perform new activities only when the change agent is around or is likely to return. Since the planner is often the (indirect) dispenser of rewards it is almost "natural" that he should become an S^D. An important part of the shaping process, then, is *the establishment of discriminative stimuli other than the planner, extension agent, peace corps volunteer, etc.* It is unfortunate, perhaps, that often it is emotionally satisfying to be an important S^D for other people's activities, whose "dependent" behavior then becomes a reinforcer; maturity on the part of the change agent, therefore, would appear to be a basic requirement.

d) Depending on whether the activity that is to be established is simple or complex, the action itself or its components can now begin to be shaped. The best procedure is a combination of instruction and modeling, with the proportion of each depending on the nature of the activity, the situation, and the characteristics of the change agent. Generally speaking, the more complex the task and the greater its difference from existing activities, the more emphasis there should be on modeling. No matter what the procedure, however, it is important that the individual *perform* the activity that is to be shaped. Two problems are likely to arise here. First, the individual may be unwilling to perform a task—especially "in public"—until he has mastered it, at least mentally. Nash,[24] for example, describes a factory in Guatemala in which new laborers simply watch experienced workers—often for many days—until they are certain that they will be able to do a good job. The fear of losing face by bungling a task results in a training period that is much longer than would be required if "practice" were included. Practice, however, would be possible only if the novice were isolated from experienced workers, or if the novices were trained together so that they would be surrounded by individuals more or less equally awkward in their actions. The second problem is that change agents often become exasperated by the slow and awkward performances of their "students." Slow and awkward performances, however, are integral parts not only of successive approximation, but of learning itself, and thus are to be expected. Furthermore, initially at least, *these performances must be rewarded.* When people "give up" halfway through learning a task, this is usually a result of inadequate reinforcement. It may be difficult for a change agent to praise a "sloppy job," and this should not be done for an extended period of time, but initially it is necessary. Care must be taken that, upon a "sloppy job," the change agent, in desperation, does not perform and complete the task himself. If he finishes the work, the "sloppy job" is in effect rewarded, and individuals will soon learn that a little effort on their part is an S^D for someone else's satisfactory completion of the task. The behavior which is established in this way, then, is not "adequate, complete performance," but rather "sloppy, incomplete attempt." Many failures of development programs, both on the level of community and region, are due to the inadvertent reinforcement and shaping of the "wrong" behavior pattern. Sadie,[25] for example, describes various unsuccessful efforts to help the South African Bantu "help themselves." It is quite apparent from his discussion that agents of the various development authorities have shaped behavior patterns that might be called "requesting help" rather than activities labeled independence, hard work, and so forth. The authorities, for example, expressed great interest in wire fences and "taught" the Bantu to build them. The people did not maintain the fences, how-

24. Nash (1958).
25. Sadie (1960).

ever, for they soon learned that a simple request to authorities to "fix the fence" resulted in the fence being repaired. The authorities' conclusion "Bantus don't care about fences" was the consequence of, and was being maintained by, the authorities' own *concern* with and repair of fences. A certain capacity for logical analysis, the understanding of other peoples' values and norms, and—above all—*patience* would appear to be among the requirements of a successful change agent.

e) Eventual success in the establishment of even simple behavior patterns depends primarily on the schedule of reinforcement that was in effect during the learning period. Not only must care be taken to reward the "right" activity, as just pointed out, but initially even those actions that merely *approach* the "right" one should be reinforced. However, such reinforcement must be handled with caution, for it is quite easy to shape incomplete acts rather than the completed activity. An incomplete act should be reinforced—in order to show the individual that he is on the right track, so to speak—but it should be indicated quite soon that full rewards can accrue only upon the adequate performance of the complete activity. It is not only the actual reinforcement, then, which is important, but also the individuals' conceptions of the *probability of future rewards*. Villagers' "trust" in the change agent, for example, concerns primarily the degree of certainty of eventual reinforcement. At the same time, such "trust" is the result of the change agent's past performance especially his proven ability to accurately predict—and produce—future rewards. Reinforcement, of course, does not come only as a result of the change agent's intervention; the activity may itself produce rewards, independent of an outsider's help. New methods of cultivation, for example, increased the potato crop in Vicos, and thus the new methods were reinforced "naturally" and permanently adopted. Other "new" activities, however, may not be as obviously beneficial. Erasmus, for example, describes the inefficiency and lengthy training involved in having villagers build their own "modern" houses.[26] Part of the length of training is due to the fact that there is only *one* reward, one's own house, with little or no further opportunities to employ one's new skills. In addition, the schedule of reinforcement must be congruent with the person's world view. If he has a conception of the universe as being capricious, reinforcers must be presented frequently, and it cannot be assumed that the possibility or *promise* of "future rewards" will play an important role.

26. Erasmus (1968).

When the universe is assumed to be systematic, however, the time between behavior and rewards can be much longer. The schedule of reinforcement which is effective in one region or for one man may therefore be quite ineffective in another area. It is possible to change schedules, however, and the frequency of rewards may thus be reduced. New change agents who cannot be trusted because their predictions have not yet been validated, and the conception of a capricious universe, would both benefit from a schedule of frequent rewards. Since the agent's predictions can then be validated in short order, he is likely to be trusted soon, and at least a part of the universe will then appear to be systematic. As a result it soon will be possible to employ a schedule with less frequent rewards. Adaptability and flexibility would appear to be prominent characteristics of effective change agents.

f) Frequent reinforcement, by itself, does not guarantee that an activity will be learned; the consistency of contingencies plays an equally important role. *"Consistent rewards" does not mean "continuous rewards,"* but refers to the fact that one action (R_1) is rewarded on one or another schedule, while another action (R_2) is punished. As a result of such consistent differential reinforcement one action (R_1) is shaped and maintained, while the other (R_2) is extinguished. When contingencies are applied inconsistently it is very difficult if not impossible to shape or extinguish any behavior. If one wanted to shape or maintain R_1, for example, and extinguish R_2, the following schedule of contingencies would practically guarantee failure (figure 10-1):

Times of Observation

	1	2	3	4	5	6	7	8	9	10
R_1	r	p	p	r	p	p	r	r	r	p
R_2	p	r	r	p	r	p	p	r	p	r

(r means reward; p means punishment)

FIGURE 10–1: Schedules of Contingencies

The major problem that is encountered in providing consistent contingencies in development programs derives from the fact that both reward and punishment can be presented consistently only if the preceding activity is *known* and if the required contingencies are *available*. In the present example, if R_1 is to be shaped, R_1 at time 2 should be reinforced, but this can be done only if one knows that R_1—rather than R_2—has occurred. A change agent living in a community has a reasonably good chance to acquire this knowledge, but regional programs often lack this information. In the shaping of complex behavior patterns, therefore, local programs will probably be more successful than those which lack personal supervision.

Even when the change agent is well acquainted with life in a community, however, he may not be able to reward and shape new behavior patterns, especially when these conflict with the requirements of the established power structure. The activities of change agents often are subject to contingencies provided by local officials, large land owners, and politicians, and thus it frequently happens that the limitations imposed on the agent in effect lead to the perpetuation of "old" activities among the villagers.[27]

Ideally, then, change agents should not only be involved in "their" communities and be aware of "their" people's actions; in addition they must be *able* to present contingencies when these are required.

g) Generalized reinforcers such as money, which can be exchanged for a number of other objects, present few problems in populations where cash and its properties are well known. Specific reinforcers, however, depend on specific state variables, and especially deprivation, for their effectiveness. In some exceptional cases, for example the Bantu described by Sadie, the existence of a cash economy does not make money a reinforcer because it cannot be exchanged for anything that would reduce deprivations—for there are no (apparent) deprivations. Since the shaping of behavior depends on differential *reinforcement,* and reinforcement cannot occur unless there are some actual or anticipated *deprivations,* it follows that some degree of deprivation, present or future, is required. In populations characterized by "constant wants," and in communities where "invidious sanctions" prevail or wealth equalization devices are the norm,[28] there will be few deprivations and hence few reinforcers. There may be objective deprivations in nutrition, housing, and health, for example, but since most human deprivations are subjective and culturally defined, objective standards introduced by outsiders cannot be used to

27. For several good examples, see Niehoff (1966), Spicer (1952), Whyte and Williams (1968).
28. As described, for example, by Erasmus (1961) and Nash (1964a).

determine them. In short, members of one culture must *learn* what is considered to be a deprivation, and thus a reinforcer, in another. This logical, easily apparent, almost self-evident point, to which it is so easy to pay lip service, is an important cause of development program failures, for all too often it is forgotten or disregarded. The forgetfulness takes two principal forms. First, change agents may assume that what was rewarding "at home" is also a reward in the community or region in which they now work. Europeans employed in African development projects, for example, often consider "fat, healthy cattle" to be rewarding, and initiate agricultural programs designed to produce such animals. But in many tribes status accrues to him who has "many animals," no matter how scrawny or sickly they may be. The reinforcer, in other words, is the *number,* not the *shape* of cattle. Bascom and Herskovits [29] provide abundant evidence of cattle improvement programs that have failed because the program designers and directors employed European, rather than tribal, definitions of deprivations and thus rewards. Such cattle programs will be successful only when "fat, healthy" cattle become reinforcers—as they have in some communities. Sadie summarizes the efforts to change Bantu life as follows: "the untiring efforts of the developing authority rather than those of the inhabitants themselves have been responsible for the measure of development that has taken place. There has been no fundamental change in the social structure, habits and institutions of the people." [30] In large part this is due to the absence of strong deprivations —and thus of possible reinforcers—that characterizes the population. In the words of Sadie, the people's "needs are relatively few. There is no strong urge to attain ever-increasing standards of material welfare. They do not have an acquisitive instinct." [31] Building and maintaining fences to improve cattle, to return to a previous point, therefore is not reinforced except by the avoidance of Europeans' displeasure—a poor reward indeed! Second, a change agent may be so aware of being in a different culture that he assumes all the deprivations, and thus reinforcers, *are* different—or *should* be different. The administrators of the Zande Scheme, for example, would not pay a higher price for the cotton grown by the people because they thought that the Azande either did not know how to spend money "wisely" (i.e. in European fashion), or should not

29. Bascom and Herskovits (1959).
30. Sadie (1960:301).
31. Ibid. p. 297. In other words, there are few learned deprivations.

be perverted by decadent cash (i.e. as had the Europeans). In short, it cannot be assumed that deprivations and reinforcers are the same in all cultures. Instead, the specific deprivations and reinforcers that prevail in a particular community or region have to be carefully analyzed, without preconceptions. It would appear, therefore, that a good change agent is not blinded by ethnocentrism.

h) However well a new activity has been shaped, its *maintenance* depends on the continued provision of consistent reinforcers, some degree of deprivation, and the occurrence of the discriminative stimulus that has been established. The most important factor is the continuation of (intermittent) reinforcement. Even after an activity has been learned it must be rewarded for a time at a moderately high rate, for both the activity and the schedule of reinforcement are new. A schedule that is effective for members of the well-educated middle class of an industrial nation cannot be transferred to a developing country, and development programs which concentrate on the shaping of behavior and neglect the planning of later reinforcers are not likely to be effective. For example, some of Mexico's "rural cultural missions" designed to bring education and national contacts to the more isolated areas of the nation, are not effective because there are few reinforcers for the new activities after the mission has left the village. The missions which emphasize skills that are "useful" in daily life, however, are more likely to be successful in the sense of firmly establishing new behavior patterns.[32] Since rewards are likely to be provided somewhat more frequently during the shaping process than is necessary for long-term maintenance, *the schedule must be changed—but gradually;* if it is changed rapidly, the activity is in danger of being extinguished. It would appear, in short, that a change agent will require the same characteristics and should employ similar procedures for both the shaping and maintenance of behavior.

i. Illogical though it may sound, a development program can be termed "successful" only when the need for its existence has disappeared. As Erasmus[33] has shown, few programs or agencies are ever judged to be unnecessary, if only because this would imply that the human beings who run them are no longer needed; and no one wants to admit being useless. Ideally, a development program from the very first day of its existence is geared to achieve its own extinction. The most important

32. Fisher (1953:79–84).
33. Erasmus (1968).

aspect of this extinction is the withdrawal of personnel and temporary services from the community or nation. Even in perfectly operating development programs at least some of the rewards originate with the change agent and other outside sources, and their rapid withdrawal would abruptly change the schedule of reinforcement. The gradual and carefully controlled withdrawal of men and programs is required if the transition from one schedule and source of reinforcers to another is to be successful and uneventful, that is, if it is to leave the associated behavior patterns undisturbed. The schedule and sources of reinforcers that remain are, of course, associated with the new activities themselves. A valid sign of success, and a sure indication that termination is both necessary and possible, is the transition from reinforcers provided by the change agent or the program itself to reinforcers associated with the newly established behavior patterns, and the transition from a schedule determined by the change agent to one that is "natural" to the newly shaped activities. It would appear, then, that the competent change agent has sufficient foresight, wisdom—and altruism—to adequately plan his own timely and gradual disappearance. As an alternative, success criteria can be built into a program—for example a certain percentage of peasants who are employing new methods of cultivation. The change agent whose village or region meets these criteria would be required to leave the community and might be rewarded in some measure, for example by a promotion.

9. THE COMBINATION OF ELEMENTS INTO SOCIAL, ECONOMIC, AND POLITICAL PROGRAMS

In the course of outlining the specific procedures involved in the various steps, an extensive list of state variables, schedules of reinforcements, discriminative and contingent stimuli, will have been created. Some of these phenomena are behavior patterns, others are material objects of various kinds, and a few may be ideas such as "the good of the nation." Most of the elements will fall into three categories, depending on the institutions in which they originate or which influence them. A large proportion of the rewards and many schedules of reinforcement will be associated with the operation of a nation's economic system. A smaller number of rewards, at least in the initial stages of a development program, fall into the "social" category. A nation's or community's political institutions, finally, are responsible for a few direct reinforcers, most aversive consequences, and the schedules of many contingencies in general. There are, of course, no clear-cut divisions among these categories, and it is often difficult—and irrelevant—to determine whether the presentation of a reinforcer, for example, is the consequence of political, economic, or social institutions. In fact, the distinction is more a reflection of laymen's thinking than of the operation or requirement of development programs. In peasant communities where distrust and poverty are the dominant themes, for example, material reinforcers and high frequency schedules will be required for the shaping and maintenance of activities. The *combination* of economic and social projects, with the specifics and proportions depending on village requirements and national capabilities, and operating within a regional political and religious framework, must be determined anew for each community. The case of Vicos illustrates how the behavioral requirements of changed contingencies were translated into effective economic and social programs. The role of a national government in the shaping and maintenance of entrepreneurial activities—by establishing S^D, rewards and schedules of presentation—is illustrated by the case of Pakistan. A protected internal market made high profits possible, and the possibility of recouping investments in two or three years in effect produced a schedule of reinforcement that was practically continuous. National economic and social policies, then, *can* be as effective as community programs in the presentation of new contingencies and schedules for new behavior patterns.

A NOTE OF CAUTION

While it is easy to outline the procedures of behavior modification which have been proven effective in small group experiments, clinical settings, and a few projects in a free environment, it cannot be concluded that the general *application* of these procedures will be simply a matter of introducing them into a community. Any project and change agent operates within a pre-existing social context, and every village, town, or subculture is part of local and regional economic and political structures. There may be a publicly expressed goal of "development," of improving the lives of peasants, and so forth, but the privately held goals of land owners, village officials, and other powerful figures are likely to be different. No change agent will be successful in modifying the behavior of ordinary men unless the operations of the formal and informal power structures—designed to preserve the status quo—are neutralized. Since these structures consist of men and their actions, an alteration of the contingencies to which they are subject will lead to an alteration of activities and goals. National policies, regional governments, fiscal institutions, and political parties are some of the more peaceful means by which the contingencies of powerful individuals' activities can be changed. However, if present or future changes in contingencies are not perceived as *real* [34] —for example the belief that a government will talk about but never institute a land reform program—no behavior change is likely, for men learn easily to live with empty threats. Violence then becomes a reasonable alternative, and as Hirschman points out, at least in Latin America violence has been an important ingredient of reform.[35]

The economic development of rural areas, in short, involves the modification of behavior on the part of both peasant and land owner, of villager and official. The ordinary change agent, with control over contingencies that are meaningful to peasants, may be successful in some of his efforts of behavior modification. But if he has no power over land owners, officials, and other powerful individuals—for example by having some control over the contingencies of their actions—the ultimate success of his project is in doubt. A successful development program therefore must include not only village-level projects but also some ways of influencing powerful individuals.

The generally slow pace of rural development in many parts of the world is due not so much to the peasant's inability to change his ways as to the land owner's unwillingness to change his views. It may be useful, therefore, to speak of a social and behavioral "critical minimum effort," just as Leibenstein describes an economic one.[36] Concern with changing the behavior patterns of peasants will not be sufficient, and general social programs without the application of behavioral principles will not lead to success. Learning principles and especially *contingencies* must be applied if significant behavior modification in substantial segments of a population is to be attempted, but success depends, in addition, on the *opportunity to express the new activities.*

The Behavioral Perspective and Conventional Wisdom

Just as many of the principles and procedures of the behavioral model of man are not new—everybody "knows" that rewards affect a person's actions—so its implications for development programs should

---

34. Hirschman (1963:chapter 5), Rajfel (1969).
35. Hirschman (1963:256ff); for an alternative, see Holmberg (1959).
36. Leibenstein (1957).

startle few practitioners. What the behavioral model provides is a *rationale* for some of the conventional wisdom of development programs, and a more scientific basis for the structuring of specific projects. When the above procedures are followed, the behavior changes required by a project can be practically guaranteed. Failures are almost always due to the deliberate neglect of a step or its implications—for example, relying on aversive rather than reinforcing stimuli; or to the accidental disregard of a basic procedure—for example, employing European rather than native definitions of "reinforcer"; or to the inability to schedule and provide rewards and define discriminative stimuli because of insufficient control over the relevant aspects of the social system. The problem of insufficient control may take a variety of forms. Hostility of local religious officials, opposition by the formal or informal power structures of a community, and wavering or inconsistent support by national or regional governmental agencies, are some of the more common factors that reduce the change agent's power to define S^D and schedule contingencies for the new activities of villagers.

Much of the information contained in the nine steps is already part of the development literature, indicating that the behavioral perspective complements existing knowledge and increases the specificity of current dicta; it does not necessarily require the radical change of all current procedures. For example, the ideas that a successful program must "involve the peasant" and be concerned with *his* needs, that a change agent should "work *with* men, not *for* men," or that programs should involve "self-help" wherever possible, make good sense to the behaviorally-oriented change agent.[37] The utilization of learning principles makes it possible to indicate not only *why* this conventional wisdom often leads to success, but how and which efficient procedures might be employed in specific situations. The admonition to "invoke the peasant, and employ self-help programs" in effect summarizes Step Eight: the *individual* should perform the actions that are supposed to be established, there must be *rewards* which are relevant to his deprivation characteristics, and these *rewards* should be associated with the *activity* rather than the program. The proposition that plans are useless and doomed to failure unless there is a national, and especially a governmental, commitment to economic development—argued persuasively and illustrated especially well by Water-

37. For good summaries of the conventional wisdom, see Arensberg and Niehoff (1964), Foster (1962), Spicer (1952), Biddle and Biddle (1965, 1968).

ston [38]—again can be made more specific by the employment of a behavioral model of man. In order for behavior change to come about, discriminative and contingent stimuli must be altered, rewards for new activities must be presented *consistently,* and this can be accomplished best—at least on a national or regional scale—by governmental action that reflects "commitment" to development. Commitment refers to firmness, consistency, the long-range point of view, and willingness to pay the price for behavior change, whether it be the offering of material rewards to peasants or the readiness to accept the abuse of powerful groups such as land owners. Much of the conventional wisdom of development programs, in short, represents behavioral principles couched in the language of everyday life. The employment of a behavioral model of man, however, makes it possible to disregard inaccurate elements of the conventional wisdom—for example the idea that personality must be changed *before* action can be altered—and to substitute propositions with a firm empirical base. Furthermore, a knowledge of learning principles makes it possible to institute new procedures in situations not covered by the conventional wisdom and to solve problems to which extensions of the wisdom appear to be inapplicable.

Doing Good and Evil

Programs designed to "help the unfortunate" or to "help others help themselves" have long been popular among individuals and private agencies, and since World War II they have become respectable on the international level as well. No matter how lofty the ultimate goal may be and no matter how inspiring the rhetoric surrounding the methods, the purposes and procedures are concerned essentially with behavior and more specifically, the *alteration* of various activities. The behavioral approach therefore provides a useful means for the specification, analysis, and evaluation of such programs.

Any project of "helping others help themselves," be it in housing, education, agriculture, or other aspects of life, consists of two major parts. One is a set of activities performed by the subjects or clients, the other is the set of actions in which the change agents engage. A project can be successful only if the combination of these activities is congruent with the requirements of learning procedures.

38. Waterston (1965).

How does one "help others?" Primarily by shaping and maintaining new behavior patterns. The employment of new tools and new construction or cultivation methods, for example, may be taught by means of instruction or modeling. If the initial consequences, while favorable, do not become apparent for some time—such as next year's harvest—intermediate rewards such as praise or some type of payment may need to be provided in order to maintain the new activities.

How do "others help themselves?" Primarily by changing their behavior patterns. These changes can take a myriad of forms, such as the use of new tools or techniques, the construction and maintenance of better houses, the taking advantage of educational opportunities, or the use of improved seeds, new crops, or modern methods of agriculture. These activities are shaped by the (often unrecognized) employment of learning principles, and are maintained, in turn, by the presumably beneficial consequences of the various activities, such as better houses, improved means of dealing with merchants, better and larger crops, and so forth.

In short, any program designed to "help others" should be built around most if not all of the nine steps outlined above. The problems that are encountered in the process—for example the question of whose conception of "reinforcer" is to be used—must be solved if the program is to be successful, and thus any "helper" should have the qualities of change agents sketched in Step Eight. While many a "helper" is intelligent and educated, few are aware of learning principles and the problems of their application in situations and cultures which differ from those of the person who is bent on helping others. Hirschman's description of the "motivation-outruns-understanding style of problem-solving" [39] is as applicable to personal and small-scale projects as it is to national endeavors. The problem and its causes, along with the procedures for solution and their applications, should be reasonably well understood before action is initiated. "Motivation" may lead the helper to study a problem and analyze possible solutions, and it may sustain him when the results of his efforts are not immediately apparent, but it cannot by itself produce solutions. By emphasizing motivation rather than understanding, programs and individuals are often unable to help others by establishing new and more effective behavior patterns—they can only "do good."

Ideal goals and procedures of "doing good." While the over-all goal may be quite abstract—for example, "increasing the quality of life"—its

39. Hirschman (1963:chapter 4).

specific components consist mainly of new activities or material goods that are the results of various new actions. The procedures which should be employed, therefore, may be summarized as the *successive approxima- tion and differential reinforcement* of these activities. The essential factor, as mentioned a number of times throughout the book, is *the consistent and selective reinforcement of specific behavior patterns in particular circumstances.* This implies knowledge of deprivation, control over rein- forcers, etc. as described in previous chapters. It may be concluded, then, that both ideal goals and ideal procedures can be easily specified, but that the effective employment of the procedures requires extensive training and the careful analysis of each situation in which "good" is to be done.

Actual goals and procedures of "doing good." No matter how the ideal goal is defined, it often is little more than a euphemism for one or another actual goal. Among the major types of actual goals—which usually become apparent only upon the specification of ideal goal com- ponents—are the shaping of behavior patterns in other people that a) are defined by oneself as "right" or "good"; b) one considers to be "better for them" in terms of often quite ethnocentric criteria; c) are replications of one's own actions; or d) do *not* replicate certain of one's actions that one considers to be "decadent." The ideal goal of "increasing the quality of life," for example, may include such elements as improving health and nutrition, literacy, and leisure activities; but it can also mean the replace- ment of loin cloths by "decent" trousers, detribalization, the defamation of native religions, or the payment of low wages in order to "protect the natives" from the "perverting influences" of cash. As Turnbull [40] and others have shown, few ideal goals are congruent with actual purposes and procedures.

Furthermore, it is apparent from the literature of deliberate social change [41] that few men who have the urge to "do good" have long-range perspectives, a knowledge of behavioral principles, and the willingness, training and perspicacity to apply them. The methodology involved in successive approximation is often thought to be too slow, and selective reinforcement is not only cumbersome but at times may appear to be inhuman. The Bantus NEED fences NOW, to return to an earlier exam- ple, and thus it would be cruel to not GIVE them fences NOW.

In short, "doing good" all too often involves the haphazard, unselec-

40. Turnbull (1962).
41. For a sample, see Spicer (1952).

tive, and, in terms of behavioral antecedents, inconsistent provision of reinforcers. Food, medicine, seeds, buildings, money, tools, educational facilities, and so forth are provided, largely in terms of the "deprivations" assumed and defined by the helper who "does good." Yet behavior change in villagers—be it the growing of cotton or the maintaining of fences— and thus the ideal and actual goal of the program, is only rarely observed. Some administrators may be content with postulating an "inner change" in these villagers, but from the behavioral perspective there arises the following intriguing question: "why *should* villagers change their behavior when the old activities have resulted in all of these improvements (or in unnecessary complications from which there is no apparent escape)?"

Ideal consequences of "doing good." Theoretically, the behavior patterns that have been newly established will be maintained by their "successful" consequences, if people's deprivations have been accurately determined and rewards have been defined in terms of criteria that are valid as far as the people themselves are concerned. Better housing and health, increased harvests and improved nutrition, the advantages of literacy, and so forth, should maintain preceding behavior chains. Such a result can be expected only, however, if behavioral principles are rigorously applied within the social, ecological, technological, and demographic parameters which operate in a community, region, or nation.

Actual consequences of "doing good." If "doing good" means the provision of reinforcers without regard to preceding activities—and this appears to be the most common procedure—it cannot be expected that behavior will be changed or that new activities will be maintained. Rather, the activity preceding the reward—for example the phrase "please give me _____"—will be strengthened. In short, by "doing good" it is quite easy to inadvertently reinforce precisely those activities that one wishes to change, for example "dependence." He who "does good" may *think* or fervently *hope* that he is rewarding the "right" activity, or he may find the whole topic of "reward and punishment" more applicable to pigeons than people and thus disgusting and inhuman, yet his actions *do* reinforce the preceding, and not necessarily "right," behavior pattern. By "doing good" blindly, then, one often is "doing evil," in effect, by reinforcing and thus strengthening precisely those actions which made the program of "doing good" necessary in the first place.

This discussion of "doing good" does not lead to the conclusion that one should terminate one's efforts to "do good." Projects designed to "do good," if their behavioral goals have been specified and if their procedures take learning principles and the sociocultural environment into account, are likely to be successful and to benefit the people for whom they are designed. Conversely, projects which are simply designed to "do good," without delineating *specific* goals and without regard to learning principles and behavioral procedures, are practically guaranteed to be unsuccessful and to "do evil." Finally, it must not be forgotten that the tasks involved in a development program are performed by men, and that it is quite possible for a theoretically sound and perfectly designed project to fail unless the men who are part of it are well trained.

The Training of Program Personnel

The argument of the preceding pages may be summarized in this hypothesis: *the knowledge and application of behavioral principles makes the success of a development program possible, while ignorance guarantees its failure unless there is a generous portion of luck.* Furthermore, it must be concluded that mere dreams of the future, concern, good will, commitment, empathy, compassion, and a heart full of love and justice will count for nothing unless these qualities are combined with accurate knowledge of the social and psychological determinants of bebehavior. The training of competent development program personnel will therefore involve several phases, as follows.

THE PERSONAL CHARACTERISTICS OF CHANGE AGENTS

In the discussion of Step Eight of ideal-type development programs the characteristics of change agents were briefly indicated. There it was pointed out that change agents—be they planners, extension agents, community developers, or Peace Corps volunteers—must be able to engage in careful, logical analysis, have insight and a touch of wisdom, and have sufficient maturity so that they will not be flattered or overcome by villagers' dependence upon them. Furthermore, the change agent should be patient, flexible, aware of other people's values, and have enough foresight and altruism to withdraw from the community when he is no longer a necessary part of it. Finally, he must have a definite contribution to make to the village or region, a specific skill relevant to the population's actual deprivations. Many of these characteristics refer, basically, to behavior. "Patience," for example, is a summary label for a wide variety of reactions to other people's activities, such as a smile when another man does not keep an appointment. An important component of any training program, then, is the shaping of these activities.

KNOWLEDGE OF BEHAVIORAL PRINCIPLES

As long as development programs emphasize behavior change, the determinants of behavior must be clearly understood. Only a firm grasp of learning principles can bring about the selective shaping and maintenance of new activities in others. Abstract knowledge, however, is not enough; practice in the application of differential reinforcement and other procedures is required if they are to be used with a modicum of familiarity. Intensive training in, and an extensive practicum of, psychological (learning) principles and procedures would appear to be basic to any training program.

ANALYSIS OF SOCIAL STRUCTURES

The behavior patterns that are to be shaped, along with those that are to be extinguished, will be or are being maintained by the community's or nation's social structure. In order to change men's activities, then, the discriminative and contingent stimuli of various behavior patterns have to be ascertained so that the program can be directed toward their selective retention and alteration. The accurate analysis of general social structures, involving knowledge of sociological and economic relationships and principles, should be a basic skill of any change agent. The procedures described in Chapters Six and Seven provide a firm basis for such an analysis.

ANALYSIS OF SPECIFIC SYSTEMS

Abstract principles and skill in general social analysis can provide no more than the basic framework for the outlining of action. Specific actions cannot be delineated until the characteristics of a specific village, region, or nation have been fitted into the general framework. It is therefore necessary to determine the deprivations, and thus the possible reinforcers, which operate in a community. In addition, the specific discriminative and contingent stimuli associated with the activities that are to be shaped and extinguished must be ascertained in order to determine the possible procedures that might be employed toward this end. The number of procedures for shaping and extinguishing behavior will be affected by the change agent's often limited ability to alter contingencies or to control reinforcers. The evaluation of alternative rewards, in terms of their effectiveness and his control over them, cannot proceed until there is abundant knowledge of the local situation, and thus some anthropological training would benefit any change agent.

COMMAND OF SPECIFIC SKILLS

As long as development programs emphasize behavior alteration, the change agent should be able to exhibit and teach the new activities. If successive approximation is to be employed, he must have sufficient knowledge of the new activities so that he can determine which existing and new acts are part of the final pattern and therefore should be rewarded. While this is self-evident in the case of house construction, for example, it is often thought that other skills, such as "community development," require less training on the part of the change agent. However, *there is little empirical support for the belief that the building of houses is more difficult, and hence requires more training, than the building of communities.*

EFFECTIVE COMMITMENT

Idealists, action-oriented young men and women, humanitarians, and those who are committed to one or another cause related to economic development, may find this outline of a training program singularly lacking in fervor and brotherly love. Yet this schema for training, and the preceding schema for development programs, arises from the proposition that, if economic development is to occur—and the philosophical questions involved here have by no means been settled—*developing nations require effective, successful programs;* efficacy and success are based on accurate information, valid principles, a logical program, and knowledgeable men. Mere commitment to a cause, no matter how lofty—for example to "help others"—is little more than a psychological palliative for the individual so committed; it is worthless in the larger scheme of bringing about behavior change in isolated communities or developing nations. *Effective* commitment, combining a *specific* goal with *accurate* information, *validated* procedures and the *willingness* and *ability* to employ them, while perhaps less emotionally satisfying and certainly more difficult intellectually, produces a higher probability of change and success.

SUMMARY

From the preceding discussion it is evident that a training program designed to produce well qualified change agents will be as rigorous and intellectually challenging as the training for any scientific discipline. To repair communities requires little that is different—in essence—from repairing bridges or bodies; all three tasks demand not only a thorough knowledge of complex basic principles and their ingenious applications in various local situations, but also accurate and exhaustive information concerning the characteristics of the basic material—be it men, metal, or metabolism. *He whose intellectual limitations prevent him from becoming a good physician or engineer cannot become an effective change agent either, for a competent change agent must have many of the skills of both.*

The Behavioral Perspective and Community Development

"Community development" is a popular idea that has provided inspiration for thousands of men and hundreds of projects all over the world.[42] In recent years it has been legitimized by becoming an integral part of the Peace Corps program, and has been expanded to include a variety of projects in poverty-stricken parts of urban-industrial nations as well. The dominant themes of the idea are self-help, co-operation, community participation, self-reliance, democracy, and higher living standards. Material changes and external improvements, however, are often considered to be of secondary importance. The Biddles, for example, speak of community development as "a social process by which human beings can become more competent to live with and gain some control over local aspects of a frustrating and changing world. It is a group method for expediting personality growth."[43] According to a comprehensive analysis of the recent community development literature, concern with material goals is definitely secondary, while changes in men's ideas, beliefs and minds are of major interest.[44]

According to the behavioral perspective, "co-operation" has empirical referents, the standard of living can be measured, but changes in men's

42. Biddle and Biddle (1965), Brokenshaw and Hodge (1969). For an example of problems that are often encountered, see Mayer (1958).
43. Biddle and Biddle (1965:78).
44. Erasmus (1968). For a good example of the psychodynamic approach, see Goodenough (1963).

minds can only be inferred from words or action. To the extent to which the success of community development programs is measured in terms of "inside changes," the behavioral approach is of little use. When success is viewed as behavior change, however, the nine steps outlined above become applicable. Since the only referents of internal changes are activities, however, it may be argued that attempts to change men's minds will also benefit from the application of learning principles.

Theoretically, at least, communitywide projects should be more successful and easier to carry out than national programs, for the only "advantage" of the latter, and even this is often not the case, is control over very general discriminative and contingent stimuli. The size of national programs, and the frequent remoteness of its controlling agencies from the behavior that is to be shaped and maintained, often make it difficult to follow up the advantages of such control. Conversely, local programs may not have the degree of control over discriminative and contingent stimuli that is ideally required. However, the ability to provide reinforcers consistently and selectively, the accurate knowledge of local variations in state variables, and the presence of change agents as at least initial dispensers of differential reinforcement more than make up for the sometimes inadequate control over individuals' environment.

In a recent critical analysis of the major theoretical and methodological perspectives that appear to underlie community development efforts, Erasmus concludes that there have been very few successes.[45] Neither the cases described in the literature [46] nor his own and others' experiences provide much ground for optimism concerning future programs, at least as long as the old perspectives and procedures remain dominant. There is little chance of altering these procedures, however; "Community Development without tangible results is now so acceptable it can be publicly advertised at public expense" in Peace Corps recruitment.[47] While it may be argued that changes in men's minds are by nature intangible, such changes cannot be proven to have occurred until there are observable and measurable—and in the case of men in developing nations this means behavioral—manifestations. The question, then, is "why do many community development programs produce so few tangible changes in the activities of the population?"

45. Erasmus (1968).
46. Niehoff (1966), Spicer (1952).
47. Erasmus (1968:72).

From a behavioral perspective the answer is to be found in the definitions of goals and the procedures that have been employed in many of
these programs. If the goal of the program is the alteration of selected
aspects of villagers' internal states, and as long as internal changes are
assumed to precede—and determine—behavior change, only a limited
number of procedures, most of them extensions of psychoanalytical principles, will be available.

When psychoanalytical procedures are applied in order to change the
behavior patterns of individuals, for example in psychotherapy, success
rates are not only difficult to determine and substantiate, but they are also
far from impressive.[48] According to Knight,[49] for example, only about 45
per cent of the cases in several well-known clinics and institutes could be
considered as much improved or apparently cured. A later study, performed by a committee appointed by the American Psychoanalytic Association,[50] showed that of 595 patients who began psychoanalysis, 306
were "completely analyzed"; of these, 210 were followed up after completion of analysis, and 126 (or 60 per cent) were considered to be
greatly improved or cured. An optimist might look at the 60 per cent
figure, but a pessimist might emphasize that of the original 595 patients
fewer than one quarter were treated successfully. Furthermore, each of
the markedly improved cases required not only considerable efforts,
around 600 hours of therapy, but also neither study presented conclusive
evidence that the "recovery" was actually due to therapy, rather than
some other unknown or uncontrolled factors. These and other studies of
the efficacy of psychotherapy have prompted Eysenck to conclude that
"all methods of psychotherapy fail to improve on the recovery rate obtained through ordinary life experiences and nonspecific treatment." [51]
Finally, Bergin [52] has presented evidence which suggests that psychotherapy at times aggravates rather than relieves the conditions that lead
patients to seek help in the first place.

Since psychiatrists with their internal-state oriented theories and
methodologies evidently fail in a large percentage of their cases in spite of
considerable training and prolonged efforts, what can be expected of

48. As described, for example, in Wolpe (1964).

49. Knight (1941).

50. Brody (1962).

51. Eysenck (1961:721). Additional evidence is presented in Bandura (1969: chapters 1 and 2).

52. Bergin (1966).

change agents with a similar orientation but who deal with *communities* rather than *individuals?* Furthermore, change agents usually have less training than psychiatrists, less knowledge of the individuals with whom they are concerned, and less time to spend on individuals or in the community. One should not expect a success rate that is higher than that obtained by psychiatrists working with individuals in therapeutically more adequate surroundings, and thus a community-development project based on internal-state theories and methodologies may well start out with rather poor chances of success.

Even when one or another behavioral model of man provides the theoretical orientation of a program, the probability of failure is high unless the change agent has the characteristics outlined in connection with Step Eight. Accurate logical analysis rather than pity, perspicacity rather than mere commitment, patience and knowledge rather than vacuous "empathy," provide the best foundation for success. One can only hope that Charles Erasmus is making an overstatement when he writes: "Community Development educators, however, are seldom equipped with knowledge-intensive skills. I am reminded of those of my students who show an interest in the Peace Corps simply out of an irresistible urge to serve their fellow men in the backward areas. When I suggest they train themselves to meet the educational deficiencies of those areas in such knowledge-intensive subjects as medicine, plant pathology, engineering, and the like, they grimace and confess their dislike of math and science. When I ask them what sort of humanitarian endeavors they have in mind, they explain that they want to help people "progress" through education programs such as Community Development. And from what I have seen of Community Development personnel, I am convinced that just such knowledge-free individuals as these eventually find their way into that knowledge-free field." [53]

The use of a behavioral model of man by knowledgeable change agents does not assure the success of community development programs, for often it is inconvenient, difficult, or impossible to employ the procedures outlined in the nine steps.[54] The very first step requires a specification of goals that is more precise than is usually the case with such

53. Erasmus (1968:93–94).
54. For a discussion of difficulties encountered in the employment of behavioral principles in a free environment, see Wolpe, Salter and Reyna (1964). Bandura (1969) presents a number of solutions to these problems.

programs. Yet it is the specificity of the goal that limits the specificity of the behavior patterns that are to be shaped. And if the activities that are to be established are not precisely defined, no specific procedures for their shaping can be delineated, no reinforcers can be attached to behavior, and no discriminative stimuli can be created. Mistakes are easily made, and the errors of any step are likely to jeopardize the whole attempt. For example, if a change agent disregards—or misunderstands—the villagers' conceptions of what constitutes a reward, or uses instead his own definitions, no theoretically perfect schedule of reinforcement will be of any importance. A mere knowledge of learning principles, then, is not enough. Anthropological and sociological observations—together with an occasional dash of insight—appear to be additional necessary ingredients for the successful shaping of new activities.

The Behavioral Perspective and National Development Programs

The behavioral approach to planning and action, as outlined in the several steps described in a previous section, does not present an *alternative* to existing methods of large-scale planned development; rather, it indicates a number of *additional elements* that should be considered when such an effort is made.[55]

The behavioral approach to development programs proceeds, so to speak, from the bottom up. That is, it begins with the observable, discrete activities of individuals, considers the general determinants of behavior, and then concentrates on the operation of specific norms, laws and regulations, and their formulations. It ends with the description of the abstract principles and overriding ideals from which they were derived. The initial steps are usually quite concrete—for example, in order to establish activity R_1 a specific reinforcer S^r_1 and a particular schedule are required. But the later steps—for example the laws that should be instituted in order to present consistent contingencies—often are considerably more vague, if only because there is a wider range of possible procedures.

Most national formulations of development programs begin at the top and work downward, so to speak. The goal is described first, for example a higher standard of living. Then the means for its achievement are delineated, such as the establishment of certain industries and production

55. For a discussion and evaluation of national planning, see Gross (1967).

goals. While these early steps can be specified in great detail, the final steps—involving the exact procedures that are to be employed in the establishment and operation of specific enterprises—are usually somewhat vague.

Both the behavioral and the national approaches begin their formulations rather strongly, with considerable support of theory and empirical evidence. However, both approaches end up with weak, or at least amorphous and often unmanageable, recommendations. A *combination of the two approaches,* therefore, would increase the probability of success of large-scale programs. The behavioral approach, for example, delineates the type and amount of control that will be required and the kinds of reinforcers that might be applied in the course of shaping and maintaining the new behavior patterns involved in the enterprises associated with the overall goal of the development program. The national approach would then determine how the required control over contingencies might be achieved, and which of the possible rewards are or will be available.

Although the behavioral perspective focuses on the individual and the determinants of his actions, it contributes to national development programs as long as their goals are defined at least partly in terms of human activities and as long as "success" is measured at least partly in terms of changed behavior patterns or their consequences. Every national or regional policy, no matter how abstractly it may be formulated, will have an eventual effect on the behavior patterns of men in one or another subculture or population segment. The ideal of "justice for peasants," for example, *if instituted,* helps reduce the conception of a capricious universe and thus contributes to the shaping of new, complex activities. If this ideal remains no more than a group of words, however, the conception of a capricious universe will find continued support in the peasant's daily experiences, thus maintaining another set of activities. This is not to say that a policy will necessarily have direct consequences for behavior. "Justice for peasants," for example, can be effected only through the operation of the judicial system, and this would involve the behavior of policemen, lawyers, and judges. Furthermore, the activities of these men are also affected by the structure and operation of the community, and thus "honesty in municipal government" may well be a necessary companion to "justice."

The major contributions of the behavioral perspective to national development programs, then, can be summarized in the form of a set of questions and answers. The major questions, to be asked of every component of a national development program, would be the following:

1. What behavior patterns of which population segment will be affected? More specifically, which actions of which men will continue to be maintained, which will be extinguished, and what actions of which men are to be newly shaped?
2. By what specific means will all of these actions be influenced? and
3. How will these activities—whether they be maintained, newly established, or extinguished—contribute to the success of local and regional projects of economic development?

In short, the specific behavioral consequences of various policies, such as tax incentives, consumer protection, or the fostering of small-scale manufacturing enterprises, must be determined. When it is ascertained that a particular policy is likely to have behavioral consequences that conflict with what is desired, the policy, or at least its applications and interpretations, may have to be changed.

The answers to this set of questions are circumscribed by the learning principles that constitute the behavioral model of man. An activity that is reinforced by the operation of a particular policy cannot be extinguished until the policy is changed, and a new behavior pattern cannot be established until the development program sets up reinforcers for it. The large proportion of failures in both national and regional development programs is due at least partly to the prevailing lack of concern with the social and psychological factors that influence the behavior patterns associated with the successful completion of these plans.

National development programs that include the behavior patterns of men in their various projects, and which combine economic, social, and psychological (learning) factors, provide both the planner and the change agent with a host of procedures that *can* be applied *now*. It is true, of course, that such applications do not add up to an *easy* task, but they certainly do add up to one that is *possible*.

xi *The Call of the Future*

Economic development as a major theme of recent history derives its force from exalted visions of the future and its slow pace from the stark reality of human and social conditions. Today, after decades of efforts, it is becoming increasingly evident that the dreams of many are in danger of being shattered—perhaps permanently—by overwhelming economic, political, and social realities. Myrdal has described one continent's battle for a better future, waged today against the deadly shadows of the past, as the "Asian Drama." But the dramas that are unfolding in other parts of the world include identical plots and characters:

> Urged on by aspirations but curbed by material conditions and their own inhibitions, articulate individuals and groups in all these countries continually make decisions with the objective of resolving or accommodating the conflicts. The drama gains its fast pace from the terrific strength of the forces creating the conflicts. The lofty aspirations of the leading actors are separated by a wide gap from the abysmal reality— including the unreadiness of leaders, followers, and the more inert masses to accept the consequences of attempting to attain these aspirations. And that gap is widening. The movement of the drama is intensified as, through time, aspirations

325

are inflated by almost everything that is printed and preached and demonstrated, be it planned or not, while positive achievements lag. Meanwhile, populations are increasing at an ever faster pace, making the realization of aspirations still more difficult.[1]

Men in developing nations have heard the call of the future—a life of material ease and spiritual satisfaction. But those who hear do not always listen attentively, and often they hear only a small part of the message while the larger part comes not from the future at all but rather from within—their momentary dreams and fears. It is here that the drama begins, for heeding the call of the future means not only that men have visions of a new arcadia, but also that the roads leading to the new life be known, accepted, and traveled. And it is in the knowledge, acceptance, and traveling of the torturous roads that men's dreams and fears endanger the triumphant success of the journey. The road that has been sketched in this book encounters many obstacles; some of them have already been described, but two others, mainly of a philosophical nature, need to be detailed. More than any purely technical difficulties these problems illustrate how contemporary fears, often held by only a few, can imperil the dreams of the future held by the many.

Means and Ends

The old question of whether the ends justify the means underlies much of the controversy surrounding both economic growth and the difficulties encountered in the design and implementation of development programs. The answer depends not only on the nature of the ends and the availability of means, but also, in the case of rapid industrialization, on the men who are committed to the fast pace and who evaluate the results.

First, *the ends of economic development are unclear.* Many idealistic conceptions and goals of industrialism are subject to personal interpretations and often approach the impossible dreams of utopians. No one has yet experienced the totality of an "industrialized way of life," and countries which come closest to it, for example western Europe and the United States, are among the first to recognize shortcomings and admit

1. Myrdal (1968:34–5).

to difficulties in the quest for a "good life." Furthermore, industrialism is a complex set of many elements, each an integral part of the whole but subject to independent assessment on moral, ethical, and philosophical grounds. A lower infant mortality rate is easy to evaluate, and most men would consider it an asset and a goal worth striving for. Factory labor, city life, and impersonal social relations are also part of industrialism, however, but their evaluation is not likely to be positive or unanimous. Even when the debate concerning the ends of economic growth has been resolved, questions remain, and the most important of these is: *Does a nation want economic development?* The answer depends not only on the definition and evaluation of development, but also on the person who is asked. Government officials, intellectuals of various philosophical persuasions, members of different professional elites, students, peasants, the young and the old, are likely to use their own criteria and to come up with different answers.[2] And to the indigenous cacophony are added the voices of men in urban-industrial nations whose views are similarly divided.

Second, *the number of possible means to achieve economic development is great.* Governmental industries or private enterprise, taxation or investment incentives, free or controlled mass media, education for all or the fostering of educated elites, democratic procedures or "temporary" authoritarian governments, illustrate the range and variety of means available for the fostering and acceleration of economic growth. These means can be evaluated in terms of at least three criteria: efficacy, philosophical acceptability, and political advisability.

Limited experience and the impossibility of controlled experimentation make it difficult to assess the efficacy of many possible procedures, and thus the judgment and prediction of efficacy is often based on theory, preconception, hope, or a combination of these. In most nations the moral, ethical, and religious standards for judging philosophical acceptability vary among subcultures, and it is unlikely that there are means which will be acceptable to all. Some opposition, then, is almost built into any attempt to encourage economic growth. Finally, the political characteristics of both new and older developing nations are likely to produce rather narrow definitions of political advisability, especially for democratically-oriented or popularly-based governments. Consequently, there is little chance of finding and employing effective, acceptable, *and* politi-

2. Inayatullah (1967).

cally advisable procedures. The methods outlined in this book, for example, while they promise to be more effective than many others that have been used so far, may not meet political or philosophical criteria, and so the question arises: *Is the nation willing to employ the most effective procedures?* While the label "empirically tested" cannot be applied to many programs, the objective criteria presently in use and the methods now available can be combined to yield "presently most likely to be effective" programs of concerted action on the levels of both the community and nation. Such programs, to the extent to which they are concerned with behavior modification, would probably employ a behavioral model of man and the systematic alteration of contingencies. However, philosophical and moral questions, the limitations arising from political realities, and the sheer size and complexity of such programs, may lead a nation or its governing elite to conclude that it is neither willing nor able to attempt or perform the task.[3] But when the answer is finally determined to be "no," then the answer to the earlier question should also be changed. For the raising of human hopes without doing everything humanly possible to realize these hopes, especially when the hopes are raised and shattered by men not immediately affected by them, is politically and morally indefensible.

Third, *most men are human.* That is, most people tend to evaluate ends and means in terms of personal experiences, the criterion of selfishness, and the short-range perspective. Leaders whose major interest is self-aggrandizement, planners whose perspective is limited to one narrow theoretical system, peasants whose frame of reference is the village, and students whose goal is a prestigious position, for example, are not likely to define ends and evaluate means so as to further the *long-term* economic growth of their *nation.* While it may be argued that western economic development had its share of these individuals and may indeed have profited from their activities, it must be remembered that more than two hundred years have passed since the "beginning" of European industrialization and that for many decades the pace was slow indeed. When the goal is *rapid* development and industrialism *now,* it is possible that *common men may not be up to this uncommon task.*

The question of whether ends justify means, then, must be left open until the ends and means have been delineated, and the specific criteria of evaluation have been determined. In the case of economic development,

3. For a discussion of some ethical problems of social control, see Spiller (1960).

no answer can be borrowed from other fields or other times, and every nation must seek anew the answers that are compatible with its visions of both dreams and realities.

Moral Aspects of the Behavioral Perspective

The behavioral model of man can be attacked from a number of directions, even though few critics doubt that men learn or that rewards and punishment affect behavior. Most attacks on the model seem to have a philosophical base and appear to be designed primarily to discredit or deny the major implications for both behavior and social phenomena which follow from a learning approach. Among the major criticisms and answers relevant to the analysis and programs of economic development are the following:

First, the behavioral model may be accused of providing a distorted, animalistic conception of man. By emphasizing operant conditioning procedures, much of man's "humanity" is overlooked, and thus a significant part of human beings is never incorporated into development analysis. Men's dreams, hopes, aspirations, and fears are left out, and economic growth becomes an almost mechanical process. Second, by emphasizing the role of external factors such as the individual's social context, a behavioral model makes men subject to the manipulation and control by others. Finally, the emphasis on differential reinforcement opens man to the designs of unscrupulous manipulators and leads to the employment of drastic measures and inhuman treatment.

In answer it should be pointed out that the behavioral model of man is an undeniably limited set of scientific hypotheses, not an all-encompassing religious dogma. The behavioral perspective admittedly emphasizes only a part of man, but it does not deny that there are other parts. Its major purpose is the explanation and prediction of the recurring behavior patterns of daily life. It is not designed to explain individualistic or creative acts such as the writing of Hesse's *Glasperlenspiel,* the charm of Exupery's *Wind, Sand, and Stars,* or men's reactions to Unamuno's *Tragic Sense of Life.* It is designed to explain why the inhabitants of Vicos used to do so little work, or why few villagers in developing nations have a long-range point of view. If one were interested in a complete picture of man, one would have to include not only learning principles but some additional philosophical and physiological propositions as well.

As long as economic growth involves drastic changes in the activities of many men, any development program must include procedures for the modification of behavior. The moral questions revolving around manipulation, "drastic" measures, and "inhuman" treatment thus are part of any development analysis. Unfortunately, the answers provided by studies of individuals' behavior modification are not necessarily applicable to large-scale programs.

An increasing number of psychologists are employing one or another behavioral model in the treatment of a large variety of abnormal individuals. A starving psychotic who refused to eat, for example, was treated successfully by depriving the patient of everything she enjoyed.[4] These things were returned to her only upon eating and evidence of weight gain, and within eight weeks she was discharged. Other severe cases have benefited from similar applications of differential reinforcement. The dangerous and self-destructive behavior patterns of autistic children, for instance, have been markedly altered by the use of conditioning procedures involving electric shock.[5]

In these and similar cases, where the danger of death and severe physical injury can be reduced only by the drastic alteration of behavior, drastic measures can be defended easily, especially since these are usually employed only when other "normal" methods—such as psychotherapy— have proven ineffective. Depriving a "dying" patient of what she enjoys or submitting autistic children to electric shock contingent on behavior at first glance may seem "inhuman," but the alternatives in the form of more conventional and "humane" therapies had proven futile. It can be argued, therefore, that *it is not the employment of behavioral procedures that is inhuman, but the unwillingness to use them when the situation is desperate.*

The controversy surrounding "inhuman procedures" and "drastic measures" can be resolved rather easily in the case of *individuals* whose life or limb is in *objective* danger.[6] But the problems involved in a *nation's* efforts of economic growth, when much of the eventual future and many of the available procedures are evaluated in terms of essentially *subjective* criteria, are much more difficult to solve. While it can be argued that the ends of the Vicos Project justified the means that were

4. Bachrach *et al.* (1965).
5. Lovaas *et al.* (1965).
6. For a discussion of ethical and other problems involved in the manipulation of human behavior, see Biderman and Zimmer (1961), Kelman (1965). The best treatment of this subject is found in Bandura (1969).

used, and while "austerity programs" are defended in terms of the greater "economic health" of nations, it is difficult to extend these conclusions to other major and nationwide programs. *Or is it?*

The behavioral model provides some answers to the question of what determines behavior, and it outlines some procedures for shaping, maintaining, and altering human activities; but it cannot answer the two questions which are involved in any program or analysis of economic development: "do we have the right to manipulate others?" and "do we have the right to shape or extinguish particular activities?" The answers provided by clinical psychologists, parents, and teachers—an unequivocal "yes"—cannot be transferred when the same questions are asked within the context of economic growth. *Or can they?* The difficulty lies in the fact that whereas the modification of "abnormal" behavior and the development of reading skills are clearly beneficial to the individuals concerned and desirable for the nation, the assessment of personal and national "benefits" and "costs" accruing from economic development is far from complete.

Curtain

The drama of economic development takes on tragic proportions not only because aspirations outpace achievements—for this has always been part of the human condition—but also, and perhaps mainly, because of men's inability and unwillingness to employ the most effective methods for the transformation of aspirations into achievement. While there are no perfect procedures as yet, even the best of those presently available are not employed to their full measure. The behavioral perspective cannot answer the questions responsible for half-hearted and inappropriate efforts, and it cannot reduce the conflicts and ambiguities that characterize the decisions and programs of many nations in all parts of the world. Procedures of behavior modification will increase the specificity of objectively "effective" programs and the probability of success, but it is men who ultimately are the agents responsible for failure or success, stagnation or change. In spite of the disappointments that have characterized postwar efforts to improve the conditions of human existence, another attempt with new procedures would seem justified. Then there will be at least a chance that the overall evaluation of development programs will be significantly different from Simon Bolivar's evaluation of his life's work—that he had plowed in the sea.

References

ABELSON, ROBERT P.
1968   "Simulation of Social Behavior," in Gardner Lindzey and Elliot
            Aronson (eds.), *The Handbook of Social Psychology*, 2nd edition
            (Reading: Addison-Wesley Publishing Company), II:274–356.

ADAMS, J. S. AND A. K. ROMNEY
1959   "A Functional Analysis of Authority," *Psychological Review*, 66:
            234–51.

ADELMAN, IRMA AND CYNTHIA TAFT MORRIS
1966   "A Quantitative Study of Social and Political Determinants of Fer-
            tility," *Economic Development and Cultural Change*, 14:129–57.

ADLER, FRANZ
1956   "The Value Concept in Sociology," *American Journal of Sociology*,
            62:272–79.
1960   "A Unit Concept for Sociology," *American Journal of Sociology*,
            65:356–64.

AKERS, RONALD L.
1968   "Problems in the Sociology of Deviance: Social Definitions and
            Behavior," *Social Forces*, 46:455–65.

ALDABA-LIM, ESTEFANIA AND GLORIA V. JAVILLONAR
1968   "Achievement Motivation in Filipino Entrepreneurship," *Interna-
            tional Social Science Journal*, 20:397–411.

ALEXANDER, ALEC P.
1960   "Industrial Entrepreneurship in Turkey: Origins and Growth,"
            Economic Development and Cultural Change, 8:349–64.

333

1967   "The Supply of Industrial Entrepreneurship," *Explorations in Entre-preneurial History,* 4:136–49.

ALLPORT, GORDON W.
1937   *Personality: A Psychological Interpretation* (New York: Henry Holt and Company).
1955   *Becoming: Basic Considerations for a Psychology of Personality* (New Haven: Yale University Press).

ALMOND, GABRIEL A. AND JAMES S. COLEMAN (eds.)
1960   *The Politics of the Developing Areas* (Princeton: Princeton University Press).

ANDERSON, C. ARNOLD
1963   "The Impact of the Educational System on Technological Change and Modernization," in Bert F. Hoselitz and Wilbert E. Moore (eds.), *Industrialization and Society* (The Hague: UNESCO), 259–78.

ANDERSON, C. ARNOLD AND MARY J. BOWMAN (eds.)
1965   *Education and Economic Development* (Chicago: Aldine Publishing Company).

ANDERSON, ROBERT T.
1966   "Rotating Credit Associations in India," *Economic Development and Cultural Change,* 14:334–39.

ANDERSON, ROBERT T. AND GALLATIN ANDERSON
1962   "The Indirect Social Structure of European Village Communities," *American Anthropologist,* 64:1016–27.

APTER, DAVID E.
1963   "System, Process, and Politics of Economic Development," in Bert F. Hoselitz and Wilbert E. Moore (eds.), *Industrialization and Society* (The Hague: UNESCO), 135–58.
1965   *The Politics of Modernization* (Chicago: University of Chicago Press).

APTER, DAVID E. (ed.)
1964   *Ideology and Discontent* (New York: Free Press).

ARENSBERG, CONRAD M. AND ARTHUR H. NIEHOFF
1964   *Introducing Social Change: A Manual for Americans Overseas* (Chicago: Aldine Publishing Company).

ARONFREED, JUSTIN
1968   "The Concept of Internalization," in David A. Goslin (ed.), *Handbook of Socialization Theory and Research* (Chicago: Rand McNally and Company), 263–323.

AUBREY, HENRY G.
1951   "Small Industry in Economic Development," *Social Research,* 18:269–312.

AYAL, ELIEZER B.
1963   "Value Systems and Economic Development in Japan and Thailand," *Journal of Social Issues,* 19:35–51.

AYLLON, TEODORO AND NATHAN H. AZRIN
1968   *The Token Economy: A Motivational System for Therapy and Rehabilitation* (New York: Appleton-Century-Crofts).

AZRIN, NATHAN H. AND W. C. HOLZ
1966   "Punishment," in Werner K. Honig (ed.), *Operant Behavior: Areas of Research and Application* (New York: Appleton-Century-Crofts), 213–70.

AZRIN, NATHAN H. AND OGDEN R. LINDSLEY
1956   "The Reinforcement of Cooperation between Children," *Journal of Abnormal and Social Psychology*, 52:100–102.

BACHRACH, ARTHUR J. (ed.)
1962   *Experimental Foundations of Clinical Psychology* (New York: Basic Books).

BACHRACH, ARTHUR J., WILLIAM J. ERWIN, AND JAY P. MOHR
1965   "The Control of Eating Behavior in an Anorexic by Operant Conditioning Techniques," in Leonard P. Ullmann and Leonard Krasner (eds.), *Case Studies in Behavior Modification* (New York: Holt, Rinehart and Winston), 153–63.

BAILEY, F. G.
1963   *Politics and Social Change: Orissa in 1959* (Berkeley: University of California Press).

BALL, RICHARD A.
1968   "A Poverty Case: The Analgesic Subculture of the Southern Appalachians," *American Sociological Review*, 33:885–95.

BANDURA, ALBERT
1969   *Principles of Behavior Modification* (New York: Holt, Rinehart and Winston).

BANDURA, ALBERT AND RICHARD H. WALTERS
1963   *Social Learning and Personality Development* (New York: Holt, Rinehart and Winston).

BANFIELD, EDWARD C.
1958   *The Moral Basis of a Backward Society* (Glencoe: Free Press).

BARNETT, H. G.
1953   *Innovation* (New York: McGraw-Hill).

BARRINGER, HERBERT R., GEORGE I. BLANKSTEN, AND RAYMOND W. MACK (eds.)
1965   *Social Change in Developing Areas: A Reinterpretation of Evolutionary Theory* (Cambridge: Schenkman Publishing Company).

BARRY, HERBERT, IRVIN L. CHILD, AND MARGARET K. BACON
1959   "Relation of Child Training to Subsistence Economy," *American Anthropologist*, 61:51–63.

BASCOM, WILLIAM R. AND M. J. HERSKOVITS (eds.)
1959   *Continuity and Change in African Cultures* (Chicago: University of Chicago Press).

BECKER, HOWARD S.
1963   *Outsiders: Studies in the Sociology of Deviance* (New York: Free Press).

BELSHAW, CYRIL S.
1955   "In Search of Wealth," *American Anthropologist* (Memoir No. 80).

BENNETT, JOHN W.
1966   "Further Remarks on Foster's 'Image of Limited Good'," *American Anthropologist*, 68:206–10.

BENNIS, WARREN G., KENNETH D. BENNE, AND ROBERT CHIN (eds.)
1969   *The Planning of Change*, 2nd edition (New York: Holt, Rinehart and Winston).

BERELSON, BERNARD AND RONALD FREEDMAN
1964   "A Study in Fertility Control," *Scientific American*, 210:29–37.

BERGIN, A.
1966   "Some Implications of Psychotherapy Research for Therapeutic Practice," *Journal of Abnormal Psychology*, 71:235–46.

BERKOWITZ, LEONARD
1969   "Social Motivation," in Gardner Lindzey and Elliot Aronson (eds.), *The Handbook of Social Psychology*, 2nd edition (Reading: Addison-Wesley Publishing Company), III:50–135.

BERLYNE, D. E.
1968   "Behavior Theory as Personality Theory," in Edgar F. Borgatta and William W. Lambert (eds.), *Handbook of Personality Theory and Research* (Chicago: Rand McNally and Company), 629–90.

BERTALANFFY, LUDWIG VON
1952   *Problems of Life: An Evaluation of Modern Biological Thought* (New York: John Wiley and Sons).
1962   "General Systems Theory—A Critical Review," *General Systems*, 7:1–20.

BIDDLE, WILLIAM W. AND LOUREIDE J. BIDDLE
1965   *The Community Development Process: The Rediscovery of Local Initiative* (New York: Holt, Rinehart and Winston).
1968   *Encouraging Community Development: A Training Guide for Local Workers* (New York: Holt, Rinehart and Winston).

BIDERMAN, ALBERT D. AND HERBERT ZIMMER (eds.)
1961   *The Manipulation of Human Behavior* (New York: John Wiley and Sons).

BLACK, C. E.
1966   *The Dynamics of Modernization* (New York: Harper and Row).

BLAKE, JUDITH AND KINGSLEY DAVIS
1964   "Norms, Values, and Sanctions," in Robert E. L. Faris (ed.), *Handbook of Modern Sociology* (New York: Rand McNally), 456–84.

BLAU, PETER M.
1964a   "Justice in Social Exchange," *Sociological Inquiry*, 34:193–206.
1964b   *Exchange and Power in Social Life* (New York: Wiley and Sons).

BOGUSLAW, ROBERT
1965   *The New Utopians: A Study of System Design and Social Change* (Englewood Cliffs: Prentice-Hall).

BRADBURN, NORMAN M.
1963   "Interpersonal Relations within Formal Organizations in Turkey,"
            Journal of Social Issues, 19:61–67.

BRADBURN, NORMAN M. AND DAVID E. BERLEW
1961   "Need for Achievement and English Industrial Growth," *Economic
            Development and Cultural Change,* 10:8–20.

BRAIBANTI, RALPH AND JOSEPH J. SPENGLER (eds.)
1960   *Tradition, Values and Socio-Economic Development* (Durham:
            Duke University Press).

BREHM, JACK W. AND ARTHUR R. COHEN
1962   *Explorations in Cognitive Dissonance* (New York: John Wiley and
            Sons).

BRODY, MORRIS W.
1962   "Prognosis and Results of a Psychoanalysis," in J. H. Nodine and
            J. H. Moyer (eds.), *Psychosomatic Medicine* (Philadelphia: Lea
            and Febiger).

BROKENSHAW, DAVID AND PETER HODGE
1969   *Community Development: An Interpretation* (Chicago: Science Re-
            search Associates, Inc.).

BUCHANAN, NORMAN S. AND HOWARD S. ELLIS
1955   *Approaches to Economic Development* (New York: Twentieth Cen-
            tury Fund).

BUCKLEY, WALTER
1967   *Sociology and Modern Systems Analysis* (Englewood Cliffs: Pren-
            tice-Hall).

BURGESS, ROBERT L. AND RONALD L. AKERS
1966   "Are Operant Principles Tautological?" *The Psychological Record,*
            16:305–12.
1967   "A Differential Reinforcement Theory of Criminal Behavior," *Social
            Problems,* 14:128–47.

CADWALLADER, MERVYN L.
1959   "The Cybernetic Analysis of Change in Complex Social Organizations,"
            American Journal of Sociology, 65:154–57.

CALDWELL, J. C.
1967   "Fertility Attitudes in Three Economically Contrasting Rural Re-
            gions of Ghana," *Economic Development and Cultural Change,*
            15:217–38.

CHASE, STUART
1962   *The Proper Study of Mankind,* 2nd revised edition (New York:
            Harper and Row).

CHOMSKY, NOAM
1959   "Review of *Verbal Behavior,*" *Language,* 35:26–58.

CLOWARD, RICHARD A.
1959   "Illegitimate Means, Anomie, and Deviant Behavior," *American
            Sociological Review,* 24:164–76.

COALE, ANSLEY J.
1963   "Population and Economic Development," in American Assembly, *The Population Dilemma* (Englewood Cliffs: Prentice-Hall), 46–69.

COALE, ANSLEY J. AND EDGAR M. HOOVER
1958   *Population Growth and Economic Development in Low Income Countries* (Princeton: Princeton University Press).

COHEN, ARTHUR R.
1964   *Attitude Change and Social Influence* (New York: Basic Books).

COLEMAN, JAMES S.
1964   "Collective Decisions," *Sociological Inquiry*, 34:166–81.

COLLIER, JOHN AND MARY COLLIER
1957   "An Experiment in Anthropology," *Scientific American*, 196:37–45.

CORTES, JUAN B.
1961   "The Achievement Motive in the Spanish Economy between the 13th and 18th Centuries," *Economic Development and Cultural Change*, 9:144–63.

COTTRELL, FRED
1955   *Energy and Society: The Relation between Energy, Social Change, and Economic Development* (New York: McGraw-Hill).

COULT, ALLAN D.
1963   "Unconscious Inference and Cultural Origins," *American Anthropologist*, 65:32–35.

CURRIE, LAUCHLIN B.
1966   *Accelerating Development: The Necessity and the Means* (New York: McGraw-Hill).
1967   *Obstacles to Development* (East Lansing: Michigan State University Press).

DAVIS, KINGSLEY AND JUDITH BLAKE
1956   "Social Structure and Fertility: An Analytical Framework," *Economic Development and Cultural Change*, 4:211–35.

DEFLEUR, MELVIN L. AND FRANK R. WESTIE
1958   "Verbal Attitudes and Overt Acts: An Experiment on the Salience of Attitudes," *American Sociological Review*, 23:667–73.
1963   "Attitude as a Scientific Concept," *Social Forces*, 42:17–31.

DELAMATER, JOHN
1968   "On the Nature of Deviance," *Social Forces*, 46:445–55.

DEUTSCH, KARL W.
1953   *Nationalism and Social Communication: An Inquiry into the Foundations of Nationality* (Cambridge: Massachusetts Institute of Technology).
1963   *The Nerves of Government* (New York: Free Press).

DOOB, LEONARD W.
1968   "Psychological Aspects of Planned Developmental Change," in Art Gallaher (ed.), *Perspectives in Developmental Change* (Lexington: University of Kentucky Press), 36–70.

DUBE, S. C.
1967a   "A Note on Communication in Economic Development," in Daniel
Lerner and Wilbur Schramm (eds.), *Communication and Change in
the Developing Countries* (Honolulu: East-West Center Press), 92–
97.
1967b   "Communication, Innovation, and Planned Change in India," in
Daniel Lerner and Wilbur Schramm (eds.), *Communication and
Change in the Developing Countries* (Honolulu: East-West Center
Press), 129–67.

DUBIN, ROBERT
1959   "Deviant Behavior and Social Structure: Continuities in Social
Theory," *American Sociological Review*, 24:147–64.

DUMONT, RICHARD G. AND WILLIAM J. WILSON
1967   "Aspects of Concept Formation, Explication, and Theory Construction in Sociology," *American Sociological Review*, 32:985–95.

DUNCAN, OTIS D. AND LEO F. SCHNORE
1959   "Cultural, Behavioral, and Ecological Perspectives in the Study of
Social Organization," *American Journal of Sociology*, 65:132–53.

EASTERBROOK, W. THOMAS
1963   "The Entrepreneurial Function in Relation to Technological and
Economic Change," in Bert F. Hoselitz and Wilbert E. Moore
(eds.), *Industrialization and Society* (The Hague: UNESCO), 57–
73.

EASTON, DAVID
1965a   *A Framework for Political Analysis* (Englewood Cliffs: Prentice-
Hall).
1965b   *A Systems Analysis of Political Life* (New York: John Wiley and
Sons).

EHRLICH, HOWARD J.
1969   "Attitudes, Behavior, and the Intervening Variables," *American
Sociologist*, 4:29–34.

EISENSTADT, S. N.
1964   "Social Change, Differentiation, and Evolution," *American Sociological Review*, 29:375–86.
1966   *Modernization: Protest and Change* (Englewood Cliffs: Prentice-
Hall).

ENKE, STEPHEN
1960   "The Economics of Government Payments to Limit Population,"
Economic Development and Cultural Change, 8:339–48.
1962   "Some Misconceptions of Krueger and Sjaastad Regarding the Vas-
ectomy—Bonus Plan to Reduce Births in Overpopulated and Poor
Countries," *Economic Development and Cultural Change*, 10:427–
31.
1963   *Economics for Development* (Englewood Cliffs: Prentice-Hall).

ERASMUS, CHARLES J.
1956   "Culture Structure and Process: The Occurrence and Disappearance

of Reciprocal Farm Labor," *Southwestern Journal of Anthropology*, 12:444–69.

1961   *Man Takes Control* (Minneapolis: University of Minnesota Press).

1967   "Upper Limits of Peasantry and Agrarian Reform: Bolivia, Venezuela and Mexico Compared," *Ethnology*, 6:349–80.

1968   "Community Development and the Encogido Syndrome," *Human Organization*, 27:65–74, 91–4.

ETZIONI, AMITAI

1964   *Modern Organizations* (Englewood Cliffs: Prentice-Hall).

1968   *The Active Society: A Theory of Societal and Political Processes* (New York: Free Press).

EYSENCK, HANS J.

1961   "The Effects of Psychotherapy," in Hans J. Eysenck (ed.), *Handbook of Abnormal Psychology* (New York: Basic Books), pp. 697–725.

FEIBLEMAN, JAMES K.

1963   *Mankind Behaving: Human Needs and Material Culture* (Springfield: Charles C. Thomas).

FENDRICH, JAMES M.

1967   "Perceived Reference Group Support: Racial Attitudes and Overt Behavior," *American Sociological Review*, 32:960–70.

FESTINGER, LEON AND HAROLD H. KELLY

1951   *Changing Attitudes through Social Contact* (Ann Arbor: Research Center for Group Dynamics).

FILLOL, TOMÁS ROBERTO

1961   *Social Factors in Economic Development: The Argentine Case* (Cambridge: The M.I.T. Press, an M.I.T. research monograph).

FIRTH, RAYMOND

1951   *Elements of Social Organization* (London: Watts and Company).

1957   *We, the Tikopia* (London: George Allen and Unwin).

1964   *Essays on Social Organization and Values* (London: Athlone Press).

FIRTH, RAYMOND AND BASIL S. YAMEY (eds.)

1964   *Capital, Saving and Credit in Peasant Societies* (Chicago: Aldine Publishing Company).

FISHER, DOUGLAS

1967   "Modern Small Industry for Developing Countries: A Paradox in Planning Economics," *Economic Development and Cultural Change*, 15:341–46.

FISHER, GLEN

1953   *Directed Culture Change in Nayarit, Mexico* (New Orleans: Middle American Research Institute, Tulane University).

FORTES, MEYER

1953   "The Structure of Unilineal Descent Groups," *American Anthropologist*, 55:17–41.

FORTES, MEYER (ed.)

1949   *Social Structure: Studies Presented to A. R. Radcliffe-Brown* (Oxford: Clarendon Press).

FOSTER, GEORGE M.
1960 "Interpersonal Relations in Peasant Society," *Human Organization,* 19:174–78.
1962 *Traditional Cultures: And the Impact of Technological Change* (New York: Harper and Brothers).
1965 "Peasant Society and the Image of Limited Good," *American Anthropologist,* 67:293–315.
1967 *Tzintzuntzan: Mexican Peasants in a Changing World* (Boston: Little, Brown and Company).

FRANKS, CYRIL M.
1964 "Individual Differences in Conditioning and Associated Techniques," in Joseph Wolpe, Andrew Salter, and L. J. Reyna (eds.), *The Conditioning Therapies* (New York: Holt, Rinehart and Winston), 149–65.

FREEDMAN, RONALD AND JOHN Y. TAKESHITA
1969 *Family Planning in Taiwan: An Experiment in Social Change* (Princeton: Princeton University Press).

FRIED, JACOB
1959 "Acculturation and Mental Health among Indian Migrants in Peru," in Marvin K. Opler (ed.), *Culture and Mental Health* (New York: Macmillan).
1962 "Social Organization and Personal Security in a Peruvian Hacienda Indian Community: Vicos," *American Anthropologist,* 64:771–80.

GAGNÉ, ROBERT M.
1965 *The Conditions of Learning* (New York: Holt, Rinehart and Winston).

GEERTZ, CLIFFORD
1962 "The Rotating Credit Association: A 'Middle Rung' in Development," *Economic Development and Cultural Change,* 10:241–63.
1963 *Peddlers and Princes: Social Development and Economic Change in Two Indonesian Towns* (Chicago: University of Chicago Press).

GERSCHENKRON, ALEXANDER
1962 *Economic Backwardness in Historical Perspective* (Cambridge: Harvard University Press).

GERTH, HANS AND C. WRIGHT MILLS
1953 *Character and Social Structure* (New York: Harcourt, Brace and World).

GIBBS, JACK P.
1968 "The Issue in Sociology," *Pacific Sociological Review,* 11:65–74.

GLADE, WILLIAM P.
1967 "Approaches to a Theory of Entrepreneurial Formation," *Explorations in Entrepreneurial History,* 4:245–59.

GLASS, DAVID
1963 "Population Growth and Structure: A Socio-demographic Study," in Egbert DeVries and José Medina Echavarría (eds.), *Social Aspects of Economic Development in Latin America* (Paris: UNESCO), I:94–111.

GOHEEN, JOHN
1958   "A Comment on Professor Singer's 'Cultural Values in India's Eco-
            nomic Development'," *Economic Development and Cultural Change,*
            7:1–3.

GOLDSCHMIDT, WALTER
1966   *Comparative Functionalism* (Berkeley: University of California
            Press).

GOODENOUGH, WARD H.
1963   *Cooperation in Change* (New York: Russell Sage Foundation).

GOULDNER, ALVIN W.
1959   "Reciprocity and Autonomy in Functional Theory," in Llewellyn
            Gross (ed.), *Symposium on Sociological Theory* (New York: Row,
            Peterson).

GREEN, BERT F.
1954   "Attitude Measurement," in Gardner Lindzey (ed.), *Handbook of
            Social Psychology* (Cambridge: Addison-Wesley).

GROSS, BERTRAM M. (ed.)
1967   *Action under Planning: The Guidance of Economic Development*
            (New York: McGraw-Hill).

GROSS, LLEWELLYN (ed.)
1959   *Symposium on Sociological Theory* (New York: Row, Peterson).

GUITERAS-HOLMES, CALIXTA
1961   *Perils of the Soul: The World View of a Tzotzil Indian* (New York:
            Free Press).

HAGEN, EVERETT E.
1962   *On the Theory of Social Change: How Economic Growth Begins*
            (Homewood: The Dorsey Press, Inc. A study from the Center for
            International Studies, Massachusetts Institute of Technology).
1963   "Comment," *American Economic Review,* 52:58–63.

HAGEN, EVERETT, E. (ed.)
1963   *Planning Economic Development* (Homewood: Richard D. Irwin,
            Inc. A study from the Center for International Studies, Massachu-
            setts Institute of Technology).

HALL, CALVIN S. AND GARDNER LINDZEY
1957   *Theories of Personality* (New York: John Wiley and Sons).

HALL, EDWARD T.
1959   *The Silent Language* (Garden City: Doubleday and Company).

HALLOWELL, A. IRVING
1954   "Psychology and Anthropology," in John Gillin (ed.), *For a Science
            of Social Man* (New York: MacMillan).

HALPERN, MANFRED
1963   *The Politics of Social Change in the Middle East and North Africa*
            (Princeton: Princeton University Press).

HARBISON, FREDERICK H. AND CHARLES A. MYERS
1964   *Education, Manpower, and Economic Growth* (New York: Mc-
            Graw-Hill).

HARRIS, MARVIN
1964 *The Nature of Cultural Things* (New York: Random House).

HARVEY, O. J., DAVID E. HUNT, AND HAROLD M. SCHRODER
1961 *Conceptual Systems and Personality Organization* (New York: John Wiley and Sons).

HAUSER, PHILIP M.
1959a "Demographic Indicators of Economic Development," *Economic Development and Cultural Change,* 7:98–116.
1959b "Cultural and Personal Obstacles to Economic Development in the Less Developed Areas," *Human Organization,* 18:78–84.

HEBB, D. O.
1949 *The Organization of Behavior* (New York: John Wiley and Sons).

HEILBRONER, ROBERT L.
1963 *The Great Ascent: The Struggle for Economic Development in Our Time* (New York: Harper and Row).

HEMPEL, CARL G.
1965 *Aspects of Scientific Exploration and Other Essays in the Philosophy of Science* (New York: Free Press).

HENDRY, JAMES B.
1964 *The Small World of Khanh Hau* (Chicago: Aldine Publishing Company).

HERMAN, THEODORE
1956 "The Role of Cottage and Small-Scale Industries in Asian Economic Development," *Economic Development and Cultural Change,* 4:356–70.

HIGGINS, BENJAMIN
1968 *Economic Development: Principles, Problems and Policies,* revised edition (New York: Norton).

HILGARD, ERNEST R.
1956 *Theories of Learning* (New York: Appleton-Century-Crofts).

HIRSCHMAN, ALBERT O.
1958 *The Strategy of Economic Development* (New Haven: Yale University Press).
1963 *Journeys toward Progress: Studies of Economic Policy-making in Latin America* (New York: The Twentieth Century Fund).
1965 "Obstacles to Development: A Classification and a Quasi-vanishing Act," *Economic Development and Cultural Change,* 13:385–93.
1967 *Development Projects Observed* (Washington: The Brookings Institution).

HOGBIN, H. IAN
1958 *Social Change* (London: Watts).

HOLLAND, JAMES G. AND B. F. SKINNER
1961 *The Analysis of Behavior* (New York: McGraw-Hill).

HOLLERMAN, LEON
1964 "Japan's Place in the Scale of Economic Development," *Economic Development and Cultural Change,* 12:139–57.

Holmberg, Allan R.
1959   "Land Tenure and Planned Social Change: A Case from Vicos, Peru," *Human Organization,* 18:7–10.
1960a   "Changing Community Attitudes and Values in Peru: A Case Study in Guided Change," in Richard N. Adams, *et al.* (eds.), *Social Change in Latin America Today: Its Implications for United States Policy* (New York: Harper and Brothers. © Council on Foreign Relations, Inc.), 63–107.
1960b   "The Research and Development Approach to Change," in Richard N. Adams and John J. Price (eds.), *Human Organization Research* (Homewood: Dorsey Press), 76–89.

Homans, George C.
1951   *The Human Group* (New York: Harcourt, Brace).
1961   *Social Behavior: Its Elementary Forms* (New York: Harcourt, Brace and World).
1964a   "Contemporary Theory in Sociology," in Robert E. L. Faris (ed.), *Handbook of Modern Sociology* (Chicago: Rand McNally and Company). 951–77.
1964b   "Bringing Men Back In," *American Sociological Review,* 29:809–18.
1967   *The Nature of Social Science* (New York: Harcourt, Brace and World).

Horowitz, Irving Louis
1966   *Three Worlds of Development: The Theory and Practice of International Stratification* (New York: Oxford University Press).

Hoselitz, Bert F.
1952   "Entrepreneurship and Economic Growth," *The American Journal of Economics and Sociology,* 12:97–110.
1956   "Nationalism, Economic Development, and Democracy," *Annals of the American Academy of Political and Social Science,* 305:1–11.
1960a   "A Sociological Approach to Economic Development," in his *Sociological Aspects of Economic Growth* (Glencoe: Free Press), 53–84.
1960b   "Social Structure and Economic Growth," in his *Sociological Aspects of Economic Growth* (Glencoe: Free Press), 23–51.

Hovland, Carl I. and Walter Weiss
1952   "The Influence of Source Credibility on Communication Effectiveness," *Public Opinion Quarterly,* 15:635–50.

Hull, Clark L.
1951   *Essentials of Behavior* (New Haven: Yale University Press).

Hunter, Holland
1961   "Optimum Tautness in Developmental Planning," *Economic Development and Cultural Change,* 9:561–72.

Inayatullah
1967   "Toward a Non-Western Model of Development," in Daniel Lerner and Wilbur Schramm (eds.), *Communication and Change in the Developing Countries* (Honolulu: East-West Center Press), 98–102.

INKELES, ALEX
1959   "Personality and Social Structure," in Robert K. Merton, Leonard
            Broom, and Leonard S. Cottrell, Jr. (eds.), *Sociology Today:
            Problems and Prospects* (New York: Basic Books), 249–76.

JACOBS, NORMAN
1966   *The Sociology of Development: Iran as an Asian Case Study* (New
            York: Frederick A. Praeger).

JAFFE, A. J.
1959   *People, Jobs, and Economic Development* (Glencoe: Free Press).

JAFFE, A. J. AND K. AZUMI
1960   "The Birth Rate and Cottage Industries in Underdeveloped Coun-
            tries," *Economic Development and Cultural Change,* 9:52–63.

JAGUARIBE, HELIO
1968   *Economic and Political Development: A Theoretical Approach and
            a Brazilian Case Study* (Cambridge: Harvard University Press).

JAYASURIYA, J. E.
1968   "Educational Dilemmas of a Developing Country: Ceylon," *Journal
            of Social Issues,* vol. 24 no. 2, 199–205.

JESSOR, RICHARD
1962   "A Social Learning Approach to Culture and Behavior," in Thomas
            Gladwin and William C. Sturtevant (eds.), *Anthropology and Hu-
            man Behavior* (Washington: The Anthropological Society of Wash-
            ington), 94–114.

JONES, ERNEST
1953–57   *The Life and Work of Sigmund Freud* (New York: Basic Books),
            vols. I–III.

JUENGER, FRIEDRICH GEORG
1956   *The Failure of Technology* (Chicago: Henry Regnery Company).

KAHL, JOSEPH A.
1959   "Some Social Concomitants of Industrialization and Urbanization,"
            Human Organization, 18:53–74.
1968   *The Measurement of Modernism: A Study of Values in Brazil and
            Mexico* (Austin: University of Texas Press).

KALDOR, NICHOLAS
1967   *Strategic Factors in Economic Development* (Ithaca: New York
            State School of Industrial and Labor Relations, Cornell University).

KAPLAN, DAVID AND BENSON SALER
1966   "Foster's 'Image of Limited Good': An Example of Anthropological
            Explanation," *American Anthropologist,* 68:202–6.

KARVE, D. G.
1958   "Comments," *Economic Development and Cultural Change,* 7:7–9.

KATZ, ELIHU
1957   "The Two-Step Flow of Communication: An Up-to-Date Report on
            an Hypothesis," *Public Opinion Quarterly,* 21:61–78.

J

Katz, Elihu and Paul F. Lazarsfeld
1955   *Personal Influence* (Glencoe: Free Press).

Kelley, Allen C. and Jeffrey G. Williamson
1968   "Household Saving Behavior in the Developing Economies: The Indonesian Case," *Economic Development and Cultural Change,* 16:385–403.

Kelley, Harold H.
1952   "Two Functions of Reference Groups," in G. E. Swanson, T. M. Newcomb, and E. L. Hartley (eds.), *Readings in Social Psychology,* revised edition (New York: Holt, Rinehart and Winston), 140–44.

Kelley, Harold H. and Edmund H. Volkart
1952   "The Resistance to Change of Group-anchored Attitudes," *American Sociological Review,* 17:453–56.

Kelman, Herbert C.
1958   "Compliance, Identification, and Internalization: Three Processes of Attitude Change," *Journal of Conflict Resolution,* 2:51–60.
1965   "Manipulation of Human Behavior: An Ethical Dilemma for the Social Scientist," *Journal of Social Issues,* 21:31–46.

Kemper, Theodore D.
1968   "Reference Groups, Socialization, and Achievement," *American Sociological Review,* 33:31–45.

Kennedy, John G.
1966   "Peasant Society and the Image of Limited Good: A Critique," *American Anthropologist,* 68:1212–25.

Kerr, Clark, John T. Dunlop, Frederick H. Harbison, and Charles A. Meyers
1960   *Industrialism and Industrial Man* (Cambridge: Harvard University Press).

Keyfitz, Nathan
1963   "The Impact of Technological Change on Demographic Patterns," in Bert F. Hoselitz and Wilbert E. Moore (eds.), *Industrialization and Society* (The Hague: UNESCO), 218–36.

Kindleberger, Charles P.
1964   *Economic Development,* 2nd edition (New York: McGraw-Hill).

King, Jr., John A.
1967   *Economic Development Projects and Their Appraisal* (Baltimore: The Johns Hopkins Press).

Kiray, Mubeccel B.
1968   "Values, Social Stratification, and Development," *Journal of Social Issues,* vol. 24 no. 2, pp. 87–100.

Kirk, Dudley and Dorothy Nortman
1967   "Population Policies in Developing Countries," *Economic Development and Cultural Change,* 15:129–42.

Kluckhohn, Clyde
1951   "Values and Value-Orientations in the Theory of Action," in Talcott Parsons and Edward A. Shils (eds.), *Toward a General Theory of Action* (Cambridge: Harvard University Press), 388–433.

KLUCKHOHN, CLYDE AND HENRY A. MURRAY
1953   *Personality in Nature, Society, and Culture* (New York: Alfred A. Knopf).

KNIGHT, R. P.
1941   "Evaluation of the Results of Psychoanalytic Therapy," *American Journal of Psychiatry*, 98:434–46.

KRASNER, LEONARD AND LEONARD P. ULLMANN
1965   *Research in Behavior Modification: New Developments and Implications* (New York: Holt, Rinehart and Winston).

KRISHNAMURTY, K.
1966   "Economic Development and Population Growth in Low Income Countries: An Empirical Study for India," *Economic Development and Cultural Change*, 15:70–75.

KRUTCH, JOSEPH WOOD
1953   *The Measure of Man* (New York: Grosset and Dunlap).

KUNKEL, JOHN H.
1961   "Economic Autonomy and Social Change in Mexican Villages," *Economic Development and Cultural Change*, 10:51–63.
1963   "Psychological Factors in the Analysis of Economic Development," *Journal of Social Issues*, 19:68–87.
1965   "Values and Behavior in Economic Development," *Economic Development and Cultural Change*, 13:257–77.
1966   "Individuals, Behavior, and Social Change," *Pacific Sociological Review*, 9:48–56.
1967   "Some Behavioral Aspects of the Ecological Approach to Social Organization," *American Journal of Sociology*, 73:12–29.
1969   "Some Behavioral Aspects of Systems Analysis," *Pacific Sociological Review*, 12:12–22.

KUNKEL, JOHN H. AND MICHAEL A. GARRICK
1969   "Models of Man in Sociological Analysis," *Social Science Quarterly*, 50:136–152.

KUSHNER, GILBERT, *et al.*
1962   *What Accounts for Sociocultural Change?* (Chapel Hill: Institute for Research in Social Science, University of North Carolina).

KUZNETS, SIMON
1956–67   "Quantitative Aspects of the Economic Growth of Nations, I–X," *Economic Development and Cultural Change*, vols. 8–11, 13, and 15.

LAMBERT, RICHARD D.
1963   "The Social and Psychological Determinants of Savings and Investments in Developing Societies," in Bert F. Hoselitz and Wilbert E. Moore (eds.), *Industrialization and Society* (The Hague: UNESCO), 116–32.

LAPIERE, RICHARD T.
1965   *Social Change* (New York: McGraw-Hill).

LEACH, E. R.
1961   *Pul Eliya: A Village in Ceylon* (Cambridge: Cambridge University Press).
1964   *Political Systems of Highland Burma: A Study of Kachin Social Structure* (London: G. Bell and Sons).

LEIBENSTEIN, HARVEY
1957   *Economic Backwardness and Economic Growth* (New York: John Wiley and Sons).

LENSKI, GERHARD D.
1966   *Power and Privilege: A Theory of Social Stratification* (New York: McGraw-Hill).

LERNER, DANIEL
1958   *The Passing of Traditional Society* (Glencoe: Free Press).
1963   "Toward a Communication Theory of Modernization: A Set of Considerations," in Lucian W. Pye (ed.), *Communications and Political Development* (Princeton: Princeton University Press), 327–50.

LERNER, DANIEL AND WILBUR SCHRAMM (eds.)
1967   *Communication and Change in Developing Countries* (Honolulu: East-West Center Press).

LEVI-STRAUSS, CLAUDE
1961   *Tristes Tropiques: An Anthropological Study of Primitive Societies in Brazil* (New York: Atheneum).
1963   *Structural Anthropology* (New York: Basic Books).

LEVINE, DONALD N.
1965   *Wax and Gold: Tradition and Innovation in Ethiopian Culture* (Chicago: University of Chicago Press).

LEVY, MARION J., JR.
1949   *The Family Revolution in Modern China* (Cambridge: Harvard University Press).
1952   *The Structure of Society* (Princeton: Princeton University Press).
1962   "Some Aspects of 'Individualism' and the Problem of Modernization in China and Japan," *Economic Development and Cultural Change*, 10:225–40.
1966   *Modernization and the Structure of Societies* (Princeton: Princeton University Press).

LEWIS, OSCAR
1961   *The Children of Sanchez* (New York: Random House).
1964   *Pedro Martinez* (New York: Random House).
1965   *La Vida* (New York: Random House).

LEWIS, W. ARTHUR
1955   *The Theory of Economic Growth* (Homewood: Richard Irwin).
1966   *Development Planning: The Essentials of Economic Policy* (New York: Harper and Row).

LIEBERMAN, SEYMOUR
1956   "The Effects of Changes in Roles on the Attitudes of Role Occupants," *Human Relations*, 9:385–402.

LINDESMITH, ALFRED R. AND ANSELM L. STRAUSS
1956   *Social Psychology* (New York: Henry Holt).

LIPSET SEYMOUR M.
1960   *Political Man: The Social Bases of Politics* (New York: Double-day).

LITWAK, EUGENE
1960a   "Occupational Mobility and Extended Family Cohesion," *American Sociological Review,* 25:9–21.
1960b   "Geographic Mobility and Extended Family Cohesion," *American Sociological Review,* 25:385–94.

LOPREATO, JOSEPH
1967   *Peasants No More: Social Class and Social Change in an Under-developed Society* (San Francisco: Chandler Publishing Company).

LORENZ, KONRAD
1966   *On Aggression* (New York: Harcourt, Brace and World).

LOVASS, O. I., B. SCHAEFFER, AND J. Q. SIMMONS
1965   "Building Social Behavior in Autistic Children by Use of Electric Shock," *Journal of Experimental Research in Personality,* 1:99–109.

LUCE, R. DUNCAN AND HOWARD RAIFFA
1957   *Games and Decisions: Introduction and Critical Survey* (New York: John Wiley and Sons).

LUNDBERG, GEORGE A.
1939   *Foundations of Sociology* (New York: MacMillan).
1961   *Can Science Save Us?* 2nd edition (New York: Longmans, Green).

LUNDIN, ROBERT W.
1961   *Personality: An Experimental Approach* (New York: MacMillan).

MAHONY, FRANK J.
1960   "The Innovation of a Savings System in Truk," *American Anthropologist,* 62:465–82.

MAIER, JOSEPH AND RICHARD W. WEATHERHEAD (eds.)
1964   *Politics of Change in Latin America* (New York: Frederick A. Praeger).

MALINOWSKI, BRONISLAW
1959   *Crime and Custom in Savage Society* (Paterson: Littlefield, Adams).

MALTHUS, THOMAS
1960   *A Summary View of the Principle of Population* (New York: New American Library of World Literature).

MALTZMAN, IRVING
1967   "Thinking: From a Behavioristic Point of View," in Carl P. Duncan (ed.), *Thinking: Current Experimental Studies* (Philadelphia: J. B. Lippincott Company), 4–18.

MANGIN, WILLIAM
1957   "Haciendas, Communidades, and Strategic Acculturations in the Peruvian Sierra," *Sociologus,* 7:142–46.

MARLOWE, DAVID AND KENNETH J. GERGEN
1969   "Personality and Social Interactions," in Gardner Lindzey and Elliot
            Aronson (eds.), *The Handbook of Social Psychology*, 2nd edition
            (Reading: Addison-Wesley Publishing Company), III:590–665.

MARTINDALE, DON
1962   *Social Life and Cultural Change* (Princeton: D. Van Nostrand).

MARUYAMA, MAGOROH
1963   "The Second Cybernetics: Deviation-amplifying Mutual Causal Proc-
            esses," *American Scientist*, 51:164–79.

MARX, MELVIN H. (ed.)
1963   *Theories in Contemporary Psychology* (New York: MacMillan).
1969   *Learning: Processes* (New York: MacMillan Company).

MAYER, ALBERT
1958   *Pilot Project, India: The Story of Rural Development at Etawah,
            Uttar Pradesh* (Berkeley: University of California Press).

MCCLELLAND, DAVID C.
1961   *The Achieving Society* (Princeton: D. Van Nostrand).
1963   "Motivational Patterns in Southeast Asia with Special Reference to
            the Chinese Case," *Journal of Social Issues*, 19:6–19.
1964   "Review of E. E. Hagen, *On the Theory of Social Change*," *Eco-
            nomic Development and Cultural Change*, 12:320–24.
1966   "Does Education Accelerate Economic Growth?" *Economic Devel-
            opment and Cultural Change*, 14:257–78.

MCCLELLAND, DAVID C. AND DAVID G. WINTER
1969   *Motivating Economic Achievement* (New York: The Free Press).

MCCORD, WILLIAM
1965   *The Springtime of Freedom: The Evolution of Developing Societies*
            (New York: Oxford University Press).

MCGUIRE, WILLIAM J.
1969   "The Nature of Attitudes and Attitude Change," in Gardner Lind-
            zey and Elliot Aronson (eds.), *The Handbook of Social Psychology*,
            2nd edition (Reading: Addison-Wesley Publishing Company), III:
            136–314.

MCQUEEN, ALBERT J.
1968   "Education and Marginality of African Youth," *Journal of Social
            Issues*, vol. 24 no. 2, pp. 179–94.

MEAD, GEORGE HERBERT
1934   *Mind, Self, and Society: From the Standpoint of a Social Behavior-
            ist*, edited by Charles W. Morris (Chicago: University of Chicago
            Press).

MEIER, GERALD M.
1964   *Leading Issues in Development Economics: Selected Materials and
            Commentary* (New York: Oxford University Press).

MEIER, GERALD M. AND ROBERT E. BALDWIN
1957   *Economic Development: Theory, History, Policy* (New York: John
            Wiley and Sons).

MEIER, RICHARD I.
1965   *Developmental Planning* (New York: McGraw-Hill).

MERTON, ROBERT K.
1957a   "Continuities in the Theory of Reference Groups and Social Struc-
        ture," in his *Social Theory and Social Structure,* revised edition
        (Glencoe: Free Press), 281–386.
1957b   "Social Structure and Anomie," in his *Social Theory and Social
        Structure,* revised edition (Glencoe: Free Press), 131–60.
1957c   "Introduction," to his *Social Theory and Social Structure,* revised
        edition (Glencoe: Free Press), 3–16.

1959   "Social Conformity, Deviation, and Opportunity Structures: A Com-
        ment on the Contributions of Dubin and Cloward," *American So-
        ciological Review,* 24:177–89.

MILLER, GEORGE A., EUGENE GALANTER, AND KARL H. PRIBAM
1960   *Plans and the Structure of Behavior* (New York: Holt, Rinehart and
        Winston).

MILLER, NEAL AND JOHN DOLLARD
1941   *Social Learning and Imitation* (New Haven: Yale University Press).

MONTAGU, M. F. ASHLEY (ed.)
1968   *Man and Aggression* (New York: Oxford University Press).

MOORE, WILBERT E.
1951   *Industrialization and Labor: Social Aspects of Economic Develop-
        ment* (Ithaca: Cornell University Press).
1960   "A Reconsideration of Theories of Social Change," *American So-
        ciological Review,* 25:810–18.
1963a   "Industrialization and Social Change," in Bert F. Hoselitz and Wil-
        bert E. Moore (eds.), *Industrialization and Society* (The Hague:
        UNESCO), 299–370.
1963b   "The Strategy of Fostering Performance and Responsibility," in
        Egbert DeVries and José Medina Echavarría (eds.), *Social Aspects
        of Economic Development in Latin America* (New York: UNESCO),
        I:231–42.
1963c   *Social Change* (Englewood Cliffs: Prentice-Hall).
1964   "Predicting Discontinuities in Social Change," *American Sociologi-
        cal Review,* 29:331–38.
1967   *Order and Change: Essays in Comparative Sociology* (New York:
        John Wiley and Sons).

MOORE, WILBERT E. AND ARNOLD S. FELDMAN (eds.)
1960   *Labor Commitment and Social Change in Developing Areas* (New
        York: Social Science Research Council).

MOREIRA, J. ROBERTO
1963   "Education and Development in Latin America," in Egbert DeVries
        and Jose Medina Echavarria (eds.), *Social Aspects of Economic
        Development in Latin America* (New York: UNESCO), I:308–44.

MORGAN, JAMES N.
1964   "The Achievement Motive and Economic Behavior," *Economic De-
        velopment and Cultural Change,* 12:243–67.

MORRIS, BRUCE R.
1967   *Economic Growth and Development* (New York: Pitman Publishing Company).

MUNROE, RUTH L.
1955   *Schools of Psychoanalytic Thought* (New York: Holt, Rinehart and Winston).

MURDOCK, GEORGE PETER
1949   *Social Structure* (New York: MacMillan).

MURPHY, ROBERT F.
1960   *Headhunter's Heritage* (Berkeley: University of California Press).

MURPHY, ROBERT F. AND JULIAN H. STEWARD
1956   "Tappers and Trappers: Parallel Process in Acculturation," *Economic Development and Cultural Change*, 4:335–55.

MYRDAL, GUNNAR
1957   *Rich Lands and Poor: The Road to World Prosperity* (New York: Harper and Brothers).
1968   *Asian Drama: An Inquiry into the Poverty of Nations* (New York: Twentieth Century Fund).

NADEL, SIEGFRIED F.
1947   *The Nuba: An Anthropological Study of the Hill Tribes in Kordofan* (New York: Oxford University Press).
1953   "Social Control and Self-Regulation," *Social Forces*, 31:265–73.
1957   *The Theory of Social Structure* (Glencoe: Free Press).

NAROLL, RAOUL
1956   "A Preliminary Index of Social Development," *American Anthropologist*, 58:687–715.

NASH, MANNING
1957   "The Multiple Society in Economic Development: Mexico and Guatemala," *American Anthropologist*, 59:825–33.
1958   "Machine Age Maya: The Industrialization of a Guatemalan Community," *American Anthropologist* (Memoir no. 87).
1959   "Some Social and Cultural Aspects of Economic Development," *Economic Development and Cultural Change*, 7:137–50.
1961   "The Social Context of Economic Choice in a Small Society," *Man*, 219:186–91.
1963   "Burmese Buddhism in Everyday Life," *American Anthropologist*, 65:285–95.
1964a   "Capital, Saving, and Credit in a Guatemalan and a Mexican Indian Peasant Society," in Raymond Firth and Basil L. Yamey (eds.), *Capital, Saving and Credit in Peasant Societies* (Chicago: Aldine Publishing Company), 287–304.
1964b   "Social Prerequisites to Economic Growth in Latin America and Southeast Asia," *Economic Development and Cultural Change*, 12:225–42.

NEEDHAM, RODNEY
1960   "Chawte Social Structure," *American Anthropologist*, 62:236–53.
1962   *Structure and Sentiment* (Chicago: University of Chicago Press).

NELSON, CYNTHIA
1967   "Analysis of World View in a Mexican Peasant Village: An Illustration," *Social Forces*, 46:52–61.

NESS, GAYL D.
1962   "Population Growth and Economic Development," *American Sociological Review*, 27:552–53.

NEWCOMB, THEODORE M.
1950   *Social Psychology* (New York: Dryden Press).
1952   "Attitude Development as a Function of Reference Groups: The Bennington Study," in G. E. Swanson, T. M. Newcomb, and E. L. Hartley (eds.), *Readings in Social Psychology* (New York: Holt, Rinehart and Winston).

NIEHOFF, ARTHUR H. (ed.)
1966   *A Casebook of Social Change* (Chicago: Aldine Publishing Company).

NURKSE, RAGNAR
1953   *Problems of Capital Formation in Underdeveloped Countries* (New York: Oxford University Press).

NUTINI, HUGO G.
1965   "Some Considerations on the Nature of Social Structure and Model Building: A Critique of Claude Levi-Strauss and Edmund Leach," *American Anthropologist*, 67:707–31.

OGBURN, WILLIAM F.
1950   *Social Change with Respect to Culture and Original Nature*, revised edition (New York: Viking Press).

OLSEN, MARVIN E.
1968   "Multivariate Analysis of National Political Development," *American Sociological Review*, 33:699–712.

OPLER, MORRIS E.
1964   "The Human Being in Culture Theory," *American Anthropologist*, 66:507, 528.
1968   "Developmental Change and the Nature of Man," in Art Gallaher (ed.), *Perspectives in Developmental Change* (Lexington: University of Kentucky Press), 17–35.

PANIKAR, P. G. K.
1961   "Rural Savings in India," *Economic Development and Cultural Change*, 10:64–85.

PAPANEK, GUSTAV F.
1967   *Pakistan's Development: Social Goals and Private Incentives* (Cambridge: Harvard University Press).

PAREEK, UDAI
1968   "Motivational Patterns and Planned Social Change," *International Social Science Journal*, 20:464–73.

PARNES, HERBERT S. (ed.)
1962   *Planning Education for Economic and Social Development* (Paris: Organization for Economic Co-operation and Development).

PARSONS, TALCOTT
1951   *The Social System* (Glencoe: Free Press).
1954   *Essays in Sociological Theory,* revised edition (Glencoe: Free Press).
1960   "Some Reflections on the Institutional Framework of Economic Development," in his *Structure and Process in Modern Societies* (Glencoe: Free Press).
1961   "An Outline of the Social System," in Talcott Parsons *et al.* (eds.), *Theories of Society* (New York: Free Press), 30–79.
1964   "Evolutionary Universals in Society," *American Sociological Review,* 29:339–57.

PARSONS, TALCOTT AND EDWARD A. SHILS (eds.)
1951   *Toward a General Theory of Action* (Cambridge: Harvard University Press).

PEPELASIS, ADAMANTIOS, LEON MEARS, AND IRMA ADELMAN (eds.)
1961   *Economic Development: Analysis and Case Studies* (New York: Harper and Brothers).

PESEK, BORIS P.
1961   "Economic Growth and Its Measurement," *Economic Development and Cultural Change,* 9:295–315.

PHILLIPS, HERBERT P.
1965   *Thai Peasant Personality* (Berkeley: University of California Press).

PIKER, STEVEN
1966   "The Image of Limited Good: Comments on an Exercise in Description and Interpretation," *American Anthropologist,* 68:1202–11.

POOL, ITHIEL DE SOLA
1963   "The Role of Communication in the Process of Modernization and Technological Change," in Bert F. Hoselitz and Wilbert E. Moore (eds.), *Industrialization and Society* (The Hague: UNESCO), 279–95.

POTTER, JACK M., MAY N. DIAZ, AND GEORGE M. FOSTER (eds.)
1968   *Peasant Society* (Boston: Little, Brown and Company).

PROSHANSKY, HAROLD AND BERNARD SEIDENBERG (eds.)
1965   *Basic Studies in Social Psychology* (New York: Holt, Rinehart and Winston).

PYE, LUCIAN W. (ed.)
1962   *Communication and Political Development* (Princeton: Princeton University Press).

RADCLIFFE-BROWN, A. R.
1952   *Structure and Function in Primitive Society* (Glencoe: Free Press).
1964   *The Andaman Islanders* (Glencoe: Free Press).

RAJFEL, HENRI
1969   "Social and Cultural Factors in Perception," in Gardner Lindzey and Elliot Aronson (eds.), *The Handbook of Social Psychology,* 2nd edition (Reading: Addison-Wesley Publishing Company), III:315–94.

RAO, K. NAGARAJA
1956   "Small Scale Industry and Economic Development in Indonesia,"
            Economic Development and Cultural Change, 4:159–70.

RAPOPORT, ANATOL
1966   *Two-Person Game Theory: The Essential Ideas* (Ann Arbor: University of Michigan Press).

RASER, JOHN R.
1968   *Simulation and Society: An Exploration of Scientific Gaming* (Boston: Allyn and Bacon).

REDFIELD, ROBERT
1941   *The Folk Culture of Yucatan* (Chicago: University of Chicago Press).
1952   "The Primitive World View," *Proceedings of the American Philosophical Society*, 96:30–36.
1956   *Peasant Society and Culture: An Anthropological Approach to Civilization* (Chicago: University of Chicago Press).

REINING, CONRAD C.
1966   *The Zande Scheme: An Anthropological Case Study of Economic Development in Africa* (Evanston: Northwestern University Press).

RISLEY, TODD R.
1968   "The Effects and Side Effects of Punishing the Autistic Behaviors of a Deviant Child," *Journal of Applied Behavior Analysis*, 1:21–34.

ROGERS, EVERETT M.
1962   *Diffusion of Innovations* (New York: Free Press).

ROSE, ARNOLD M.
1962   "A Systematic Summary of Symbolic Interaction Theory," in Arnold M. Rose (ed.), *Human Behavior and Social Processes* (Boston: Houghton Mifflin), 3–19.

ROSTOW, WALT W.
1956   "The Take-Off into Self-Sustained Growth," *Economic Journal*, 66:25–48.
1960   *The Stages of Economic Growth: A Non-Communist Manifesto* (Cambridge: Cambridge University Press).

ROTTER, JULIAN B.
1954   *Social Learning and Clinical Psychology* (Englewood Cliffs: Prentice-Hall).

SADIE, J. L.
1960   "The Social Anthropology of Economic Underdevelopment," *Economic Journal*, 70:294–303.

SALZ, BEATE R.
1955   "The Human Element in Industrialization," *Economic Development and Cultural Change*, 4:1–265.

SAMUELSON, KURT
1961   *Religion and Economic Action: A Critique of Max Weber* (New York: Basic Books).

SARNOFF, IRVING, DANIEL KATZ, AND CHARLES MCCLINTOCK
1965   "Attitude-Change Procedures and Motivating Patterns," in Harold
            Proshansky and Bernard Seidenberg (eds.), *Basic Studies in Social
            Psychology* (New York: Holt, Rinehart and Winston), 121–29.

SCHNEIDER, LOUIS AND SVERRE LYSGAARD
1953   "The Deferred Gratification Pattern: A Preliminary Study," *American Sociological Review*, 18:142–49.

SCHRAMM, WILBUR
1967   "Communication and Change," in Daniel Lerner and Wilbur
            Schramm (eds.), *Communication and Change in the Developing
            Countries* (Honolulu: East-West Center Press), 5–32.

SCHUMANN, HOWARD
1967   *Economic Development and Individual Change* (Cambridge: Harvard University Press).

SCHUMPETER, JOSEPH A.
1961   *The Theory of Economic Development* (Cambridge: Harvard University Press).

SCOTT, ANDREW M., WILLIAM A. LUCAS, AND TRUDI M. LUCAS
1966   *Simulation and National Development* (New York: John Wiley and
            Sons).

SCOTT, WILLIAM A.
1968   "Attitude Measurement," in Gardner Lindzey and Elliot Aronson
            (eds.), *The Handbook of Social Psychology*, 2nd edition (Reading:
            Addison-Wesley Publishing Company), II:204–73.

SENIOR, CLARENCE
1958   *Land Reform and Democracy* (Gainesville: University of Florida
            Press).

SHORTER, FREDERIC C.
1966   "The Application of Development Hypotheses in Middle Eastern
            Studies," *Economic Development and Cultural Change*, 14:340–54.

SIEGEL, ALBERTA E. AND SIDNEY SIEGEL
1957   "Reference Groups, Membership Groups, and Attitude Change,"
            Journal of Abnormal and Social Psychology, 55:360–64.

SIGMUND, PAUL E. (ed.)
1963   *The Ideologies of the Developing Nations* (New York: Frederick A.
            Praeger).

SILVERMAN, SYDEL F.
1968   "Agricultural Organization, Social Structure, and Values in Italy:
            Amoral Familism Reconsidered," *American Anthropologist*, 70:1–
            20.

SIMON, HERBERT A.
1957   *Models of Man* (New York: John Wiley and Sons).

SINGER, MILTON
1956   "Cultural Values in India's Economic Development," *Annals of the
            American Academy of Political and Social Science*, 305:81–91.

1958   "India's Cultural Values and Economic Development: A Discussion: A Postscript," *Economic Development and Cultural Change,* 7:10–12.

SMELSER, NEIL J.
1959   *Social Change in the Industrial Revolution* (Chicago: University of Chicago Press).
1963   "Mechanism of Change and Adjustment to Change," in Bert F. Hoselitz and Wilbert E. Moore (eds.), *Industrialization and Society* (The Hague: UNESCO), 32–54.

SPENGLER, JOSEPH J.
1956   "Capital Requirements and Population Growth in Underdeveloped Countries: Their Interrelations," *Economic Development and Cultural Change,* 4:305–34.
1960   "Population and World Economic Development," *Science,* 131: 1497–1502.
1961   "Population Change: Cause, Effect, Indicator," *Economic Development and Cultural Change,* 9:249–66.

SPICER, EDWARD H. (ed.)
1952   *Human Problems in Technological Change: A Casebook* (New York: Russell Sage Foundation).

SPILLER, ROBERT A. (ed.)
1960   *Social Control in a Free Society* (Philadelphia: University of Pennsylvania Press).

SPIRO, MELFORD E.
1954   "Human Nature in Its Psychological Dimensions," *American Anthropologist,* 56:19–30.
1965   "A Typology of Social Structure and the Patterning of Social Institutions: A Cross-Cultural Study," *American Anthropologist,* 67: 1097–1119.

SRINIVAS, M. N.
1958   "A Note on Mr. Goheen's Note," *Economic Development and Cultural Change,* 7:3–6.

STAATS, ARTHUR W. (ed.)
1964   *Human Learning: Studies Extending Conditioning Principles to Complex Behavior* (New York: Holt, Rinehart and Winston).

STAATS, ARTHUR W. AND CAROLYN K. STAATS
1963   *Complex Human Behavior* (New York: Holt, Rinehart and Winston).

STEWARD, JULIAN H.
1955   *Theory of Culture Change: The Methodology of Multilinear Evolution* (Urbana: University of Illinois Press).

STOCKWELL, EDWARD G.
1960   "The Measurement of Economic Development," *Economic Development and Cultural Change,* 8:419–32.
1962   "The Relationship between Population Growth and Economic Development," *American Sociological Review,* 27:250–52.

STRAUSS, ANSELM (ed.)
1964   *George Herbert Mead: On Social Psychology* (Chicago: University of Chicago Press).

STYCOS, J. MAYONE
1968   *Human Fertility in Latin America: Sociological Perspectives* (Ithaca: Cornell University Press).

SUPPLE, BARRY E. (ed.)
1963   *The Experience of Economic Growth* (New York: Random House).

SUTTON, FRANCIS X.
1961   "Planning and Rationality in the Newly Independent States in Africa," *Economic Development and Cultural Change,* 10:42–50.

SWIFT, MICHAEL G.
1957   "The Accumulation of Capital in a Peasant Economy," *Economic Development and Cultural Change,* 5:325–37.

TAJFEL, HENRI
1969   "Social and Cultural Factors in Perception," in Gardner Lindzey and Elliot Aronson (eds.), *The Handbook of Social Psychology,* 2nd edition (Reading: Addison-Wesley Publishing Company), III: 315–94.

TANGRI, SHANTI S. AND H. PETER GRAY (eds.)
1967   *Capital Accumulation and Economic Development* (Boston: D. C. Heath).

THIBAUT, JOHN W. AND HAROLD H. KELLEY
1959   *The Social Psychology of Groups* (New York: John Wiley and Sons).

THOMAS, DON R., WESLEY C. BECKER, AND MARIANNE ARMSTRONG
1968   "Production and Elimination of Disruptive Classroom Behavior by Systematically Varying Teacher's Behavior," *Journal of Applied Behavior Analysis,* 1:35–45.

TURNBULL, COLIN M.
1962   *The Lonely African* (New York: Simon and Schuster).

UNAMUNO, MIGUEL DE
n.d.   *Del Sentimiento Tragico de la Vida* (New York: Las Americas Publishing Co.).

ULLMAN, ALBERT D.
1965   *Sociocultural Foundations of Personality* (New York: Houghton-Mifflin).

ULLMANN, LEONARD P. AND LEONARD KRASNER (eds.)
1965   *Case Studies in Behavior Modification* (New York: Holt, Rinehart and Winston).

VAIZEY, JOHN
1962   "The Role of Education in Economic Development," in Herbert S. Parnes (eds.), *Planning Education for Economic and Social Development* (Paris: Organization for Economic Co-operation and Development), 39–47.

VERA, OSCAR
1963 "The Educational Situation and Requirements in Latin America," in Egbert De Vries and José Medína Echavarría (eds.), *Social Aspects of Economic Development in Latin America* (New York: UNESCO), I:279–307.

VOGET, FRED W.
1960 "Man and Culture: An Essay in Changing Anthropological Interpretation," *American Anthropologist*, 62:943–65.

VOGT, EVON Z.
1960 "On the Concepts of Structure and Process in Cultural Anthropology," *American Anthropologist*, 62:18–33.

DE VRIES, EGBERT AND JOSÉ MEDÍNA ECHAVARRÍA (eds.)
1963 *Social Aspects of Economic Development in Latin America* (New York: UNESCO).

WARRINER, CHARLES K.
1956 "Groups Are Real: A Reaffirmation," *American Sociological Review*, 21:549–54.

WATERSTON, ALBERT
1965 *Development Planning: Lessons of Experience* (Baltimore: Johns Hopkins Press).

WEBER, MAX
1947 *The Theory of Social and Economic Organization*, translated by A. M. Henderson and Talcott Parsons (New York: Oxford University Press).
1958 *The Protestant Ethic and the Spirit of Capitalism*, translated by Talcott Parsons (New York: Charles Scribner's Sons).

WHITING, BEATRICE B. (ed.)
1963 *Six Cultures: Studies in Child Rearing* (New York: John Wiley and Sons).

WHITING, JOHN W. M. AND IRVING L. CHILD
1953 *Child Training and Personality* (New Haven: Yale University Press).

WHYTE, WILLIAM F. AND ALLAN R. HOLMBERG
1956 "From Paternalism to Democracy: the Vicos Project," *Human Organization*, 15:15–18.

WHYTE, WILLIAM F. AND LAWRENCE K. WILLIAMS
1968 *Toward an Integrated Theory of Development* (Ithaca: Cornell University Press).

WILLIAMS, JR., ROBIN M.
1951 *American Society: A Sociological Interpretation* (New York: Alfred A. Knopf).

WILSON, GODFREY AND MONICA WILSON
1945 *The Analysis of Social Change* (Cambridge: Cambridge University Press).

WOLF, ERIC R.
1955 "Types of Latin-American Peasantry: A Preliminary Discussion," *American Anthropologist*, 57:452–71.

1957   "Closed Corporate Peasant Communities in Mesoamerica and Central Java," *Southwestern Journal of Anthropology*, 13:1–18.

1966   *Peasants* (Englewood Cliffs: Prentice-Hall).

WOLMAN, BENJAMIN B.

1960   *Contemporary Theories and Systems in Psychology* (New York: Harper and Brothers).

WOLPE, JOSEPH

1964   "The Comparative Clinical Status of Conditioning Therapies and Psychoanalysis," in Joseph Wolpe, Andrew Salter, and L. J. Reyna (eds.), *The Conditioning Therapies* (New York: Holt, Rinehart and Winston).

WOLPE, JOSEPH, ANDREW SALTER, AND L. J. REYNA (eds.)

1964   *The Conditioning Therapies: The Challenge in Psychotherapy* (New York: Holt, Rinehart and Winston).

WORSLEY, PETER

1964   *The Third World* (Chicago: University of Chicago Press).

YINGER, J. MILTON

1965   *Toward a Field Theory of Behavior: Personality and Social Structure* (New York: McGraw-Hill).

YOUNG, FRANK W. AND ISAO FUJIMOTO

1965   "Social Differentiation in Latin American Communities," *Economic Development and Cultural Change*, 13:344–52.

YOUNG, FRANK W. AND RUTH C. YOUNG

1960   "Two Determinants of Community Reaction to Industrialization in Rural Mexico," *Economic Development and Cultural Change*, 8:257–64.

ZEILBERGER, JANE, SUE E. SAMPEN, AND HOWARD N. SLOANE, JR.

1968   "Modification of a Child's Problem Behavior in the Home with the Mother as Therapist," *Journal of Applied Behavior Analysis*, 1:47–53.

ZETTERBERG, HANS L.

1965   *On Theory and Verification in Sociology*, 3rd edition (Totowa: Bedminster Press).

ZIMMERMAN, L. J.

1965   *Poor Lands, Rich Lands: The Widening Gap* (New York: Random House).

ZOLLSCHAN, GEORGE K. AND WALTER HIRSCH (eds.)

1964   *Explorations in Social Change* (Boston: Houghton Mifflin).

Index